ON THE TRINITY
AND THE BIBLE

MICHAEL SERVETUS
ON THE TRINITY AND THE BIBLE

AN ANNOTATED TRANSLATION OF
THE RESTORATION OF CHRISTIANITY
BOOKS 1 AND 2 ON THE DIVINE TRINITY

translated by
Peter Zerner and Peter Hughes

edited with an introduction by
Peter Hughes

Blackstone Editions
Toronto, Ontario, Canada
www.BlackstoneEditions.com

© 2023 by Peter Hughes
All rights reserved
Published 2023

978-1-7753556-9-4

Front cover image: *St. Michael and the Dragon*
Walters Art Museum, Baltimore, MD
Creative Commons W.26.131R

In Memoriam
Peter Zerner

Lector, si monumentum requiris, circumspice

Books in This Series

Volume 1: *On the Trinity and the Bible*
   The Restoration of Christianity:
     On the Divine Trinity, books 1 and 2
     Translated by Peter Zerner and Peter Hughes

Volume 2: *On the Mysteries of the Word*
   The Restoration of Christianity:
     On the Divine Trinity, books 3 and 4
     Translated by Peter Zerner and Peter Hughes

Volume 3: *On the Holy Spirit*
   The Restoration of Christianity:
     On the Divine Trinity, book 5
     Translated by Peter Zerner, Peter Hughes, and
     Lynn Gordon Hughes

Contents

Translator's Preface *by Peter Hughes*	ix
Key to Annotations, Symbols, and Abbreviations	xxi
A Note on the Text	xxix
Introduction	1
The Restoration of Christianity	
Introduction	63
On the Divine Trinity, book 1	72
On the Divine Trinity, book 2	159
Appendixes	
A. *On the Errors of the Trinity*, book 1	225
B. Servetus's Introduction, Selected Marginal Notes and Chapter Headings for the Pagnini Bible	311
Annotations	335
Bibliography	418
Index of Biblical References	439
Index of Authorities Cited	454

Translator's Preface
by Peter Hughes

The Road to Restoration

I first became acquainted with the case of Michael Servetus in 1980, when I was preparing to study for the Unitarian Universalist ministry. My minister, Charles Magistro, lent me a copy of Roland Bainton's biography of Servetus, *Hunted Heretic*. I was immediately captivated by Bainton's engaging relation of Servetus's tragic and dramatic story. Here was a creative and original religious thinker whose passion for reform took him well beyond the revolutionary changes instituted by the leaders of the Reformation; who aspired to formulate a religious vision that could inspire and unite people of different faiths, only to encounter incomprehension and deadly persecution at the hands of both Roman Catholics and Protestants.

I went to theological school in Chicago determined to enhance my knowledge of Servetus. I studied under John Godbey, a professor whose specialty was the Radical Reformation, writing a paper for him on the early stages of the troubled relationship between Servetus and John Calvin. Using the resources of the seminary and the University of Chicago I was able to study many of the documents in French pertaining to Servetus, and those Latin items that had already been rendered into English. But I was frustrated

Translator's Preface

in coming to grips with Servetus's main work, *The Restoration of Christianity*, because of my inability to read the intellectual *lingua franca* of his time. I sought out books that contained translated extracts from *Restoration*, photocopied the pages, and pasted them into a sort of scrapbook. When this proved utterly inadequate I began to study Latin, a course of action that was unheard of at a Unitarian Universalist theological school.

I wrote my Doctor of Ministry thesis on the appropriation of the story of the life and death of Servetus by modern Unitarian Universalists. I hoped to have the opportunity to make a more historical contribution, but that would have to wait. I was called to a New England Universalist church, where I was ideally placed to investigate the history of early American Universalism. What time I had for historical research was fully occupied by this study.

After I retired on disability in 1999, I took on the task of editing the online *Dictionary of Unitarian and Universalist Biography*. Still having the books, notes, and photocopies accumulated during my Chicago days, I composed the entry on Servetus myself. As a result I was invited to speak at the 450th Anniversary Conference on Servetus held by the International Council of Unitarians and Universalists at Geneva in October, 2003.

By then I had returned to the study of Servetus, as editor of a revised edition of *Hunted Heretic*. In 2002 my wife Lynn Gordon Hughes had started a small publishing company, Blackstone Editions, and was working with the Unitarian Universalist Historical Society on a project to reprint classic works of Unitarian and Universalist history. I proposed a reissue of *Hunted Heretic*, then still the best English-language biography of Servetus. Having been invited by Ángel Alcalá to take advantage of the enhancements to *Hunted Heretic* offered by his 1973 Spanish translation, and with the permission of the Bainton family, I prepared a new edition with updated notes and bibliography.

Meanwhile, work was proceeding on the first English translation of *Christianismi Restitutio*, under the leadership of translator Christopher Hoffman and project director Alicia McNary Forsey. They approached Lynn and me to explore the idea of having the translation published by Blackstone Editions. In the end, Blackstone Editions proved to be unable to work within the timetable and guidelines that had been set for this project. The Forsey team found another publisher and issued their translation beginning in 2007.[1] But this experience had rekindled my interest in translating Servetus, and clarified my vision of how I wanted to do it. I did not just want to render Servetus's words into English; I wanted to situate the text within its intellectual and theological context, noting and exploring its connections to the works of the Church Fathers, medieval scholastics, Renaissance humanists, and all the other influences that made Servetus the person and the theologian that he became. This, clearly, would take a vast amount of time. But I felt that I had time, as I was retired — physically disabled, but still capable of intellectual work — and then not much more than fifty years old.

A Conversation of Translators

A translation is a dialogue between translator and author. But it is also a conversation among translators. If earlier translations of a work exist, these become part of the conversation — even if they are translations into different languages. The present translation has been enriched by the opportunity to consult translations into English, French, and Spanish. But this kind of dialogue flows largely one way. The translator may listen to others, but will always have the last word. What, on the other hand, if a translation were done by two translators, or by an even larger team? Then in each selection of word or phrasing there could be a true dialogue, a give and take in real time. This would allow the original author's voice to be heard

---

[1] *The Restoration of Christianity: An English Translation of Christianismi Restitutio, 1553*, translated by Christopher Hoffman and Marian Hillar, with notes by Marian Hillar, was published by The Edwin Mellen Press in 2007. Three additional volumes were issued as *Treatise on Faith and Justice of Christ's Kingdom* (2008), *Treatise Concerning the Supernatural Regeneration and the Kingdom of the Antichrist* (2008), and *Thirty Letters to Calvin, Preacher to the Genevans, and Sixty Signs of the Kingdom of the Antichrist and His Revelation Which Is Now at Hand* (2010).

more clearly — not just in the words of each translator, but in the objections that each raises to the words of the other.

My initial attempts at translating Servetus were reviewed by my wife Lynn, who used her editorial skills to help render my English text more smooth and readable. She cross-examined my portrayal of Servetus's theology (and the theologies of those Servetus quoted) until she was satisfied that I understood the theology well enough to explain it to her clearly. She also, it turned out, had a good ear for detecting biblical language, and thus was able to identify many previously unrecognized wordings and quotations. For Servetus naturally spoke and wrote in the language of the Bible and, except when he was interested in highlighting a specific text as an authority, did not always feel that there was a need to identify verses and phrases that he expected his readers to find exceedingly familiar.

However, what turned this project into a full collaboration — a true dialogue of translations — was a fortuitous circumstance. In 2005, while I was in the early stages of working on *Restoration*, I received word, through the offices of my denomination, that a scholar, Peter Zerner, had volunteered to translate Reformation-era works from Latin. Peter had degrees in Classics and had already made translations from Greek and Latin. He had taught Latin, had lived in Greece, knew French and Hebrew, and — a bonus when we came to work on book 5 — was expert in technical medical language. He had experience with Bible translation, so that he could not only identify biblical passages, but could point out the ones that were especially tricky to translate from Hebrew or Greek. I wasted no time in recruiting him for this Servetus project. We worked closely together for the next fourteen years.

We soon settled into a routine of co-translation. Peter Zerner usually made the first draft translation, adding commentary on the biblical and other ancient references, and occasionally a little multilingual humour. I then compared his version with the Latin, tracked down quotations, compared Servetus's Bible translations with other contemporary Latin editions, and wrote up my counter-proposals. Following this, we met for long sessions on Skype and went through the text together, phrase by phrase, arguing about words and meaning, discussing each passage until we had agreement about what Servetus was trying to say, debating each critical word, consulting dictionaries, lexicons, thesauruses, and internet resources, taking into account what Servetus said elsewhere and judging it in the context of the times, trying to eliminate unintended ambiguity, until we were both happy with the text. We each had our own ideas about English style, so we each learned to avoid the locutions that the other disliked.

It was a fruitful collaboration in many ways. In the course of our work Peter developed a more sophisticated appreciation of the theologies of the Church Fathers and medieval philosophers, while my Latin improved. In addition to our work on *Restoration*, we translated related texts by Laelio Sozzini, John Calvin, and others, which I hope will eventually see the light of day. Together we translated a mysterious manuscript, *Declarationis Jesu Christi Filii Dei*, which had been discovered in 1953 and was thought to be a lost work by Servetus. Peter and I analyzed the work and concluded that it was actually by Matteo Gribaldi, an Italian law professor who was a contemporary and admirer of Servetus. Our edition of this work was published in 2010 as *Declaratio: Michael Servetus's Revelation of Jesus Christ the Son of God; and Other Antitrinitarian Works by Matteo Gribaldi*.

In the course of our long collaboration Peter Zerner and I became good friends, although we only saw each other in person much later. Those long Skype calls came to include discussions of our families, politics, health problems, philosophies of life, and various extreme weather events. We did finally meet, briefly, once in 2013 and once in 2015. We and our spouses, Lynn and Carol, hoped to be able to gather again, but this was not to be.

Sadly, in 2019, *in media vita*, Peter Zerner passed away. We had translated most, but not all, of the five books and two dialogues that make up the first part of *Restoration*, "On the Trinity." Dialogue 2 remains incomplete. I hope to be able to finish it, and eventually to publish the complete annotated translation of "On the Trinity."

Principles of Translation

Our aim in this translation has been to convey the force of Servetus's theological arguments as clearly and unambiguously as we can, for people who are not experts in theology or philosophy. We realized early on that our success as translators was dependent on our own success in coming to grips with Servetus's thought. For translators cannot help inserting themselves into the texts they create: the translation consists of words they have chosen, and they can convey only ideas that they themselves have understood.

The following sections outline some of the challenges we encountered when working with this text, and some of the key decisions we made along the way.

Servetus's Latin. Servetus wrote in a form of neo-Latin, which is stylistically different from classical Latin. He was not of the Renaissance school of thinking, which maintains that the only good Latin is a style that is modelled on Cicero and his ilk. Accordingly his writing has sometimes been disparaged as defective or "barbarous." But a great deal depends on a translator's attitude towards the text. If the translator thinks that the original author was a bad writer or confused in his thinking, this prejudice may well be confirmed in the translated result. As we have worked with this material, however, we have found that Servetus's ideas are coherent and reasonably well-organized, and that his Latin style, though perhaps not of the highest literary quality, is effective in conveying his ideas, his passion, and his wit. These are qualities that we have tried to bring to this English translation. We respect our author and have tried to treat his works, which were intended to bring people back to a pure and simple religion, with equal respect.

Parallel translations. One of our earliest decisions was to translate *Restoration* in parallel with the corresponding sections of *On the Errors of the Trinity*, even though we were not necessarily planning to publish a complete translation of *Errors*. By translating both works side by side, we would be able to see — and to convey to our readers — the complex relationship between the two works. In our translation of *Restoration* we use marginal notes to point out the corresponding passages in *Errors*.

There is a particularly close relationship between book 1 of *Restoration* and book 1 of *Errors*. For this reason we decided to include book 1 of *Errors* in this volume as an appendix. By translating both of these texts in a consistent manner, readers will be able to compare them readily and to view them chronologically as documents in the stages of Servetus's intellectual biography.

Filling in the blanks. A key decision we made at an early stage was that we would continue to examine and research each part of the text until we felt that we understood it. At the risk of being wrong, we decided to make our text as unambiguous as we could. We did not let caution hold us back from making our translation declare exactly what we thought Servetus meant. For this reason we have added to the translation words and phrases for which there is no explicit justification in the Latin, but which are required in order to complete sentences or thoughts, fill in quotations, or supply missing information. These insertions are enclosed in square brackets. Readers are, of course, welcome to question our choice of words or information, and to supply their own.

Highlighting the structure. To help guide the reader through the text, we have broken up long paragraphs whenever we detected a change in subject or when we encountered Latin guide words (e.g. *item*) indicating the introduction of a new topic. For the same reason we have added subheadings, as needed, to bring out the structure of the book and to call attention to the parallels between *Restoration* and *Errors*. Some of these headings are taken from the occasional headings and marginal notes in the original works; those that we added, like our other interpolations, are marked with square brackets.

Annotations. One challenge in reading Servetus is that his style often seems mysteriously elliptical. For, like any author in any age, Servetus made assumptions about what his readers could be expected to know. He could quote a fragment of a biblical quotation and be confident that the whole passage would be instantly called forth in the minds of his readers. He could assume that certain important philosophical and theological controversies — Platonists vs. Aristotelians, Church Fathers vs. ancient heretics, realists vs.

nominalists, Erasmus vs. the Roman Catholic church, and free will vs. determinism — were well-known and at least partly understood. He could presume that his readers' vocabulary would include theological terms like *communicatio idiomatum* and *hypostasis*. Consequently, except perhaps for specialists, even well-educated twenty-first century readers will find themselves deficient by sixteenth-century standards.

In addition there are many things that Servetus and his contemporaries thought they knew, but that from our perspective represent outdated, incomplete, or false information. Among these are biblical passages taken from what are now considered less than reliable manuscripts, the attribution of many works to the Church Fathers — notably Ignatius, Athanasius, and Augustine — which are now considered pseudepigraphal, and ancient and medieval conceptions of the function of the parts of the human body.

The ideal readers of Servetus's works would be people immersed in a Renaissance-era curriculum and steeped in a Reformation-era state of mind. Since this is not possible, we must accept that the past will always be something of a foreign country. We therefore embarked on this project as explorers, seeing each puzzling expression or mysterious allusion as a potential pathway into this unknown territory. Sometimes tracking down these allusions has led us into surprising byways. In order to share with the reader the results of these excursions, we have included over 200 annotations to shed light on specific aspects of the text.

Technical terminology. In presenting the technical philosophical terms of the Church Fathers and the scholastics, which appear with some frequency in Servetus's works, we have followed common modern scholarly practice and left words and phrases such as *suppositum, communicatio idiomatum,* and *ousia* in Latin (or Latinized Greek), providing parenthetical translations and annotations to help elucidate their complexities.

Quotations and borrowings. One thing that we discovered in the course of our translation was that Servetus often used information, vocabulary, and even whole blocks of text from other sources,

Translator's Preface

and did not always signal his borrowings with a citation. This may strike the modern reader as careless scholarship or even plagiarism. But it is unreasonable to expect Servetus to follow twenty-first century standards of scholarly citation. And even to believe that he was applying Renaissance standards of scholarship in his writing is to make a mistake about the kind of literature that he was composing. For he was writing a theological and apologetic work, meant to convince not by scholarly rigour, but through the marshalling of religious authorities. When Servetus cited a source it was because he wished to invoke that name as an authority in spiritual matters. And the most solid religious authorities, as far as he was concerned, are the earliest ones. To this end he would quote a later writer who is quoting an earlier one, but cite only the embedded quotation. For example, book 2 includes a long quotation from Marsilio Ficino's *Platonic Theology*, a work dating from the late fifteenth century. In Ficino's text there is an unacknowledged quotation from the fourth-century writer Eusebius, who cited the more ancient philosopher Numenius. Servetus preserved only the mention of Numenius, for that is the authority that he was interested in presenting.

If plagiarism is not an issue, why should we care whether or not Servetus borrowed some text from Ficino? The answer is that we now know, for certain, that Servetus read Ficino. Put on the alert, we have gone on to find many more instances of borrowing from *Platonic Theology* and from other works written or translated by Ficino. This provides significant information about Servetus's intellectual and spiritual development.

Therefore, as we prepared our translation, we had to watch out for clues that might signal the presence of borrowed text. We could not accurately translate a passage until we knew whether it was a quotation, a paraphrase, or piece of purely Servetan text. Fishing expeditions on the internet often yielded surprising results. Sometimes the only way we detected a quotation was by sensing a subtle change in vocabulary or style. Once we had identified a quotation, we had to find out what the original author meant in his own time, and also how he was generally understood in Servetus's time.

Quotations, References, and Sources

All translations from Latin, including those in the introduction and annotations, are ours.

In verifying and translating Bible quotations and paraphrases we have consulted the Vulgate Bible, both in period and modern editions;[2] the five editions of Erasmus's *New Testament* (1516-1535); several editions of Santes Pagnini's *Biblia sacra*, including the one edited by Servetus; the Septuagint, in the Aldine edition (1518) and in its Latin translation (1526); the Münster Bible (1534-36); and a variety of modern English Bibles, including, but not restricted to, those in the tradition of the 1611 Authorized Version. To shed light on the interpretation of controversial Bible passages we have consulted volumes of the Anchor Bible and other modern commentaries, as well as Erasmus's *Annotations*, works written in critique of Erasmus's interpretations (by Edward Lee, Diego de Zúñiga, and others), and Calvin's Bible commentaries.

To find Servetus's quotations from, and references to, the Quran we have employed the version he used, the twelfth-century Robert of Ketton translation into Latin. For a modern perspective we have consulted two English Qurans, M. A. S. Abdel Haleem's *The Qur'an* (2004) and Seyyed Hossein Nasr, ed., *The Study Quran* (2015).

For Servetus's reference to non-scriptural sources such as the Church Fathers, medieval scholastics, and Renaissance writers such as Erasmus and Ficino, we have tried to identify and, when possible, examine the editions that he might have used. These are listed in the bibliography. However, in our notes on Servetus's references to Church Fathers and early scholastic writers like Peter Lombard, we generally direct the reader to the nineteenth-century Migné *Patrologia Graeca* (PG) and *Patrologia Latina* (PL) editions, even though these do not necessarily represent the latest or best versions of these texts. These collections, PG and PL, have two distinct advantages.

---

[2] Including but not restricted to versions of the *Glossa Ordinaria* (including *Biblia Sacra cum glossis*, 1545), the *Complutensian Polyglot* (1520), Nestle-Aland *Novum Testamentum: Graece et Latine* (2002), and *Biblia sacra iuxta vulgatam versionem* (1984).

First, they are widely available in libraries and all of their volumes can be accessed on the Internet. Secondly, they are comprehensive, standardized collections. Thus we can send readers to PG and PL using a simple system of volume and page numbers, rather than having to direct them to a haphazard collection of sixteenth-century or modern editions, some of which the reader might find it difficult to locate. Moreover, many of the early editions are hard to read, even for a reader who knows Latin. Some may be in a gothic font and many are full of arcane abbreviations. Pagination may be absent or may follow a system strange to modern eyes. In cases where Servetus, in his citations, used a different chapter and section numbering than is found in PG or PL — as is, for example, the case for Irenaeus — we have verified the reference in the editions that Servetus could have read and ascertained that he was not mistaken in his citations.

Acknowledgements

On behalf of the translation team, I would like to express our gratitude toward those who provided support and assistance in the long process of bringing this book to fruition.

I have received institutional support from the Centre for Renaissance and Reformation Studies at the University of Toronto. The fellowship I have been given has allowed me the use of the University libraries as well as electronic resources such as the *Patrologia Latina* searchable database. The library at the Pontifical Institute of Medieval Studies (PIMS) on the University of Toronto campus was also invaluable. In the early days of my work on this project I had access to the Rockefeller Library at Brown University and the special collections held at Harvard University. My co-translator, Peter Zerner, was able to use the Z. Smith Reynolds Library at Wake Forest University. We were able to study the Edinburgh manuscript thanks to a copy provided by the University of Edinburgh. I was able to look at parts of the 1541 edition of the Pagnini Bible thanks to copies sent to me by the librarians at the Jean-Léon Allie Library and Archives at Saint Paul University in Ottawa.

Previous translators of *Restoration* — Ángel Alcalá, Christopher Hoffman, and Marian Hillar — have, in various ways, provided materials, leads, or support. The Michael Servetus Institute, especially Sergio Baches Opi and Jaume de Marcos, have given us encouragement and promoted our work. We have also been supported by the Unitarian Universalist Historical Society and its successor organizations. Parts of the introduction were adapted from articles previously published in the *Journal of Unitarian Universalist History*.

My friend Paul Howard provided computer programming that allowed me to identify matching texts throughout *Errors* and *Restoration*. Our friends Pat Falcon and Gwendolyn Howard provided encouragement and stimulating exchanges of ideas over the years.

This book would not have been possible without the long-time support and assistance of our spouses, Carol Zerner and Lynn Hughes. Carol provided editing, proofreading, and translation advice and checking. Lynn did project organization, editing, proofreading, translation checking, and book design as well as creating or co-creating much of the apparatus of this book.

Key to Annotations, Symbols, and Abbreviations

Bible Books, Chapters, and Verses

In referring to the books of the Bible we have adopted the names commonly used in English Protestant Bibles. In particular, the four books called 1-4 Kings in the Vulgate we call 1-2 Samuel and 1-2 Kings.

For the convenience of modern readers who would like to track down Servetus's biblical citations and allusions, we have provided verse numbers, to the extent that they can be ascertained. Since Servetus wrote before versification had become established, he did not have the same sense of pinpoint location that later writers would develop. Some of his references are to a whole chapter, or to several verses scattered throughout. In quotations he occasionally stitched together several disjoint phrases from different verses in a particular chapter, adding connecting words of his own.

Sometimes chapters within books of the Bible are divided in different places in various versions of the Bible. In particular, there are two ways of numbering the Psalms: Roman Catholic Bibles use the Septuagint numbering, while Protestant Bibles follow the Masoretic Hebrew numbering. In most cases the Protestant psalm numbers can be obtained by adding one to the number that Servetus cited. In the translation, we have retained the numbers

Key to Annotations, Symbols, and Abbreviations

that Servetus used, but in our footnotes we refer the reader to the English Protestant chapters and verses.

> Of Joseph's stock was Joshua, who established the tabernacle in Shiloh. But, as Psalm 77 says, God spurned the tabernacle of Joseph, that is, Shiloh.ᵈ
>
> ---
>
> ᵃ Gen 49:11-12. ᵇ Gen 49:8. ᶜ Gen 48:5; 1 Chr 5:1-2. ᵈ Ps 78:60.

Servetus cited Psalm 77 (Vulgate numbering),
but the footnote is to Psalm 78

Abbreviations

The following abbreviations are used when referring to frequently-cited works and collections of works.

Alcoran	Latin translation of the Quran by Robert of Ketton (1143), in *Machumetis Saracenorum … ipseque Alcoran,* ed. T. Bibliander (1543)
Calvini opera	*Ioannis Calvini Opera quae supersunt omnia* (vol. 29-87 of *Corpus reformatorum,* 1863-1900)
Dialogues	Servetus, *Dialogorum de trinitate libri duo*
Erasmus, *Opera omnia*	*Desiderii Erasmi Roterodami Opera omnia,* Amsterdam edition (1969 –)
Errors	Servetus, *De Trinitatis Erroribus*
Institutes	Calvin, *Institutio Christianae religionis*
PG	*Patrologia Graeca,* ed. J.-P. Migne (1857-1866)
PL	*Patrologia Latina,* ed. J.-P. Migne (1841-1855)
Restoration	Servetus, *Christianismi Restitutio*
Sentences	Peter Lombard, *Sententiarum libri quatuor*

Key to Annotations, Symbols, and Abbreviations

Typographical Conventions and Punctuation

The following conventions are used in all translated text.

Page Numbers

Page numbers in the translated text show the location of page breaks in the original sixteenth-century publications. The 1531 printing of *Errors* uses folio numbers instead of page numbers, so alternate pages are designated as "r" (recto) or "v" (verso). Page numbers are printed in boldface and enclosed in square brackets, e.g. **[10]** or **[32r]**.

Note that **all** references to page numbers in *Errors* and *Restoration* (in annotations, cross references, index, etc.) refer to these standard page numbers.

Text Supplied by Editors

Square brackets are used to identify text added to the translation to improve clarity. This includes section headings and subheadings that have been added in order to bring out the structure of the text.

> [*Other Objections to the Trinity*]
>
> [*The Trinity is Contrary to Reason*]
>
> It now remains for me to demonstrate, by means of reasoned argument and authoritative texts, that these three beings cannot coexist in one God.
>
> First of all, I could attack this imaginary triad by using the sixteen arguments [showing the logical inconsistencies in the idea of the Trinity] raised by Robert Holkot **[32v]** in distinction 5 of book 1 of his *Sentences*.[c] He does not give

In this passage, square brackets designate a heading, a subheading, and some additional text added by the editors, as well as a page break.

Quotations

Quotations from the Bible are printed in italics; quotation marks are used only if the quoted passage includes direct speech. Quotation marks are used for non-biblical quotations.

Key to Annotations, Symbols, and Abbreviations

> *them one heart, and one way.*[a] Also, in Acts 4, [we read] that *the multitude of believers were of one heart and of one soul.*[b] And in book 8 of *Against Celsus*, Origen expressly says that the passage ["*I and the Father are one*"] should be understood in accordance with [Acts 4]. He says that the Father and the Son are one, for, "although it is apparent that they are two beings in substance, they are one in agreement, harmony, and oneness of will."[c]

This passage includes quotations from the Bible, shown in italics. "I and the Father are one" is also in quotation marks because it is spoken by Jesus. The quotation from Origen is in quotation marks. Note unrelated use of italics for the book title, Against Celsus.

Marginal Notes

The original printings of both *Errors* and *Restoration* include occasional marginal notes. In this volume, these notes are indicated by curly brackets.

In both books, marginal notes such as "The First Objection of the Pharisees" or "The Second Argument of the Sophists" are used to indicate divisions of the text. In such cases we have formatted them as headings or subheadings. These headings are enclosed in curly brackets, instead of the square brackets that indicate headings supplied by the editors.

On the Errors of the Trinity also includes marginal notes that are not headings, but general comments such as "The words of Christ are especially to be heeded" or "All of their arguments are turned back upon them." Marginal notes of this type are shown in italics and right-justified.

> The debate about the equality or inequality of natures was unknown to the apostles.
>
> *{Ignorance of the [Hebrew] names for the divine has misled philosophers}*
>
> Some philosophize about an equality of nature [in divinity], because the same word [*dominus*, lord] is used

An example of a marginal note that is not a subheading

Cross References

Marginal notes are used to cross-reference parallel passages in *Errors* and *Restoration*.

> which [**42**] is continuously bringing forth the second, so that those two beings can then continuously breathe out a third from within themselves; and that "on the throne of majesty" this set of triplets "would be seated on the triclinium."ᶜ
>
> *Err, 40v*   Despite all these deviations and deformities, the three beings are said to be equal and of equal power. Indeed, as Augustine says in *Against Maximinus*, the Son has the

> Despite all these [**40v**] deviations, [Augustine] says,   *Rest, 42* in *Against Donatus*, that the three beings are equal and of equal power. For according to Augustine, the Son has the power to spew out a son for himself and a grandson for

Marginal notes link Restoration, page 42, with Errors, page 40v.

The Edinburgh Manuscript

There is a manuscript, held by the University of Edinburgh, containing an early version of the first sixteen pages of *The Restoration of Christianity*. This is described in more detail in the Introduction.

In this edition, we have printed the Edinburgh manuscript version and the final printed version on facing pages. The text is arranged so that parallel passages are printed side by side, showing which sections are common to both versions and which are found in only one or the other. The pages containing text from the Edinburgh manuscript are shaded so they can be identified easily.

Page numbers in the Edinburgh manuscript are prefaced with the letter E, for example [**E3**].

The Edinburgh Manuscript	The 1553 Printed Edition
God himself! *With our faces unveiled* we shall now behold God, whom we previously could not see. And we shall observe him clearly within ourselves, if only we open the door and set forth along the path. It is now time to open the door onto this path of light, *without which* nothing can be *seen, without which no one can* read the sacred writings, or know God, or be a Christian. This is the only path to truth that has been laid out for us — genuine, unerring, and easy to follow. If you, reader, begin to follow it, it will reveal the secrets of God to you. It is the only path that fully reveals the divine generation of Christ in the Word, and the true procession of the Holy Spirit; and shows that both [the Word and the Spirit] share the same substance in God. This path will lie open before you. It will lead you to all that is heavenly, and place the true God before your eyes. Come, therefore, pious reader, all you who yearn for Christ and have a sincere desire for his truth, gird yourself for the journey you are about to take with me. Always keep Christ before you as the goal. Always strive to understand who he is. Defend his honour and his glory everywhere. Commit yourself entirely to him. Always intent upon him [2] ... I am here diligently undertaking this work, which is pleasing to Christ and useful to ..., not ...[a] I have divided the whole path into five books, with some dialogues appended, so that we might ascend, step by step, to a full understanding of Christ. The first book contains three basic ἀξιώματα (*axiomata*, propositions) about Christ, three arguments of the Pharisees, and three of the sophists, as well as refutations of their extremely illogical inferences about invisible beings. The second book explains twenty passages of scripture. The third deals with the prefiguration of the	God himself! *With our faces unveiled*[a] we shall now behold God, whom we previously could not see. And we shall observe him shining within ourselves, if only we open the door and set forth along the path. It is now time to open the door onto this path of light, *without which* nothing can be *seen, without which no one can* read the sacred scriptures, [4] or understand God,[b] or be a Christian. This is the path to truth — genuine, unerring, and easy to follow. It is the only path that fully reveals the divine generation of Christ in the Word, and the true procession of the Holy Spirit; and shows that both [the Word and the Spirit] share the same substance in God. It is the only path that places God himself right before our eyes. I have divided the whole path into five books, with some dialogues appended, so that we might ascend, step by step, to a full understanding of Christ. The first book contains three basic propositions about Christ, three arguments of the Pharisees, and three of the sophists, as well as refutations of their extremely illogical inferences about invisible beings. The second book explains twenty passages of scripture. The third deals with the prefiguration of the

A sample of the Edinburgh manuscript and final printed text, in parallel columns. In this case the Edinburgh manuscript includes a paragraph that is not included in the printed edition.

Footnotes

In editorial content, such as the introduction and annotations, footnotes are numbered sequentially within each document. In translated text, footnotes are identified by superscript letters, starting over with "a" on every page. Note that the Edinburgh manuscript pages do not repeat footnotes that are found in the parallel text.

Identification of Works Cited

Works cited in footnotes may be identified in several different ways.

1. The most frequently cited sources are identified by abbreviations such as *Errors, Restoration, Sentences*. See the list of abbreviations above.

2. Works that are listed in the bibliography are identified by author and title, sometimes in shortened forms. Full publication details are found in the bibliography.

3. For works not in the bibliography, full publication details are supplied in the footnote.

Titles of works written in Latin (or in other languages using the Latin alphabet) are given in the original language in the footnotes, even though they are referred to in the main text by their English translations. For works written in languages using other character sets, such as Greek and Hebrew, English titles are used throughout.

Square brackets around the name of an author indicates that the work is no longer believed to have been written by the supposed author. Context should be sufficient to distinguish between the use of square brackets to indicate pseudepigrapha vs. the use of square brackets to indicate text supplied by the editors.

Use of Page Numbers and Section Numbers in Footnotes

Most of the primary sources cited in this book use some type of section numbers, so that they can be identified without having to specify a particular edition. Where this is not possible, page or folio numbers are used. For works that are in the standard collections *Patrologia Latina* (PL) or *Patrologia Graeca* (PG), the location information is included in the footnote.

---

[a] Augustine, *Enchiridion* 38 (PL 40 251-252).   [b] [Athanasius], *De ariana et catholica confessione* (PL 62 302C, 303D-304A).   [c] Basil, *Contra Eunomium* 2.8 (PG 29 586B-587B).   [d] Gregory of Nazianzus, *Orationes* 31.7 (PG 36 139C-D).   [e] *Sentences* 1.13.5 (PL 192 556), quoting Augustine, *De Trinitate* 15.47 (PL 42 1094-1095) and [Augustine], *Dialogus quaestionum XLV* 2 (PL 40 734).   [f] *Restoration*, 189 (book 5).   [g] De Oria, *De enunciatione* 2.2.6, quoting Aristotle, *Metaphysics* 5.2 (1013b 9-10) and *Physics* 2.3 (195a 9-10).   [h] Isa 48:16.

Example of various types of footnotes:
- *Abbreviation (footnotes e, f)*
- *Short Latin titles for works found in bibliography (footnotes a, b, c, d, e, g)*
- *English title for works written in Greek (footnote g)*
- *Square brackets to indicate pseudo author (footnotes b, e)*
- *Biblical citation (footnote h)*
- *Page number (footnote f)*
- *Section numbers (footnotes a, c, d, e, g)*
- *PL/PG locations (footnotes a, b, c, d, e)*

Key to Annotations, Symbols, and Abbreviations

Annotations

Annotations are explanatory notes, varying in length from a few sentences to multi-paragraph mini-essays. They are located at the end of the volume, after the appendixes. Annotations are numbered sequentially within each translated document. They are identified by superscript numbers in the translated text.

> Hilary's *On the Councils*, [where he writes] that, in God, "there are three in terms of substance."[67] The Master himself admits as much in [book 1] distinction 25,[d] and the rest follow him.

In translated text, superscript numbers indicate annotations (and letters indicate footnotes).

When annotations are referenced (in other annotations or in footnotes) they are identified as follows:

[a] Matt 2:13-15.   [b] Matt 2:15, quoting Hos 11:1.   [c] See A.R1.20.

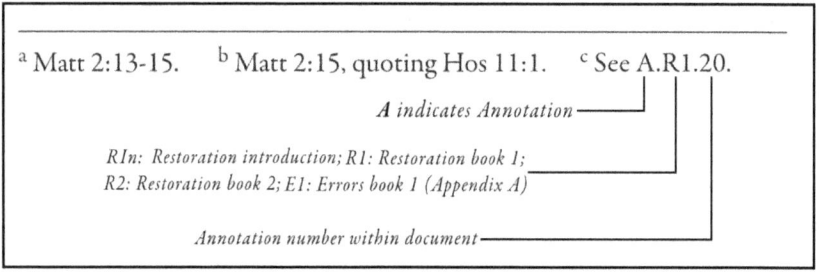

A indicates Annotation

RIn: Restoration introduction; R1: Restoration book 1; R2: Restoration book 2; E1: Errors book 1 (Appendix A)

Annotation number within document

In this example, A.R1.20 indicates annotation 20 for Restoration book 1.

A Note on the Text

The Restoration of Christianity

Only three copies of the original printing of *The Restoration of Christianity* are known to remain in existence. They reside at the Bibliothèque Nationale in Paris, the Österreichische Nationalbibliothek in Vienna, and the University of Edinburgh. In 1790 a transcription based on the Vienna copy, made to match the original pagination, was published in Nuremberg by Christoph Gottlieb von Murr. This was reprinted by Minerva of Frankfurt in 1966.

Until recently most scholars who have consulted *Restoration* have used the Murr transcription, which contains a number of copying mistakes, a few of which are significant. Fortunately, in recent years the Paris copy has been made available online on Gallica Bibliothèque Numérique, and the first 576 pages of the Vienna copy are reprinted in Ángel Alcalá, ed., *Miguel Servet: Obras Completas*, vols. 5 and 6 (Zaragoza: Larumbe, 2006). As these two copies of *Restoration* are defaced or damaged in different ways, it is helpful to be able to inspect both.

The Edinburgh Manuscript

At a very early stage, the first quire (pages 1-16) of the copy now in Edinburgh was replaced by a manuscript whose text varies significantly from that printed in 1553. The translation team was able to get a .pdf copy of the replacement manuscript from the University of Edinburgh Library. This helped us to verify and revise David Wright's useful 1989 transcription published in "The Edinburgh Manuscript Pages of Servetus' *Christianismi Restitutio*," in Elsie Anne McKee and Brian G. Armstrong (eds.), *Probing the Reformed Tradition* (Louisville: Westminster/John Knox, 1989).

On the Errors of the Trinity

In 1965 Minerva made a reprint of the original pages of both *On the Errors of the Trinity* and *Dialogues on the Trinity / On the Righteousness of Christ's Kingdom*. This volume is, unfortunately, missing pages 54v-55r from book 2 of *Errors*. Transcriptions of *Errors* are available in two bilingual editions: the Latin-Spanish edition in *Obras Completas*, volume 2-2 (2004), and the Latin-French edition translated by Rolande-Michelle Bénin and Marie-Louise Gicquel, *Sept Livres sur les erreurs de la Trinité* (Paris: Champion, 2008).

Pagnini Biblia Sacra

More than a half dozen copies of the 1542 Pagnini Bible, edited by Servetus, are available online via Google Books. One of these preserves a text that was censored by the Inquisition in Spain.

The fine print in Servetus's marginal notes is poorly inked and difficult to read, even when computer enlarged. The chapter headings, some of which Servetus modified, being more centrally located on the page, are more cleanly inked. The inking quality varies from copy to copy, so looking at more than one is sometimes required.

For comparative purposes, it is also possible to find online a 1528 Pagnini Bible, one of the several printings of his first edition, and several editions from after 1542, whose biblical text is closer to the 1527-28 original than the text as edited by Servetus. So far, the unauthorized 1541 version, from which Servetus adapted chapter headings, can only be consulted in a few scattered research libraries.

Introduction

Michael Servetus is best known as a victim of religious intolerance. In *The Decline and Fall of the Roman Empire* Edward Gibbon famously said, "I am more deeply scandalized at the single execution of Servetus than at the hecatombs which have blazed in the auto-da-fés of Spain and Portugal."[1] This is a sentiment that has resonated with many others, who have been shocked by the unjust and horrific treatment of Servetus, who, in 1553, was betrayed to the Inquisition by John Calvin and burned at the stake by the Protestant citizens of Geneva.

Servetus is also remembered for his contribution to the history of medicine. Two generations before the discovery of the circulatory system by William Harvey, Servetus described the passage of the blood through the lungs. He appears to have been the first European to publish a description of the so-called "lesser circulation." However, since the work that contains this revolutionary information was almost entirely suppressed and remained unread by scientists until well after Harvey's time, Servetus's description cannot be said to be an essential link in the history of the advance

---

[1] Edward Gibbon, *Decline and Fall of the Roman Empire* (London, 1776-1798), chap. 54, note 36.

of physiology. Nor was it intended as such. What Servetus wrote was conceived as a contribution to theology, describing how the Holy Spirit enters the body and forms the soul of a human being.

This brings us to what Servetus really cared about: how to picture God, how to understand God's plan for the world, how to become one of the children of God, and how to enlist on the right side in the cosmic struggle of good versus evil. These are the issues with which we must eventually engage if we are to come to terms with what Servetus actually wrote.

This volume contains a fresh translation of books 1 and 2 of the opening section, "On the Trinity," of Servetus's greatest theological work, *The Restoration of Christianity* (1553). It is the first volume of a projected multi-volume translation of "On the Trinity." It includes, as an appendix, book 1 of Servetus's first work, *On the Errors of the Trinity* (1531), completed when he was only about twenty-five years old. The similarities and differences between the opening books of the two works help us to understand the spiritual and intellectual growth that took place over two decades of Servetus's adult life. In another, more modest, appendix, we have provided material from the 1542 edition of Santes Pagnini's translation of the Bible, which was edited by Servetus. Servetus's introduction outlines his principles of biblical interpretation, and a selection of his marginal notes demonstrates his application of these principles. Also included in this book is a translation of the "Edinburgh manuscript," a variant version of the opening portion of book 1 of *Restoration*, which contains, among other things, personal information that Servetus later decided to exclude.

The Challenge of Understanding Servetus's Thought

Servetus's ideas have not been taken seriously by the great majority of theologians and scholars. Having been hunted by Roman Catholics and executed by Protestants, he is considered something of an embarrassment by many mainstream Christians. Accordingly, few of these writers have been motivated to make any careful investigation or analysis of his theology. His thought has been misrepresented by his theological enemies, deprecated by later confessional scholars, and considered beside the point by most of those who deplore the intolerance that led to his execution. And since Servetus's works contain many ideas with which modern religious liberals have little sympathy, even Unitarians, who claim him as a spiritual ancestor, have so far evinced little interest in undertaking the formidable task of coming to terms with his ideas. Most people know Servetus's theology only through capsule summaries, sometimes wildly inaccurate, found in histories and reference works written by scholars who have not studied Servetus's works first-hand.

Understanding Servetus's theology may appear to be an unmanageable task. He wrote in Latin and his chief work, *The Restoration of Christianity*, at 734 pages, is dauntingly massive. Servetus's writings have long had a reputation for being confusing, difficult to understand, and even incoherent. Early in the nineteenth century the Unitarian minister Andrews Norton, who had not himself read Servetus's works, reported, "It is said indeed, that his opinions on the subject of the person of our Saviour, as they appear in his writings, are not always intelligible, and his meaning does not always seem to be such as could be clearly explained."[2] A century later, Ephraim Emerton — professor of Ecclesiastical History at Harvard, an expert in translating from medieval Latin, and the author of a celebrated book on Erasmus — said that Servetus's "manner of expressing himself is confusing and intricate to the last degree, so much so that neither in his own time nor since has any one quite dared to say that he understood it ... to those who have studied him, even sympathetically, his thought remains to a great extent enigmatical."[3] Emerton's colleague at Harvard, George Foot

---

[2] Andrews Norton, "Life of Michael Servetus," *General Repository and Review* 4 (1813), 35.

[3] Ephraim Emerton, "Calvin and Servetus," *Harvard Theological Review* 2:2 (April 1909), 145. More recently David Bumbaugh, a Unitarian Universalist minister and historian, has seconded this sentiment, saying, "[Servetus's] teachings on the Trinity are difficult and tortuous to the modern mind." David Bumbaugh, *Unitarian Universalism: A Narrative History* (Chicago: Meadville Lombard Theological School, 2001), 19.

Moore, agreed, saying, "Servetus's theories of the constitution of the Godhead are not easy to define," and laid down prerequisites for Servetus study: "Even an intelligent misunderstanding of [Servetus's theology] requires more than a superficial acquaintance with the transient phase of philosophy to which he was addicted, and a first-hand knowledge of the history of doctrine, heresy, and controversy, from the Fathers to the Reformers."[4] As the Radical Reformation scholar John Godbey more recently remarked, "Most persons lack sufficient understanding of [Servetus's] views to make defensible statements about him."[5]

A modest goal, then, might be to try to make a few "defensible statements" about Servetus's "confusing," "intricate," and "enigmatical" thought, in hopes of approaching the "intelligent misunderstanding" that, given the passage of centuries and the differences in culture and education between Servetus and ourselves, is about all that we are entitled to expect. Nevertheless, it is my hope that this fresh reading of his works might accomplish something more.

Whatever else people think of Servetus, few could call him derivative. He is *sui generis*, almost a theological universe to himself. Although his theology was biblical, he interpreted Bible texts in his own way. And although he was influenced by many who went before him — ancients like Irenaeus and Tertullian and moderns like Ficino and Erasmus — he selected, from each of these, ideas that suited his plan and set aside the rest. To read Servetus, then, is to get an education in the history of religion and philosophy while, at the same time, learning something new.

Interest in Servetus has increased in recent years.[6] Religious intolerance, although deplored by the majority, remains a problem.

---

[4] George Foot Moore, review of Louis Israel Newman, *Jewish Influence on Christian Reform Movements*, in *American Historical Review* 32:1 (October 1926), 100.

[5] John Godbey, "Michael Servetus," unpublished paper (c.1987), 1.

[6] In the last two decades I have attended a number of conferences where Servetus was on the program. The topics discussed ranged widely: Servetus and Islam, Servetus and blood circulation, Servetus as a geographer, the authorship of a manuscript attributed to Servetus, Servetus and Unitarianism, Servetus and humour.

Introduction

Servetus's story continues to remind us of the horrors to which such hatreds inevitably lead. Beyond this, his curiosity and openness to evaluating potential truth wherever it might be found — whether it be in the Bible, the Quran, or in the words of Hermes Trismegistus, Zoroaster, Philo of Alexandria, or Moses Maimonides — is an inspiration to those who would not merely tolerate those with different religions, but welcome them for whatever spiritual insight they might have to share.

In his religious mission and his theological approach Servetus now stands as one of the principal pioneers of the Spanish Reformation. We may have to concede that he was a one-man reformation, a reformation that sadly went nowhere, as Spain remained virtually untouched by anything resembling Protestantism. But we must also note that Servetus was not really a Protestant. His ideas, neither welcome nor understood north of the Pyrenees, represented another potential branch from Roman Catholicism, a kind of reform quite different from that of the Lutherans and Calvinists. In the event, this Spanish reformer, like the Italian reformers of his time, ended up having more influence in eastern Europe (and much later in Britain and America) than in his homeland.

But this religious influence has become, over the years, much diluted and distorted. It is time that his theology began to be better understood. Servetus scholar and translator Earl Morse Wilbur hoped that, if the confusion surrounding his theology could be cleared up, "Servetus's proposed reconstruction of Christianity would be found to present some very attractive features, and regret might be aroused that some at least of his reforms were not adopted."[7] Acquiring a true picture of Servetus's religious thought leads us, I believe, to a portrait of a special kind of Christianity that is both liberal and grounded in the essential core of Christian revelation, one that encourages us to seek out the face of God in each other and to know that we are all children of God.

---

[7] Wilbur, *History of Unitarianism,* 1:208-209.

Introduction

Outline of a Life

We know far less about Servetus's life than we would like to know. In fact, we know far less than we think we know. Except for the few months when he was in prison and on trial for his life, hardly anything is known with certainty. Much of what we think we know about his earlier life is based on the testimony he offered under interrogation in Vienne and Geneva in 1553. These testimonies are contradictory and often demonstrably (and understandably) mendacious. For example, at Vienne he was trying to convince the French Inquisition that he was not Servetus at all, but a somewhat younger man who could not possibly have been old enough to have written *On the Errors of the Trinity* in 1531. Beyond this perjured testimony there are very few surviving documents that can definitely establish any detailed — or even general — information about the first ninety-five percent of his life.

Even the length of his life is controversial. Was he born in 1506, 1509, or 1511? The answer is important because we would like to know how educated and mature he was when he first emerged on the scene as the author of heretical published works, and whether he had time to accomplish all, or only some, of the activities he mentioned in his testimony. There are good reasons to believe that the earlier birthdate might be at least approximately correct, but the fact that 1509 and 1511 derive from his interrogation testimony has caused many scholars to prefer one or other of those later dates.[8]

Why is Servetus's life veiled in such obscurity? The first answer is that, in this respect, Servetus is not unique. Details of the life of William Shakespeare, who lived half a century later, are equally obscure, forcing biographers into much wild speculation.[9] Even John Calvin, whose later years are recorded in minute detail, has a youth whose record is broken by great lacunae.[10] Much of the

---

[8] Hughes, "In Search of Servetus's True Birthdate."

[9] See, for example, Bill Bryson, *Shakespeare: The World as Stage* (New York: HarperCollins, 2008), chap. 1.

[10] Noted in, for example, Alexandre Ganoczy, *The Young Calvin* (Philadelphia: Westminster Press, 1987), 60-61, 86; Bernard Cottret, *Calvin: A Biography* (Grand Rapids: Eerdmans, 1995), 65.

Introduction

information we lack is missing because it was never recorded. In the sixteenth century it was not dreamt that very much information would be required by posterity about people of such humble origin. And, of the records that once existed, many have been lost or destroyed in the intervening years. In particular, the Spanish Civil War was very hard on buildings in Aragon that may have contained archives and other evidence.[11]

We know particularly little about Servetus's life because he deliberately and continuously concealed the truth. Living much of his life in hiding, he did his best to erase the record of his early life and create a new identity, one designed to deflect both biographical and inquisitorial investigation. When he was discovered and identified, his enemies had no desire to publicize his ideas or his life story. As far as they were concerned, it would have been better if his very existence, together with his heresies, could have been expunged from the historical record. If he were lost to memory, then perhaps the very poor figure that Calvin cut, in the whole affair of Servetus's apprehension and execution, could be forgotten as well.

With these considerations in mind, then, let us summarize what we can know with reasonable certainty about Servetus's life.[12]

Miguel Serveto was born in Spain, early in the sixteenth century, and grew up in a small town, Villaneuva de Sijena, in Aragon. His parents were Antón Serveto, a notary, and Catalina Conesa. Among his siblings was Juan, who became a priest in the nearby town of

---

[11] Alcalá, introduction to *Obras Completas*, 1:xli-xlii. Hillar, *Michael Servetus*, 3.

[12] A large portion of the evidence upon which we base our conjectures about the outline of Servetus's life story is derived from the records of Servetus's interrogations in Vienne and Geneva, which are collected in *Calvini opera*, vol. 8. Roland Bainton's biography, *Hunted Heretic*, first published in 1953, remains a reasonably reliable source, less speculative than most. Also well-balanced is Ángel Alcalá's introduction to *Miguel Servet: Obras Completas,* vol. 1, as well as his introductions to subsequent volumes. A recent book by Miguel González Ancín and Otis Towns, *Miguel Servet en España*, presents documents that shed new light on Servetus's family constellation and early education. The authors rightly question some of the assumptions others, including Bainton, have made, yet, notably on the question of Servetus's birth and ancestry, engage in speculation of their own. See also Hillar, *Michael Servetus*.

Introduction

Poleñino.¹³ Miguel took his Master of Arts degree from the studium (proto-university) at Zaragoza, where Gaspar Lax, a relative, was senior master.¹⁴ In his youth Miguel was well-acquainted with Juan de Quintana, a chaplain in the Aragonese court of Emperor Charles V, and later imperial confessor. At some point — Servetus said that it was while he was studying law in Toulouse — he was introduced to the study of the Bible in its original languages.¹⁵

In 1530 Servetus arrived in Switzerland, where he lived for a time with the chief reformer in Basel, Johannes Oecolampadius. Because of his heretical beliefs he wore out his welcome there and in 1531 moved to Strasbourg, where he was briefly sponsored by the reformer Martin Bucer.¹⁶ Any support that Servetus enjoyed, however, ended later that year when he published *On the Errors of the Trinity*. In this work he did not (as is sometimes claimed) argue against the concept of the Trinity, as such. He was, however, severely critical of the doctrine as it was commonly taught, which he considered both gnostic and tritheistic. After this publication he was nearly universally condemned by both Protestants and Catholics,¹⁷ and hunted by the French and Spanish Inquisitions. The latter dispatched Juan Serveto to Germany to try to lure his brother back to Spain.¹⁸ There is no evidence that Servetus's attempt at a more moderate restatement, *Dialogues on the Trinity* (1532), did anything to mollify his critics.

In fear of his life, Servetus fled to France, where he took on a new identity under the name of Michel de Villeneuve. During the 1530s he was a student at the University of Paris, studying mathematics and medicine.¹⁹ Some time around 1534 Servetus, in his

---

[13] José Castro y Calvo, *Contribución al estudio de Miguel Servet* (Zaragoza, 1932), 30.

[14] Ancín and Towns, *Miguel Servet en España*, 269-272.

[15] *Calvini opera*, 8:846, 767.

[16] *Calvini opera*, 8:767.

[17] These reactions are surveyed in Bainton, *Hunted Heretic*, 37-47.

[18] Marcel Bataillon, "Honneur et inquisition: Michel Servet poursuivi par l'Inquisition espagnole," *Bulletin Hispanique* 27 (Jan.-Mar. 1925).

[19] *Calvini opera*, 8:848.

own persona, had an engagement to meet and debate with Calvin, who was then also a student in Paris. Servetus, for some reason, did not show up, and Calvin ever afterwards held this against him.[20]

To support himself during and after his student years, Servetus worked as a proofreader and editor for publishers in Lyons. He is known to have edited two editions of Ptolemy's *Geography* (1535 and 1541) and the second edition of Santes Pagnini's translation of the Bible (1542). In Lyons he became a disciple of the Neoplatonist physician Symphorien Champier, whose medical opinions he defended in a pamphlet, *Apology against Leonard Fuchs* (1536). His own principal medical work, written in Paris, was the monograph *On Syrups* (1537), in which he demonstrated his extensive knowledge of Greek and Islamic medical literature. His studies at Paris ended as a result of his being disciplined by the university and by the Parlement of Paris for his lectures on judicial astrology.[21] In the course of this controversy Servetus published a defence, *A Discourse in Favour of Astrology* (1538). There is no record of him taking a medical degree, in Paris or elsewhere, though he subsequently behaved as if he had one.[22]

Michel de Villeneuve practised medicine in a small town, Charlieu, for a few years. Beginning around 1541, he was taken on as physician by the Archbishop of Vienne, Pierre Palmier, who had been impressed by his lectures in Paris.[23] As an active and beloved citizen of Vienne, he helped supervise the construction of a bridge across the Rhône and volunteered to treat the hospitalized poor.[24]

---

[20] Calvin, *Déclaration*, 8-9, 58. Theodore Beza and Germain Colladon, *Vie de Calvin* (1565), in *Calvini opera*, 21:57.

[21] Juan Antonio Cremades Sanz-Pastor, *Miguel Servet en Francia* (Zaragoza: El Justicia de Aragon, 2008), 35-92.

[22] He appears to have gone briefly to Montpellier after Paris, and may have obtained his professional degree there. Alcalá, introduction to *Obras Completas*, lxxx.

[23] *Calvini opera*, 8: 767, 769, 777, 781, 846. Jérôme-Hermès Bolsec, *Histoire de la vie de Calvin* (Paris, 1577), 4r. Dedication to Ptolemy's Geography (1541).

[24] Cavard, *Le procès de Michel Servet*, 31-45.

By the early 1540s Servetus had revived his project of reforming the Christian faith. He reworked *On the Errors of the Trinity* and *Dialogues on the Trinity* into the first seven books of a new and much larger work. To these he added further books on the sacraments and on justification. Much of the theology of his early works was retained, but it was refined and backed up with better supporting scholarship. Added to this was the fruit of his growing enthusiasm for ancient and modern Neoplatonic and esoteric literature and his new espousal of anabaptism. A draft of this work, *The Restoration of Christianity*, was ready by the time he began a correspondence with Calvin in 1546.

This exchange of letters, facilitated by the Lyons publisher Jean Frellon, also included an exchange of books. Calvin sent Servetus a copy of the latest edition of his *Institutes,* and Servetus sent back a draft manuscript of *Restoration*. Expressing impatience, Calvin called off the correspondence after a few letters.[25] Servetus, still eager for debate, sent at least two dozen more letters, which the reformer set aside unanswered. Servetus sent back the *Institutes*, marked up with critical comments, and asked for the return of his draft. Calvin did not comply.[26] He retained all of the heretical papers sent to him in Servetus's handwriting as evidence that might be useful in the future. In a now notorious letter, Calvin reported to his friend Guillaume Farel that Servetus had sent him "a tedious volume of his deranged ideas" and had offered to come to Geneva to meet with him. He confided to Farel, "if he does come, as long as I continue to possess any authority, I will never allow him to go away alive."[27] In the French version of *On Obstacles* (1550) Calvin publicly revealed that the physician Michel de Villeneuve was really the heretic Servetus. This work, circulated among Protestants, did not come to the attention of the Inquisition. However, around this time Servetus believed that the leader of the Genevan Protestants

---

[25] D'Artigny, "Mémoires," 68. *Calvini opera*, 8:748-749, 833-834, 848-849.

[26] *Calvini opera*, 8:xxxi, 751.

[27] Calvin to Farel, 13 February 1546, in *Calvini opera*, 12:283.

had indeed informed on him to the Roman Catholic authorities.[28] To another Geneva minister, Abel Poupin, Servetus disclosed, "I know that in that cause I will certainly die."[29]

In the early fall of 1552 Servetus decided that *The Restoration of Christianity* was essentially finished and arranged to have a thousand copies printed in a secret location. In early 1553 Calvin received a pre-publication copy, from which, through intermediaries, he sent a quire to the French Inquisition in Lyons. He followed up with documents in Servetus's own handwriting.[30] In April, Michel de Villeneuve was arrested and interrogated. He denied being Servetus, and related a life history in which he attempted to show that he was just someone who had at one time been impressed by Servetus and who had taken on Servetus's persona only in order to debate Calvin.[31] When it became clear to him that, in spite of his efforts, the identity of Servetus and de Villeneuve would soon be established, he escaped from jail, possibly with the connivance of friends.[32]

We next hear about Servetus when, on August 13, 1553, he was arrested in Geneva. Calvin, again through an intermediary, provided the accusations that resulted in the fugitive's detention. This time Servetus did not deny his identity, but told a story that emphasized his Protestant credentials. He was interrogated by the ruling council of the city, the public prosecutor, and Calvin himself.[33] He also engaged in a written debate with Calvin and the other Geneva ministers.[34] The Genevans then sent away for advice from the other Protestant churches in Switzerland.[35] With these answers in hand,

---

[28] Calvin, *Des Scandales*, 98. Calvin, *Déclaration*, 53-54.

[29] *Calvini opera*, 8:751.

[30] D'Artigny, "Mémoires," 78-79, 82-83, 93-94.

[31] D'Artigny, "Mémoires," 98-100. *Calvini opera*, 8:848-849.

[32] D'Artigny, "Mémoires," 111-114. *Calvini opera*, 8:746, 788.

[33] *Calvini opera*, 8:725-782.

[34] Philip E. Hughes, *The Register of the Company of Pastors of Geneva in the Time of Calvin* (Grand Rapids: Eerdmans, 1966), 223-284.

[35] *Calvini opera*, 8:803.

the council declared Servetus guilty of blasphemy and condemned him to death.[36] On October 27, 1553, he was burned at the stake. By this time all of the bales of *Restoration* had been rounded up and burned. In the end, only three printed copies survived.[37]

Although biographical data about Servetus is frustratingly sparse, and often based on documents of doubtful veracity, his theological writings constitute a rich and, I believe, underused source of biographical information. By this I do not refer to the occasional nuggets of possible personal information found in *Restoration* (or the Edinburgh manuscript draft).[38] What I mean is a different kind of information: evidence of what Servetus read and when he read it, what he learned and when he knew it. His books are a record of his intellectual biography.

One might ask, if Servetus published only in 1531-32 and 1553, how can we know what he was reading and learning in the years leading up to the publication of these books? One way is to look for patterns in his use of sources. It is sometimes possible to determine the date or place of writing of a particular passage by ascertaining the collection of books that he likely had at hand at the time. Another way is to look carefully into the availability of the books that he cited. Servetus lived in an interesting time in this respect. Printed books had been in existence for less than a hundred years. Many important works were first set in print during his lifetime. Since it is unlikely that he had much access to manuscript editions, we can be fairly confident that he became familiar with the contents of a work only after its first printing. Sometimes we can even identify the particular edition that Servetus used, based on a close scrutiny of the variances in his quotations of a text. And if we

---

[36] *Calvini opera*, 8:827-830.

[37] *Calvini opera*, 14:599-600, 8:755-756. Émile Doumergue, *Jean Calvin* (Lausanne, 1926), 6:269-275. Madeline E. Stanton, "Bibliography of Servetus," in John F. Fulton, *Michael Servetus* (New York: Reichner, 1953), 84-86.

[38] For example, what appears to be an eyewitness account of the imperial coronation in Bologna in 1530; or the description of Servetus's feelings as a fugitive after he went into hiding following the nearly universally hostile reception of *Errors* and *Dialogues*. See *Restoration*, 462; *Restoration* (Edinburgh manuscript), 3.

know that he used an item in a particular collection, we can guess that he used other items in the same collection. These methods, in coordination with the differences between the printed copies and the partial manuscripts of *Restoration*, can give us a surprisingly detailed chronology of Servetus's reading and a stratification of many of the passages in his text.

On the Errors of the Trinity and *The Restoration of Christianity* take us as close to Servetus as we can get. The biographical information gathered by reading and analyzing his books is the internal story of his education, the itinerary of his intellectual journey, the evolution of his thought, and the *bildungsroman* narrating the emergence of his hopes and dreams.

The Development of On the Errors of the Trinity

The book that Servetus produced in 1531, *On the Errors of the Trinity*, was a remarkable achievement for a young man of twenty-five or so. It might justly be compared to the first version of Calvin's *Institutes of the Christian Religion*, published in 1536 when its author was just twenty-seven. And, like the *Institutes*, which grew more than four-fold in size by the time it reached its final form in 1559, Servetus's *Errors* was greatly augmented by the time it had been reshaped as *The Restoration of Christianity* in 1553. Of course these two books had different fates. *Institutes* became, even to this day, a perennial seller, serving as the theological manual and spiritual guide for the Reformed Church. Servetus's contribution to the Reformation was anathematized and, in its final form, almost completely suppressed.

Book 1 of *On the Errors of the Trinity* — roughly the first third of the text—is designed for a Spanish audience. In it Servetus addressed the issue of the reluctance of Jewish and Muslim monotheists to genuinely convert to Christianity[39] — a major concern in Spain, but a subject of minor interest and importance elsewhere.

Spain, unlike France, Germany, and Switzerland, was territory that had until recently been shared, and fought over, by Christian

---

[39] *Errors*, 37v, 42v-43r.

and Muslim princes. In the Muslim principalities that existed in the Iberian peninsula there had been a kind of toleration extended towards the other two Abrahamic religions, which allowed the Jews, in particular, to flourish. But in the years leading up to the reconquest by the Christian kingdoms, completed in 1492, the situation changed. In that year, all Jews who did not consent to convert to Christianity were expelled. Those who did become Christians — the *conversos* — remained under suspicion, for it was widely believed that many former Jews had not converted whole-heartedly and that they secretly practiced Judaism. The institution of the Spanish Inquisition was created to police the "New Christians" and to eradicate any who were found to be guilty, or even suspected, of backsliding. The same harsh treatment — forced conversion, suspicion, persecution — was soon afterwards extended to the *Moriscos*, the former Muslims who remained in Spain when those who refused to renounce their faith were driven into exile.

Why, Servetus must have wondered, would whole populations allow themselves to be deprived of most of their possessions and driven out of their country, to face deadly peril in strange lands, rather than embrace Christianity? And why was it that so many of those who converted did so only reluctantly, and afterwards longed for the religious rituals, customs, and ideas that they had formerly embraced? He concluded that there must be some flaw at the heart of the Christian faith that was a stumbling-block for these other, stricter monotheists. For many Muslims and Jews did not consider Christianity to be a proper monotheism at all. Accordingly, Servetus identified the orthodox doctrine of the Trinity as the reason for this hesitancy. How could Christianity claim to be a true monotheism if its adherents worshipped what appeared to be three gods?

On the Errors of the Trinity was the fruit of these early speculations. Servetus wrote: "This cause presented itself to me when I was but a young man, about twenty years old. Without any human instruction, I was driven by a divine impulse to write on this subject."[40] If he was born around 1506, this would have been around

---

[40] *Restoration* (Edinburgh manuscript), 2.

Introduction

1526 — which is also the earliest date he could have come across the editions that he used of Irenaeus's *Against Heresies* and pseudo-Clement's *Recognitions*, first printed in that year. Both of these works were important to him, and, as we shall see, Irenaeus was central in the development of his theology. In fact, discovering and reading Irenaeus may have been an essential part of the "divine impulse" that set his project in motion.

In writing *Errors*, Servetus does not appear to have been working from a comprehensive plan made at the outset. Rather, he started with book 1 and then added to it by a process of accretion. He would begin by proposing a major idea and then, in subsequent books, would refine it and clarify it, as additional ways of thinking about it occurred to him. Occasionally one of these explanations evolved into a new major idea that would then itself require expansion, restatement, and clarification. Apparently Servetus did not do much revision of his earlier text as he went along. The clarifications were not inserted next to the earlier sections that they modified, but were added at the end of *Errors* in the form of a new book. The later books were lightly integrated into the whole by a system of forward and backward references. The only substantial attempt to put his arguments into better order happened many years later when he rearranged and transformed *Errors*, together with much new material, in order to create the opening five books of *The Restoration of Christianity*.

This process can be more readily grasped by surveying an outline of *Errors*. (Asterisks flag Servetus's major ideas. The rest constitute clarifications, developments, and restatements of earlier themes.)

Book 1 *Christ, who is God and the Son of God, is a real human being.
Arguments against Servetus's assertions and refutations, including discussion of the name Elohim.
*The Holy Spirit is not a separate being, but an activity of God.
*The doctrine of the Trinity is not mentioned in Scripture, and is incoherent.

Book 2 *Christ was first the Word and then the Son.
The Holy Spirit is God's Spirit working within us.

Introduction

Book 3   The Word was first uttered in the creation of the world, then made incarnate.
The Father did not suffer as a consequence of Christ's embodiment.
Christ is the Wisdom of God.
The Word, a disposition of God, is not the Spirit of God.

Book 4   God shows himself to us in three dispositions.
*Christ is the image, or appearance, of God.
With the appearance of Christ, the Word no longer exists.

Book 5   A discussion of the Hebrew words for God, and how they apply to Christ.

Book 6   Christ is the way that we see God.

Book 7   The Son is the word spoken by God.
Christ is a blend of God and a human being.
The Word is a disposition of God.
The Holy Spirit is a disposition of God.
The Word showed God in bodily form.

This outline shows Servetus stating ideas, defending them, evolving and expanding them in the course of his defence — and defending them yet again. You will not find all of his ideas about Christ, the Word, or the Holy Spirit gathered into one place in *Errors*. For example, the Word is discussed in book 2, then again in book 3, and clarifications are added in books 4 and 7. Many of the books, being agglomerations of a variety of ideas, cannot possibly be given a helpful thematic title. Rather, each book represents a new stage in the progressive refinement of Servetus's theology.

Most of Servetus's major ideas are laid out in book 1, including his well-known critique of the Trinity. But two important doctrines come later. In book 2 he puts forth his exposition of the history of Christ, telling of the transformation of the Word into the Son of God. And book 4 contains the first major statement of the central Servetan concept that the man Christ is the appearance of God, the way that we humans encounter divinity. As we read further and

Introduction

further into *Errors*, we witness Servetus refining his apologetic to meet new objections that arose in his own reflection on these subjects or that he encountered in discussing his work with others. The irony is that in order to respond to others' objections and to try to better accommodate his teachings to mainstream theology, Servetus sometimes introduced ideas — like his history of the mutually exclusive stages of Christ — that were viewed as even more heretical than those he was trying to explain away.

Thus it appears that *On the Errors of the Trinity*, though a work of fairly modest dimension, was written over a relatively long period of time. This analysis confirms the general outline of the theory proposed by the nineteenth-century German Servetus enthusiast, Henri Tollin, that *Errors* was written in several distinct stages, at different times, in different places, and with different audiences in mind.[41]

As we have seen, book 1 of *Errors* — about a third of the whole — appears to have been written for a Spanish, Roman Catholic audience. Accordingly, Servetus felt that he needed to address Peter Lombard's authoritative compilation, *Sentences*, full of quotations from Hilary, Augustine, and the later Church Fathers. He also challenged the medieval church philosophers and theologians. Most of his non-biblical citations and quotations — Peter Lombard's *Sentences*, Isidore of Seville's *Etymologies*, the Church Fathers, the medieval scholastics — are to be found in book 1. It seems that, when writing the first part of *Errors*, Servetus had ready access to a lot of books, perhaps a library. While living in Spain, he may have had the resources of a university at his disposal. Or perhaps he availed himself of the substantial personal collection of Juan de Quintana. Tollin proposed that book 1 may have been written as a letter addressed to Quintana. Certainly this distinguished cleric, who was an expert on Duns Scotus, could well have been the target of Servetus's discussion of late scholastic philosophers. However, when Quintana was asked in 1532 to comment on the recently

---

[41] Henri Tollin, *Das Lehrsystem Michael Servets* (Gütersloh, 1876), 1:135.

published *Errors*, he did not admit to his interlocutor, the papal nuncio Girolamo Aleandro, that the notoriously heretical book had been written while Servetus was under his tutelage.[42]

Book 2 has far fewer non-biblical citations, relative to the length of the book, and the density of them is even less in books 3 to 7. It is likely that Servetus no longer had reliable access to a library and was constantly on the move when writing the later books of *Errors*. He may then have been able to consult only the few volumes that he could carry in his luggage, together with those he might have found on the shelves at the residences where he visited. Furthermore, while sojourning in Protestant lands, he may have calculated that he could better appeal to evangelical minds by basing his arguments more completely on the Bible — almost, but not quite, *sola scriptura*.

References to rabbinic Jewish sources appear only in the second and subsequent books of *Errors*. The relatively late appearance of such sources indicates that Servetus did not, as some have contended, have a Jewish upbringing and education. It is clear that his interest in Hebrew arose only in young adulthood, after he was exposed to humanistic and evangelical thinking, which gave him the desire to read the Bible in its original languages.

The idea that the disposition known as the Word ceases to exist, and that the Son only begins to exist with the incarnation, is first enunciated in book 2, then developed further in books 3 and 4. In his letters to Servetus, Johannes Oecolampadius complained about the denial that the Son is eternal or co-eternal with the Father.[43] Thus these books were probably either already completed, or in the process of being written, in late 1530 and early 1531, when Servetus was lodging with Oecolampadius in Basel. Willingness to take up certain already-discussed theological points and to restate them in alternative ways may have been Servetus's attempt to win over the ecumenical and relatively open-minded and tolerant Martin Bucer,

---

[42] Girolamo Aleandro to Pope Clement VII, 17 April 1532, in *Monumenta Vaticana historiam ecclesiasticam saeculi XVI* (Freiburg im Breisgau, 1861), 109.

[43] Oecolampadius to Servetus, in *Calvini opera*, 8:857-861.

with whom he stayed later in 1531. In the event neither Oecolampadius nor Bucer was willing or able to entertain, or tolerate, any of Servetus's reformulations.

In 1532, after *On the Errors of the Trinity* had been printed and then condemned, Servetus tried — unsuccessfully yet again — to put forth his ideas in a way that he hoped might render them relevant to Protestants. In a new work, *Dialogues on the Trinity*, he added his take on the Eucharist and justification, doctrines much discussed and contested by Reformation thinkers. To *Dialogues* Servetus appended a very short work, *On the Righteousness of Christ's Kingdom*, which dealt with justification in more detail. He tried to overcome the Protestant-Catholic divide over the relative merits of faith versus works by coming down on the side of love. Unfortunately this promotion of ecumenism, known to have come from the same pen that had produced what were considered dangerous and egregious heresies, did not inspire either Catholic or Protestants to reconsider. The many forces arrayed to resist Servetus's irenic appeal were far too committed to their own directions of advance.

For several years, until it became too dangerous to do so, Servetus persisted in trying to search out new formulas that would give his theology general appeal. The record of these various futile attempts is recorded in *On the Errors of the Trinity* and *Dialogues on the Trinity*, which together constitute the intellectual autobiography of Servetus during the years 1526-32.

The Plan of The Restoration of Christianity

The work that Servetus began in the early 1540s was, at the same time, a new book and a revision of his earlier writings. In the decade since he completed his youthful theological works, Servetus had studied the Bible intensively in the course of his editorial labours. His theological ideas had been strengthened and extended by his study of occult and Neoplatonic writings. He had embraced anabaptism and millenarianism. And, having witnessed the erratic progress of the Reformation, particularly the events in Geneva and the career of Calvin, Servetus felt that there was still much work to be done to renovate Christianity and to steer church reform onto the proper course.

Introduction

Servetus's general plan was to reshape *On the Errors of the Trinity* by excising its weaker arguments, firming up the old material with the results of more careful research, and adding the new apologetic that he had been developing throughout the decade. His earlier works had been written hastily and with relatively few resources. For example, in *Errors*, many Church Fathers and other authorities had, of necessity, been quoted at second-hand. Being more settled in the 1540s, he had long-term access to libraries and was able to amass a modest personal collection of books. Also, with more ancient authors having been edited, translated, and published, he was now able to employ a more careful and consistent level of scholarship. As a result it appears that, though his theological views were not substantially changed, they were clarified and enhanced, and given deeper and more solid foundations. He also had a sense of the wider audience to whom his arguments were now directed.

To the end that his main points might stand out more clearly and not be misunderstood, he set about reorganizing his material. The seven books of *On the Errors of the Trinity* and the two books of *Dialogues on the Trinity* were transformed into the five books and two dialogues that comprised "On the Trinity," the first major section of *The Restoration of Christianity*.

Book 1

Book 1 of *The Restoration of Christianity* is similar in content to book 1 of *On the Errors of the Trinity*. They both survey ways of thinking, about the Trinity and about Christ, that Servetus felt to be both incorrect and pernicious. A little more than a third of the text in book 1 of *Restoration* is taken directly from *Errors*, including nearly half of the text in the first half of the book. The general outline of the book is also retained, including three propositions, three objections of the Pharisees, and three arguments of the sophists. Thus this is the book where comparisons with *Errors* can most readily be made.

The opposition to Peter Lombard (and, by extension, official Roman Catholic theology) is largely confined to book 1 of both *Errors* and *Restoration*. Peter Lombard's *Sentences* is Servetus's source for much material from the Latin post-Nicene Church Fathers, particularly Hilary and Augustine, who are rarely mentioned in the later books. There is a sprinkling of late Greek Fathers. Of these, the one mentioned most is Athanasius, a natural target in any critique of the Trinity. However, most of Servetus's quotations from Athanasius are actually from works now known not to have been written by Athanasius. There are many citations of the ante-Nicene Fathers, particularly Irenaeus and Tertullian, but since these writers are formative in Servetus's theology, references to them can be found throughout his works. In *Restoration*, in addition to adding much that was new from his study of the Church Fathers, he rechecked and revised the many patristic quotations he had previously taken from secondary sources. He also trimmed back, eliminated, or revised passages that could be interpreted as advocating Arianism.

In both *Errors* and *Restoration*, book 1 contains arguments based upon medieval scholastics, terminist logic, and the Quran. The scholastic section from *Errors* was incorporated into *Restoration* without much change, and there is no evidence that Servetus attempted any double-checking of this material. The passing reference in *Errors* book 1 to terminist logic, a late medieval development, is expanded in *Restoration* to a couple of paragraphs, with several examples of paradoxical syllogisms. In the case of the Quran, in *Restoration* he retained the secondary material from *Errors*, but added copious quotations drawn directly from the Latin translation of the Quran. In these books references to ancient Greek philosophers are largely confined to Aristotle and Plato, unlike later books (especially *Restoration* book 4 and dialogue 1) in which Servetus dropped quite a variety of names. The references to Plato, all in *Errors*, are quite general; for example, turning the philosopher into a verb: to platonize. The quotations from Aristotle (or pseudo-Aristotle), found in both of Servetus's works, are well-known nuggets that may have been gathered from secondary works.

Book 2

Formally, book 2 of *The Restoration of Christianity* is unique in Servetus's work. It consists of twenty mini-essays of varying length, each discussing a biblical passage, or a set of related passages, all bearing on his understanding of the nature of Christ. No other book in *On the Errors of the Trinity* or *The Restoration of Christianity* has the peculiar structure of *Restoration*, book 2. It must be noted, however, that much of the content, or at least the seeds of the content, of the great majority of these essays can be found in *Errors* (mostly in books 2 and 3). Only passages 4 and 18 are entirely new.[44]

When considering the construction and contents of book 2 of *Restoration*, we ought to look back to portions of the more structurally heterogeneous book 1. The sections labeled "three objections of the Pharisees" and "three arguments of the sophists," and the discussion of two scriptural passages between these sections, constitute eight additional mini-essays on biblical proof-texts. These portions of book 1 should be considered an important part of Servetus's overall biblical demonstration, presented in book 1 because they were needed immediately as part of the argument against the orthodox portrayal of the Trinity. Accordingly, those Bible passages featured in book 2 may be viewed as preparation for subsequent books. To this end, the text of book 2 is full of forward references. These passages stand as a set of proof-texts that, among other things, shed light on book 3 of *Restoration*, which presents Christ as the face or appearance of God.

By organizing book 2 as he has done, and by placing it in such a prominent location near the beginning of the work, Servetus was also highlighting the centrality of Bible study for the development of his theology, and its importance in the education of anyone who aspired to contribute to Christian religious thought. He may also have wished to demonstrate how naturally his main theological tenets flowed from a study of key scriptural passages. By piling evidence upon evidence, he hoped to lead readers to discover for themselves the conclusions to which he was eventually going to lead them.

---

[44] Passage 1 is drawn from books 2 and 3 of *Errors*; passages 2, 3, 9, and 11 from book 2; and passages 7, 8, 12, 13, 14, 15, and 19 from book 3. There are small contributions from book 3 in passages 16 and 17, and seeds of passages 5 and 20 in book 4. Passage 6 takes a little from books 1 and 5, and passage 10 takes something from book 7.

The Rest of "On the Trinity"

Book 3 of *The Restoration of Christianity* collects and focuses Christological ideas that had been spread out over books 2, 3, 4, 6, and 7 of *On the Errors of the Trinity* and the original *Dialogues on the Trinity*. Although book 1, being more critical and focused on the Trinity, is more notorious, book 3 is actually more central to Servetus's way of thinking, and is the book that might give readers the most accurate idea of what Servetus was about. Much of book 1 is negative theology, clearing away the underbrush, explaining what he does not think, and proving others wrong. Book 3 is more constructive and makes it easier to see that Servetus's idea of Christ is not intricate, complicated, or confused, but simply stated, coherent, and elegant. Christ is God's self-revelation in the form human beings can best understand: as a human being. Christ is a real human being with a single nature, but at the same time he is entirely God and inherently celestial.

Book 4 of *Restoration*, lightly seeded by the discussion of the Old Testament names of God in book 5 of *Errors*, contains a great deal of new material that Servetus drew from pre-Christian, Hermetic, Neoplatonic, and Renaissance writings (for example, those of Marsilio Ficino and Agostino Steuco). This book is most interesting to those who wish to know what Servetus had learned since he wrote *Errors* and to discover in what new directions his theology might have been heading. Although his central ideas are unchanged, this new book provides a broader basis of proof and evidence for his central thesis and, as well, a more extensive foundation for spiritual knowledge that includes information drawn from outside the Abrahamic faiths, notably Greece, Persia, and Egypt.

In book 5 of *Restoration*, things become even more interesting to modern readers. Here Servetus brings together his ideas about the Holy Spirit, which had been spread through several unconnected sections in *Errors*. The major addition in the first half of the book is a long account of how the Holy Spirit enters a human being, which includes the celebrated description of the pulmonary transit of the blood. This was in aid of showing that the Holy Spirit, though a disposition of God, has no real personality, as we might understand it, but is more akin to air: actually something contained in the air that comes from God, from Christ, to enter into us. Servetus's physiological explanation of how the spirit goes from the heart to the brain and operates within the cavities in the head is not at all ground-breaking; on the contrary, it is largely in accordance with old theories which, in his time, were beginning to be questioned and cast aside.

The two dialogues of *Restoration* are formally similar to those published in 1532, but are longer and pursue new topics. In both dialogues there is much Neoplatonic and Hermetic material, following up on book 4. Dialogue 1 has new long discussions of angels and hell. Dialogue 2 contains more arguments drawn from Servetus's scientific and medical studies, combined with Neoplatonic emanationism. Using his knowledge of embryology and obstetrics, he discusses the development of unborn children and the process by which the soul enters the newborn child at birth.

The Treatises on the Sacraments and Salvation

The five books and two dialogues that make up the "On the Trinity" section of *The Restoration of Christianity* are substantial enough to form a complete volume by themselves. But Servetus had much more to say than could be contained within the bounds of this new work on Christology. He also wished to adjudicate the Protestant-Catholic debates on salvation and the sacraments. Accordingly, he composed two new treatises, "On Faith and the Righteousness of Christ's Kingdom, Surpassing the Righteousness of the Law, and on Love," and "On the Heavenly Rebirth and the Kingdom of the Antichrist."

The first of these is an twofold expansion of his 1532 treatise, "On the Righteousness of Christ's Kingdom," which had been published with his *Two Dialogues*. In these, while paying lip-service to the Protestant emphasis on the priority of faith over works, he teaches that good works are also required if the person who has been saved through faith is to acquire any merit in the sight of God. In 1532 he claimed that he had found a position between that of Protestantism and Catholicism, that mediated between the two and avoided the errors attached to each of them. Moreover, he proposed that the path out of this false dichotomy, greater than faith or works, was love. For faith without deeds, and, even more, faith without love, is empty. Faith is merely the doorway to the kingdom, but the whole path to eternal life is love.[45] Since Servetus believed that grace is breathed in through the air, he thought that good works and love can emerge in human beings apart from any particular intellectual faith.[46]

The second item, "On Heavenly Rebirth and the Kingdom of the Antichrist," in four books, is a work of the same order of magnitude as "On the Trinity." It features two of Servetus's new ideas, acquired since he wrote his 1531-1532 works: millenarianism and anabaptism. He thought that Armageddon, the great battle between good and evil, between Christ and Antichrist, would commence in 1585.[47] This struggle would be led by the archangel Michael, with whom Miguel Serveto/Michel de Villeneuve naturally identified.

Servetus came to believe strongly in adult baptism, and deplored paedobaptism. He thought that the proper time for this important sacrament was not physical maturity, but intellectual and spiritual maturity, at thirty years of age.[48] In book 3, "On Heavenly Rebirth," he discussed the three services provided by the church: preaching, baptism, and communion. In book 4 he listed twenty arguments against the baptism of children and then enumerated twenty-five true descriptions of baptism. His penchant for such lists continued in a later section, on the Antichrist.

Signs of the Antichrist

Restoration includes a very short work, actually no more than a pamphlet of a few pages, "Sixty Signs of the Kingdom of the Antichrist." Although thematically it is closely related to part of "On Heavenly Rebirth and the Kingdom of the Antichrist," it is situated

---

[45] Servetus, *De justicia regni Christi*, F7v, F5v. *Restoration*, 350.

[46] Servetus, *De justicia regni Christi*, F4r. *Restoration*, 349.

[47] *Restoration*, 396. The date of 1585 was calculated by adding 1260 (from Rev 11:3, "And I will grant my two witnesses power to prophesy for 1260 days") to 325 (the year of the council of Nicaea).

[48] *Restoration*, 372, 413.

Introduction

later in the book, between the "Letters to Calvin" and the "Apology to Melanchthon." Servetus had it carefully placed in the printed volume so that part of it falls on page 666.

The Letters to Calvin and Melanchthon

To all of this Servetus eventually added two further works as a kind of appendix. One was a set of thirty unanswered letters addressed to Calvin, written in the wake of his 1546 correspondence with that reformer. In published form, they act as "open letters" to Calvin, and cover much ground gone over elsewhere. The final section of *The Restoration of Christianity* was, in effect, another open letter, "Apology to Melanchthon." This constitutes a long discussion of Servetus's use of the Apostolic and ante-Nicene Fathers, which Melanchthon had criticized in several editions of his *Loci Communes*. Here Servetus discussed authors like Irenaeus and Ignatius, at greater length than was offered in the earlier books.

To Melanchthon, and many other Reformation theologians, including Calvin, the early Church Fathers, before the later days when trinitarian doctrine was fully elaborated, spoke with the same voice, even if they lacked the terminology to express it. Servetus, on the other hand, thought that Irenaeus and the other early Church Fathers used different terms, and spoke in a different way, because they, being closer to the time of Christ, had a clearer and less degenerate picture of what the incarnation was all about. Each of these approaches, to Calvin and to Melanchthon, involving some measure of sarcasm and abuse—for example, accusing Calvin of being drunk—was ultimately viewed as a form of *lèse majesté*.[49]

The Edinburgh and Paris Manuscripts

We are fortunate to possess, though also frustratingly tantalized by, two partial early versions of *The Restoration of Christianity*. These are found in two manuscripts, one now held at the University of Edinburgh and the other at the Bibliothèque Nationale in Paris. The Edinburgh manuscript covers the opening of *Restoration*, the first

---

[49] *Restoration*, 675. *Calvini opera*, 8:728, 730-731. It should be noted that the abuse went both ways.

Introduction

16 pages of book 1. The Paris manuscript, which I plan to discuss in more detail in the next volume, contains a version of books 3 through 5 and dialogue 1 of "On the Trinity," pages 92-246, with the books copied out in a different order. These two manuscripts are not in Servetus's hand, but have been copied from earlier exemplars. The texts they contain vary in interesting ways from those in the printed edition, giving us glimpses of two earlier stages in Servetus's composition.

We cannot be sure exactly how these manuscripts came to be in the forms that we now have. How did the copyists who made them come to be in possession of Servetus's drafts? We do know of a draft that was at one time in Calvin's hands: the manuscript book that Servetus sent to Calvin in the course of their 1546 correspondence. It has been speculated (but is by no means certain) that this "book," retained by Calvin, is the source from which the Edinburgh manuscript was eventually copied.[50]

There is no internal evidence in the Edinburgh manuscript that could date it precisely, except to say that the language looks a little less polished than that of the printed version, and that the text appears to be at an intermediate stage between that in *Errors* and that in *Restoration*. The most fascinating thing, entirely unique to the Edinburgh manuscript, is a bit of biographical detail, describing Servetus's feelings when, early in the 1530s, he first went into hiding from the inquisition and thought of fleeing to the New World.[51] He likely removed this passage before the final version that was sent to the printer because it was too personal and self-revelatory for a work of theology.

Calvin is known to have sent pages from a printed copy of *Restoration* to the Inquisition in France. This would have left him in

---

[50] Leonard L. Mackall, "A Manuscript of the *Christianismi Restitutio* of Servetus, placing the Discovery of the Pulmonary Circulation Anterior to 1546," *Proceedings of the Royal Society of Medicine* (17 October 1923), 35-38. Roland Bainton, "The Smaller Circulation: Servetus and Colombo," *Sudhoffs Archiv für Geschichte der Medizin* (October 1931), 371-374. Wright, "The Edinburgh Manuscript Pages," 283-285.

[51] *Restoration* (Edinburgh manuscript), 3.

possession of a mutilated copy of the print edition, to set alongside the draft he received in 1546. It seems reasonable to suppose that Calvin, or someone else who later came into possession of these items, commissioned a new manuscript, copied from the one sent by Servetus, shaped to replace the missing quire in the (by then rare) print volume.

Servetus and the Bible

Everyone who treasures or studies the Bible really only masters and values a portion of that compendium. It is not so much that people necessarily consciously reject some portions of Scripture (though in fact many do), but that the collection of biblical books is so copious and heterogeneous that it is impossible for even the most enthusiastic or learned students of the Bible to hold it all in their heads. Given the variety of minds that encounter the Bible, each with their own predispositions and interests, it is not surprising that different individuals will sift the scriptures and identify different sets of the most valuable books and passages, while other parts may be dismissed as irrelevant or forgettable, perhaps even repellent. As a result, every reader, Christian or not, believer or skeptic, has a personal Bible, which is a subset of the whole. Each personal Bible expresses a different outlook on the Bible as a whole, giving it a unique valuation and emphasis, and, if it is regarded as scripture, supporting a particular theology.

Servetus was a theologian unique in his time, yet he did not beat an entirely new trail through the jungle of scriptural text. Rather, to a significant degree, he was following pathways well-travelled by the orthodox, but with the intent of reading these texts in a different way. In his use of the Bible, we can observe Servetus gathering up what had, in his time and before, been viewed as proof-texts for the existing consensus of Christian theology. He then read these passages in context and, if they pointed to locations in the Old Testament, he studied those and learned to interpret them in their context. He was eager to find and re-interpret any passages drawn from Hebrew scriptures that had been used by orthodox Christians to prop up traditional Christology and to find others that could be deployed as counter-arguments. One might say with some justification that Servetus was reading the Bible in a new way, all the while believing that he was reading it in a very old way, one that restored the Christian belief of the apostolic period.

What, then, is in Servetus's Bible? To begin with, he cited the New Testament more often than the Old. Of the Gospels, he was most interested in John — understandably, for John is more overtly theological than Matthew, Mark, or Luke. He often quoted the Acts of the Apostles and, among the Pauline epistles, the letters to the Romans, Corinthians, Ephesians, Philippians, and Colossians. He was conversant with the Epistle to the Hebrews, the two epistles of Peter, and the first epistle of John. Given his millenarian disposition, it is only to be expected that he was quite familiar with the entire book of Revelation, citing almost every chapter.

Servetus was interested in the early Hebrews' experiences of epiphany and in the names that they applied to God. Accordingly he read much in Genesis and the early part of Exodus. Considering the kingship of ancient Israel and Judah as parallels to the reign of Christ, he looked to Old Testament history to foreshadow more recent events. He often cited the books of Kings and Chronicles, mentioning the books of Samuel a little less.

Like many Christians, Servetus was familiar with a subset of the psalms. He was most interested in psalms about royal enthronement and temple ceremonies, and those that celebrated the power and deeds of God. Among the prophets, he cited Isaiah more than all of the rest of the prophets combined. He made the most intensive use of what we now know as Second and Third Isaiah (chapters 40-55 and 56-66), as well as chapters 6-14 in First Isaiah (chapters 1-39). His interest in Psalms, Isaiah, and the other prophets is also indicated in the marginal notes that he provided for these books in his edition of the Pagnini Bible.

Biblical Languages and Translations

Servetus started with the fundamental idea that the Bible needs to be consulted in its original languages, especially Hebrew. He deplored the loss of meaning that is suffered when a Hebrew text is translated, and ripped out of its network of allusions to other texts in that language.[52] He thought the Bible would be misunderstood if readers were unable to recognize conventions of Hebrew style, such as its frequent use of exaggeration, which would have been understood by its original readers.[53] Moreover, as Servetus pointed out, even the Greek New Testament contains Semiticisms that can be properly understood only by a reader who is trained in Hebrew.[54] Accordingly, he said, "Those who discuss sacred scripture without knowing the sacred language will fall into dangerous errors."[55] And he went even beyond that, asserting that there is something unique about the Hebrew tongue. It is "the holy language spoken by God himself." Only Hebrew contains "the true mysteries of God."[56]

Servetus considered Greek an important language, in two senses. First of all, it was written by the apostles, and was the language in which the New Testament was preserved. Although not written in God's own language, the Greek documents that form the New Testament are the best witness we have to events and teachings that took place in a world where almost all spoke Aramaic. Secondly, during the centuries around the time of Christ, Greek was an official language of the Hebrew scriptures. For much of the Jewish diaspora, for gentile converts to Judaism, and for the early Christian evangelists, the Greek translation of the Old Testament, the Septuagint, was held to be divinely inspired and thus constituted Scripture.

However, Servetus was not entirely enamoured with the Greek of the Septuagint. He felt it necessary to apologize for its quotation by Peter as it was "the only Greek version then in use."[57] However, he thought use of the Septuagint when the Hebrew was available was

---

[52] Pagnini Bible (1542), introduction.

[53] Pagnini Bible (1542), introduction. *Errors*, 117r. *Restoration*, 53, 89.

[54] *Restoration*, 87-89, 611, 615.

[55] *Restoration*, 67.

[56] *Restoration*, 89.

[57] *Restoration*, 80.

less to be blamed than misreading the Greek.[58] He regretted that even the Greek-writing apostles had an impoverished vocabulary as they were not sufficiently well-versed in Hebrew.[59]

Nevertheless, when citing the Bible, Servetus explicitly quoted Greek or Hebrew texts only occasionally. Even in Book 2 of *The Restoration of Christianity*, which is devoted to close reading of biblical texts, he cited the original languages for only about half of the passages. However, thoroughgoing consultation of original languages is implicit in all of his analyses. Servetus's Latin biblical quotations, in book 2 and elsewhere, often deviate from those in any established translation. He favoured the official Vulgate Latin wording in about half of his quotations of the Bible, but he was almost as likely to have obtained wording from Erasmus's translation of the New Testament (which he used even more frequently in *On the Errors of the Trinity*) or from Pagnini's Latin translation of the Old Testament. Frequently Servetus produced a Bible text that looks like a combination of Vulgate phrasing and wording taken from either Erasmus or Pagnini, perhaps with a few words inspired by yet another existing translation, together with some verbiage that could only have been supplied from his own rendering of the Hebrew or Greek text. Thus, even when the locutions in Servetus's quotations originated with Jerome, Erasmus, or Pagnini, we can be confident that the quotations represent what Servetus believed to be a meaning faithful to the original Hebrew or Greek.

In book 2 of *Restoration* and elsewhere, the Bible scholarship that Servetus demonstrates is impressive. He read the passages he studied in the original languages, even (in book 2, passage 3) making use of the Aramaic Targums. He consulted commentaries by the Church Fathers, including Augustine, Jerome, and John Chrysostom; apologetic works by Church Fathers, including Irenaeus, Tertullian, and Origen, among many others; Rabbinic scholars, such as Ibn Ezra, David Kimhi, and Moses Maimonides; and recent writers such as Erasmus, Pagnini, and Sebastian Münster. At the end of all this, the

---

[58] *Restoration*, 67.

[59] *Errors*, 15v.

Introduction

results of his early modern critical method are often surprisingly consistent with those of recent scholarship.

Bible Typology

Having claimed Servetus as in some ways modern, we must nevertheless remember that he was a man of his time and shared ways of thinking that are less well-accepted nowadays. Among these is thinking of Bible history as organized by "types." Typology, in terms of history — in particular, the kind of history that the Bible relates — organizes people and events into categories that, across intervals of time, in some ways resemble one another. For many Christians, including Servetus, it has been important to track these resemblances from the Old Testament to the New. This binds the two scriptures into one and justifies the retention of the Hebrew Scriptures by Christians who no longer identify themselves as Jews. And it puts forth a sense of prophecy not only in the pronouncements of Isaiah and his ilk, but in the character of historical actors and the nature of the historical events described in the Old Testament. Thus, for the believer, typology heightens the meaningfulness of everything in the scriptures.

In particular, Christians for whom typology is important look to the Old Testament to provide types for Christ and for the events culminating in his crucifixion. In the vocabulary of typology, Christ is termed the antitype for various more ancient types. Among the types for Christ that Servetus considered were various royal figures: David and Solomon, kings of Israel;[60] Hezekiah, king of Judah;[61] and Cyrus, king of Persia.[62] Servetus saw David's restoration to kingship after the revolt of Absalom as a type of the resurrection of Christ.[63]

For Servetus, typology shaped history and linked the stages of history together. The prophets could not provide the link, because

---

[60] *Restoration*, 60, 66, 68. Pagnini Bible (1542), marginal notes no. 5, 7, 15, 16, 17 (Appendix B).

[61] *Restoration*, 70-72. Pagnini Bible (1542), marginal notes no. 20, 24, 28.

[62] *Restoration*, 71. Pagnini Bible (1542), marginal notes no. 35, 39, 41, 42, 48.

[63] *Restoration*, 59. *Errors*, 56r.

they could only see what was in their era, according to the stage of revelation that God had so far provided.[64] Prophecies, to the extent that they did predict the distant future, did so because their utterances were actually types.[65]

Servetus described the connections across the years, provided by typology, as a "mystical" or "spiritual" influence.[66] But typology, understood correctly, is a way of describing real phenomena and does not require resorting to mystery. It is evident that later events are shaped by earlier ones, particularly if people are trained to look for these patterns in their history. For example, the modern democratic developments coming out of the revolutions in America and France were conditioned by knowledge of the constitutions and politics of ancient Athens and Rome.

The Bible as History

Although the aims of Servetus's Bible study were theological and apologetic rather than scholarly, his approach had features in common with modern scholarship: he wanted to know what the biblical texts meant to the people who wrote them, and to those who first heard them. He assumed that real Christianity was to be found by getting into the minds of the ancient Jews and the earliest generations of Christians. Thus the answer to the scholar's question would largely fulfil the theologian's quest.

This meant that he had to take seriously what was meant by the texts in their original historical context: "For each prophet, according to the literal sense, was focused on his own time in history."[67] Even when constructing a Christian typology based upon the Old Testament, it is necessary to understand the stories of the original types before these figures can be connected with their New Testament antitypes. Servetus thought it would be a great loss to

---

[64] *Restoration*, 60, 318. *Errors*, 114r.

[65] For example, David "foretold the people's future freewill offering to Christ" by means of typology. *Restoration*, 67.

[66] *Restoration*, 89. Pagnini Bible (1542), marginal notes no. 5, 39, 41, 44, 46.

[67] Pagnini Bible (1542), introduction.

neglect the literal portion of the twofold nature of Scripture. He regarded this outward meaning as the more important one, because "unaided, it brings the other, mystical sense to light."[68]

Jerome Friedman, in *Michael Servetus: A Case Study in Total Heresy*, proposed that Servetus looked at divine history in five stages. In the first stage, before and after creation, the inaccessible and unknown God was yet to be revealed. In the second stage, the time of the patriarchs and of Moses, God was manifested through angels and epiphanies, culminating in the handing down of the Law to the people of Israel. In the third, the times of the kingdoms of Israel and Judah, those who witnessed the mysterious divine appearances, and transmitted God's message, were the prophets. The fourth stage was an encounter with God himself, the human face of God, Jesus Christ. The last stage will take humanity beyond its finite limits towards an even more complete knowledge of God.[69]

Thus the Bible may be seen as recording the ongoing relationship between God and humankind, a relationship that evolves and progresses from something basic and primitive towards something more interactive and sophisticated. It could, as well, be likened to human growth, from infancy, to childhood, youth, maturity, and the wisdom of age. What is appropriate to be presented to human beings in childhood is quite different from what they can absorb as adults. But the earlier stages of education are not wrong, only incomplete.

Thus the way Servetus read the Bible revealed a tolerant attitude towards pre-Christian religion. For he believed that the epiphanies witnessed by the patriarchs and prophets, as described in the Old Testament, were genuine religious revelations of their own era, revealing God in the way that God wished to be seen and heard in that place and at that time. Although these messengers from on high may, in addition, have been typological anticipations of a greater incarnation yet to come, they were in themselves important contacts between the divine and the human spheres, meant to have an immediate impact on human affairs. The great majority of

---

[68] Pagnini Bible (1542), introduction.

[69] Friedman, *Michael Servetus: A Case Study in Total Heresy*, 31.

Servetus's marginal notes to the Pagnini Bible were employed to make this point. He believed that the Old Testament was, in itself, an important revelation, even before the New Testament which followed it. Consequently, the "Law" of Judaism existed not just to be superseded, but constituted, on its own, a valuable gift from God. The religion of the Jews was not to be deprecated, but was an earlier part of the treasure bestowed from on high by God. While the Jews might be blamed for rejecting Christian revelation (though not so much for declining its trinitarian presentation), their interpretation and elucidation of pre-Christian scripture was to be respected.

Freedom of the Will

Servetus's preference for typology over prophecy helps to account for his preference for free will over predestination. For a world in which prophets can foretell the distant future is clearly predetermined. But a world in which the future is shaped by earlier events, and by our present perception and analysis of them, is one that is somewhat determined — we cannot escape history — but that also leaves room for an element of choice, of free will. Looking back with the mindset of typology shapes our thinking and channels our activities by restricting our options. At the same time it allows us rational choice among various courses of action. And as all these choices are being made within a culture of types, even though there are countless individual free choices being made, it is as if God were herding or funnelling humanity to some predetermined end. So that, as Servetus describes it, when God looks at all of history from the perspective of eternity — that is, outside of time — he sees it as a complete and finished thing, as if he could see it all in "the present moment."[70]

According to Servetus, God lives outside of time, in an eternal present, where nothing is past or future; everything just is. God has created time for his creatures, and within this time, since their intelligences reflect the divine mind, they have a portion of the divine free will, the ability to make choices within the constraints

---

[70] *Restoration*, 53-56.

that hedge them about.[71] "Just as Christ has free will in heaven, so do we ourselves, who have been enlightened by him, possess it. By the freedom by which Christ is free, we are free, having been given his spirit and freedom."[72]

Servetus thought that it was free will that made us sentient and human. He believed that human beings are responsible for their acts. They will succeed or fail, will be punished or rewarded based upon the things that they decide to do or not to do. Such punishments would not be fair if people were predestined to sin and had no ability to do what was right.[73] In the course of the controversies associated with his trial, he told the Geneva ministers that "by holding to the bondage of the will, you make us into sticks and stones."[74]

Servetus's Theology

Servetus's theology has been described in many ways: as unitarian or proto-unitarian, Arian, Sabellian, even as trinitarian. Let us examine some of the characterizations that have been made of his Christology and his views on the Trinity.

Servetus as Trinitarian

Is it possible that Servetus was just a heretical trinitarian? After all, in his discussion of God, he used the terms 'Father," "Son," and "Holy Spirit." Moreover, it is a well-known phenomenon that minor deviations from orthodoxy are often treated more seriously than major apostasy, for what they lack in egregiousness they more than make up by being dangerously insidious. His title *On the Errors of the Trinity* might be thought to indicate, not that the basic idea of a trinity in the Godhead was itself an error, but that that there were serious errors in the way the Trinity had been presented by orthodox Christians — errors which could be corrected, placing Christianity upon a firmer ground, making the religion more accessible to the faithful and more appealing to potential converts.

---

[71] *Restoration*, 53-55. *Errors*, 80v-81r.

[72] *Restoration*, 570.

[73] *Restoration*, 55-56.

[74] *Calvini opera* 8:518.

Introduction

Let us, then, first look at the theological teaching of the trinitarian Christian churches to ascertain what the Trinity consists of. Then we can measure Servetus's departure from this doctrine, and determine whether Servetus can be said to be, in any way, trinitarian.

The Trinity is a description of the Godhead as three persons — the Father, the Son, and the Holy Spirit — in one divine essence. The three persons act in different ways with respect to creation, though they are in accord with respect to their will and intentions. Substantially, and in nature, however, it is claimed that they are one God, and this tripartite unity is enough to make worship of the Trinity a form of monotheism.

Along with this there is a division of Christian theology called Christology, and this makes trinitarianism even more complex. Christology analyzes Christ, who is said to be both God and man. Unlike God as a whole, Christ has two natures, one fully divine and the other entirely human. These two natures are mysteriously connected and combined. This is articulated in a doctrine called *communicatio idiomatum*, which states that whatever properties belong to one of the two natures is shared with the other. The suffering of Jesus in his human life is then communicated to the divine nature, but only to the second person, the Son. The idea that the first person, the Father, could suffer is a heresy known as patripassianism.

Furthermore, all three persons of the Trinity existed from before the beginning of time. The second person, the Son, was the Logos, or the Word, long before he became incarnated as Jesus Christ. It was actually the Word that created the universe. When the Word itself entered the universe as a particular man, it still remained ubiquitous, like God as a whole. The Son was begotten as a man in time, but existed as the Word before all time. The third person, the Holy Spirit, was not begotten, but "proceeded" from the Father and the Son (or, in the Greek Orthodox church, from the Father alone).

What did Servetus make of all this? First of all, he found trinitarian theology to be too complicated and artificial. Almost no one really understands it. Any detailed analysis of it will show it to be logically inconsistent. The vast majority of Christians, even if they could understand it, would derive no religious knowledge or inspiration from it.

Servetus objected to the whole idea of there being "persons" in God. If these persons have any reality, he argued, then trinitarians are tritheists, worshipping three separate gods. And if they are invisible, incorporeal, and indistinct, then they are inconsequential. Servetus mocks the persons of the Trinity as "the first being," "the second being," and "the third being," calling them "metaphysical" or "mathematical."[75] And if there are three, why can there not be four, five, or more? Such distinctions within God are not what personhood is about. For Servetus, a person in God is not a metaphysical distinction, but a mode of manifestation.

According to Servetus, there is really only one person in God, and that is the Son. Jesus Christ is God, as human beings can see and interact with him. The Father is the same God, in no way distinct, but viewed impersonally, remote and unapproachable. The Holy Spirit is not actually God himself, and certainly not a person, but merely an activity of God. And even the Son's personality is somewhat temporary. In the beginning, the Word was an activity of God, God's way of creating the universe. The Word was not properly the Son, until, with the incarnation, it took on personality. Though the Son remains fully God, fully the one God and not part of it, he is at the same time fully human. There are not two natures in this Christ. He was born and grew to maturity in the normal way for human beings. But since he was begotten by God and not by a human father, he was the Son of God. By saying that the Father and the Son (or God and Christ) are just two ways of viewing the Godhead and not two parts of God, and relegating the Holy Spirit to an activity, Servetus claimed to preserve pure monotheism.

Thus Servetus deviated from the doctrine of the Trinity not just in detail, but systematically. For he rejected the idea of three persons in one God and two natures in Christ. With it goes a lot of doctrinal apparatus and controversy that has characterized orthodox Christian thinking: *communicatio idiomatum*, the question of the

---

[75] Servetus considered the "mathematical unity of natures ... a mere philosophical flight of fancy, and one that is never expressed in sacred literature." *Errors*, 24r

ubiquity of Christ, the debate over procession of the Holy Spirit, fear of patripassianism, and so on. Though he used a fair portion of the vocabulary associated with trinitarian theology, and though he believed that Jesus Christ is God (this merely makes him a Christian), he cannot be viewed as a trinitarian, even a very heretical one.

Servetus as Unitarian

The adoption of Servetus as a unitarian hero began as soon as Unitarianism came into existence. Sixteenth-century proto-unitarians Matteo Gribaldi and Francis Dávid incorporated much of Servetus's writing in their works, subtly reshaping his theology in order to support their own more Arian or adoptionist messages. Gribaldi copied a great deal of text from *On the Errors of the Trinity* into his *Revelation of Jesus Christ the Son of God* (c. 1557), while Dávid took almost half of *On the Kingdom of Christ* (1569) from *The Restoration of Christianity*.[76] However, Servetus's theology, while sharing certain characteristics with modern liberal religion, has other features that are foreign to most people's conception of unitarianism, notably the identification of Jesus as God and the idea that that he entered the world garbed in celestial flesh.[77]

It might be contended that Servetus was a unitarian because his ideas tended to lead to unitarianism. But this argument can also be applied to John Calvin. The twentieth-century Reformed theologian, Karl Barth, thought that, if the doctrine of the Trinity had never existed, Calvin could have articulated his theology in roughly the same way that he did. He wrote, "[The Trinity] has an honorary place [in the *Institutes*], but we cannot possibly maintain that [Calvin's] heart beat faster when he dealt with it." Because of his lack of enthusiasm for the doctrine of the Trinity, Calvin unwittingly created an opportunity for the emergence of a Socinian "neighbour on the left."[78] But no one argues that this makes Calvin a unitarian.

---

[76] Introduction to Gribaldi, *Declaratio*, xxii-xxv. Rezi, "The Influence of Michael Servetus on Dávid Ferencz," 27.

[77] *Restoration*, 14-15, 73-74.

[78] Barth, *The Theology of John Calvin*, 311-312.

Introduction

Servetus as Arian

Although a large variety of heresies emerged in early Christian times, it was principally Arianism that came to stand for effective opposition to Roman ecclesiastical authority and its trinitarian theology. According to the Arians, Christ was a lesser divine being than God the Father. Since Servetus opposed the orthodox formulation of the Trinity, it is not surprising that many, from the time of Servetus's youth to the present day, have jumped to the conclusion that he must have been an Arian.[79]

Much of the idea that Servetus was an Arian seems to derive from the fact that he paid a good deal of critical attention to the biblical proof-texts long held to be important supports of orthodoxy against Arianism, such as Romans 9:5, Philippians 2:6, and 1 John 5:7-8. However, Arianism, with its binitarian belief in a separate and subordinate divinity, would have been useless in Servetus's project of reformulating Christianity to make it more attractive to strictly monotheistic Muslims and Jews.

Servetus explicitly denied being an Arian. In *Errors* he wrote, "What if I say that Jesus Christ is indeed the great God, and at the same time, I say what he, speaking with the utmost simplicity, said, *'The Father is greater than I'*? Does that make me an Arian?" Servetus acknowledged that he often cited passages that Arians used to dispute with the orthodox, but denied that this made him an Arian: "Nor should anyone be amazed when I introduce passages of scripture that have been cited by heretics for their own purposes. For, although the scriptures have been misused by heretics, they have not on that account lost their soundness, so that they cannot ever be used again."[80]

Servetus considered the whole Arian controversy "devised by Satan in order to turn people's minds away from knowledge of the true Christ, and to fashion for us a tripartite God."[81] That is, he

---

[79] Two examples: Oecolampadius, quoted in *Calvini opera* 8.744; Hans J. Hillerbrand, *A New History of Christianity* (Nashville: Abingdon Press, 2012), 314.

[80] *Errors*, 13r.

[81] *Restoration*, 22.

believed that the Arians, far from being heroic critics of orthodoxy, were, through their perverse theology, responsible for the defensive reaction which took the form of the newly-invented, and deeply mistaken, orthodox doctrines of the Trinity.

Servetus as Modalist

Calvin, who was familiar with Servetus's writings, coupled Servetus's theology not only with Arianism, but also with Sabellianism, or modalism.[82] This heresy is in many respects at the opposite extreme from Arianism in the spectrum of Christian theology.

Modalism is a radically monotheistic form of Christianity, whose most famous exponent was the early third-century theologian Sabellius of Libya. Modalists taught that the Father and the Son have no separate identities within the Godhead and are merely different manifestations, or modes, of the undivided Godhead. While modalism solved the problem of making Christ fully divine within a purely monotheistic system, the consequent total identification of Christ with God, and the Son with the Father, left modalists open to the criticism that they believed that when the Son suffered and died on the cross, the Father suffered and died as well. This idea, called patripassianism, was unacceptable and abhorrent to most Christian theologians.

Many modern scholars depict Servetus as largely Sabellian.[83] There is, in fact, a fair amount of evidence in Servetus's works to suggest that he was a modalist. He strongly identified Christ with God. The third of the three propositions with which he begins both *Errors* and *Restoration* is: Christ is God.[84] Though human in form, Servetus believed, Christ was entirely divine, and to see him was to see God, insofar as that was possible for human beings: "All the deity of the Father, the adoration owed to God, and the visible form of God, are in Christ, who is truly God."[85]

---

[82] Calvin, *Institutes*, 5th ed. (1559) 1.13.22.
[83] Friedman, *Michael Servetus*, 41-42, 48. Bainton, *Hunted Heretic*, 27-28. Williams, *Radical Reformation*, 401. Hillar, *Michael Servetus*, 25-26.
[84] *Errors*, 2r. *Restoration*, 5.
[85] *Restoration*, 16.

Although Servetus referred to Christ, the Word, and the Spirit as modes,[86] he, like the orthodox, he dismissed Sabellianism as a monstrosity.[87] "Sabellius," he wrote, "adhering to the unity of God, was unacquainted with [God's] modes of communication and dispensation."[88] The word "dispensation" gives us a hint as to the reason why we cannot entirely claim Servetus as a modalist.

The Economy of God

Servetus believed that the most reliable information about Christ was to be obtained from the earliest sources. He considered trinitarianism, which fully developed only during the fourth and fifth centuries, too remote from the incarnation to tell us anything about the nature of Christ. The post-biblical writings Servetus valued most were those that he believed to have been written in the late first century and during the second: those of Clement of Rome, Polycarp, Ignatius of Antioch, Justin Martyr, Irenaeus, and Tertullian. Using concepts provided by Irenaeus and others, Servetus described the persons of God as "three modes of manifestation ... through God's economy (οἰκονομία)."[89] The key word is "economy," which is used here in quite a different way from the way it is employed in the modern world. Tertullian rendered the Greek word οἰκονομία into Latin as "dispensation" (*dispensatio*).

There are two principal approaches to reconciling the ideas "Christ is God" and "God is one." One approach is to venture a description of the inner workings of the Godhead, the "immanent Trinity." Thinking metaphysically, theologians envision, or believe they can deduce, different beings or persons and the ways that these beings interact or are in relationship with one another. This is the metaphysical and philosophical approach to which Servetus objected.[90] The other way of portraying the deity is to describe

---

[86] *Errors*, 37r. *Restoration*, 164-165, 183-184.

[87] *Errors*, 38r-39r. *Restoration*, 37-38.

[88] *Restoration*, 37.

[89] *Restoration*, 24. See *Errors*, 29r.

[90] For example: *Errors*, 8r, 19r, 23r (metaphysical); 5v, 6v, 7v (philosophical). *Restoration*, 10-12, 20-21, 24-26.

Introduction

the "economic Trinity," or, since the word "Trinity" was unknown prior to Tertullian, "the economy of God." The word "economy" here means the way that God interacts with his creatures in order to fulfill his plans for them. Thus the "economic" approach is to see God exclusively from the outside, from the point of view of a finite creature.

The second-century theologian Irenaeus, whose work Servetus often cited, believed that God, being infinite and transcendent, cannot be perceived by mortal senses or comprehended by human understanding.[91] In order to become visible and understandable by finite creatures, God must make himself finite.[92] Accordingly, the Son takes the form of a human being — a real human being, not an apparition — who reveals the divinity of God as directly and completely as human beings can stand. Knowing the human Jesus Christ does not give human beings a complete grasp of God, because finite creatures can never possess that, but it does advance human knowledge of God, a knowledge that is susceptible to endless increase.[93]

Irenaeus spoke metaphorically of the Word as one of the "hands of God" that God used to make humanity. The other hand was Wisdom, or the Holy Spirit.[94] God's plan is to bring all creatures to him so that, while remaining creatures, they share in God's immortality and glory.[95] The "hands of God" that bring this about are not separate beings,[96] any more than human hands are separate beings. We only distinguish between these aspects of God in order to understand the economy of God, that is, God's plan for our salvation. Apart from their role in this project, the aspects of God cannot be described as persons, or even functions.

The theology of Irenaeus has been considered orthodox by Christian churches ever since it was first propounded. Although

---

[91] Irenaeus, *Adversus haereses* 2.28.2 (PG 7 804B-805C).

[92] Irenaeus, *Adversus haereses* 4.4.2 (PG 7 982B 1032A-B, 1136D-1138C).

[93] Irenaeus, *Adversus haereses* 2.28.3, 4.20.7 (PG 7 1037A-B).

[94] Irenaeus, *Adversus haereses* 4.pref.4, 4.20.1, 5.6.1, 5.28.4 (PG 7).

[95] Irenaeus, *Adversus haereses* 4.38.3 (PG 7 1107B-1108C).

[96] Irenaeus, *Adversus haereses* 2.30.9 (PG 7 821C-823A).

he did not mention the Trinity by name, Irenaeus talked about the component parts — Father, Son/Word, and Holy Spirit. His theology is, in fact, an early stage along the path from the Messianic Judaism of Jesus of Nazareth and his followers to the creedal trinitarian Christianity established by the post-Nicene Church Fathers and the Church councils of late antiquity. But the later elaborations that give trinitarianism its familiar shape — three persons in one essence, two natures for the person of Christ, the sharing of properties (*communicatio idiomatum*) between Christ as God and Christ as man — are not required in Irenaeus's economic theology, because it is concerned only with the human experience of God and not with knowledge of God's inner workings. Thus Irenaeus's vision of God, while largely consistent with the theology of later orthodoxy, could also be adapted to serve the different needs of quite unorthodox interpreters.

While pursuing his youthful quest for a truly monotheistic Christianity, Servetus experienced the pre-trinitarian theology of Irenaeus as a major revelation. Like this ancient mentor, Servetus saw Christ, not as a separate personality, but as a feature of God: the face, or appearance, that God presents to his human creatures. Servetus frequently called Christ the form (*forma*), appearance (*species*), or face (*facies*) of God.[97] In both *Errors* and *Restoration*, Servetus contended that Christ is God and, at the same time, a real human being. When we look at the human Christ we see God. Concerned primarily with how we encounter and respond to God's overtures to us through Christ, Servetus had no tolerance for any proposed invisible, incorporeal, and "metaphysical" sons of God. Rather, he says, "This man whom you see is the Lamb of God, the Son of God, visible to our eyes, touchable by our hands, and perceptible by all the other senses."[98]

Irenaeus's image of the two hands of God was also taken up by Servetus. But, since, like the modalists, Servetus strongly identified Christ with the Father, he described the two hands, the Word

---

[97] *Errors*, 9v, 18r-v, 19v-20r. *Restoration*, 15-16, 19-22, 36.

[98] *Restoration*, 12.

and the Holy Spirit, as extending from Christ himself.[99] The task of these hands — God's plan, or economy, of our salvation — is for Servetus, as it was for Irenaeus, to elevate human creatures to a more divine status, making them true "children of God."[100]

Servetus also frequently cited Tertullian. Despite being the one who named the Trinity, Tertullian was also a theologian of the divine economy. Unlike later theologians, he did not identify two natures in Christ — one invisible and divine, the other human and visible — but said that the Son was "both man and God."[101] Similarly, Servetus said that there was a single "twofold nature in Christ, both divine and human."[102] According to Tertullian, both aspects of Christ's nature come from the substance of the Father. Likewise Servetus claimed that Christ's flesh is divine substance.[103]

Back to the Beginning

In order to get an overall feeling for Servetus's God, we could not do better than to go back to the beginning: the beginning of *On the Errors of the Trinity* and the inception of *The Restoration of Christianity*. In both of those places Servetus starts with three assertions: that Jesus Christ is a human being, that he is the Son of God, and that he is God. This is not a theology of three persons, but three ways of describing the single person who is the interface between God and humanity. Since we cannot relate directly to God in his infinitude, God has exhibited himself as a man, a real human being who was born and who did not escape death. Being born, with an origin both human and divine, he had to have been a son: a son of man and Son of God.

The important thing is that there is only one God. Jesus Christ, the Son of God, is, for humanity, the only person of God. He is what we can see when we see God, or experience God in any way. He is

---

[99] *Restoration*, 694-695.

[100] *Errors*, 9r. *Restoration*, 7, 13.

[101] Tertullian, *Adversus Praxean* 2 (PL 2 157A).

[102] *Restoration*, 16.

[103] *Dialogues*, B6v-B7r.

the face of God, the face that we can look upon and yet survive. But he is not less than God, just God accommodated to our minds and senses. Thus Servetus avoids the problem for which the Trinity was the rather imperfect solution: how to incorporate Christ as a part of God while retaining monotheism. For Servetus there are no parts of God. Christ and God are the same being: "I and the Father are one" (John 10:30).

Servetus and Islam

Servetus recognized that the Bible was not the only valid record of God's interaction with humanity. There were other repositories of divine wisdom that Servetus cited as if their status was, if not precisely scriptural, at least closely akin to it. Among these was the holy book of the Muslims, the Quran. Although his attitude did not approach the modern interfaith ideal of granting other religions, in principle, the same value as one's own, he did suppose that Islam and Judaism had some value, and that these religions had information to impart, useful to Christianity as a corrective to wrong ideas and misinformation that had entered Christendom since the time of Jesus. According to Servetus, Muhammad said that "the Christian people, who were originally one group, were afterwards torn asunder by various schisms because they had allowed themselves to be turned aside to more than one god."[104] And he said that Muhammad "was gravely offended by these three incorporeal gods, or three distinct, invisible, and equal beings in one God. Because of this perverse trinitarian doctrine, he parted ways with Christianity, which was an extremely sad and lamentable thing for the entire world."[105]

It has sometimes been speculated that Servetus was acquainted with Spanish Muslims, learned Arabic from them, and was consequently able to read the Quran.[106] It has even been suggested that he traveled to Africa, where he acquired training in Arabic and

---

[104] *Restoration*, 35.

[105] *Restoration*, 36.

[106] For example: John Edwards, *The Socinian Creed* (London, 1697), 227. Lawrence and Nancy Goldstone, *Out of the Flames* (New York: Broadway, 2002), 56.

Islam.[107] However, there is no evidence that Servetus studied under Muslims, was ever in Africa, or had even a rudimentary knowledge of Arabic. The only basis for such claims is that Servetus shows some knowledge of Islam and the Quran in book 1 of *On the Errors of the Trinity* and in book 1 of *The Restoration of Christianity*.[108] For, it has been asked, how could Servetus speak about the contents of the Quran without knowing any Arabic?

There are, however, two possible ways that Servetus could have obtained information on the Quran without being able to read Arabic. One is by reading secondary sources: specifically, Christian apologetic literature, describing Islamic belief and the content of the Quran. The other is by reading the Quran in translation. In the event, Servetus availed himself of both these resources.

Everything that Servetus said about Islam in *Errors* can be found in Marsilio Ficino's *On the Christian Religion* (1474). Moreover, he lifted substantial chunks of text directly from this book. Thus it is almost certain that this is the major — and likely the only — source of Servetus's early information about Islam.[109]

The newly added text in the section on the Islam in *Restoration* is largely based on reading the Quran in a translation made in the twelfth century by Robert of Ketton. This was available only in manuscript until 1543, when it was printed in Basel by Theodore Bibliander as part of his three-volume collection, *The Lives of*

---

[107] The idea that Servetus went to Africa surfaces chiefly among Servetus's opponents and detractors, who wish to demonstrate that Servetus was, to some extent, an apostate and was at least partially converted to Islam. For example: Louis Moreri, *Le Grand Dictionnaire Historique* (Lyons, 1683), 644. Alphonsus Liguori, *The History of Heresies and their Refutation* (2nd ed., Dublin, 1857), 350.

[108] *Errors*, 43r; *Restoration*, 35-36. More recently it has been claimed that Servetus had to know Arabic in order to read the material on the pulmonary transit by the thirteenth-century Arab physician Ibn an-Nafis. e.g., Plinio Prioreschi, *A History of Medicine: Renaissance Medicine* (Omaha: Horatius, 1996), 351. But there are several other, more plausible, explanations for how Servetus could have come across this breakthrough idea in physiology, and it is yet to be explained how Servetus could have had access to the work of Ibn an-Nafis.

[109] See *Errors*, 43r. Ficino, *De Christiana religione* 12, 29, 34, 36.

Muhammad, the Chief of the Saracens, and of His Successors, Their Teachings, and the Quran Itself. Based upon the wording in Servetus's quotations, and the particular non-standard sura numbering in his citations, it is clear that he was using not only Robert's translation, but Robert's translation as presented in Bibliander's publication.[110] Furthermore it appears that, in *Restoration*, Servetus also used other works that were printed by Bibliander in the 1543 collection: Ricoldo of Monte Croce's *Refutation of the Quran* (c.1300), Nicholas of Cusa's *Sifting of the Quran* (1461), and *A Summary of the Teachings of Muhammad*, translated by Herman of Carinthia.[111]

The citations of the Quran in *Restoration* were a red flag to Servetus's accusers at his trial in Geneva. An interrogator asked him, "As you well knew the Quran to be an evil book full of blasphemies, why did you cite passages from it to support your doctrine and excuse the Turks?" Servetus replied, "I cited it as claiming the glory of our Lord Jesus Christ, because the Quran shows that most plainly and makes Christ greater than Muhammad" and "From an evil book, one can well take good things."[112] Moreover, he said, "the Quran ... was published in Basel and it was permitted to read it, and there were letters from the ministers of the Zurich church printed with it."[113]

Servetus greatly overestimated the appeal in the Muslim world of any form of Christianity, much less one that includes a divine Jesus. He was misled both by his unfamiliarity with living Islam and by the four-hundred-year-old Robert of Ketton translation, which, by subtle choices in wording, greatly overstates the power and importance of Jesus in the Quran. Had Servetus developed his arguments and his theology into a proselytizing tool for converting Muslims, and had he ventured to undertake a mission into the Islamic world, he would have discovered that his basic assumptions were gravely mistaken.

---

[110] Hughes, "Servetus and the Quran," 68.

[111] *Restoration*, 35-36.

[112] *Calvini opera*, 8:782.34-35.

[113] *Calvini opera*, 8:770.21.

Introduction

Servetus's Opponents

Because of the heated epistolary debate between Servetus and Calvin in 1546, followed by Servetus's trial and execution in 1553 by Genevans under the sway of Calvin, we tend to think of Calvin as Servetus's chief antagonist. But when he was writing *On the Errors of the Trinity*, Servetus had not yet heard of Calvin. At that time Calvin, himself still a very young man, was neither well-known nor even a Protestant. And in book 1 of *The Restoration of Christianity*, though it was written after Calvin had become the celebrated reformer of Geneva, Servetus was largely revising and improving the argument of *Errors*, while retaining many of the same ideas. So who was it that Servetus had in mind as his opposition when he wrote *Errors*? And who beside Calvin did he still have in mind, when he incorporated a revision of book 1 of *Errors* into *Restoration*?

Roman Catholic Orthodoxy

Young Servetus was aware of the early Lutherans and their writings. He was personally acquainted with French evangelicals as early as his stay in Toulouse.[114] But he did not at first seek to contend with these early Protestants. Rather, he took from them the inspiration to prepare his own complementary critique of Roman Catholic orthodoxy. Just as Lutheranism was, in part, a protest against clergy abuses and papal exactions upon the people of Germany, Servetus's concerns grew out of the special circumstances of Christianity in Spain. Here the resistance of the Jewish and newly conquered Muslim populations to Christian proselytization was a central social issue, and thus a major impetus for Servetus's very Spanish version of the Reformation.

Ironically, such a Spanish Reformation could not flourish in Spain itself. Due to the efforts of the Inquisition, the plan of religious reform inspired by conditions in Spain could only be discussed beyond the borders of Spain. Yet, as might have been expected, when Servetus left Spain and travelled north he found there little interest

---

[114] *Calvini opera*, 8:767.

Introduction

in the aspects of his theological program that addressed the unique Spanish situation. His trinitarian revisionism found sympathetic readers only among other refugees from the Catholic south, most notably the evangelicals fleeing Italy.

Even as Servetus completed *On the Errors of the Trinity* north of the Pyrenees, and visited with and debated Protestant divines, his theological views remained conditioned by his initial call to religious testimony. Moreover, he initially had a sense of fellow-feeling with his anti-Catholic hosts. Thus his image of the views that he wished to counter in his earliest writing remained those of Roman Catholic orthodoxy.

In the course of the time that he was writing *Errors*, Servetus did develop an opposition to Lutheranism, which emerges as a subordinate theme. In books 3 through 6 Lutherans come up for criticism five times. In book 3 he took issue with Luther's teaching on the bondage of the will in a passage on God's relation to time (which he later reworked, minus any explicit reference to Luther or Lutherans, in book 2 of *Restoration*).[115] In the later books of *Errors*, Servetus's most frequent Lutheran target is the doctrine of justification by faith.[116] A little later, in *On the Righteousness of Christ's Kingdom*, he devoted a whole tract to the subject. In his medical pamphlet, *Apology against Fuchs* (1536), before attacking the Lutheran physician Fuchs's views on medication and disease, he took him to task for his views on justification.[117]

In *Restoration*, Servetus still opposed justification by faith and wrote at length against it, but he omitted any mention of the Lutherans, likely because by then he knew that Calvin and others in the Reformed Church also promoted it.[118] The only references to Luther himself in *Restoration* are one in Servetus's letters to Calvin and five in his "Apology to Melanchthon."[119] The addressee of the

---

[115] *Errors*, 80v-81r. *Restoration*, 53-55.
[116] *Errors*, 82v, 96r, 99r-v, 109v.
[117] *In Leonardum Fuchsium apologia*, A2v-A4v.
[118] *Restoration*, 287-354.
[119] *Restoration*, 651, 672-674, 701.

latter was, of course, the second most celebrated Lutheran. Servetus paid special attention to him because of the sharp criticism of *Errors* contained in Melanchthon's *Loci Communes*.[120]

In the course of his student years Servetus had also absorbed Erasmian humanism, which was a potent intellectual force in early sixteenth-century Spain. The humanists portrayed themselves as opponents of scholasticism, which was the philosophy and theology of the Church that emanated from the universities, particularly the Sorbonne in Paris. While the height of scholasticism was in the thirteenth and fourteenth centuries, with philosophers like Thomas Aquinas, Duns Scotus, and William of Ockham, the foundation of the traditions of the schools was in the twelfth, with teachers like Peter Abelard and Peter Lombard. It was an opus of the latter, the first volume of which was devoted to the Trinity, that was adopted for centuries as the official theology of the Catholic Church. During this period, Peter Lombard's *Sentences* was, along with the Bible, the focus of theological instruction. As a humanist, and a rebel against the orthodox conception of the Trinity, Servetus felt that he had to take on the great official scholastic teacher. Accordingly, in book 1 of *Errors*, and even in book 1 of *Restoration*, Servetus's principal opponent was Peter Lombard.

Peter Lombard's theology was built upon a systematically organized collection of texts gathered largely from the post-Nicene Latin Church Fathers. If *Sentences* is a kind of *summa*, then it is a *summa* of the Christian thought of late antiquity as filtered through a medieval mind. In book 1 of *Errors* and book 1 of *Restoration*, when Servetus appears to be arguing against Augustine, Hilary, and the other Church Fathers, he is actually responding to Christian theology as presented in *Sentences*.

In addition, many of the later scholastic philosophers wrote commentaries on *Sentences*, or expansions on its themes. Servetus discussed passages from commentaries by Duns Scotus, William of Ockham, Henry of Ghent, Robert Holkot, Pierre d'Ailly and

---

[120] Melanchthon, *Loci communes* (1535), C5v-6r.

Introduction

John Mair.[121] Thus, a significant portion of Servetus's energy in book 1 of *Errors*, as well as in the corresponding book 1 of *Restoration*, was taken up with arguing with Peter Lombard, with the authorities brought forward by Peter Lombard, and with philosophers following in the footsteps of Peter Lombard. This focus on the Catholic Church's scholastic teaching is perhaps what most defines these opening books and separates them from the remaining portions of these two theological works.

One might ask why, if Servetus's arguments were so directed against the scholastics, he did not target, mention, or even indirectly refer to Thomas Aquinas, who is in our day is most celebrated of the scholastics. Aquinas seems to us conspicuous by his absence in Servetus's works, all the more so because he wrote his own commentary on Peter Lombard's *Sentences*.

While Aquinas was by no means obscure in Servetus's time, he was not then the dominating figure that he is today. Today Aquinas's *Summa Theologiae* is recognized as the official teaching of the Roman Catholic Church. But in Servetus's day that honour still belonged to Peter Lombard's *Sentences*. So if Servetus wanted to challenge the doctrines of the Church, Peter Lombard, not Thomas Aquinas, was the acknowledged champion that he had to confront. Moreover, in the sixteenth century, Aquinas was the preserve of Dominican scholars and theologians. Servetus's mentor, Juan de Quintana, was not a Dominican and his scholarly speciality was the Franciscan philosopher, Duns Scotus,[122] to whom Servetus frequently alludes in book 1 of *Errors* and *Restoration*.

The Sophists

In reading the opening books of both *On the Errors of the Trinity* and *The Restoration of Christianity*, one immediately notices the frequent pejorative use of the label "sophists." Who, one wonders, are these "sophists" that Servetus despised so much? The litera-

---

[121] *Errors*, 21r, 31v-32v. *Restoration*, 29-30, 42.

[122] James K. Farge, *Biographical Register of Paris Doctors of Theology, 1500-1536* (Toronto: Pontifical Institute of Medieval Studies, 1980), 385-386.

ture of Servetus's time sheds little direct light on the subject, for almost everyone disparaged opponents by calling them sophists or describing their reasoning as sophistical.

The term "sophist" was first used in fifth-century BCE Athens to denote professional rhetoricians and teachers of rhetoric. Greeks in those days were of two minds regarding these articulate, learned, clever, and charismatic speakers. On one hand they trained people to speak and to argue coherently and persuasively. On the other, sophists were trained to be able to argue any side of a question with equal skill and effectiveness. They were tools that could be applied to the attainment of any end, by any person who had the money to hire them. Sophists did not constitute a philosophical school whose teaching had specific content. They did not collectively present any information about the organization of the world. The distrust they engendered by their mercenary ways was passed on to later ages by Aristotle and Plato, who worried about the danger of over-persuasive people. Aristotle, in his *Sophistical Refutations*, portrayed sophists as devious manipulators of argumentation, who employed hard-to-spot logical fallacies to help them win debates.

In the Renaissance, humanists revived an emphasis on speaking well and writing with good Latin style, modeled on the ancient Roman classical authors, notably Cicero. But Cicero was a politician and a lawyer, whose stock-in-trade was the ability to persuade juries and the Senate to accept his point of view, or that of the clients who hired him. Moreover, many of the Renaissance humanists, such as Leonardo Bruni, Poggio Bracciolini, and Lorenzo Valla, were employed as secretaries, diplomats, and publicists by secular rulers, or by the Pope or other ecclesiastical potentates. Highly proficient in Latin, and sometimes able to read Greek, these humanists used their eloquence to promote the interests of their employers. Accordingly, they were distrusted, and labelled sophistical, by those not in sympathy with the humanist program.

Humanists and evangelicals, for their part, saw scholasticism as a way of thinking that stood in the way of the ordinary Christian's engagement with the Bible. Scholastic philosophy was a highly technical subject, which the ordinary believer found difficult and confusing. It had been a useful intellectual discipline in the days when literacy was restricted to scholars who were mainly friars and the clergy, but with the dawn of printing in the late fifteenth century and the spread of literacy into the middle classes, many desired a simpler and more straightforward path to religious learning. Reading the Bible in translation (in Latin or in the vernacular), or studying it in the original languages, humanists and evangelicals began to consider scholasticism, and the Roman Catholic orthodoxy that supported it, a form of obfuscation, a way of battering the less learned into submission with their tricky, "sophistical" argumentation.

Thus, while the later scholastics and the representatives of the Catholic establishment argued that the humanists were deploying their skill at rhetoric in a sophistical way, the humanists and evangelicals considered the scholastic teaching, with its arcane vocabulary, the intricate distinctions within its logic, and its speculations on questions that seemed far removed from ordinary life, to be sophistry in the extreme.

Servetus could have absorbed his disdain for "sophists" from the humanists with whom he was familiar, such as Erasmus and Juan Luis Vives, or from early Protestants like Luther and Melanchthon. Erasmus thought that most of "the common crowd of theologians nowadays... have learned nothing but sophisms."[123] Servetus might have taken as a motto Erasmus's pronouncement: "it is better to be a little less of a sophist than to understand less of the Gospel and the Apostolic letters."[124] Vives, in *Against the Pseudo-dialecticians*, called sophistic discipline "nitpicking based on perverted meanings of words."[125] In the first version of *Loci Communes* (1521), Melanchthon deployed the term "sophist" more than thirty times, and called his opponents "impious sophistic

---

[123] Erasmus, *Antibarbarorum* (Basel, 1520), 127.

[124] Erasmus, *Ratio seu methodus compendio perveniendi ad veram theologiam* (Basel, 1520), 216.

[125] Vives, *Adversus pseudodialecticos*, B4r.

professers of theology."[126] In the 1543 edition he included Servetus among those who were guilty of "sophistries and corruptions of the Gospel."[127] Luther, in *On the Bondage of the Will*, called Peter Lombard the father of the sophists.[128] Perhaps Luther's characterization is what inspired Servetus to use the label "sophists" for his opponents when be began composing *On the Errors of the Trinity*.

In *Errors* (though not in *Restoration*) Servetus often accused opponents of "philosophizing." This usage indicates that Servetus, like the humanists, had the scholastic philosophers in mind. Of course he criticized Greek philosophy as well, considering it a baneful influence on Christian thought. In addition, he characterized the theological ideas of the philosophizing sophists as "metaphysical" and "mathematical." Other relevant terms that he employed are *moderni* (the nominalist school of philosophy), "schools," and "scholastics."

Servetus's Spanish Mentors

We have seen that Servetus was personally acquainted with, and perhaps engaged in some study under, two Spanish scholars, Juan de Quintana and Gaspar Lax. The latter was a leading voice in the development of terminist logic, a rather arcane late medieval development in the study of logic. Although the value of this field of study has begun to be reconsidered by modern logicians, it was widely seen in Servetus's time as a dead end. Even Lax ultimately gave it up as a waste of his time. For these apparently vain efforts Lax was dubbed "the prince of sophists."[129]

Interestingly, in 1532 Quintana applied the label "sophist" to Servetus himself. This many have been a recognition of the power of Servetus's rhetoric. But Quintana is also recorded as saying that he did not think that Servetus, unaided, could have achieved the eloquent and persuasive style found in *On the Errors of the*

---

[126] Melanchthon, *Loci communes* (1521), H2v.

[127] Melanchthon, *Loci communes* (1543), B6v.

[128] Luther, *De servo arbitrio*, H3v.

[129] Noreña, *Studies in Spanish Renaissance Thought*, 17.

Trinity.[130] Quintana may have called Servetus a "great sophist"[131] not on the basis of his eloquence, but because he associated him with the school of logic of Lax. Yet, based upon the vague and superficial understanding of terminist logic demonstrated in both *Errors* and *Restoration*, Servetus could never have been a serious disciple of Lax. If he did study briefly with the "prince of sophists," it is clear that Servetus — like Lax's well-known student, Juan Luis Vives, who rejected this development of scholasticism for the humanism of Erasmus — came to see this brand of sophistry as a great error.

Servetus was much better trained in theology than he was in logic. His reaction to Peter Lombard, and the late Church Fathers whom he cited, inspired the core of his argument in the first book of each of his major works. He treated the sophistry of the later scholastics and logicians, including his contemporaries, as merely supplemental evidence of the kind of mistaken reasoning that led to errors in the conceptions of the Trinity.

Augustine and Calvin

When Servetus quoted Augustine, Hilary, and other Church Fathers in *The Restoration of Christianity*, he depended less on Peter Lombard than he had previously. Even when he retained material from *On the Errors of the Trinity*, he often took the trouble to check the meaning, the wording, and the citations in current printed editions of the Church Fathers. This was not just an improvement in scholarship, but also indicated a shift in focus. For while Peter Lombard had stood for the kind of Roman Catholic orthodoxy that was the target of Servetus's early attempt at reformation, his later vision was meant to counter the arguments of Calvinists, and Protestants in general, as well.

The landscape of reform changed radically during the decade after the publication of *Errors*, notably with the emergence and growth of Reformed churches, including the one led by Calvin in Geneva. And Servetus's perception of who his chief theological

---

[130] Girolamo Aleandro to Pope Clement VII, 17 April 1532, 109. See note 42.

[131] *Errors*, 42r. *Restoration*, 45.

Introduction

enemies were must have been reshaped by the widespread negative reaction to the works he published in 1531 and 1532. By looking through Servetus's text, noting the addressees of two of the later sections of *The Restoration of Christianity*, and considering the writings of the reformers, we can get an indication of which contemporary "sophists" he had in mind, while he was talking of the Church Fathers and the scholastics.

Protestants, in general, valued Augustine even more than Catholics did. But just as they liked to read the Bible for themselves and make their own interpretations, they also liked to read Augustine's works in their original form, rather than in excerpts selected and interpreted by such as Peter Lombard. They absorbed Augustine in his entirety, finding much to criticize when comparing him with scripture, but discovering even more to appreciate and to use in combating their theological adversaries.

The Lutheran leaders, critical as they were of Roman Catholic worthies and scholastic teachers, were relatively fond of the works of Augustine and only moderately severe in their critique of Peter Lombard. Luther, originally an Augustinian friar, quoted Augustine more than any other non-scriptural source of authority. Nevertheless "when the door was opened to me by Paul," he told his dinner companions, "I was done with [Augustine]."[132] His evaluation of Peter Lombard was laced with sarcasm: "He was a great man. If he had looked into the Bible he would undoubtedly have been the greatest."[133] These comments were first published after Servetus's death. But Servetus is known to have been very much aware of Melanchthon's *Loci Communes*, in which Servetus himself was singled out for criticism. Melanchthon, though often critical of Augustine or measured in his praise,[134] sometimes granted him the kind of authority he reserved for Luther himself.[135] Peter Lombard,

---

[132] Luther, *Tischreden* no. 347.
[133] Luther, *Tischreden* no. 192.
[134] *Loci Communes* (1543), H8v.
[135] *Loci Communes* (Basel, 1521), N5v.

according to Melanchthon, although he fell short because he did not rely enough on scripture, was more nearly correct than the sophists (that is, the scholastics) who commented on his *Sentences*.[136]

When Calvin referred to Peter Lombard, it was generally to criticize him or his doctrines and only a few times to allow him a small measure of approval. According to Calvin, Peter Lombard was the Pythagoras of the sophists.[137] Calvin was critical of the use of authorities in *Sentences*: "Many of [the authorities in the *Sentences*], which Lombard, leader of [the scholastics], stitched together in his patchwork quilt, are culled from the deranged ideas of [later] monks and attributed to Ambrose, Jerome, Augustine, and Chrysostom."[138] And he too was unimpressed by the Master's biblical knowledge: "Apparently he was not well trained in this."[139]

Among the major reformers, Augustine received the greatest approval from Calvin. Augustine is mentioned increasingly in the various editions of *The Institutes of the Christian Religion*, starting with a few dozen citations in 1536 and increasing to around 250 by 1553. More than half of Calvin's patristic citations are to Augustine.[140] In the 1539 edition he wrote, "Let Augustine's testimony prevail among those who willingly submit to the [Church] Fathers' authority."[141] He later added this self-justification: "Lest anyone reject this as a new invention, [I am telling you that] Augustine did not think or speak in any other way."[142] In *On God's Eternal Predestination* (1552) he identified so completely with his favourite Father that he claimed, "if I were to pen a confession [of faith], I would be exceedingly satisfied with text woven together from his

---

[136] *Loci Communes* (Basel, 1521), A3r, H5v.

[137] Calvin, *Institutes*, 2nd ed. (1539), 209.

[138] Calvin, *Institutes*, 1st ed. (1536), 357.

[139] Calvin, *Institutes*, 2nd ed. (1539), 209.

[140] S. J. Han, "An Investigation into Calvin's Use of Augustine," *Acta Theologica Supplementum* 10 (2008), 79.

[141] Calvin, *Institutes* (1539), 249.

[142] Calvin, *Institutes* (1543), 433.

writings."[143] In his epistle to King Francis I of France at the beginning of the *Institutes*, Calvin embraced the authority of Augustine together with that of all the other Church Fathers: "All the Fathers, with one heart, have loathed and, with one voice, have detested the corruption of the holy word of God by the verbal trickery of sophists and by subjection to the disputes of dialecticians."[144]

We may observe that Servetus differed from Calvin here only in having moved Augustine and the rest of the later Church Fathers into the sophist category. Thus, to the extent that Calvin continued to take ideas from Augustine, in Servetus's eyes, he too was a sophist.

Augustine's works (including pseudepigraphal ones) are mentioned 17 times in book 1 of *On the Errors of the Trinity* and more than 50 times in book 1 of *The Restoration of Christianity* — a threefold increase. There are also some 30 references to Augustine in the later books of *Restoration*, but none at all in the later books of *Errors*. This reflects an increasing emphasis, in Servetus's work, on his debate with Calvin, and to a lesser extent, other Protestant reformers. Thus, in *Restoration*, when Servetus talked of Augustine he was actually addressing a contemporary — his most obdurate opponent, the one that he most wished to convince.

Reading Servetus Today

Modern Christians may be reassured to find out that Servetus was not against every tripartite understanding of God, but only against those that he thought tended towards tritheism and/or gnosticism. Like other Christians, Servetus spoke of God in terms of Father, Son, and Holy Spirit, but he did not consider this grouping an essential pillar of the faith. What is essential, in his view, is the incarnation: the presentation of God to humanity in a way that human beings can comprehend and to which they can relate. For Servetus, faith in Jesus Christ was vital, for Christ was the very face of God, our pathway to knowledge about God, and our connec-

---

[143] *Calvini opera* 8:266.

[144] Calvin, *Institutes* (1536), 23.

tion to the divine. The Anglican biblical scholar John Barton calls the modern version of Christian faith "allegiance to Christ as the self-expression of God."[145] This, in a nutshell, also encapsulates Servetus's five-hundred-year-old faith.

For Servetus, the core of Christianity is very simple — something that, unlike the Trinity, can be grasped by ordinary human beings, not just learned intellectuals. "Think then not of the sophists," Servetus instructed, "but think of the Jews in those places, fishermen and women, in pure simplicity acknowledging that Jesus was the Christ."[146] And after a lengthy explanation of the Logos, he says:

> Faithful reader, even if you do not achieve an understanding of the manner of Christ's begetting and of his divinity in all its fullness, nevertheless always believe that he is the Messiah, your saviour, begotten by God. This is all you need to believe, in order to live in Christ.[147]

The chief error of the Trinity, from Servetus's point of view, is that, conceive it how you may, the Trinity has an unfortunate tendency to obstruct, obscure, and distract from what should be the *kerygma*, the core teaching, the essential message, of the Christian church. Thus evangelicals, as well as unitarians, may find inspiration in the life and teachings of this daring and reckless soul who had the effrontery to preach even to the leaders of the Reformation.

---

[145] John Barton, *A History of the Bible: The Book and its Faiths* (Penguin, 2019), 488.
[146] *Restoration*, 6.
[147] *Restoration*, 51.

THE RESTORATION OF CHRISTIANITY

Books 1 and 2

CHRISTIANI-SMI RESTITV-TIO.

Totius ecclesiæ apostolicæ est ad sua limina vocatio, in integrum restituta cognitione Dei, fidei Christi, iustificationis nostræ, regenerationis baptismi, & cœnæ domini manducationis. Restituto denique nobis regno cælesti, Babylonis impiæ captiuitate soluta, & Antichristo cum suis penitus destructo.

בעת ההיא יעמוד מיכאל חשר
καὶ ἐγένετο πόλεμος ἐν τῷ οὐρανῷ.

M. D. LIII.

Danielis Márkos Szent-Ivani Transylvano-Hungari.

Londini 1665 die 13 Maij

Nunc Michaelis Almasi Futuro Episcopo d'anius.

THE RESTORATION OF CHRISTIANITY

A summoning of the entire apostolic church back to the way it was in the beginning, with our understanding of God, faith in Christ, our justification, regeneration in baptism, and partaking of the Lord's supper restored to soundness. And with the Antichrist and his minions utterly destroyed, the restoration to us of the heavenly kingdom, released from the captivity of impious Babylon.

ובעת ההיא יעמד׳ מיכאל השר

[*At that time Michael the great prince will arise — Daniel 12:1*]

καὶ ἐγένετο πόλεμος ἐν τῷ οὐρανῷ

[*And there was war in heaven — Revelation 12:7*]

1553

| The Edinburgh Manuscript |

Introduction

[E1] The manifestation of God through the Word, and his communication by means of the Spirit, both become substance in Christ alone. It is only in Christ that we shall be able to see, since the entire divinity of the Word and of the Spirit can be discerned only in this human being.

I shall unfold what is *unquestionably the great mystery of our religion*: how divinity has been made manifest throughout the ages, and how God, who was once revealed in the Word, has now been *manifested in the flesh* and *seen by angels* and human beings.

A vision formerly concealed has now been revealed. We shall clearly describe the actual modes in which God has presented himself to us: outwardly visible in the Word, and inwardly perceptible through the Spirit. Each way it is a great mystery, that human beings can both see and possess

> The 1553 Printed Edition

Seven Books
On the Divine Trinity
in which no illusion of three invisible beings will be taught, but only the true manifestation of the substance of God in the Word and its communication in the Spirit

Introduction

[3] The object of our inquiry, majestically sublime though it may be, is easy to grasp and can be conclusively proven. The most important things, dear reader, are the recognition of God as he is revealed in substance, and the way in which the divine nature is actually communicated. The manifestation of God himself through the Word, and his communication by means of the Spirit, both become substance in Christ alone. It is only in Christ that we shall be able to see clearly, since the entire divinity of the Word and of the Spirit can be discerned only in this human being.

I shall unfold what is *unquestionably the great mystery of our religion*: how divinity has been made manifest throughout the ages, and how God, who was once revealed in the Word, has now been *manifested in the flesh*, communicated *by the Spirit*, and *seen by angels* and human beings.[a]

A vision formerly concealed has now been revealed. We shall clearly describe the actual modes in which God has presented himself to us: outwardly visible in the Word, and inwardly perceptible through the Spirit. Each way it is a great mystery, that human beings can both see and possess

---

[a] 1 Tim 3:16.

The Edinburgh Manuscript

God himself! *With his face unveiled* we shall now behold God, whom we previously could not see. And we shall observe him clearly within ourselves, if only we open the door and set forth along the path.

It is now time to open the door onto this path of light, *without which* nothing can be *seen, without which no one can* read the sacred writings, or know God, or be a Christian. This is the only path to truth that has been laid out for us — genuine, unerring, and easy to follow. If you, reader, begin to follow it, it will reveal the secrets of God to you. It is the only path that fully reveals the divine generation of Christ in the Word, and the true procession of the Holy Spirit; and shows that both [the Word and the Spirit] share the same substance in God. This path will lie open before you. It will lead you to all that is heavenly, and place the true God before your eyes.

Come, therefore, pious reader, all you who yearn for Christ and have a sincere desire for his truth, gird yourself for the journey you are about to take with me. Always keep Christ before you as the goal. Always strive to understand who he is. Defend his honour and his glory everywhere. Commit yourself entirely to him. Always intent upon him [E2] ... I am here diligently undertaking this work, which is pleasing to Christ and useful to ..., not ... [a]

I have divided the whole path into five books, with some dialogues appended, so that we might ascend, step by step, to a full understanding of Christ. The first book contains three basic αξιώματα (*axiomata*, propositions) about Christ, three arguments of the Pharisees and three of the sophists, as well as refutations of their extremely illogical inferences about invisible beings. The second book explains twenty passages of scripture. The third deals with the prefiguration of the

---

[a] The manuscript is damaged at this point.

> The 1553 Printed Edition

God himself! *With his face unveiled*[a] we shall now behold God,[1] whom we previously could not see. And we shall observe him shining within ourselves, if only we open the door and set forth along the path.

It is now time to open the door onto this path of light, *without which* nothing can be *seen, without which no one can* read the sacred scriptures, [4] or understand God,[b] or be a Christian. This is the path to truth — genuine, unerring, and easy to follow. It is the only path that fully reveals the divine generation of Christ in the Word, and the true procession of the Holy Spirit; and shows that both [the Word and the Spirit] share the same substance in God. It is the only path that places God himself right before our eyes.

I have divided the whole path into five books, with some dialogues appended, so that we might ascend, step by step, to a full understanding of Christ. The first book contains three basic propositions about Christ, three arguments of the Pharisees and three of the sophists, as well as refutations of their extremely illogical inferences about invisible beings. The second book explains twenty passages of scripture. The third deals with the prefiguration of the

---

[a] 2 Cor 3:18. [b] See Heb 12:14.

> **The Edinburgh Manuscript**

person of Christ in the Word, seeing God visibly, and the hypostasis of the Word. The fourth concerns the names of God, his essence, and the origins of all things. The fifth book deals with the Holy Spirit. Following this, the first dialogue reveals Christ's fulfillment in all things after the shadows of the Law have passed away, and investigates the essential nature of angels, souls, and hell. The second dialogue teaches the way in which Christ was begotten, and that he is neither a created being nor a being of finite power, but is truly worthy of adoration and is truly God.

O Christ Jesus, do not forsake your servant who labours for your cause and who is oppressed by fear and tormented by his enemies. Grant me now the encouragement of your *good spirit* and give me strength.

Guide my mind and my pen, so that I may describe the glory of your divinity and express true faith in you. This is your cause: to display your true glory and the salvation of your people.

This cause presented itself to me when I was but a young man, about twenty years old. Without any human instruction, I was driven by a divine impulse to write on this subject. I set about doing this before and (such is the world's blindness) I was soon hunted far and wide so that I might be seized and put to death. [E3] Filled with terror, I fled into exile and, my heart filled with tremendous sorrow, for many years I concealed my identity among strangers. Realizing, however, that I was but an immature youth, lacking eloquence and as yet insufficiently educated, I abandoned my original undertaking almost completely. But, lo and behold, most merciful Jesus, you are once again appearing as an advocate, full of encouragement, pleading on behalf of your afflicted client. And you are commanding me to summon up my courage once again and to press forward with alacrity, this time fortified

> ## The 1553 Printed Edition

person of Christ in the Word, seeing God visibly, and the hypostasis of the Word. The fourth concerns the names of God, his essence, and the origins of all things. The fifth book deals with the Holy Spirit. Following this, the first dialogue reveals Christ's fulfillment in all things after the shadows of the Law have passed away,[2] and explains the essential nature of angels, souls, and hell. The second dialogue teaches the way in which Christ was begotten, and that he is neither a created being nor a being of finite power, but is truly worthy of adoration and is the true God.

O Christ Jesus, Son of God, you who were given to us from heaven, you who in yourself visibly reveal deity, show yourself to your servant so that such a marvellous manifestation may be truly brought to light. *Give* me now, I *entreat* you, your *good spirit*[a] and your *potent word*.[b]

Guide my mind and my pen, so that I may describe the glory of your divinity and express true faith in you. This is your cause, even yours from the Father: to display the glory of your spirit.

This cause was presented to me by a divine impulse. I take it up because I am zealous for your truth. I set about doing this once before[c] but now I am compelled do so again. For, given my certainty about this matter and the unmistakable *signs of the times*,[d] the time has truly come for me to make it known to all the faithful.

---

[a] See Luke 11:13 (11:12 in Vulgate): "the heavenly Father [will] give the good spirit to those who ask him." Most modern Bibles say "holy spirit," but in Servetus's time the Vulgate used "good spirit." [b] Heb 4:12.
[c] In *On the Errors of the Trinity* and *Two Dialogues on the Trinity*.
[d] Matt 16:3.

> **The Edinburgh Manuscript**

by the study of many authors, and above all, by complete confidence in your truth. You yourself are my witness in this — lest anyone consider me a mere innovator driven by vain ambition. Again, as God is my witness, this is the reason that I have postponed my task. And it is also because of the persecution which so loomed over me, that, like Jonah, I wanted instead to take flight upon the sea,[a] or to escape to some newly discovered island.[3] But I cannot do this, since you, whose cause this is, have forbidden me to do so. Thus I can no longer put off this task, for the end of time is now at hand, as I shall make clear from the *signs of the times*.[b]

A lamp should not be hidden, you taught us, and *woe to me if I do not preach the gospel!* This is the common cause of all Christians, to which we are all obligated.

It remains for you, reader, for the sake of Christ, to kindly bear with me. For then you shall hear the subject discussed in that simple speech in which truth delights, without any exaggeration.

---

[a] See Jonah 1:3.   [b] Matt 16:3.

Introduction

The 1553 Printed Edition

A lamp should not be hidden, you taught us,[a] and *woe to me if I do not preach the gospel!*[b] This is the common cause of all Christians, to which we are all obligated.

It remains for you, reader, for the sake of Christ, to kindly bear with me to the end of this work. For then you shall hear the entire subject discussed truthfully, without any exaggeration.

---

[a] See Matt 5:15; Luke 8:16. [b] 1 Cor 9:16.

| The Edinburgh Manuscript |

Book 1

About the man Jesus Christ and the false images

In order to get off to a good start on our path, in this, the first book of my account of the Son of God, as in the preaching of the first apostles, I shall begin with the most well-known facts. These facts, which have been publicly proclaimed to everyone, should be obvious to anyone of good sense.

I shall begin with the man Jesus Christ himself, in order to refute the sophists and because he is our current subject. [E4] Embarking on speculation about the Word, but lacking a foundation [of knowledge about the man Jesus], [the sophists] are led to [believe in] some other son and consign the true Son of God to oblivion. I will try to remind them who that true Son is.

Since the [masculine singular] demonstrative pronoun [*hic*, this] refers to a man who was beaten and whipped, I submit that the following three statements are the plain and simple truth: 1) this [man] is Jesus Christ; 2) this [man] is the Son of God; and 3) this [man] is God.

| The 1553 Printed Edition |

Book 1

About the man Jesus Christ and the false images

[5] In order to get off to a good start on our path, in this, the first book of my account of the Son of God, as in the preaching of the first apostles, I shall begin with the most well-known facts. These facts, which have been publicly proclaimed to everyone, should be obvious to anyone of good sense.

The man Jesus is himself the door and the path. I shall begin with him in order to refute the sophists and because he is our current subject. Aspiring to knowledge about the Word, but lacking a foundation [of knowledge about the man Jesus], [the sophists] are led to [believe in] some other son and consign the true Son of God to oblivion. I intend to remind them who that true Son is.

Since the [masculine singular] demonstrative pronoun [*hic*, this] refers to a man[1] who was beaten and whipped, I submit that the following three statements are the plain and simple truth: 1) this [man] is Jesus Christ; 2) this [man] is the Son of God; and 3) this [man] is God.

Err, 2r

Err, 2r

The Edinburgh Manuscript

Behold the door! Behold the path on which alone is that illumination that leads to knowledge of the glory of God. This glory is reflected in the face of Jesus Christ.

{First Proposition} [*This Man is Jesus Christ*]

In the first place, this man was called Jesus, as the first postulate clearly and self-evidently shows. For that was the name given to him as a boy on the day of his circumcision (Luke 1 and 2), just as your name, for instance, is John, and his, Peter. Jesus, as the early Church Fathers teach, is a masculine proper name, while Christ is a title.

The Jews all admitted that he was Jesus, but when [Pilate] asked them about *"Jesus who is called Christ,"* they denied that he was the Christ. And they *put out of the synagogue* those who *confessed him to be the Christ*. The apostles frequently argued with them about whether Jesus was the Messiah. But there was never any doubt or question that he was Jesus, nor did anyone ever deny this.

Weigh carefully the intent of Paul's words, and the zeal with which he *testified to the Jews that Jesus was the Messiah* (Acts 9, 17, and 18). With what *spiritual fervour Apollos of Alexandria confuted the Jews, proving* this [man] *Jesus to be the Christ*! These things were said of the man, without any sophistical qualifications. Think then not of the sophists, but think of the Jews in those places, fishermen and women, in pure simplicity believing that this man Jesus was the Christ. Likewise *the blind, when they heard* the report *that Jesus* of Nazareth *was passing* their way, immediately began *shouting,* [E5] "Jesus, *son of David, have mercy on us.*"[a] If you had been there, what conception would you have had in your mind of Jesus of Nazareth as he passed by?

---

[a] Matt 20:30.

| The 1553 Printed Edition |

{*First Proposition*} [*This Man is Jesus Christ*]

To begin with, nothing can be demonstrated with greater certainty than this self-evident first postulate: this man is called Jesus. That was the name given to him as a boy on the day of his circumcision (Luke 1 and 2),[a] just as your name, for instance, is John, and his, Peter. The name Jesus, as the early Church Fathers[2] teach, is a masculine proper name, while Christ is a title.[3]   *Err, 2v*

The Jews all admitted that he was Jesus, but when [Pilate] asked them about *Jesus who is called Christ*,[b] they denied that he was the Christ. And they *put out of the synagogue* those who *confessed him to be the Christ*.[c] The apostles frequently argued with them about whether Jesus was the Messiah. But there was never any doubt or question that he was Jesus, nor did anyone ever deny this.   *Err, 2v*

Consider the intent of Paul's words, [6] and the zeal with which he *testified to the Jews that Jesus was the Messiah* (Acts 9, 27, and 18).[d] With what *spiritual fervour Apollos of Alexandria confuted the Jews, proving* this [man] *Jesus to be the Christ*![e] These things were said of the man, without any sophistical qualifications. Think then not of the sophists, but think of the Jews in those places, fishermen and women, in pure simplicity acknowledging that Jesus was the Christ[f] — this man, Jesus of Nazareth, Jesus the son of David.   *Err, 2v*

---

[a] Luke 1:31, 2:21.   [b] Matt 27:17, 22.   [c] John 9:22. See also John 12:42, 16:2.   [d] Acts 9:22, 17:3, 18:5. The printed text erroneously has Acts 27 instead of Acts 17; the Edinburgh manuscript is correct.
[e] Acts 18:24-25, 28.   [f] Matt 14:32-33 (fishermen); John 11:27 (Martha); John 4:29 (the Samaritan woman).

| The Edinburgh Manuscript |

Granting, therefore, that the man is Jesus, and having granted that he was anointed by God, we are then forced to concede that he is the Christ. For he himself is *your holy child, whom you have anointed* (Acts 4). He is the *holy of holies* whose anointing was predicted in Daniel 9. Moreover, in Acts 10, Peter said, "*You know*," as if it were something abundantly clear to everyone. For what was said about Jesus was common knowledge: how *God anointed Jesus*, that [man] *of Nazareth, with the Holy Spirit and with power, for God was with him, the one established by God as the judge of the living and the dead.* "*Let all the house of Israel know assuredly,*" [Peter says] in Acts 2, "*that God has made this Jesus, whom you crucified, both Lord and Christ*" — that is, the anointed one.

These people did not take the word "Christ" to mean some incorporeal being, but applied it to a [human] body that was anointed by God and possessed the substance of deity. As you will see, this body was anointed by the Holy Spirit.

Clement, Justin, Irenaeus, Tertullian, and the rest of the early Church Fathers all affirm that the word "Christ" is a noun pertaining to "a human nature." The meaning of the word ["Christ," or the anointed one] demonstrates that very thing. For "to be anointed" can only refer to a human nature. Who, therefore, will deny that it was a man who was anointed? *He who denies that Jesus is the Christ is the Antichrist,* while *every one who believes that* [Jesus] is the anointed one *is born of God.*

Book 1

> **The 1553 Printed Edition**

But granting that this [man] is Jesus, we have to concede that he is the Christ, the one who was in truth anointed by God. For he is *your holy child, whom you have anointed* (Acts 4).[a] He is the *holy of holies* whose anointing was predicted in Daniel 9.[b] Moreover, in Acts 10, Peter said, "*You know*," as if it were something abundantly clear to everyone.[c] For what was said about Jesus was common knowledge: *how God anointed Jesus, that man of Nazareth, with the Holy Spirit and with power, for God was with him,* and *he is the one established by God as the judge of the living and the dead.*[d] "*Let all the house of Israel know assuredly,*" [Peter] says in Acts 2, "*that God has made this Jesus, whom you crucified, both Lord and Christ*"[e] — that is, the anointed one.

Err, 2v

Err, 3r

Clement, Justin,[4] Irenaeus, Tertullian, and the rest of the early Church Fathers all affirm that the word "Christ" is a noun pertaining to "a human nature."[f] The meaning of the word ["Christ," or the anointed one] demonstrates that very thing. For "to be anointed" can only refer to a human nature. Who, therefore, will deny that it was a man who was anointed? *He who denies that Jesus is the Christ is the Antichrist,* while *every one who believes that* [Jesus] *himself is the anointed one is born of God.*[g]

Err, 3r

---

[a] Acts 4:27. [b] Dan 9:24. [c] Acts 10:36-37. [d] Acts 10:38, 42.
[e] Acts 2:36. This argument — that Christ is a human being because only a human being can be anointed — is based on Tertullian, *Adversus Praxean* 28 (PL 2 192C-193A). Tertullian even added "that is, the anointed one" to his quotation of Acts 2:36. [f] [Clement], *Recognitiones* 1.45-46 (PG 1 1233A-1234B). Irenaeus, *Adversus haereses* 3.9.3 (PG 7 871A-C). Tertullian, *Adversus Praxean* 29 (PL 2 194A).
[g] 1 John 2:22, 5:1.

The Edinburgh Manuscript

Furthermore, in book 1 of Clement's *Recognitions*, Peter explains the true meaning of the word ["anointed"]: "Because kings were commonly called Christs, therefore, [Jesus], on account of the superior nature of his anointing, above all others, is anointed Christ, the King." For "just as God made an angel first among angels, a beast first among beasts, and a star first among stars, so, too, did he make Christ first among men." The authority of the Old Testament also teaches us that it was a man who was called Christ, since even an earthly king can be called Christ (1 Samuel 12 and 24 and Isaiah 45).

Similarly in Matthew 1: [Mary], *of whom Jesus was born, that man who is called Christ*. Note the article [*ille*, that man] and note the title [Christ], which are to be understood to concern the begetting of the man. Note also the pronouns, which are to be understood here as pointing to something perceived by the senses.

[E6] He is a man, who was begotten by the Holy Spirit. Luke, in chapter 3, is clearly describing Christ the man when he says: *And Jesus was entering his thirtieth year and was thought to be the son of Joseph*. This man, who was *thought to be the son of Joseph*, was Jesus Christ, the son of God.

In Acts 13 Paul says to the Jews: "*God, as he promised, brought forth from the seed of* David, Christ, the man you had put to death." In the same passage in Acts and also in John 1, John the Baptist says, "Do not *suppose that I am* the Christ." How ridiculous John's disavowal would have been if the word "Christ" could not refer to a human being! [In that case], Christ's question and Peter's response in Matthew 16 would have been meaningless: Christ *said, "Who do*

Book 1

The 1553 Printed Edition

In book 1 of Clement's *Recognitions*,[5] Peter explains the true meaning of the word ["anointed"]: "Because kings were commonly called Christs, therefore [Jesus], on account of the superior nature of his anointing, above all others, is called Christ the King." For "just as God made an angel first among angels, a beast first among beasts, and a star first among stars, so too did he make Christ first among men."[a] The authority of the Old Testament also clearly teaches us that it was a man who was called Christ, since even an earthly king can be called Christ[6] (1 Samuel 12 and 24 and Isaiah 45).[b]

Err, 3r-v

Similarly in Matthew 1: [Mary], *of whom Jesus was born, that man who is called Christ*.[c] Note here the article [*ille*, that man] and the title [Christ].

Err, 3v

[7] He is a man, who was begotten by the Holy Spirit. Luke, in chapter 3, is clearly describing Christ the man when he says: *And Jesus was entering his thirtieth year and was thought to be the son of Joseph*.[d] This same man, who was *thought to be the son of Joseph*, was Jesus Christ, the son of God.

Err, 3v

In Acts 13 Paul says to the Jews: "*God, as he promised, brought forth from the seed of* David, Christ, the man you had put to death."[e] In the same passage in Acts and also in John 1, John the Baptist says, "Do not *suppose that I am* the Christ."[f] How ridiculous John's disavowal would have been if the word "Christ" could not refer to a human being! [In that case], Christ's question and Peter's response in Matthew 16 would have been meaningless: Christ *said, "Who do*

Err, 3v

---

[a] [Clement], *Recognitiones* 1.45 (PG 1 1233B).   [b] 1 Sam 12:1-5, 24:6; Isa 45:1.   [c] Matt 1:16.   [d] Luke 3:23.   [e] Acts 13:23, 28.   [f] Acts 13:25; John 1:20.

| The Edinburgh Manuscript |

people say that I am?" and *Peter replied, "You are the Christ, you are the Son of the living God."* The man whom some supposed to be *Elijah and others Jeremiah*, Peter said was *Christ, the Son of God.* He did not say, "The incorporeal son is in you," but *"You are the Son."* And when Christ *charged [the disciples] to tell no one that he himself was the Christ*, what do you think he was indicating by means of that pronoun [*ipse*, he himself]? If he is not the Christ, how does he make us his anointed ones?

I would not have belaboured this at such length, proving what is clearer than the noonday sun, except that I see that the minds of some have been led astray. For, not understanding the mystery of the incarnation, they consider Christ to be both an incorporeal being and a real son, although throughout history it has always been an actual human being who has been called Christ [that is, anointed]. Hear the testimony of Christ, calling himself a human being: *"You seek to kill me, a human being who has told you the truth"* (John 8). And in 1 Timothy 2 [Paul calls him] *the mediator between God and humanity, the human being, Christ Jesus.*

But if you find the word *homo* [human being] to be objectionable, because the sophists have corrupted its meaning by using it as a connotative term, then consider the word *vir* [man]. And listen to what Peter says in Acts 2: *"Jesus of Nazareth* was *a man appointed by God."* In the last chapter of Luke: *Concerning Jesus of Nazareth,* [E7] *who was a man, a prophet, mighty [in deed and word].* In John 1 [John the Baptist says], *"After me will come a man."* In Isaiah 53: *the lowliest of men, a man of sorrows.* In Zechariah 6: *Behold the man whose name is the Branch.* And in Acts 17: *God will judge the world by that man* — that is to say, Christ.

> The 1553 Printed Edition

*people say that I am?"*⁷ and *Peter replied, "You are the Christ, you are the Son of the living God."*ᵃ The man whom some supposed to be *Elijah and others Jeremiah*,ᵇ Peter said was *Christ, the Son of God*. He did not say, "The incorporeal son is in you," but "*You are the Son.*" And when Christ *charged [the disciples] to tell no one that he himself was the Christ*,ᶜ what do you think he was indicating by means of that pronoun [*ipse*, he himself]? If he is not the Christ, how does he make us his anointed ones?

This is something so obvious that we would not need to belabour it at length, except that the minds of some have been led astray. For, not understanding the mystery of the incarnation, they consider Christ to be both an incorporeal being and a real son, although throughout history it has always been an actual human being who has been called Christ [that is, anointed]. Hear the testimony of Christ, calling himself a human being: "*You seek to kill me, a human being who has told you the truth*" (John 8).ᵈ And in 1 Timothy 2 [Paul calls him] *the mediator between God and humanity, the human being, Christ Jesus.*ᵉ

But if you find the word *homo* [human being] to be objectionable, because the sophists have corrupted its meaning by using it as a connotative term, then consider the word *vir* [man].⁸ And listen to what Peter says in Acts 2: "*Jesus of Nazareth* was *a man appointed by God.*"ᶠ In the last chapter of Luke: *Concerning Jesus of Nazareth, who was a man, a prophet, mighty [in deed and word].*ᵍ In John 1 [John the Baptist says], "*After me will come a man.*"ʰ In Isaiah 53: *the lowliest of men, a man of sorrows.*ⁱ In Zechariah 6: *Behold the man whose name is the Branch.*ʲ And in Acts 17: *God will judge the world by that man*ᵏ — that is to say, Christ.

ᵃ Matt 16:13, 15, 16. ᵇ Matt 16:14. ᶜ Matt 16:20. ᵈ John 8:40.
ᵉ 1 Tim 2:5. ᶠ Acts 2:22. ᵍ Luke 24:19. ʰ John 1:30. ⁱ Isa 53:3.
ʲ Zech 6:12. ᵏ Acts 17:31.

The Edinburgh Manuscript

If you have common sense, reader, and are fully convinced of [what I say about] the nature of the demonstrative pronoun, it will be obvious to you that [pointing to something] is the true and original meaning of the word "this." For when [Jesus] was pointed out for people to see, it was generally accepted that "*this is the Christ*" and "*you are Jesus.*" And he spoke, asked and answered questions, and felt hunger, and they saw him walking on water.

[When he asked] "*Whom do you seek?*" [they answered,] "*Jesus of Nazareth.*" [Jesus said to them,] "*I am he.*" [And Judas said,] "*Whomever I shall kiss is the one; seize him.*" [Jesus said,] "*It is I myself, touch me, and see.*" When Peter is addressing the Jews, he says, "*this Jesus, whom you* put to death, *God raised up, of which we all are witnesses.*" If you had been engaged in a debate with one of the Jews, what would you have been trying to point out by the use of such pronouns? For none of them had ever heard about either the Trinity or an invisible son.

[Due to the false ideas we hold about the Trinity] are we not in a worse condition than the Samaritan woman in John 4, who said, "*Come and see the man who told me all that I ever did. Is this not the Christ?*" Christ had confirmed the impression of the woman, who knew nothing at all about incorporeal beings. For, when she asked about the Messiah to come, *he who is called the Christ*, he answered, "*I who am speaking to you am he.*" I whom you see speaking. Not some incorporeal being, but I, the one who is speaking now, am the true and natural son of God.

Likewise, the blind man who received sight in John 9 conceived a similar faith in Jesus, saying, "*The man who is*

> **The 1553 Printed Edition**

If you have common sense, reader, and are fully convinced of [what I say about] [8] the nature of the demonstrative pronoun, it will be obvious to you that [pointing to something] is the true and original meaning of the word "this."⁹ For when [Jesus] was pointed out for people to see, it was generally accepted that "*this is the Christ*"[a] and "you are Jesus."[b] And he spoke, asked and answered questions, and felt hunger, and they saw him walking on water.¹⁰

Err, 4v

[When he asked] *"Whom do you seek?"* [they answered,] *"Jesus of Nazareth."* [Jesus said to them,] *"I am he."*[c] And Judas said,] *"Whomever I shall kiss is the one; seize him."*[d] [Jesus said,] *"It is I myself, touch me, and see."*[e] In Acts 2, when Peter is addressing the Jews, he says, "*this Jesus, whom you* put to death, *God raised up, of which we all are witnesses.*"[f] If you had been engaged in a debate with one of the Jews, what would you have been trying to point out by the use of such pronouns? For none of them had ever heard anything about either the Trinity or an invisible son.

[Due to the false ideas we hold about the Trinity] are we not in a worse condition than the Samaritan woman in John 4, who said, *"Come and see the man who told me all that I ever did. Is this not the Christ?"*[g] [Christ] had just confirmed the impression of the woman, who knew nothing at all about incorporeal beings. For, when she asked about the Messiah to come, *he who is called the Christ*, he answered, *"I who am speaking to you am he."*[h] I whom you see speaking. Not some incorporeal being, but I, the one who is speaking now, am the true and natural son of God.

Err, 4v-5r

Likewise, the blind man who received sight in John 9 conceived a similar faith in Jesus, saying, "*The man who is*

---

[a] John 7:41. [b] There are numerous instances in the Gospels of "you are Christ." However, "you are Jesus" is not found. [c] John 18:4-5. [d] Matt 26:48; Mark 14:44. [e] Luke 24:39. [f] Acts 2:32, 36. [g] John 4:29. [h] John 4:25-26.

The Edinburgh Manuscript

called Jesus made clay [*and anointed my eyes*]." Because he had faith in Christ, he received sight; and he did not believe anything false about Christ.

In addition, you understand, what the Apostle says refers to an actual human being: as *by one man's trespass*, etc., so by *the grace of one man, Jesus Christ. For as by a man came death*, so *by a man has come also the resurrection of the dead.* Either he is using the word "man" in the absolute sense in both cases, or in both cases he is using it connotatively; otherwise there can be no comparison. Here he is speaking of the first [**E8**] Adam and the second, so it profits the sophists nothing to take [the word "man"] in a connotative sense.

Finally, in John 20, *Jesus performed miracles in order that we might believe that he is the Christ, the Son of God.* What is essential about Jesus, then, is that we believe that Jesus was begotten by God and died for our salvation. Nathanael concludes that [Jesus] is the Son of God, because [Jesus displays divine knowledge when] he says about him, "*I saw you under the fig tree.*" In Matthew 14 others come to the same conclusion, because he chased the wind away.

{*Second Proposition*} [*This Man is the Son of God*]

These conclusions [reached by those who witnessed Christ's miracles] clearly prove my second proposition: that this very man, whom I call Christ, is the Son of God. For, based on the miracles that he performed, [the witnesses] concluded that he was the Son of God. Once it has been proven that he is Jesus Christ, [the second proposition] is also proven, since scripture always proclaims that Jesus Christ is the Son of God.

> The 1553 Printed Edition

called Jesus made clay [and anointed my eyes]."ᵃ Because he had faith in Christ, he received sight; and he did not believe anything false about Christ.

What the Apostle says ought to be understood as referring to an actual human being: as *by one man's trespass*, so by *the grace of one man, Jesus Christ*.ᵇ *For as by a man came death, by a man has come also the resurrection of the dead*.ᶜ Either he is using the word "man" in the absolute sense in both cases, or in both cases he is using it connotatively; otherwise there can be no comparison. Here he is speaking of the first Adam and the second Adam, so it profits the sophists nothing to take [the word] "man" in a connotative sense.

Err, 5r

Finally, in John 20, *Jesus performed miracles in order that we might believe that he is the Christ, the Son of God.*ᵈ What is essential about Jesus, then, is that we believe that Jesus was begotten by God and anointed for our salvation. Nathanael concludes that [Jesus] is the Son of God, because [Jesus displays divine knowledge when] he says about him, "*I saw you under the fig tree.*"ᵉ In Matthew 14 [the disciples] come to the same conclusion, because he chased the wind away.ᶠ

Err, 5v

[9] {*Second Proposition*} [*This Man is the Son of God*]

These conclusions [reached by those who witnessed Christ's miracles] very clearly prove my second proposition: that this very man, whom I call Christ, is the Son of God. For, based on the miracles that he performed, [the witnesses] concluded that this man was the Son of God. If one accepts that this man is Jesus Christ, it follows that this man is the Son of God, since scripture always teaches that Jesus Christ is the Son of God. It then surely follows that God, the father of Jesus Christ, is God, the father of a man.

Err, 6r

ᵃ John 9:11.   ᵇ Rom 5:15.   ᶜ 1 Cor 15:21.   ᵈ John 20:30-31.
ᵉ John 1:47-50.   ᶠ Matt 14:32-33. See also Luke 8:23-25.

> **The Edinburgh Manuscript**

He is publicly identified as the Son of God, and thus, in relation to him, God is called the Father. God is truly his father because Jesus was begotten in substance by him, as you were by your own father. Christ was not begotten by Joseph; rather he was begotten by the Holy Spirit, begotten from the substance of God. This body was truly and naturally begotten from [the substance of] God, without any sophistical qualification. In what follows I shall clearly explain the way in which he was begotten. For now, I shall only observe in passing that the Word of God overshadowed the Virgin like a cloud, and was the *dew* of the physical begetting of Christ, like a cloud which causes the earth to *bring forth and bud* (Psalm 71; Isaiah 45 and 55).

For this reason, in the first chapters of their respective gospels, both Matthew and Luke teach that he is called the Son [of God]. In Luke the angel says to Mary, "*The Holy Spirit will come upon you, and the power of the Most High will overshadow you.*" This is immediately followed by the words, "*and therefore the child who is to be born shall be called holy, the Son of God.*" Matthew offers the same explanation, saying that [Mary] was made pregnant by the Holy Spirit, for *that which was conceived in her was of the Holy Spirit.* What was conceived in her was a son. [Matthew] is speaking straightforwardly, not sophistically. Jesus was born of Mary, a son of the substance of Mary.

Now, if Mary is the natural **[E9]** mother, she is the mother of someone's natural son. Note what Luke says:[a] The son begotten in you, whom *you will conceive and bear, will be called the Son of the Most High. He will be great, and God will give him the throne of his father David.*" Why did [the

---

[a] Here the copyist of the Edinburgh manuscript mistakenly read the Latin word *is* (he) as "15," and inserted the word "cap." (chapter) in order to connect it to the reference to Luke. But the quotation here is from Luke chapter 1, not chapter 15.

| The 1553 Printed Edition |

This very man is everywhere clearly identified as the Son of God, and thus, in relation to him, God is truly the Father. God is truly his father because Jesus was begotten in substance by him, as you were by your own father. Christ was not begotten by Joseph; rather he was begotten by the Holy Spirit, begotten from the substance of God. This man, Jesus, was truly and naturally begotten from [the substance of] God, without any sophistical qualification. In what follows I shall clearly explain the way in which he was begotten. For now, I shall only observe in passing that the Word of God overshadowed the Virgin like a cloud,[a] and acted on her like the *dew* of the begetting [of Christ], like *rain* which causes the earth to *bring forth and bud* (Psalm 71; Isaiah 45 and 55).[b]

For this reason, in the first chapters of their respective gospels, both Matthew and Luke teach that he is called the Son [of God]. In Luke the angel says to Mary, "*The Holy Spirit will come upon you, and the power of the Most High will overshadow you.*" This is immediately followed by the words, "*and therefore the child who is to be born shall be holy*, truly *the Son of God.*"[c] Matthew offers the same explanation, saying that [Mary] was made pregnant by the Holy Spirit, for *that which was conceived in her was of the Holy Spirit.*[d] What was conceived in her was a son. [Matthew] is speaking straightforwardly, not sophistically. Jesus was born of Mary, a son of the substance of Mary.

Now, if Mary is the natural mother, she is the mother of someone's natural son. Note what Luke says: The son begotten in you, whom *you will conceive and bear, will be called the Son of the Most High. He will be great, and God will give him the throne of his father David.*"[e] Why did [the

Err, 6r

Err, 6r

Err, 6v

---

[a] Luke 1:35. [b] Ps 72:6; Isa 45:8, 55:10. [c] Luke 1:35. [d] Matt 1:20.
[e] Luke 1:31, 32.

The Edinburgh Manuscript

angel] not say, "He will be called the son of the first person," and "The first person will give him the throne"? Instead what he says is, "*The Son of God, the Most High,*" and "*God will give him the throne.*" Is one to suppose that the second incorporeal being was begotten by the Holy Spirit? Or that what was begotten by the Holy Spirit was not really a son?

It is to no avail that many people, by distorting the angel's words, twist the word "holy" to make it apply to another son, as if Christ, the firstborn, was not worthy [to be called holy]. This is especially apparent since, in the next chapter, Luke reveals why [the angel] said "holy." It was because Christ was *the male who opens the womb*. For *every [first-born] male opening the womb* shall be called *holy to [the Lord]* (Exodus 13 and 34, Numbers 8).

In addition, [the sophists] would have us believe that [in Luke 1] the *power* of God, or rather the strength *of the Most High*, which *overshadowed* Mary as the Spirit descended, was the metaphysical, invisible son, because spirit and power (that is, spirit and strength) are spoken of copulatively. To this I reply that Luke means the same thing by the word "power" (that is, "strength") as he does in chapter 24 of Luke and in Acts 1, where he uses the same word: *You will receive power* (or *strength*) *when the Holy Spirit comes down upon you*.

This is why Luke says that John [the Baptist] will come in *the spirit and power of Elijah*, and that because of this he is *more than a prophet*. The other prophets had the spirit of prophecy, but they did not have the power to perform miracles, as Elijah did. Therefore it is said that Elijah had *spirit and power*, that is to say, spirit and strength. John also possessed power, even from the womb — power approaching

> The 1553 Printed Edition

angel] not say, "He will be called the son of the first person," and "The first person will give him the throne"? Instead what he says is, "*The Son of God, the Most High*," and "*God will give him the throne*." Is one to suppose that the second incorporeal being was begotten by the Holy Spirit? Or that what was actually begotten by the Holy Spirit was not really a son?

Err, 6v

It is to no avail that many people, by distorting the angel's words, twist the word "holy" to make it apply to another son, as if [10] Christ, the firstborn, was not worthy [to be called holy]. This is especially apparent since, in the next chapter, Luke reveals why [the angel] said "holy." It was because Christ was *the male who opens the womb*.[a] For *every [first-born] male opening the womb* shall be called *holy to [the Lord]* (Exodus 13 and 34, Numbers 8).[b]

Err, 6v

What is more, [the sophists] would have us believe that [in Luke 1] the *power*, or rather the strength, *of the Most High*, which *overshadowed* Mary as the Spirit descended,[c] was the metaphysical, invisible son, because spirit and power (that is, spirit and strength) are spoken of copulatively.[11] To this I reply that Luke means the same thing by the word "power" (that is, "strength") as he does in chapter 24 of Luke and in Acts 1, where he uses the same word: *You will receive power* (or *strength*) *when the Holy Spirit comes down upon you*.[d]

This is why Luke says that John [the Baptist] will come with *the spirit and power of Elijah*,[e] and that because of this he is *more than a prophet*.[f] The other prophets had the spirit of prophecy, but they did not have the power to perform miracles, as Elijah did. Therefore it is said that Elijah had *spirit and power*, that is to say, spirit and strength. John also possessed power from the womb — power approaching

---

[a] Luke 2:23.   [b] Ex 13:2, 13:12, 34:19; Num 8:16-17.   [c] Luke 1:35.
[d] Luke 24:49; Acts 1:8.   [e] Luke 1:17.   [f] Luke 7:26.

The Edinburgh Manuscript

that of the one whose coming he prophesied. He had the power of turning the faithless back to their God through miracles, [E10] just as Elijah had. To bear witness to the truth, fire descended from heaven at Elijah's command, even though the altar had been flooded with water (1 Kings 18). Similarly, *the Holy Spirit* miraculously *descended* from *heaven* when John *baptized* in water, bearing witness to the truth of Christ (Matthew 3 and Luke 3).

Thus power added to spirit indicates a certain degree of [spiritual] power, not two separate metaphysical beings. There is a difference between spirit and power, because there is not equal power, or equal strength, in every spirit. [Power added to spirit] is the *double share of* Elijah's *spirit* that Elisha sought; namely, the spirit of prophecy and the spirit of miracles. It was in this way that the apostles *received the Holy Spirit* and *power*, that is, the *Holy Spirit* and *strength*, so that, thus divinely inspired *with great potency* and the power to perform miracles, they were able to *bear witness to the resurrection of Christ* (Acts 1 and 4). The conjunction ["and"] adds something particular; as, for instance, when it is written, [*he will baptize you*] *with the Holy Spirit and with fire*. The addition of fire increases the power and adds to the intensity of the cleansing.

In Acts chapter 6, men *full of the Holy Spirit and of wisdom* were *appointed,* who, in addition to the gift of the Spirit common [among those early Christians], had the kind of wisdom that suited them for [particular pastoral] tasks. From this one can very clearly understand why Luke said [in Acts 1] that the Holy Spirit and power were in Christ and the apostles. Luke makes this even more plain

> **The 1553 Printed Edition**

that of the one whose coming he prophesied — the power of turning the faithless back to their God through miracles, just as Elijah had. To bear witness to the truth, fire descended from heaven at Elijah's command, even though the altar had been flooded with water (1 Kings 18).[a] Similarly, *the Holy Spirit* miraculously *descended* from *heaven* when John *baptized* in water, bearing witness to the truth of Christ (Matthew 3 and Luke 3).[b]

Thus power added to spirit indicates a certain degree of [spiritual] power, not two separate metaphysical beings. There is a difference between spirit and power, because there is not equal power, or equal strength, in every spirit. [Power added to spirit] is the *double share of* Elijah's *spirit* that Elisha sought;[c] namely, the spirit of prophecy and the power to perform miracles. It was in this way that the apostles *received the Holy Spirit* and *power*, that is, the *Holy Spirit* and *strength*, so that, thus divinely inspired *with great potency* and the power to perform miracles, they were able to *bear witness to the resurrection of Christ* (Acts 1 and 4).[d] The conjunction ["and"] adds something particular; as, for instance, when it is written, [*he will baptize you*] *with the Holy Spirit and with fire*.[e] The addition of fire increases the power and adds to the intensity of the cleansing.

In Acts chapter 6, men *full of the Holy Spirit and of wisdom* were *appointed*,[f] who, in addition to the gift of the Spirit common [among those early Christians], had the kind of wisdom that suited them for [particular pastoral] tasks. From this one can very clearly understand why **[11]** Luke said [in Acts 1] that the Holy Spirit and power were in Christ and the apostles.[g] Luke makes this even more plain

---

[a] 1 Kg 18:30-39.   [b] Matt 3:16; Luke 3:21-22; see also Mark 1:10.
[c] 2 Kg 2:9.   [d] Acts 1:8, 4:33.   [e] Matt 3:11; Luke 3:16.   [f] Acts 6:3.
[g] Acts 1:8.

| The Edinburgh Manuscript |

in Acts 10, where he writes, *God anointed Jesus of Nazareth with the Holy Spirit and with power* (that is to say, with the Holy Spirit and strength). Here the conjunction ["and" in the phrase "spirit and power"] precludes the idea that this power [to perform miracles] can be taken metaphorically as an argument for an incorporeal son. Rather [the conjunction] tells us that the spirit of Christ possesses all strength.

Furthermore, Luke did not say that this strength is to be called the Son. Rather he who was begotten in Mary by *the power of* God, *will therefore be called the son of God.* For Mary did not have sexual relations with a man; **[E11]** she was made pregnant by the power of God, in that overshadowing which fulfilled the function of a man's seed. Because of this she can be said to have been made pregnant by the Holy Spirit; and Christ himself was *begotten, sent forth*, and *anointed* by the Holy Spirit (Matthew 1, Isaiah 48 and 61). [Luke] did not claim that the second being was begotten by the third; rather [he said] that he who was born of Mary from the Holy Spirit, is the Son.

Irenaeus understood this passage in this way, for he said, at the beginning of book 5 [of *Against Heresies*] that the Son of the Most High was born of Mary. In Tractate 99 on the Gospel of John, Augustine was unable to explain the passage any other way. Thus he said that the Holy Spirit itself, God's power, was active in the begetting of Christ.

Besides, the very meaning of the word ["son"] teaches us that the Son is to be called a human being. For just as being anointed is a condition characteristic of the body, so

> The 1553 Printed Edition

in Acts 10, where he writes, *God anointed Jesus of Nazareth with the Holy Spirit and with power* (that is to say, with the Holy Spirit and strength).[a] Here the conjunction "and" [in the phrase "spirit and power"] precludes the idea that this power [to perform miracles] can be taken metaphysically as an argument for an incorporeal son. Rather [the conjunction] tells us that the spirit of Christ possesses all strength.

Furthermore, Luke did not say that this power is to be called the Son. Rather he who was begotten in Mary by *the power of* God, *will therefore be called the son of God*.[b] For Mary did not have sexual relations with a man; she was made pregnant by the power of God, in that overshadowing which fulfilled the function of a man's seed.[c] Because of this she is said to have been made pregnant by the Holy Spirit; and Christ himself was *begotten, sent forth*,[12] and *anointed* by the Holy Spirit (Matthew 1, Isaiah 48 and 61).[d] [Luke] did not claim that the second being was begotten by the third; rather [he said] that he who was born of Mary from the Holy Spirit, is the Son.

Err, 6v-7r

Irenaeus understands this passage in this way, for he says, at the beginning of book 5 [of *Against Heresies*] that the Son of God the Most High was born of Mary.[e] In Tractate 99 on the Gospel of John, Augustine was unable to explain the passage any other way. Thus he said that the Holy Spirit itself, God's power, was active in the begetting of Christ.[f]

Moreover, the very meaning of the word ["son"] teaches us that the Son, properly speaking, is a human being. For just as being anointed is characteristic of a human being, so

Err, 7r

---

[a] Acts 10:38. [b] Luke 1:35. [c] The expression *vice seminis* (the function of [a man's] seed) is found in Tertullian, *Adversus Valentinianos* 7 (PL 2 551B). [d] Matt 1:20 (begotten); Isa 48:16 (sent); Isa 61:1 (anointed).
[e] Irenaeus, *Adversus haereses* 5.1.3 (PG 7 1122C-D). [f] Augustine, *In evangelium Iohannis* 99.7 (PL 35 1889).

| The Edinburgh Manuscript |

too being born is a condition of the flesh. Certainly he came to be born through the power of the Spirit. Nevertheless, the body itself was truly begotten and truly born, and it is this very body that shares in the substance of God, as we will discuss later.

Who, I ask you, is that [man] who *was considered to be the son of Joseph*? Who is the *fruit of the womb*? Is that fruit [of the womb] not a substantial son? Who is that *male who opens the womb*? Is that male not, properly speaking, a son? Who is that little child, mentioned in Matthew 2, whom Joseph accepted as his own, led away [into Egypt], and brought home again? Is that child not the *son called out of Egypt*? You will not find any other father of that little child, that fleshly son, but God, no begetter but God. Otherwise you will have to claim that [the son] is an apparition, and not flesh. For if he is flesh, that flesh was begotten by someone. Therefore he is the son of some father. Furthermore, God is called the father of this flesh, the father of this bread (John 6), and *the vinedresser* and *father* of this [*true*] *vine* (John 15).

Therefore if this corporeal being is really the Son, and there is another real, incorporeal, invisible **[E12]** son, then there must be two actual sons, however you join them together as one; because two male children were begotten and born. For if we concede that there are two real begettings of two beings, then we cannot deny that two male children were begotten and born. Who, unless bewitched, would ever make a distinction between male children who were begotten [by a father] and sons [of that father]?

The holy scriptures speak about Jesus, the only Son of God, and they do not call the Son anything other than a man who was actually born. Every Christian should

> The 1553 Printed Edition

too being begotten and being born are human characteristics. Certainly [the incarnation] came about through the power of the Spirit. Nevertheless, the body itself was truly begotten and truly born, and it is this very body that shares in the substance of God.[13]   *Err, 7r*

Who is that [man] who *was considered to be the son of Joseph*?[a] Who is the *fruit of the womb*?[b] Is that fruit [of the womb] not a substantial son? Who is that *male who opens the womb*?[c] Is that male not, properly speaking, a son? Who is that little child, mentioned in Matthew 2, whom Joseph accepted as his own, led away [into Egypt], and brought home again?[d] Is that [child] not the *son called out of Egypt*?[e] You will not find any other father of that child, that fleshly son, but God, no begetter but God. Otherwise you will have to claim that [the son] is an apparition, and not flesh. For if he is flesh, that flesh was begotten by someone. Therefore he is the son of some father. Furthermore, God is called the father of this flesh, the father of this bread (John 6),[14] **[12]** and *the vinedresser* and *father* of this [*true*] *vine* (John 15).[f]   *Err, 7r-v*

Therefore if this corporeal being is really the Son of God, and there is another real, incorporeal, invisible son, then there must be two actual sons, however you join them together as one; because two male children were begotten and born. For if we concede that there are two real begettings of two beings, then we clearly cannot deny that two male children were begotten and born. Who, unless bewitched, would ever make a distinction between male children who were begotten [by a father] and sons [of that father]?   *Err, 7v*

The holy scriptures speak about Jesus, the only Son of God, and they do not call the Son anything other than a man who was actually born. Every Christian should   *Err, 7v*

---

[a] Luke 3:23.   [b] Luke 1:42.   [c] Luke 2:23.   [d] Matt 2:13-15.
[e] Matt 2:15, quoting Hos 11:1.   [f] John 15:1.

| The Edinburgh Manuscript |

acknowledge that Jesus of Nazareth, in this mode of being, is the Christ, the Son of God. Christ openly proclaimed that he was the Messiah, the Son of God, even to women and simple common folk. Upon hearing his straightforward proclamation, what kind of Messiah, I ask you, would a humble woman have been thinking of? Besides, such people were completely unaware of the metaphysical fictions contained in the formulas of our trinitarians. The other, metaphorical and invisible Son was conjured up later, based on a false interpretation of "the Word" in John, as I shall clearly explain.

At that time, certainly, faith in the Son of God was different than it is now, as one can now gather from the following familiar passage. God says to John [the Baptist]: "*He upon whom you see the Spirit descend and remain*, this is my son." "*And I*," [John the Baptist] says, "*have seen and have borne witness that this is the Son of God*" (John 1).

First, note that, prior to this, John did not know who the Son of God was. Now consider the way that [Jesus's sonship] was made known, and the other things that happened that day. According to the sophists' way of thinking [that the Son was an invisible, metaphysical being], John [the Baptist] must have been deceived, and he must have been deceiving others as well, when he said that the man whom he saw was the Son of God. [Before he was given the sign] he said, "*I myself did not know him.*" But when an outward sign was given, [he said,] "It has now been clearly demonstrated to me that this is the Son of God, [**E13**] in order that I might make it known to all the Jews that he is the Son of God, by proclaiming, *Behold the Lamb*, behold the Son."

Whom do you offer me as the *lamb* [*for the sacrifice*]? This man whom you see is the Lamb of God, the Son of

Book 1

The 1553 Printed Edition

---

acknowledge that Jesus of Nazareth, in this mode of being, is the Christ, the Son of God. Christ openly proclaimed that he was the Messiah and the Son of God, even to women and simple common folk. Upon hearing his straightforward proclamation, what kind of Messiah, I ask you, would a humble woman have been thinking of? Besides, such people were completely unaware of the metaphysical fictions contained in the formulas of our trinitarians. The other, metaphysical and invisible Son was conjured up later, based on a false interpretation of "the Word" in John, as I shall now clearly explain.

Err, 8r

At that time, faith in the Son was different than it is now, as one can gather from the following familiar passage. God says to John [the Baptist]: "*He upon whom you see the Spirit descend and remain*, this is my son."ᵃ "*And I*," [John the Baptist] says, "*have seen and have borne witness that this is the Son of God*" (John 1).ᵇ

Err, 8r

First, note that, prior to this, John did not know who the Son of God was. Now consider the way that [Jesus's sonship] was made known, and the other things that happened that day. According to the sophists' way of thinking [that the Son was an invisible, metaphysical being], John [the Baptist] must have been deceived, and he must have been deceiving others as well, when he said that the man whom he saw was the Son of God. [Before he was given the sign] he said, "*I myself did not know him*."ᶜ But when an outward sign was given, [he said,] "It has now been clearly demonstrated to me that this is the Son of God, in order that I might make it known to all the Jewsᵈ that he is the Son of God, by proclaiming, *Behold the Lamb*,ᵉ behold the Son."

Err, 8r

Whom will you offer me as the *lamb [for the sacrifice]*?ᶠ This man whom you see is the Lamb of God, the Son of

---

ᵃ John 1:33. ᵇ John 1:34. ᶜ John 1:31, 33. ᵈ See John 1:31.
ᵉ John 1:36. ᶠ Gen 22:7.

The Edinburgh Manuscript

God, visible to our eyes, touchable by our hands, and perceptible by all the other senses. Otherwise the voice from heaven would have been lying when it said, "*He on whom you see* [*the Spirit descend and remain*], *he is* the one." [God] must have been lying when, as [the Holy Spirit] descended upon [Jesus] in the presence of the people who were gathered there, [the voice from heaven] said, "*This is my beloved son*" or "*You are my son.*" If by the pronoun "this" [God] was indicating some other, hidden, being, then [John's] testimony would not have been clear and he would have been misleading the people, who had never heard anything about the invisible son.

Likewise, in John 9, when [the man who had been blind] asked who the Son of God was, Jesus replied, "*You have seen him, and it is he who is speaking to you.*" This very man whom you are looking at is the Son of God. Also the centurion, when he saw with his own eyes [Christ on the cross], said, "*Truly this man was the Son of God!*" The pronouns [in these statements] point to a being perceptible by the senses. The centurion was not a sophist, and he was not speaking in terms of *communicatio idiomatum* [the sharing of attributes], or using the word "man" connotatively. Instead, he said about an actual man, "*This was a righteous man,*"[a] and "*This man was the Son of God.*"

Hear the words of Paul, who, as soon as he had recovered his sight, *entered the synagogue and preached about Jesus, that he was the Son of God* (Acts 9). About these "attributes" of the sophists, [he said] not a word. The High Priest did not have in mind a second incorporeal being when he asked, "*Are you the son of the blessed God?*" Realizing what [the priest] had in mind, Jesus replied, "*I am*" (Mark 14) or "*You*

---

[a] Luke 23:47.

> **The 1553 Printed Edition**

God, visible to our eyes, touchable by our hands,[a] and perceptible by all the other senses. Otherwise the voice from heaven would have been lying when it said, "*He on whom you see* [*the Spirit descend and remain*], *he is* the one."[b] [God] must have been lying when, as [the Holy Spirit] descended upon [Jesus] in the presence of the people who were gathered there, [the voice from heaven] said, "*This is my son*" or "*You are my son.*"[c] If by the pronoun "this" [God] was indicating some other, **[13]** hidden, being, then [John's] testimony would not have been clear and he would have been misleading the people.

Err, 8r-v

Likewise, in John 9, when [the man who had been blind] asked who the Son of God was, Jesus replied, "*You have seen him, and it is he who is speaking to you.*"[d] This very man whom you are looking at is the Son of God. Also the centurion, when he saw with his own eyes [Christ on the cross], said, "*Truly this man was the Son of God!*"[e] Bear in mind that the pronouns [in these statements] point to a being perceptible by the senses. Then consider that the centurion was not a sophist, and that he was not speaking in terms of *communicatio idiomatum* [the sharing of attributes], or using the word "man" connotatively. Instead, pointing to an actual man, he said, "*This man was the Son of God.*"

Err, 8v

Hear the words of Paul, who, as soon as he had recovered his sight, *entered the synagogue and preached about Jesus, that he was the Son of God* (Acts 9).[f] About these "attributes" of the sophists, [he said] not a word. The High Priest did not have in mind a second incorporeal being when he asked, "*Are you the son of the blessed God?*" Realizing what [the priest] had in mind, Jesus replied, "*I am*" (Mark 14)[g] or "*You

Err, 8v

---

[a] 1 John 1:1.   [b] John 1:33.   [c] Matt 3:16-17; Mark 1:10-11; Luke 3:22.
[d] John 9:37.   [e] Mark 15:39; Matt. 27:54.   [f] Acts 9:20.   [g] Mark 14:61-62.

The Edinburgh Manuscript

say that I am the Son of God" (Luke 22). Therefore they all had a simple, unsophisticated faith in him, [like Martha], **[E14]** who said "*I believe that you are the Son of God.*"

The sophists might now object that it does not appear to matter much whether the man Jesus is called the Son of God, since even we are called children of God. My answer to this is that being the Son of God is a matter of supreme importance, and that more consequences arise from this than the world has ever comprehended, as I shall now show.

[Jesus] is a true and natural-born son [of God], whereas we are children [of God] by adoption. Our being called children of God is proof that he is the true Son. How could he transform human beings into children [of God], if he, a human being himself, was not the true Son? We are called children [of God] because of the gift and grace given to us through him. Therefore he himself, as the one responsible for our own adoption, is called "son" in another, and superior, way. He himself is God's natural-born son, begotten out of the true substance of God, as you will see later. No one else is a child [of God] by direct descent, but others become God's children. *By faith in Jesus Christ we are made children of God* (Galatians 3, John 1). Therefore we are called *children by adoption* (Romans 8, Ephesians 1). [Jesus] is called not merely a son, but *the true Son [of God]*. He is not a son in the ordinary sense of the word, but [*God's*] *very own Son* (Wisdom of Solomon 2, Romans 8).

Just as properly as earthly fathers are called the fathers of their own children, God is said to be the father of Jesus Christ. Otherwise God could not be called the specially efficient and productive cause of this particular effect. If he should choose to have an offspring of his very own, and acts

The 1553 Printed Edition

say that I am the Son of God" (Luke 22).ᵃ Therefore they all had a simple, unsophisticated faith in him, [like Martha], who said "*I believe that you are the Son of God.*"ᵇ

But you might say that it does not appear to matter much whether the man Jesus is called the Son of God, since even we are called children of God. My answer to this is that being the Son of God is a matter of supreme importance, and that more consequences arise from this than the world has ever comprehended, as I shall now show.

[Christ] is a true and natural-born son [of God], whereas we are children [of God] by adoption. Our being called children of God is proof that he is the true Son. How could he transform human beings into children [of God], if he, a human being himself, was not the true Son? We are called children [of God] because of his gift and grace. Therefore he himself, as the one responsible for our own adoption, is called "son" in another, and superior, way. He himself is God's natural-born son, begotten out of the true substance of God. No one else is a child [of God] by direct descent. Others become God's children; they are not born the children of God. *By faith in Jesus Christ we are made children of God* (Galatians 3, John 1).ᶜ Therefore we are called *children by adoption* (Romans 8, Ephesians 1).ᵈ [Jesus] is called not merely a son, but *the true Son [of God]*. He is not a son in the ordinary sense of the word, but [*God's*] *very own Son* (Wisdom of Solomon 2, Romans 8).ᵉ

Just as properly as earthly fathers are called the fathers of their own children, God is said to be the father of Jesus Christ. Otherwise God could not be called the specially efficient and productive cause of this particular effect.[15] If he should choose to have his very own offspring, and acts

Err, 8v

Err, 9r

Err, 9r-v

Err, 9v

ᵃ Luke 22:70. ᵇ John 11:27. ᶜ Gal 3:26; John 1:12. ᵈ Rom 8:15, 23; Eph 1:5. See also Gal 4:5. ᵉ Wisd of Sol 2:18; Rom 8:32.

The Edinburgh Manuscript

on his own to beget him, more than an earthly father could do — and also bestows his own substance upon him — then why does he not deserve [**E15**] to be called a father, just as properly [as any other father]? *"Can it be that I, who give procreation to others, shall myself be barren?" says the Lord* (Isaiah 66). By no means! Rather he is called the Father because *all fatherhood in heaven and on earth is named after him* (Ephesians 3).

[The name Father is] all the more fitting, because [God] not only begot [Christ], but also endowed him with the substance, light, and fullness of divinity, so that in this the Son would be like the Father. And there is yet another reason why [God] is even more properly called a father than mortal men are: he participates in the begetting of others' [sons], while other [fathers] contribute nothing to the begetting of his Son. Therefore, if [God] is more properly called the Father, then Christ, beyond all others, is most appropriately called the Son. But I shall have more sublime things to say about this sonship later, if it is permissible to use the term "sonship" [in this way].

And so now the argument can be turned [against the sophists]. For the Son of God shares his sonship with us; while the sonship of the second being, if it is not a human sonship, has nothing in common with ours. Christ calls us his brothers because he is a human being. He is a man who is *the first-born among brethren*, just as he is *the first-born of the dead*. Therefore this first-born human was a man who was born a son.

The sophists think themselves so magnificent that they do not even deign to gaze upon this [human] Son. They consider it a degrading and contemptible thing for the Son of God to be called a human being. The Son, they say, must be of the same "ultimate species" as the Father. But how do

> **The 1553 Printed Edition**

on his own to beget him, more than an earthly father could do — and also bestows his own **[14]** substance upon him — then why does he not deserve to be called a father, just as properly [as any other father]? *"Can it be that I, who give procreation to others, shall myself be barren?" says the Lord* (Isaiah 66).ᵃ By no means! Rather he is called the Father because *all fatherhood*¹⁶ *in heaven and on earth is named after him* (Ephesians 3).ᵇ

[The name Father is] all the more fitting, because [God] not only begot [Christ], but also endowed him with the substance, light, and fullness of divinity, so that in this the Son would be like the Father. And there is yet another reason why [God] is even more properly called a father than mortal men are: he participates in the begetting of others' [sons], while other [fathers] contribute nothing to the begetting of his Son. Therefore, if [God] is more properly called the Father, then Christ, beyond all others, is most appropriately called the Son. But I shall have other, more sublime things to say about this sonship later, if it is permissible to use the term "sonship" [in this way].

And so now the argument can be turned [against the sophists]. For the Son of God shares his sonship with us; while the sonship of the second being, if it is not a human sonship, has nothing in common with ours. Christ calls us his brothers because he is a human being. He is a man who is *the first-born among brethren*,ᶜ just as he is *the first-born of the dead*.ᵈ Therefore this first-born human was a man who was born a son.

The sophists think themselves so magnificent that they do not even deign to gaze upon this [human] Son. They consider it a degrading and contemptible thing for the Son of God to be called a human being. The Son, they say, must be of the same "ultimate species"¹⁷ as the Father. But how do

Err, 9v

Err, 9v

Err, 37v

ᵃ Isa 66:9.   ᵇ Eph 3:15.   ᶜ Rom 8:29.   ᵈ Rev 1:5; see also Col 1:18.

The Edinburgh Manuscript

they reach this conclusion? It cannot be [that the Son is of the same ultimate species as the Father], since [Christ's] parents [God and Mary] belong to completely different species.

Besides, everything in scripture condemns [the idea that the Son of God is not a human being] and Christ himself **[E16]** also rejects it. In John chapter 10 he shows that he is the Son of God by comparing himself to other human beings. He says, "Even though scripture calls other men *'gods, and the sons of God,' you claim that* I am *blaspheming because I said, 'I am the Son of God'* when *the Father has sanctified* me *above* all my other *fellows* and *companions*."

Behold, he who was sanctified is the Son of God. He is the one [who *will be called*] *holy, the Son of God*. He is the one whom the apostles call "*your holy son, Jesus*." Who is this holy one, if not the *male that opens the womb*, the true and corporeal Son of God?

{*Third Proposition*} [*This Man is God*]

I have declared this to be true: Christ is God. [In scripture] he is said to be truly God — God in substance — *for in him deity* [*dwells*] *bodily*. But, as this [proposition] will be made very clear in what follows, for now it is sufficient to say that if he is called God, [it is because] he has the form of God, the appearance of God, and the might and power of God. He is called God because of his power, just as he is called a human being because of his flesh. On account of that divine power given him by the Father, he himself is called "mighty God" in Isaiah 9: *Unto us a child is born; he will be called Mighty God*.

> ### The 1553 Printed Edition

they reach this conclusion? It is utterly impossible [for the Son to be of the same ultimate species as the Father], since [Christ's] parents [God and Mary] belong to completely different species.

Furthermore, everything in scripture condemns [the idea that the Son of God is not a human being] and Christ himself also rejects it. In John chapter 10 he shows that he is the Son of God by comparing himself to other human beings. He says, "Even though scripture calls other men *'gods, and the sons of God,' you claim that* I am *blaspheming because I said, 'I am the Son of God'*[a] when *the Father has sanctified* me *above* all my other *fellows* and *companions*."[b]

Behold, he who was sanctified is the Son of God. He is the one who *will be called holy, the Son of God*.[c] He is the one whom the apostles call "*your holy son, Jesus*."[d] Who is this holy one, if not the *male that opens the womb*,[e] the true and corporeal Son of God?

{*Third Proposition*} [*This Man is God*]

I have declared this to be true: Christ is God. [In scripture] he is said to be truly God — God in substance — *for in him deity* [*dwells*] *bodily*.[f] But, as this [proposition] will be made perfectly clear in what follows, for now it will suffice to say that if **[15]** he is called God, it is because he has the form of God, the appearance of God, and the might and power of God. He is called God because of his power, just as he is called a human being because of his flesh.[g] On account of that divine power given him by the Father, he himself is called "mighty God" in Isaiah 9: *Unto us a child is born; he will be called Mighty God*.[h]

Err, 37v

Err, 37v-38r

Err, 9v-10r

---

[a] John 10:35-36, referring to Ps 82:6. [b] Heb 1:9, referring to Ps 45:7. [c] Luke 1:35. [d] Acts 4:27. [e] Luke 2:23. [f] Col 2:9. [g] Tertullian, *Adversus Praxean* 21 (PL 2 181B): "He is the Son of Man through his flesh, just as he is also the Son of God through his spirit." [h] Isa 9:6.

The Edinburgh Manuscript

Behold, the name and the might of God are bestowed upon the newborn child, to whom *is given all power in heaven and on earth*. In Isaiah 45 he is called God of Israel. In John 20, Thomas addresses [Christ] as, *"My Lord, my God!"* In Romans 9, Christ is said to be *in everything* and *over all things, God who is to be praised, God* [**E17**] *who is blessed* and is to be blessed *forever*. His divinity is demonstrated in many other passages. For he was exalted, so that he might receive divinity and *a name which is above every name*.

The sophists not only deny that he is God, but they even deny that he was anointed. Indeed, they strip him of those things that are his by nature, denying that he was the son of Mary and finally denying that he was a man — [claiming that he was] only "a human nature." They deny that the man is a human being, and admit that God could be an ass.

Are not these [sophists] Antichrists and disparagers of Christ? Could there ever be a greater affront than if, when I am speaking to you, you were to say that I do not exist, or if you were to deny me the things that plainly belong to me?

These disparagers want all the names [given to Jesus Christ in scripture] to be applied to the second being. In the service of this fabrication, the currently prevailing school has devised a special kind of sophism, *communicatio idiomatum* [sharing of attributes]. They impose a new definition on the term "human," so that it can be taken "connotatively," as an equivalent to the phrase, "supporting a human nature." And now, by means of *communicatio idiomatum*, they will allow the proposition that the Son of God is a human being. By this they mean that the second person

> ### The 1553 Printed Edition

Behold, the name and the might of God are bestowed upon the newborn child, to whom *is given all power in heaven and on earth*.[a] In Isaiah 45[b] we read, "*I* am *the Lord who calls you by your name, the God of Israel.*"[18] In John 20, Thomas addresses [Christ] as, "*My Lord, my God!*"[c] In Romans 9, Christ is said to be *in everything over all things, God who is to be praised, God who is blessed*[d] and is to be blessed.[19] His divinity is demonstrated in many other passages. For he was exalted, so that he might receive divinity and *a name which is above every name*.[e]

Err, 10r

His adversaries so detest [the human Jesus] that they not only deny that he is God, but even that he was anointed. Indeed, they strip him of those things that are his by nature, denying that he was the son of Mary and denying that he was a man — [claiming that he was] only "a human nature." They deny that the man is a human being, and admit that God could be an ass.[20]

Err, 10r

Are not these [sophists] really Antichrists and disparagers of Christ? Could there be a greater affront than if, when I am speaking to you, you were to say that I do not exist, or if you were to deny me the things that plainly belong to me?

Err, 57v

These disparagers want all the names [given to Jesus Christ in scripture] to be applied to the second being. In the service of this fabrication, the currently prevailing school has devised a special kind of sophism, *communicatio idiomatum* [sharing of attributes]. They impose a new definition on the term "human," so that it can be taken "connotatively," as an equivalent to the phrase, "supporting a human nature."[21] And now, by means of *communicatio idiomatum*, they will allow the proposition that the Son of God is a human being. By this they mean that the second person

Err, 10v

---

[a] Matt 28:18. [b] Isa 45:3 [c] John 20:28. [d] Rom 9:5. [e] Phil 2:9.

> ## The Edinburgh Manuscript

sustains a human nature, and is [only] a connotative human being. In this way they are also admitting that it is possible for God to be an ass or for the [Holy] Spirit to be a mule, sustaining a mulish nature.

Think about it, reader: if Christ, his disciple Paul, or the other disciples were [once again] preaching, could they endure these human fabrications and this seductive verbal trickery? Are not [these sophists] making Christ into a sophist teacher by claiming that the prophets and the apostles used the word "Christ" to signify the second person of the Godhead, connoting "that which can sustain a human nature"?

But what if, everywhere [in the Bible], instead of the word "Christ," **[E18]** the word "anointed" [which means the same thing] had been used? Would they then claim that it was the [second] being who was specially *anointed* and was the recipient of *the holy spirit and power*? Or could [this second being] say, "*all things have been delivered to me by my father*"? Or was the Father speaking about him sophistically when he said, "*Behold my child, whom I have chosen, my beloved, I will put my spirit upon him*"? You will find that [these words] in Matthew 12 refer to the man Jesus. Just as whatever is written in the Bible [about the Son] refers to him, everything looks to him and is brought to fulfilment by him.

But what exactly is this *communicatio praedicatorum* [sharing of properties]? For the property, "sustaining a human nature," was not, prior [to this theological speculation], applicable to a human being. How, then, does a human being share his properties with God, if they do not actually belong to him?

> The 1553 Printed Edition

sustains a human nature, and is [only] a connotative human being. In this way they are also admitting that it is possible for God to be an ass or for the [Holy] Spirit to be a mule, sustaining a mulish nature.

Think about it, reader: if Christ, his disciple Paul, or the other disciples were [once again] preaching, could they endure these human fabrications and this seductive verbal trickery? Are not [these sophists] making Christ into a sophist teacher by claiming that the prophets and the apostles used the word "Christ" to signify the second person of the Godhead, connoting "that which can support [16] a human nature"? *Err*, 10v–11r

What if, everywhere [in the Bible], instead of the word "Christ," the word "anointed" [which means the same thing] had been used? Would they then claim that it was the [second] being who was specially *anointed* and was the recipient of *the holy spirit and power*?[a] Or could [this second being] say that *all things had been delivered* to him *by his father*?[b] Or was the Father speaking about him sophistically when he said, "*Behold my child, whom I have chosen, my beloved, I will put my spirit upon him*"?[c] You will find that [these words] in Matthew 12 refer to the man Jesus. Whatever is written in the Bible about the Son refers to him; everything looks to him and is brought to fulfilment by him. *Err*, 11r

But what exactly is this *communicatio praedicatorum* [sharing of properties]?[22] For the property, "supporting a human nature," was not, prior [to this theological speculation], applicable to a human being. How, then, does a human being share his properties with God, if they do not actually belong to him? *Err*, 11r

---

[a] Acts 10:38. [b] Matt 11:27; Luke 10:22. [c] Matt 12:18, quoting Isa 42:1.

The Edinburgh Manuscript

I shall now unreservedly acknowledge and clearly show that there is a twofold nature in Christ, both divine and human. In Christ, God and man are truly united in a single substance: *one body* and *one new man* (Ephesians 2). But because the divine nature [of Christ] depends on the mysteries of the Word, let me put it more plainly:[23] God is able to share the *fullness of deity* with a human being, and to give him his divinity, majesty, power, and glory. *Worthy is the Lamb who was slain, to receive divinity, power, wisdom, honour, and glory* (Revelation 5).

If in Exodus 7 Moses was *made a god to Pharaoh*, and in Isaiah 45 Cyrus [is addressed as] the God of Israel, then, in a far more powerful and superior way, Christ became the Lord and God of Thomas and of us all. In Psalm 44 Solomon is also literally called God. But those men were not gods by nature, but only by a gift of limited duration. Christ, on the other hand, is God by natural birth, since he was naturally begotten of the substance of God. All the deity of the Father, the adoration owed to God, and the visible form of God, are in Christ, who is truly God. For just as the Father is the true God, so, too, by bestowing his true deity solely on his only son, [God] ensures that [the man Jesus] is himself the true God.

[*The First Objection of the Pharisees*]

Having explained the three basic truths about Christ, it remains for me to refute the three objections of the Pharisees, which Christ himself will undertake for us.

First objection: "If Christ is God, there will then be more than one god." To this challenge by the Pharisees, who accused Christ of *making* himself *out to be God*, he replied, "[*Is it not written in your law*] *that, 'I have said, you are gods'?*" (John 10).

> The 1553 Printed Edition

I shall now very clearly show that there was, and continues to be, a twofold nature in Christ, both divine and human. In Christ, God and man are truly united in a single substance: *one body* and *one new man* (Ephesians 2).[a] But because the divine nature of Christ depends on the mysteries of the Word, let me put it in a simpler way: God is able to share the *fullness of deity*[b] with a human being, and to give him his divinity, majesty, power, and glory. *Worthy is the Lamb who was slain, to receive divinity,*[24] *power, wisdom, honour, and glory* (Revelation 5).[c]

Err, 11v

If in Exodus 7 Moses was *made a god to Pharaoh*,[25] and in Isaiah 45 Cyrus [is addressed as] the God of Israel,[d] then, in a far more powerful and superior way, Christ became the Lord and God of Thomas and of us all.[e] In Psalm 44[f] Solomon is literally called God.[26] But those men were not gods by nature, but only by a gift of limited duration. Christ, on the other hand, is God by natural birth, since he was naturally begotten of the substance of God. All the deity of the Father, the adoration owed to God, and the visible form of God, are in Christ, who is truly God. For just as the Father is the true God, so, too, by bestowing his true deity solely on his only son, [God] ensures that [the man Jesus] is himself the true God.

Err, 11v

{*The First Objection of the Pharisees*}

Having explained the three basic truths about Christ, it remains for me to refute the three objections of the Pharisees, which Christ himself will undertake for us.

First objection: "If Christ is God, there will then be more than one god." To this challenge by the Pharisees, who accused Christ of *making* himself *out to be God*, he replied, "[*Is it not written in your law*] *that, 'I have said, you are gods'?*" (John 10).[g]

Err, 12v

---

[a] Eph 2:15, 16. [b] Col 2:9. [c] Rev 5:12. [d] Ex 7:1 (Moses); Isa 45:3 (Cyrus). See A.R1.18. [e] John 20:28. [f] Ps 45:7 [g] John 10:34.

[17] Here Christ teaches that he is God, sanctified by God the Father. He attempts to persuade some Jews that, in the same way that others are called gods, he himself can also be called God. It was in this way that people of weaker understanding were led gradually to recognize the divine nature of Christ. He goes on to say: if scripture *calls them gods to whom the word of God was spoken*,[a] how much more, then, should the Son, *whom the Father sanctifies*[b] beyond all others, be called not just the Son of God, but God as well. Thus, although these [men] are "gods," there is only one divinity, which is communicated from the Father to the Son at his begetting. There is only one God, who is the source of all deity.

Err, 12v

The Jews should not have been offended by [what Christ said] since Moses, Solomon, and Cyrus were called gods.[c] Having seen him perform such mighty works of God and such great miracles, the Jews should not only have attributed to Christ the divinity of *Elohim*,[d] but they also should have realized that [the word "God"] suited him because of his superior nature. This is the explanation Christ gave for the preeminence of his own divinity in John 5 and 10.[e] Because of this, distinctive epithets were added to [honour] his deity, so that he is called *God of the whole earth, great God, mighty*, and *blessed over all*.[27]

I shall later speak more precisely and at greater length about the substantial nature of Christ's deity. Let it suffice for the moment to say that I do not divide God into pieces or tear him apart, as the sophists do. It is very clear that such a plurality cannot be introduced into the deity, as the trinitarians do with their so-called "real relations"[28] and their three distinct incorporeal beings. For, as I shall soon demonstrate, it is here [in these trinitarian sophisms] that there is a real and absolute plurality of gods.

---

[a] John 10:35, referring to Ps 82:6. [b] John 10:36. [c] See A.R1.18 (Cyrus), A.R1.25 (Moses), and A.R1.26 (Solomon). [d] The meaning of *Elohim* is discussed at length in *Errors*, 13v-15v. [e] John 5:36-37, 10:25.

{The Second Objection of the Pharisees}

The second objection [of the Pharisees] was: how can Christ be said *to have come down from heaven*[a] and to have come *into the world, sent by the Father?*[b] Those who raise this objection against us, like the Pharisees, are clearly reasoning incorrectly.

In John 6, the Pharisees murmured, *"Is this not the son of Joseph, whose father and mother we know? How then does he say, 'I have come down from heaven'?"*[c] On this point Christ teaches that, in order to understand his descent [from heaven], we must be *made alive by the spirit.*[d] For the understanding conveyed by *the flesh profits nothing.*[e] Since [according to John 6] the Word of God, *having come down from heaven,* is now on earth, the flesh **[18]** of Christ, you must then concede that the very flesh of Christ came down from heaven.[29] The flesh of Christ is from heaven, it is *the bread from heaven,*[f] it is of the substance of God, and it came forth from God. However, since these matters are better understood in the context of the mystery of the Word, my discussion of them must be postponed to subsequent books [in this work].[g]

In the meantime, you should be able to understand *"from heaven,"* that is, *"from on high,"* as [Christ] himself teaches in John, chapter 8 [*"You are from below, I am from on high"*].[h] You may understand Christ's words in their spiritual sense, which is that Christ, in the spirit of God, came before all time, and that his spirit was in heaven from the very beginning. His words were heavenly; for this reason alone, you must grant that he himself was from heaven. For *the baptism* [of Jesus] *by John was from heaven*[i] and the *second man was from heaven, and heavenly.*[j] Anything that

Err, 16r

Err, 16v

---

[a] John 6:33, 38, 58.   [b] John 10:36.   [c] John 6:42.   [d] 1 Pet 3:18.
[e] John 6:63.   [f] John 6:31, 32, 41.   [g] In books 2 and 3.   [h] John 8:23.
[i] Matt 21:25; Mark 11:30; Luke 20:4.   [j] 1 Cor 15:47. The "second man" is Christ, the second Adam.

is superior to flesh and blood is of heaven and is in heaven. Not only was Christ from heaven, but he even brought heaven itself to us, as you shall [presently] see.

Err, 16v-17r

There is no difficulty in responding to the objection to [Christ's claim] that he was sent by the Father, since even John is said to have been sent by God: *There was a man sent by God, whose name was John* (John 1).[a] The prophets and the apostles are all said to have been sent by God. Christ himself proclaims this in John 17: "*As you*, Father, *sent me*, your son, *into the world, so do I send* the apostles *into the world.*"[b] And in John 20: "*As the Father sent me, so I send you.*"[c]

Err, 17r

I am forced to resort to these parallels, which Christ himself used, so that the truth may be made more plain. It is true that Christ's mission, and his coming forth from the Father, are remarkable, as will become evident [in my account of] the mystery of the Word. Similarly, it should not seem wondrous when we say that *Christ came into the world*,[d] since the same thing applies to others, [that is, to] *everyone*[30] *who comes into this world* (John 1).[e]

In order to counter two heresies that were flourishing in his day, John taught that *Jesus Christ came in the flesh*.[f] The first [heresy] was that of the disciples of Simon Magus,[g] who claimed that Christ was an apparition, without actual flesh.[31] In opposition to them, John uses the word, "flesh." The second heresy, which followed soon after the first, was that of Ebion and Cerinthus, who claimed that Jesus was a completely human being, devoid of the substance of deity, and that before [he was born to] Mary he had no existence.[32] Against the latter, [John] teaches that Jesus came [*into the world*], and that before this time he was *the Word with God*.[h] In **[19]** what follows you will see clearly the truth of this

---

[a] John 1:6. [b] John 17:18. [c] John 20:21. [d] John 11:27. [e] John 1:9.
[f] 1 John 4:2. [g] For the story of Simon Magus, see Acts 8:9-24 and Irenaeus, *Adversus haereses* 1.23.1-4 (PG 7a 670B-673A). [h] John 1:1.

matter. For you will see clearly that the nonsense of our trinitarians was unknown to [the early Christians]. In his Epistle to the Philippians, Polycarp cites what John says against the heresies just mentioned.[a] Ignatius[33] does the same in several places,[b] and so does Irenaeus.[c] None of them ever taught, or even imagined, the inventions of our trinitarians. They simply proclaimed that Jesus was the true Messiah, the Son of God, and that, in his own person and substance, he had been *the Word with God*. But this is unknown to all of the trinitarian sophists. Now it must be truly understood.

{*The Third Objection of the Pharisees*}

The third objection that can be raised is: how is it that Christ, in Philippians 2,[34] *did not consider it theft*[35] *to be equal to God*?[d] Christ himself answers this. For, in John 5, the Pharisees accuse him of *making himself out to be equal to God*.[e] In his reply Christ does not deny this equality, but says that he has all power and does everything the Father does.[f] Thus, *like the Father, the Son raises the dead*; gives sight to *the blind; makes lepers clean*; and heals *the deaf*, the paralyzed, those possessed by demons, and others.[g] The Father *has given all judgement* and all power *to the Son, so that all might honour the Son even as they honour the Father*.[h]

See how Christ bears witness that he is *equal to God*. See how the μορφή (*morphe*, form), that is, the appearance of the

Err, 17r-18r

Err, 18r

---

[a] Polycarp, *Ad Philippenses* (PG 5 1011B), citing 1 John 4:2.
[b] [Ignatius], *Ad Smyrnaeos* 2 (PG 5 842B); *Ad Trallios* 9 (PG 5 790A); *Ad Ephesios* 7 (PG 5 738C).   [c] Irenaeus, *Adversus haereses* 3.19 (PG 7 938C-941C), 3.22 (PG 7 955C-960A).   [d] Phil 2:6.   [e] John 5:18.
[f] John 5:19.   [g] John 5:21; Matt 11:5; Luke 7: 22. See Erasmus, *Annotationes*, "esse se aequalem deo" (Phil 2:6), quoting Ambrosiaster's commentary on Phil 2:7-8 (PL 17 432B): "[What] is the form of God, if not the visible example? Because God was visibly apparent, when he woke the dead, gave hearing to the deaf, and made lepers clean." In *Opera omnia*, VI-9: 290.   [h] John 5:22-23.

Err, 18r Deity,[36] shone in him as he performed his great miracles. Christ also possessed the divine appearance and form from all eternity, as I shall explain later.

Err, 18r Now let us contemplate the divine appearance that is present in him; and with that divine appearance, his divine power. Paul connects Christ's great power with his humility of spirit, which he holds out to us as a model for imitation.[a] He teaches that Christ's humility was of the highest possible degree. Such was his greatness, that the more he was endowed with superior majesty and power, the more he made himself obedient and abased himself.

Err, 18r-v Power often turns people into tyrants, but this was not the case with Christ. Although *appearing in the form of God*,[37] he did not consider using his great equality to the deity to commit theft. Christ [20] refused to use his power tyrannically for theft. He declined [to participate in] a theft [of power] when he *realized that* [the people] *were going to take him by force and make him a king* (John 6).[b] Instead he conducted himself in a humble manner, since he did not want his *kingdom* to be *of this world*.[c] Christ could have everywhere displayed the divine appearance or divine form that was seen on the Mount [of Transfiguration], and lived among men and women as a heavenly king. But for our salvation he preferred *the form of a servant*,[d] even to the point of bearing the cross. He *did not consider* committing *theft* [of power]. Although he had the power of God, he refused to violently defend himself against the Jews by taking command of *twelve legions of angels*.[e] He chose, instead, to suffer humbly.

Err, 18v Thus, in John 5, Christ is said to be equal to God because of the power given to him to be equal to God.[f] *Every-*

---

[a] See Erasmus, *Annotationes*, "esse se aequalem deo" (Phil 2:6); in *Opera omnia*, VI-9:290. [b] John 6:15. [c] John 18:36. [d] Phil 2:7. [e] Matt 26:53. [f] John 5:20, 26-27.

thing the Father has is his.[a] *All things* made by the Word of God *are made through him*, since he himself is the Word of God.[b] In Luke 22, Christ himself commented on his equality of power [with God], saying, "*the Son of man shall be seated at the right hand of the power of God.*"[c] And in Ephesians 1, Paul teaches us about Christ's equality [with God] and his exaltation to the right hand of the power of God, saying that he was established *above all rule, authority, power, and dominion, and above every name that is named, not only in this world but indeed even in the world to come.* Finally, *all things have been placed under his feet and* [God] *has given him to the church to be the head over all things, he who fulfills everything in all things.*[d]

Err, 18v

[Christ's] equality of power with God is noted in Daniel 7: *Behold, the Son of man came up to the Ancient of Days, and* all kingly *power was given to him.*[e] Jeremiah also, in chapter 30, marvels at this: Who is it who thus *approaches and draws near* to God,[f] so that he approaches equality with [God]? In Zechariah 13, God calls the man Jesus עמית (*amit*), that is, my associate and my equal.[g]

Err, 18v-19r

Here I will not bother to discuss the [sophists'] fabulous inventions about the metaphysics of those three invisible beings, the inherent tendency [of those beings] to engage in thievery, and their haggling over equality. As if [metaphysical] beings could stoop to such ignoble passions! I am all the more willing to pass over these fictions, because Paul never gave them the slightest thought. He says, **[21]** *Let that state of mind be present in you which was in Christ Jesus, who* being God in substance and *being in the form of God*,[h] did not think of being equal to God in terms of theft. For Christ never contemplated using his divine power to commit

---

[a] John 16:15. [b] John 1:3; see also Col 1:16. [c] Luke 22:69.
[d] Eph 1:21-23. [e] Dan 7:13-14. [f] Jer 30:21. [g] Zech 13:7. Here Servetus translates the Hebrew word *amit* as both "associate" and "equal." [h] Phil 2:5, 6.

theft, but bore himself with humility, only later being raised on high by his resurrection.^a

But such humility, Cyril instructs us, is not consistent with the divine nature. Christ's humility, he says, is not consonant with the [divine] nature of the Word, since humility, like being raised on high, applies only to a human being (*Thesaurus*, book 8, chapter 1).^b Thus, the divine nature, in and of itself, was neither humbled nor exalted; only Christ the man was. This is how Augustine expounds [the passage from Philippians]^c at the beginning of the third book of *Against Maximinus*,[38] contradicting what he often says elsewhere.[39] As we shall later show, [Augustine] often displayed his ignorance of the [true] nature of the person [of Christ].

Err, 19v-20r

The man Christ, *established*[40] *as the appearance of God, did not think of being equal to God as theft*. He did not contemplate using his power of equality with God for tyranny or theft. For it would truly have been theft if, by the use of violence, he had renounced the work for which his Father had intended him, or if he had usurped a royal tyranny over the world. This is the real meaning of the word ἁρπαγμός (*harpagmos*, theft). Christ was never interested in anything of this kind. He never took anything from anyone by violence.

Err, 20r

The Greek article τὸ and the adverb ἴσα, "equally,"[41] make this idea clear, because they describe [Christ] in the disposition of a man, and not metaphysical and incorporeal equal natures.[42] For as Paul says, Christ did not consider [using] the fact that he was equally God to commit theft. Here we find the truest meaning [of this passage]. Paul does

---

^a See Erasmus, *Annotationes*, "esse se aequalem deo" (Phil 2:6), quoting Ambrosiaster's commentary on Phil 2:7-8 (PL 17 409A): "He did not assert equality for himself; he did not arrogantly claim it for himself, and by his own example he demonstrated humility to us." In *Opera omnia*, VI-9:290.   ^b Cyril of Alexandria, *Thesaurus* 8.1 (PG 75 119A). "These words of humbling, appropriate for a servant, do not pertain to his essence, but are only suitable when applied to the incarnation."
^c Augustine, *Contra Maximinum* 2.2 (PL 42 759-760).

no violence to [the word] "equally," but infers [equality] from the appearance of Deity. For he says that Christ, who had the appearance of God, did not consider τὸ εἶναι ἴσα θεῷ — did not consider being equally God (which, by existing in the form of God, he was) — to be theft. *Err, 20r*

Indeed, as the apostle says, Christ assumed the *form* or appearance *of a servant*.[a] He says this in order to distinguish [this form] from the form or appearance of God, about which he had just spoken. And in both places [the word] μορφή (*morphe*, form) is used. In this way he is asserting the superiority of humility. For **[22]** although [Christ] was powerful in either appearance, he used the humbler of the two. He did not use the appearance and the strength of God, but [appeared] as an ordinary human being. This very man Jesus, who earlier had the appearance of God, afterwards, as you will observe, took the appearance of a servant.[b] It is said that he was *found in the guise of a human being*.[c] As the psalmist says, "*You shall die like human beings*, even though *you are gods*" (Psalm 81).[d] And Samson, who because of his surpassing strength seemed not human but superhuman, said, "*I shall* then *be weak, like other men*."[e] *Err, 20r-v*

You have now seen all of the scriptural passages that speak about [Christ's] equality with God. These passages are completely irrelevant to the [theological] battles of our time. The conflict with the Arians over the the equality or inequality of natures of these invisible persons, which shook the entire world in [Pope] Sylvester's day,[f] was devised by Satan in order to turn people's minds away from knowledge of the true Christ, and to fashion for us a tripartite God. O Jesus, Son of God, have mercy on us now, so that we may come to recognize you as God's Son! *Err, 20v*

---

[a] Phil 2:7.   [b] See Erasmus, *Annotationes*, "esse se aequalem deo" (Phil 2:6): "For it does not seem to me, as it does to some, that he received the form of a servant when the man [Jesus] was born." In *Opera omnia*, VI-9:290.   [c] Phil 2:8.   [d] Ps 82:6-7.   [e] Judg 16:7, 17.   [f] Sylvester was Pope from 314 to 335.

{*Two Passages from Scripture*}

Err, 22v Having examined the arguments used by the Pharisees against Christ, before we come to the arguments of the sophists, I will first attempt to shed some light on two scriptural passages, from which the concept of the Trinity is derived. The first is in 1 John 5:[a] *There are three that bear witness in heaven, the Father, the Word, and the Spirit: and these three are one.*[43] The second passage is from Matthew, chapter 28: *Baptize in the name of the Father and of the Son and of the Holy Spirit.*[b]

We now must turn our attention to a simple explanation of these passages: that the very same divinity that is in the Father was communicated directly and bodily to the Son, Jesus Christ. Then, through the agency of the angelic spirit,[44] it was in turn spiritually communicated by the Mediator to the apostles on the day of Pentecost.[c] But divinity was both bodily and spiritually implanted in Christ alone from the time of his birth. He then gives this holy and substantial breath to others.[d] I shall later explain separately each mode of communication, the corporeal and the spiritual, demonstrating that the very substance of the Holy Spirit is the same divinity that is in [23] the Father and the Son.[45]

Now, the aim of the first passage, from [the Epistle of] John, is to prove that the man Jesus is the Son of God. To prove this, [John] cites six testimonies, three in heaven and three on earth, all wholeheartedly agreeing that the man Jesus is the Son of God. In this passage the Word testifies about the Son, [which shows that the Son is] a separate being; thus the sophists cannot claim that the Word is the Son. And so, to prove on the authority of heaven [that Jesus is the Son of God], John cites the heavenly testimony at the Jordan River, when the Holy Spirit, performing its angelic ministry, *descended like a dove,*[e] and a voice from heaven said, "*This is my Son.*"[f]

---

[a] 1 John 5:7-8 [b] Matt 28:19. [c] Acts 2:3-4. [d] John 20:22.
[e] John 1:32; see also Matt 3:16; Mark 1:10; Luke 3:22. [f] Matt 3:17; Mark 1:11; Luke 3:22.

John cites visible and unmistakable testimony; otherwise he would have proven nothing. The voice manifested there, and the words from heaven that were heard, testify that this [man] Jesus was the Son of God. It is the Father who is clearly present here, testifying from heaven that this [man] is his Son. And the Spirit, descending upon him from heaven, also bears clear and visible witness here. In John 5 Christ himself cites three similar testimonies about himself.[a] And all of these [testimonies] are one, because they are in agreement in their witness about the very same thing, the unity of divinity itself.

[The First Epistle of] John also cites *three* other *testimonies on earth: spirit, water, and blood.*[b] For, when the water and blood poured from Christ's side, he *let his spirit go*,[c] *commending* it to God,[d] and dying as a man on earth dies. But to what do these things bear witness? Not, surely, to some incorporeal being, but rather they testify that this human being was the Son of God, out of whom, as he was dying, these three witnesses came forth. Here one can see what John had in mind. For he left no stone unturned[e] in order that he might prove Jesus to be the Son of God.

The central focus of all scripture is Jesus, the Son of God. John exhorts us to believe this if we wish to live in Christ. *He who believes that Jesus is* the Son of God *is born of God.*[f] *Who is it that has overcome the world but he who believes that Jesus is the Son of God?*[g] Thus, whoever does not believe this is not a Christian. Whoever does not believe this is not *founded on* that firm *rock*:[h] *You are the Christ, the Son of the living God* (Matthew 16).[i] The foundation of our salvation, and the foundation of the Church, is to believe faithfully that the man Jesus Christ is the Son of God, and our saviour.

Err, 26r

---

[a] John 5:36, 37, 39. [b] 1 John 5:7-8. [c] Matt 27:50. [d] Luke 23:46.
[e] A saying discussed by Erasmus in *Adagia* 1.4.30; in *Opera omnia*, II-1:429-430. [f] 1 John 5:1. [g] 1 John 5:5. [h] See Matt 7:24-27; Luke 6:47-49. [i] Matt 16:16.

The Restoration of Christianity

[24] Regarding the second passage:[a] Baptism according to the teaching of the apostles is rightly conferred in the name of Christ, because Christ contains in himself the Father and the Holy Spirit — the anointed, the anointer, and the anointing.[46] However, Christ wanted to express all of this in a broader sense, in order to confer honour on the Father and to connect the Holy Spirit to the act of baptism. For it is in this act that the gift of the Holy Spirit is particularly apparent. Therefore, [Jesus] begins by saying, "*Baptize in the name of the Father*," because [the Father] is the original, true, and primary source of *every gift* (James 1).[b] [He says] "*in the name of the Son*," because *through him we have received reconciliation*[c] and the gift [of baptism]. *There is no other name under heaven by which we must be saved* (Acts 4).[d] [And he says,] "*in the name of the Holy Spirit*," because the gift of the Holy Spirit is given in baptism (John 3, Acts 2).[e]

Err, 28v

Err, 28v-29r

In books 3 and 6 of Clement's *Recognitions*, Peter says that this is a triple invocation of the divine name. There he calls it "a triple beatitude" and "a threefold mystery."[f] These three modes of manifestation, or personhood, are not based on metaphysical distinctions of incorporeal beings in God, but, as taught by both Irenaeus and Tertullian,[g] are present, through God's οἰκονομία (*oikonomia*, economy), in the performance of the sacrament [of baptism].[47]

Consider also what Hilary says at the beginning of book 2 of *On the Trinity*: Christ "commanded them to baptize in the name of the Father, the Son, and the Holy Spirit, that is, by acknowledging the originator, the only-begotten, and the gift." The originator is the unbegotten "God the Father, from whom all things are"; the only-begotten is "Jesus

---

[a] Matt 28:19: "Go therefore and make disciples of all nations, baptizing them in the name of the Father and of the Son and of the Holy Spirit."
[b] James 1:17. [c] Rom 5:11. [d] Acts 4:12. [e] John 3:26-27; Acts 2:38.
[f] [Clement], *Recognitiones* 3.67, 6.9 (PG 1 1311D, 1352B-C).
[g] Irenaeus, *Adversus haereses* 4.20.10, 4.33.15, 5.2.2-3 (PG 7 1038C-1039A, 1083A, 1123B-1128A). Tertullian, *Adversus Praxean* 2-3 (PL 2 156-159).

Christ, through whom all things are"; and the Holy Spirit is "the gift in all things," the unique gift of baptism. There is "infinity in the eternal, the appearance [of God] in the image, and the benefit in the gift."[a] Here is the Trinity in its truest sense, which comes from ancient teaching: God the Father, invisible in the infinite; his appearance seen in his image [Christ, the Son]; and the gift [of the Holy Spirit] proceeding [from the Father and the Son]. If only Hilary's understanding [of the Trinity] had been preserved. If only Augustine (in *On the Trinity*, book 6),[b] and the rest of the sophist crowd, had not obscured [Hilary's] words![48] See book 1, distinction 31 of [Peter Lombard's] *Sentences*.[c]

{*The First Argument of the Sophists*}

Let us now examine the kind of arguments from which [the sophists] reach the erroneous conclusion that there are several distinct incorporeal beings within God. One of the arguments [25] is based upon John, chapter 10: "*I and the Father are one*."[d] In Sermon 56 and also in Tractates 36 and 71,[49] Augustine makes use of this passage, saying "because [John] says 'one'" to counter Arius, and saying "because [John] says 'are'" to counter Sabellius.[e] Hence, when countering Sabellius, [Augustine] concludes that there are two incorporeal beings, while, when countering Arius, he concludes that they have one equal nature. And thus he applauds his own remarkable triumphs. But carefully consider, reader, that here in this passage it is Jesus himself who is speaking. He said "are," because he is both God and man. And he said "one," because there is one divinity, one power, one harmony of thought, and one will shared by the man and God.

Err, 22v

Hence it is established that there is one οὐσία (*ousia*, substance) and one ἐξουσία (*exousia*, power). We find the

---

[a] Hilary, *De Trinitate* 2.1 (PL 10 50D-51A).   [b] Augustine, *De Trinitate* 6.11 (PL 42 931).   [c] *Sentences* 1.31.3 (PL 192 604),   [d] John 10:30.
[e] Augustine, *In evangelium Iohannis* 36.9, 71.2 (PL 35 1668, 1821). See also Augustine, *De Trinitate* 7.12 (PL 42 945).

Err, 23r word *ousia* only in chapter 15 of the Gospel of Luke,[a] where it refers specifically to domestic property: resources, goods, and wealth.[50] *Exousia* is used in various places [in the Greek New Testament]. Where Christ speaks about the power given to him by the Father, the word *exousia* is used — a word which, when referring to Christ, has nearly the same meaning as *ousia*: might, abilities, and a wealth of power. All of these things Christ has in abundant measure. And he and the Father share one *ousia* and one *exousia*. He is ὁμόυσιος (*homoousios*), that is to say, truly of the same substance as God the Father, and one with God.

Err, 23v This was the early Church Fathers' straightforward understanding in their exposition of the passage, "I and the Father are one." Origen, in book 8 of *Against Celsus*,[b] and Cyprian, in his letter to Magnus,[c] both maintain that [the passage means that] the man [Jesus] is one in will with God.[51] This understanding of the passage is confirmed by the words of Christ himself, where he teaches that we may be one with him, just as he himself is one with the Father.[d]

True Christians are one with Christ, not only through their harmony of thought, but in actual substance, as I shall clearly demonstrate. Both Irenaeus and Tertullian teach this, and they do so in many places.[e] Hilary teaches this as well, in book 8 of *On the Trinity*,[f] as does Cyril in his commentary on John.[g] For we are one through the substance of Christ, just as he is one in substance with God.

{*The Second Argument of the Sophists*}

Err, 28v A second argument by which sophists seek to prove their triad of invisible beings[h] is based upon [this text from]

---

[a] Luke 15:12-13.   [b] Origen, *Contra Celsum* 8.12 (PG 11 1534B-C).
[c] Cyprian, *Ad Magnum* 5 (PL 3 1188B).   [d] John 17:22.   [e] See, for example, Irenaeus, *Adversus haereses* 4.20.4, 5.1.3, 5.2.3 (PG 7 1034B, 1123A, 1126A-B); Tertullian, *Adversus Marcionem* 2.25, 2.27 (PL 2 315A, 317C).   [f] Hilary, *De Trinitate* 8.13-15 (PL 10 246A-248A).
[g] Cyril, *In divi Joannis evangelium* 9 (PG 74 279B-C).   [h] See, for example, [Athanasius], *De unitate sanctissimae trinitatis* (PL 62 241A).

Exodus 3: *I am the God of Abraham, the God of Isaac, the God of Jacob*.[a] But nothing metaphysical [26] is being written about here, as is proven by the fact that God, when speaking to Jacob, said: "*I am the God of your father Abraham and of Isaac*" (Genesis 29 and 32).[b] Now you cannot possibly infer from this that there are two metaphysical beings. Furthermore, when [God] spoke to Isaac, he said "*I am the God of your father Abraham*" (Genesis 26).[c] If we are to understand [Exodus 3] as referring to those three beings, how can *the God of Abraham, the God of Isaac, the God of Jacob* be called the father of Jesus Christ in Acts?[d]

Can it be that this Trinity is to be called the father of that second [metaphysical] being of theirs — or is it the father of the man [Jesus Christ]? Indeed, in book 1, distinction 26 of *Sentences*, [Peter] Lombard teaches, based on Augustine and Hilary, that "the man is the son of the Trinity and the whole Trinity is the father of the man."[e] In book 11 of *On the Trinity*, Hilary explains Christ's statement, "*I ascend unto my God, my Father and your Father*,"[f] by saying that the entire Trinity "is the father of the man Christ, just as it is the father of other people."[g] And for Augustine, in book 5 of *On the Trinity*, the whole Trinity is the Father of creation.[h] Thus for [both Hilary and Augustine], the Trinity is the father of the humanity of Christ and the father of his divinity; and the whole Trinity is the father.[52] Consequently, [according to them,] both the incorporeal Son and the corporeal man are the son of the Trinity, and are begotten by all three [persons of the Trinity].

But we, rejecting all these fictions, understand that God is called "the God of Abraham, the God of Isaac, and the God of Jacob," in order to dissuade the Jews from believing in a plurality of gods. For they were prone to [worship]

Err, 29r

Err, 29v

---

[a] Ex 3:6. [b] Gen 28:13, 32:9. "Genesis 29" is a mistake; the parallel passage in *Errors* refers to Gen 28. [c] Gen 26:24. [d] Acts 3:13.
[e] *Sentences* 1.26.5 (PL 192 593). [f] John 20:17. [g] Hilary, *De Trinitate* 11.14 (PL 10 408C). [h] Augustine, *De Trinitate* 5.12 (PL 42 918-919).

Err, 29v   a plurality of gods], just as we are today. They were accustomed to multiplying their gods *according to the number of* their *cities* (Jeremiah 2 and 11).[a] Therefore, to prevent them from multiplying their gods according to the number of ages or generations of men, and lest they believe that there was one God of Abraham, another God of Isaac, and another God of Jacob, God proclaimed that he was the

Err, 29v   same God of them all. [God] makes this clear in the words immediately preceding, when he says, "*I am the God of your fathers*."[b] [And thus God said,] "*I am the God who led you out of the land of Egypt*"[c] and "*out of Ur of the Chaldeans*."[d] And in Exodus 6 God says that it was he who appeared to [the patriarchs]: "*I am God, who appeared to Abraham, to Isaac, and to Jacob*."[e] Also, in Isaiah 48, [God says], "*I am he, I am the first, and I am the last*."[f]

Err, 29v   Another reason for calling himself the God of Abraham, Isaac, and Jacob was that, **[27]** by manifesting himself to the Israelites through Moses, God was at that time beginning to fulfill the promises made to [the patriarchs]. And the third reason that he called himself the God of [those three patriarchs] was to show that [the patriarchs] were all destined to be restored to life, and indeed were already alive, living in God's presence (Luke 20).[g]

{*The Third Argument of the Sophists*}

The [sophists'] third argument is based on the three men who appeared to Abraham in Genesis 18.[h] Because "Abraham saw three, but worshipped only one," they conclude that there are three incorporeal beings in God.[53] To this I reply that what Abraham saw was [three] angels.

Everywhere throughout the Old Testament the person of Christ is prefigured by an angel. The angel was a guide,

---

[a] Jer 2:28, 11:13. [b] Ex 3:6, as quoted in Acts 7:32. [c] Ex 20:2; Ps 81:10.
[d] Gen 15:7. [e] Ex 6:2-3. [f] Isa 48:12. [g] Luke 20:37-38; see also Matt 22:32 and Mark 12:26-27. [h] Gen 18:1-3.

pointing the way toward Christ, just like the Law itself. In those days, [an angel], acting in the place of God, spoke using the words of God, and in him was the reflection of Christ. In Genesis 16 and 22, it was an angel who was speaking as God.[a] In Genesis 31 an angel said to Jacob, "*I am the God of Bethel.*"[b] And it was an angel who spoke to Moses, saying, "*I am the God of Abraham, of Isaac, and of Jacob*" (Exodus 3, Acts 7).[c]

Err, 61r

In [Genesis 18], one of the three angels spoke as God, his radiance representing the person of Christ — a reflection of the Word, as you will see later.[d] God made one angel first among angels and head of the divine council.[54] [This angel] spoke to the Jews as if he were God; therefore, he is called מיכאל (Michael), that is to say, "Who is like God?" In [Genesis] chapter 18, [this angel] spoke to Abraham as God.[e] And in the next chapter, the two attendant ministering angels who continued on to Sodom [also spoke as God].[f] When God said *my angel shall go before you*,[g] "my angel" is meant to be understood as Michael. This is shown by the Hebrew word ["my angel"], which contains the name "Michael." For מלאכי (my angel) and מיכאל (Michael) are formed from exactly the same Hebrew letters. What is more, this angel is specifically called "Prince of the Jews."[55]

Augustine's reasoning in book 2 of *On the Trinity*,[h] which is based on Lot having bowed down to the ground in the presence of the two angels,[i] is unconvincing. For Lot bowed in a gesture of hospitality to welcome his honoured guests, even though he had no idea that they were angels (see Hebrews 13).[j] That Lot calls them "my lords" does nothing to justify Augustine's fantasies, because the noun used here is not the tetragrammaton, but the word we commonly use

---

[a] Gen 16:7-13, 22:11-18. [b] Gen 31:13. [c] Ex 3:6; Acts 7:32.
[d] See *Restoration*, 47-48 and A.R2.3. [e] Gen 18:33. [f] Gen 19:1.
[g] Ex 32:34. [h] Augustine, *De Trinitate* 2.22 (PL 42 859). [i] Gen 19:1-2.
[j] Heb 13:2: "Do not neglect to show hospitality to strangers, for thereby some have entertained angels unawares."

to address men as "lords."[56] This, or some other honorific title, could with equal justice [28] have been assigned by Lot to the angels, especially since the Lord himself was present when Sodom was condemned to be destroyed by fire. Augustine is foolish to speculate about whether Lot's two guests were "the Father and the Son, or the Father and the Holy Spirit, or the Son and the Holy Spirit."[a] What ridiculous prattle!

Err, 27v   To the arguments that I have already mentioned, [Peter] Lombard adds, in book 1 of *Sentences*, at the end of distinction 2: "Almost every single syllable of the New Testament agrees in implying the Trinity" of three invisible beings.[b] To me, however, not only all the syllables, but every single letter, all the accents on the letters, *the mouths of babes and sucklings,*[c] and even *the very stones cry out*[d] that there is one God the Father and his Christ, the Lord Jesus. *For there is one God, and one mediator between God and humanity, the man Christ Jesus* (1 Timothy 2).[e] And *for us there is one God, who is the Father, and one Lord, Jesus Christ* (1 Corinthians 8).[f] Even John, to whom the heavens opened in the Apocalypse, saw only God the Father and his Christ. And only *God and the Lamb* are praised and worshipped there.[g] Stephen, to whom *the heavens* were also *opened, beheld the glory of God, and Jesus standing at his right hand.*[h]

Similarly, in Matthew 23 [Jesus says] *"There is one Father"* and *"one teacher, Christ."*[i] And in John 8 [he says] *"It is not I alone [who judge], but I and the Father [who sent*
Err, 27v   *me]."*[j] *"I am not alone,"* he says, *"because the Father is with me."*[k] *"They have not known the Father, nor me."*[l] *"[This is eternal life,] that they may know you, the only true God, and Jesus Christ, whom you have sent."*[m]

---

[a] Augustine, *De Trinitate* 2.22 (PL 42 859).   [b] *Sentences* 1.2.8 (PL 192 529).   [c] Matt 21:16, quoting Ps 8:2.   [d] Luke 19:40.   [e] 1 Tim 2:5.
[f] 1 Cor 8:6.   [g] Rev 21:22, 22:3.   [h] Acts 7:55-56.   [i] Matt 23:9-10.
[j] John 8:16.   [k] John 16:32.   [l] John 16:3.   [m] John 17:3.

Book 1

When [Jesus] said, "*No one knows the Father but the Son, nor the Son, but the Father*,"ᵃ was the third being not aware of this? John omitted any mention of this third being in his first letter, in which he expresses the desire that we be *in fellowship with the Father and with his Son Jesus Christ*.ᵇ Similarly, in 1 Timothy 5, Paul says, "*I charge you before God and the Lord Jesus Christ and the elect angels.*"ᶜ Note that Paul's solemn admonition was made before God, Christ, and the angels — not before the third being. Nevertheless, the metaphysicians want [this third being of theirs] to be the equal of the second, and seated in a position of equality with him on the throne of the Trinity, in the third corner of the [heavenly] triclinium.⁵⁷ And so they sing in their hymn: "On the throne of majesty, three were sitting on a triclinium."⁵⁸

Err, 27v-28r

But Christ teaches otherwise in Revelation 3: **[29]** "*I will confess [your name] before my Father and before the angels.*"ᵈ What a grievous affront to the third being, for Christ to say, "before the angels" and not "before [the third being]"! In Mark 8, and in Luke 9 and 12, Christ mentions only himself, the Father, and the angels.ᵉ In Revelation 1, John wishes us *grace and peace from God, the seven spirits, and Jesus Christ*.ᶠ He does not mention any third being. Irenaeus, in many places in book 3 [of *Against Heresies*] as well as in the prologue to book 4, states that in the scriptures no one is called God except the Father of all that is, and his Son Jesus.ᵍ Neither Irenaeus nor Tertullian, nor any of the early Church Fathers, spoke of a third being as God.

Err, 28r

In a later [book in this volume] you will see each of [these writers] explain the dispensation of the Holy Spirit,ʰ and you will thus come to understand the divine substance

---

ᵃ Matt 11:27. ᵇ 1 John 1:3. ᶜ 1 Tim 5:21. ᵈ Rev. 3:5. ᵉ Mark 8:38; Luke 9:26; Luke 12:8. ᶠ Rev 1:4, 5. ᵍ Irenaeus, *Adversus haereses* 3.6.2 and 4.pref.4 (PG 7 861B, 975C). ʰ In book 5.

of the Holy Spirit — although [the Spirit's] underlying nature is not that of a visible person like the Son.

[Other Objections to the Trinity]

[The Trinity is Contrary to Reason]

Err, 32r   At this point I must demonstrate, by means of reasoned argument and authoritative texts, that these three distinct, incorporeal beings cannot coexist in the unity of God.

Err, 32r-v   First of all, I could easily dismiss this imaginary triad by using the sixteen arguments [showing the logical inconsistencies in the idea of the Trinity] raised by Robert Holkot in distinction 5 of book 1 of his [*Questions on the Four Books of*] *Sentences*.[a] He does not give an adequate response to any of the objections he raises, and cannot offer anything but a sophistical response, as he himself admits.[59] See book 1 of Augustine's *On the Trinity*[b] and "preludes"[60] in Pierre d'Ailly's [*Questions*], book 1, question 5,[c] where these [two] admit that this triad of beings cannot be proven from the words of scripture, but is only a received idea based upon tradition.[61]

[The Trinity Implies Tritheism]

Err, 21r-v   In order to comprehend just how valiantly the sophists strive to defend [their conception of] one God, listen to what someone from our own century, John Mair,[62] writes on this subject in *On the First Book of Sentences*, distinction 4, in the solution of argument 6.[d] [John Mair and the other sophists] concede that the three persons are, absolutely, distinct beings. And Augustine, in book 1 of *On Christian Doctrine*, says that [the three persons] are "the beings from whom we ought to take our [spiritual] satisfaction."[e] [The sophists] also say that "person" is a substantive noun [or a

---

[a] Holkot, *Quaestiones* 1.5   [b] Augustine, *De Trinitate* 1.1-3 (PL 42 819-821).   [c] D'Ailly, *Quaestiones* 1.5 (93r col. 1).   [d] Mair, *In primum sententiarum* 4.6.   [e] Augustine, *De doctrina Christiana* 1.5 (PL 34 21).

noun denoting substance].⁶³ Augustine teaches this in book 7 of *On the Trinity*, and all the others follow him. [See Peter Lombard] *Sentences*, book 1, distinction 23.ᵃ

Reasoning, therefore, "from lesser to greater,"⁶⁴ John Mair concludes from the three persons [of the Trinity] that there are, absolutely, three hypostases,⁶⁵ "three substances," "three essences," and "three beings." Hence [he must conclude that] there are, absolutely, "three gods."ᵇ Nevertheless, he says that there is one **[30]** connotative being, and one connotative essence.⁶⁶ It is significant that [the sophists] take these words ["substances," "essences," "beings," etc.] connotatively. And this can also be gathered from the Master [Peter Lombard], in book 1, distinction 25 of *Sentences*.ᶜ

Is ours, then, a connotative God, and not an absolute God? Are not those people really tritheists⁶⁷ who create, absolutely, three actually distinct incorporeal gods? Or three actually distinct simple incorporeal beings? Or three entities? The argument from lesser to greater logically proves that there are three absolute beings — and three essences as well, since every entity is an essence. This is admitted in Hilary's *On the Councils*, [where he writes] that, in God, "there are three in terms of substance."⁶⁸ The Master himself admits as much in [book 1] distinction 25,ᵈ and the rest follow him.

Also, by the argument from convertibles, from three beings the logical conclusion is that there are three entities.⁶⁹ Hence there are three essences and three gods. In arguing against the Jews, [trinitarians] attempt to prove the truth of their Trinity, saying that since [the Hebrew word] *Elohim* is a plural and means "gods," there are two, three, or even

Err, 21v

Err, 36r

Err, 36r

ᵃ *Sentences* 1.23.8 (PL 192 585), quoting Augustine, *De Trinitate* 7.8 (PL 42 941). ᵇ Mair, *In primum sententiarum* 4.6. ᶜ *Sentences* 1.25 (PL 192 588-591), commenting on Augustine, *De Trinitate* 7.8 (PL 42 940-941).
ᵈ *Sentences* 1.25.5 (PL 192 589), quoting Hilary, *De synodis* 12, 32 (PL 10 490A, 505A).

more gods.ª If, by the logic of the Trinity, there are gods, then there are three gods: three really distinct incorporeal gods. If they are really distinct, and distinct in essence, then, by the argument from convertibles, they are to be taken as absolutes. Truly, therefore, those who do not have a single God, but only a tripartite, compound God, are tritheists, or even atheists. They have a connotative God, not an absolute one. They have imaginary gods, demonic illusions.

For Athanasius,[70] Hilary,[b] Cyril,[c] [Gregory of] Nazianzus,[d] Basil,[e] Augustine,[f] and all the rest, there is one unbegotten God, one God who is begotten, and one God who is neither begotten nor unbegotten. Therefore, there are three gods: one who cannot be born, another who is born, and yet another who "proceeds." For the unbegotten God is not the begotten one, and the one who is begotten is not the one who proceeds. Therefore we have another God and another being. One God is dead, two are not; one person is dead, two are not; one being is dead, two are not.

[*The Trinity is Inconceivable*]

Err, 32v

We can bring up yet other arguments, derived from [the sophists'] own basic principles, proving conclusively not only that these three beings cannot exist in one God, but that they are unimaginable. For in order to have [**31**] an idea of the Trinity it would be necessary to have separate ideas of each of the three beings, so that it would be possible to think of one of them without thinking of any of the others. Everyone denies [that this is possible], citing [the words of Jesus himself], "*He who sees me, sees* the Father."[g] They answer that someone might have an idea of the Trinity by having an idea of God "connotatively" as those three beings.

ª *Sentences* 1.2.6 (PL 192 527).   [b] Hilary, *De Trinitate* 2.18 (PL 10 86C).   [c] Cyril, *Thesaurus* 34 (PG 75 586A).   [d] Gregory of Nazianzus, *Orationes* 31.7-8 (PG 36 140C-142C).   [e] Basil, *Contra Eunomium* 2.28 (PG 29 635C).   [f] *Sentences* 1.13.5 (PL 192 556), quoting Augustine, *De Trinitate* 15.47 (PL 42 1094-1095) and [Augustine], *Dialogus quaestionum LXV* 2 (PL 40 734).   [g] John 12:45.

Book 1

But being entirely couched, as it is, in connotative terms, this response is clearly empty, and smacks of one of their sophistical concoctions. It is empty, and also contrary to their own principles, for three beings to be connoted by one idea, when they cannot be signified in absolute terms by three [ideas]. For, by their own well-known rules, every connotative signification presupposes something absolute.

Furthermore, Porphyry's rule applies to all things: "From any essential commonality, a concept may be abstracted, which has an absolute and irreducible meaning."[71] If there can be absolute concepts of the divine beings, what kind [of concepts] are they? Is the Trinity known to Christ and the angels? If [in the minds of Christ and the angels] there are three distinct absolute concepts of three beings, do they distinctly perceive three absolute gods? Christ plainly taught that the *angels see the face of* his *Father*;[a] but he does not say that they see other beings. At the present time in heaven Christ himself sees nothing in himself other than the Father.[b]

Err, 33r

Dream if you want to, [but when you do,] direct your gaze at those mental images, and then you will plainly see that your Trinity cannot be understood without three mental images. For "observing mental images is necessary for understanding."[72] Although you deny it in your words, in your mind you are worshipping a quaternity [of gods]. For you have four pictures [in your mind], and the fourth is a mental image representing the essence [of the divine]. For "observing some mental image is necessary for understanding" the essence. If you look carefully and pay attention, you will find that your Trinity is a tumult of false appearances in the imagination, which holds you spellbound.

Err, 33r

Actually, all trinitarians are atheists. For what does it mean to be without God, other than not to be able to think about God? A confused jumble of three beings is constantly

Err, 21v–22r

---

[a] Matt 18:10.   [b] See John 6:46: "No one has seen the Father, except he who is from God; he has seen the Father."

looming before our minds and hampering our understanding, **[32]** driving us to madness whenever we think about God. There are *three evil spirits* in the brain, which beguile people, as John says in Revelation 16.ᵃ

Err, 33v   "It is enough to believe," [the trinitarians] say, even if [what we are asked to believe] is incomprehensible.⁷³ In this they expose their own foolishness, because they accept incomprehensible things. As [the apostles] say, *they understand neither what they are saying nor what they are affirming* (1 Timothy 1), and *[like irrational beasts] they blaspheme those things about which they have no understanding* (2 Peter 2).ᵇ

Err, 33v   This is all the more [absurd], since you yourselves profess — and indeed all do profess — that what you understand is itself the object of faith. Therefore, if you have this faith, show me: what is the extent of your understanding? What is it that you think you understand? Is not your own mental confusion the [real] object of your faith?⁷⁴

We can now see how it was that Augustine could boast, in book 1 of *On the Trinity* as well as in book 1 of *On Christian Doctrine*, that he understood the Trinity and that it could be perceived by a purified mind.ᶜ For he was perceiving a shifting array of illusions, as I shall more clearly show in what follows.

In his letters to Fortunatianus and Paulina, Augustine asserts that God cannot be seen by us in our future state of blessedness, nor even by the angels themselves.ᵈ In fact he imagines that illusions within our minds depict the Trinity, thereby turning on its head the entire happiness of both men and angels. As if our souls can see more [in this life] than can be seen by the angels and the rest of the blessed ones!

ᵃ Rev 16:13.   ᵇ1 Tim 1:7; 2 Pet 2:12.   ᶜAugustine, *De Trinitate* 1.3 (PL 42 821); *De doctrina Christiana* 1.10 (PL 34 23).   ᵈAugustine, *Epistulae* 148.7-9 (PL 33 625-626) to Fortunatianus; 147.28 (PL 33 609) to Paulina.

You can add to this yet another argument against the false ideas of the trinitarians: "nothing can be in the intellect unless it"— or something similar or analogous to it —"has first been [perceived by] the senses" (*Posterior Analytics*, book 1, and *On the Soul*, book 3).[75] A deaf person cannot learn music, nor a blind person perspective, because things that cannot be perceived by their senses cannot be present in their minds. But you have never had a sensory perception, or even a mental image, of three beings of this kind, that together constitute a unity. For two, three, or more beings, coexisting as one, cannot be found anywhere. Consequently, no basis can be found in sensory perception by means of which the mind could reach such a conclusion. Indeed [the mind] is wearied and confused by [the Trinity], because it struggles to envision it, while lacking a basis in sense perception — which is like laying the foundation of a building in a void.

[33] Furthermore, let us imagine that there is a separate person of the Father, as my adversaries readily admit [that we can], since they make a formal distinction between the persons and the essence.[76] Then, I ask, since it is agreed that any being has its own essence and its own nature, how can I imagine a multiplicity of beings without a multiplicity of essences? Or that a new being can be added, without a new nature?

[*God Is One*]

We are taught to avoid such plurality, not only by reason, but by countless authorities, in the New Testament as well as in the Old. In Matthew 19 [Jesus says,] "*There is one who is good, God.*"[a] And in Mark 10: "*No one is good but one, God.*"[b] In that case, what of those who fail to acknowledge the One Itself, and, by means of their artificial connotative essence, turn to a plurality of beings and a plurality of absolute

---

[a] Matt 19:17.   [b] Mark 10:18.

gods? Are they not content with unity in name only? Note, moreover, that it is the Son who is speaking here. From [these words of Jesus] it is clear that the entire basis of the unity of God is to be found in the Father.

Err, 34r-v

In 1 Corinthians 8, [Paul writes]: *There is one God, who is the Father, and one Lord, Jesus Christ.*[a] See also Ephesians 4: *There is one God and Father of us all.*[b] And in 1 Timothy 2 he says, *There is one God, and one mediator between God and humanity.*[c] Is it not strange that the apostles never said that the first being, or the first person, is the father of the second person, but rather that God is the father of Jesus Christ? Nor did they ever say that the second being is the Son of God, but [they say] that Jesus himself is the Son of God.

Err, 34v-35r

Likewise, when Ignatius, Irenaeus, and other Church Fathers proclaim that there is one almighty God who is the God of both the Old and the New Testaments, declaring that this same [God] is the Father of Jesus Christ,[d] what then ought you, listener, to deduce from this preaching? Tertullian, also, even though he went over to Montanism,[77] nevertheless proclaims many brilliant truths drawn from apostolic tradition.[e] There is also an ancient book, said to be by Clement, the disciple of Peter, in which Christ is proclaimed with the utmost clarity.[f] [This is a work] in which you can still discover many traces of [apostolic] simplicity.

Err, 35r

Also, in his Epistle to the Philadelphians, Ignatius, the disciple of John the Evangelist, writes: "If anyone preaches that the God of the Law and the Prophets is one, but denies that Christ is his son, then he is a liar... If anyone professes faith [34] in the man Jesus Christ, while denying that the God of the Law and the Prophets is the father of Christ, then he is not established in the truth."[g] Furthermore, in his Epistle

---

[a] 1 Cor 8:6.   [b] Eph 4:6.   [c] 1 Tim 2:5.   [d] Irenaeus, *Adversus haereses* 4.2.2 (PG 7 977A-B); [Ignatius], *Ad Philadelphios* 5-6 (PG 5 830A-B); Origen, *De principiis* 2.4.1 (PG 11 198C).   [e] Tertullian, *Adversus Marcionem* 3.1 (PL 2 322C-D).   [f] [Clement], *Recognitiones* 2.40 (PG 1 1267B), 7.23 (PG 1 1364C).   [g] [Ignatius], *Ad Philadelphios* 6 (PG 5 830B).

to the Tarsians, [Ignatius] clearly teaches that Christ "is not God over all things, but [God's] son."[a] You can find similar ideas in Justin, as cited by Irenaeus and others.[b] If only the writings of all who lived in that age had survived![78]

Is it not true that, for these trinitarians of ours, the entire Trinity is the God of the [Old Testament] Law? But Jesus Christ, according to them, is not the Son of the entire Trinity. Therefore [they must believe that Jesus] is not the Son of the God of the Law. I ask you, consider why the ways of speaking employed by the early Church Fathers are not found in our trinitarians. They use very different ones, which were unknown to those in ancient times. The [original] way of thinking [about God] is the only valid one. Consider that Irenaeus's entire book, *Against All Heresies*, treats this very subject, yet never mentions the trinitarians' nonsense. For these so-called "realities" had not yet entered the consciousness of humankind. *Err*, 35r

Let us now turn our attention to the Old Testament, where we are often instructed to profess a unity, not a plurality, in God. For example, in Exodus 20: *I am your God, and you shall have no other gods apart from me.*[c] And in Deuteronomy 6: *Hear, O Israel, Yahweh*[79] *is our God and Yahweh is one.*[d] The same idea is also expressed in Deuteronomy 4, where it is written: *Know therefore this day, and ponder in your heart, that* God himself is *God in heaven above and on the earth below*;[e] there is no other apart from him. He alone is God (Deuteronomy 32, 2 Kings 19, Psalm 85, Isaiah 37, and John 17).[f] He alone is called God, which the tritheists deny, maintaining that he always had three partners. They offer this argument: since there could be "no perfect comfort in solitude," therefore "three were sitting on a triclinium."[g] *Err*, 35r-v

---

[a] [Ignatius], *Ad Tarsenses* 5 (PG 5 891B). [b] Irenaeus, *Adversus haereses* 4.6.2 (PG 7 987B); Eusebius, *Historia ecclesiastica* 4.18 (PG 20 375C).
[c] Ex 20:2, 3. [d] Deut 6:4. [e] Deut 4:39. [f] Deut 32:39; 2 Kg 19:19; Ps 86:10; Isa 37:16; John 17:3. [g] See A.R1.57-58.

Err, 37r But God himself, through the prophet [Isaiah], says, *"I am the Lord and there is no other; apart from me there is no God. Aside from me there is no Lord; I am the Lord and there is no other"* (Isaiah 43 and 45).[a] The Hebrews are supported by so many authorities that they are right to wonder at the tripartite God introduced by [the Christians]. They think that our [New] Testament is schismatic [35] because they see that the unity and simplicity of their own God is so abhorrent to us, and also because not a single one of their ancestors ever contemplated such a thing [as the Trinity].

[*The Witness of the Quran*]

What shall we say of the Muslims, who disagree with us for the same reason? How savagely they censure us! And for good reason, in the just judgement of God, because there are none who *"recall it to mind* [that *I am God and there is no other*]*.*"[b] The Trinity is subject to unreserved condemnation in their Quran, suras 11, 12, and 28,[80] where Muhammad teaches that these three Gods, or "partners of God," were "unknown to their forefathers," and that these three are the sons of Beelzebub, whom the trinitarians worship "in place of God."[c] Indeed, in Revelation, John speaks of them as *three demonic spirits emerging* [*out of the mouth of the dragon and out of the mouth of the beast and out of the mouth of the false prophet*].[d]

Err, 43r But let us now listen more fully to what Muhammad has to say about Christ and the Christians. In the suras Al 'Imran, Al-Nisa', and Al-Ma'idah,[81] and in a good many other suras, he says that Christ was the greatest of the prophets,

---

[a] Isa 43:11, 45:5-6. Similar pronouncements are found in Isa 44:6, 45:21, and other passages. [b] Isa 46:8-9. [c] Condemnation of the Trinity: Quran 4:171 (Alcoran 11); partners of God: Quran 5:72, 18:52 (Alcoran 12, 28); unknown to their forefathers: Quran 18:4-5 (Alcoran 28); sons of Beelzebub: Quran 18:50 (Alcoran 28). In Robert of Ketton's translation of the Quran, "Beelzebub" is the name used for Iblis, the fallen angel who becomes Satan. [d] Rev 16:13.

the Word of God, the spirit of God, the power of God, the very soul of God, and the Word born of a perpetual virgin by the breath of God — or by the breath of the Holy Spirit — and that the Jews behaved wickedly toward him.[a] He also says that the first disciples of Christ were the very best and noblest of men, who wrote the truth. They did not maintain the doctrine of the Trinity, but rather this was added by men from later times, who corrupted [the original] holy teaching.[b] In sura 4 [Muhammad] says that in later times countless disagreements arose over matters about which [among the earliest Christians] "there was no dissent or controversy."[c] He asserts this again in sura 20, where he says that the Christian people, who were originally one group, were afterwards torn asunder by various schisms because they had allowed themselves to be turned aside to more than one god.[d] In sura 12 and a number of other places, he says that the reason for their mistake of setting up three equal partners is that they are idolaters, worshippers of images, and, therefore lack an understanding of the true God.[e] In sura 28 he says that an incorporeal son was "unknown to their forefathers," and that those whom they call the "partners of God" are really the sons of Beelzebub.[f] In sura 29 he says that because of such great blasphemy "heaven is thrown into disorder and the mountains and the earth tremble."[g] Thus he concludes sura 50 with these words: "We believe in one God, and not in any of his supposed partners."[h]

Now hear some more of the laudatory words with which [Muhammad] praises Christ. In sura 4, he says that Christ, [36] having been raised on high, above all things, was given

Err, 43r

---

[a] Ficino, *De Christiana religione* 12, 29, 34, 36.   [b] Ficino, *De Christiana religione* 36.   [c] Quran 2:253 (Alcoran 4).   [d] Quran 10:18-19 (Alcoran 20).   [e] Quran 5:73-77 (Alcoran 12); Quran 22:30-31 (Alcoran 32).
[f] Quran 18:4-5, 50, 52 (Alcoran 28).   [g] Quran 19:88-90 (Alcoran 29).
[h] Quran 40:84 (Alcoran 50).

the power of God and the very mind of God.[a] In sura 5 he says that Christ "came [into the world] endowed with divine power and might," "to be a face beheld by all nations both in this age and in the ages to come."[82] In sura 11 he says that the peoples of the Law, Jews as well as Saracens,[83] will one day come to believe in this Jesus, the son of Mary.[b] In the same sura he says, "Believe, therefore, in God and his messenger, and cease talking about three gods."[c] In sura 12 he says that Christ "brought us the gospel, which is the light, the confirmation of the Law, a chastening, and the right way."[d] In sura 13 he says that Christ had "a pure and blessed soul" and that he had prepared a heavenly table for those who believe in him.[84] In the book *The Teachings of Muhammad*, Christ is called "the word, the spirit, and the power of God."[e] Muhammad calls Christ *Ruhallah*, "the spirit of God," the one begotten by the very breath of God.[f]

Finally, although [Muhammad] attributes almost everything to Christ, he does not acknowledge Christ as the son of God, in the way the word "son" was used by the tritheists in his own time. On the contrary, he was gravely offended by these three incorporeal gods, or three distinct, invisible, and equal beings in one God. Because of this perverse trinitarian doctrine, he parted ways with Christianity, which was an extremely sad and lamentable thing for the entire world. This incorporeal deity, with real distinctions [among the three persons], caused him to deny that Christ was God. As one can gather from suras 100[85] and 122, when Muhammad denied [that Jesus was] the Son of God,[g] he was denying what was being put forward at the time: an invisible son similar to the Father. [If not for the doctrine of the

---

[a] Quran 2:253 (Alcoran 4).   [b] Quran 4:159 (Alcoran 11).   [c] Quran 4:171 (Alcoran 11).   [d] Quran 5:46 (Alcoran 12).   [e] Herman of Carinthia, *Doctrina Machumetis*, 199.   [f] Nicholas of Cusa, *Cribratio Alcorani* 1.20, discusses how the Arabic word *ruhallah* (spirit or breath) is applied to Christ.   [g] Quran 112:3-4 (Alcoran 122). For other denials of the divinity of Jesus, see Quran 5:17, 72,116; 19:35.

Trinity, Muhammad] would have conceded readily that the man Jesus Christ was the son of God, since he granted that [Christ] was begotten by God of a virgin.[86]

[*The Trinity Leads to Heresy*]

From the public witness of the first Christians, as well as from the testimony of their opponents, you may easily conclude, reader, that the Trinity was unknown to them. You will gather exactly the same thing by comparing the first Christian writings with the monstrosities that followed later.

Now let us consider the monstrous ideas that have resulted from trinitarian thinking, so that you may understand that "one absurdity always leads to many others."[87] Once the imaginary mental image of three beings [**37**] had taken hold of people's minds, the tritheists said, "there are three gods."[a] This is what our [trinitarians] profess: three absolute [gods] and one connotative.

Err, 38r-v

The Arians created an inequality among these three beings, by separating the second substance from the first.[b] Macedonius said that the third being, which is unlike the other two, is not God, but merely a created being.[c] It is no wonder that, having gone astray at the very outset, they would subsequently be tossed about on the high seas, forever drifting in a state of hallucination, and forever [as Irenaeus says][d] "bringing in a greater question [in order to resolve] a lesser one."[88]

Err, 38v

The Aëtians and Eunomians[89] made the [three] beings so unlike each other that the third being now becomes the creation of a created being, with the result that the third being is not able to see the other two, since scripture says that *no one knows the Father except the Son, and no one knows the Son except the Father*.[e] In this Aëtius and Eunomius differ

Err, 38v

---

[a] Isidore, *Etymologiae* 8.5.68 (PL 82 304C).   [b] Isidore, *Etymologiae* 8.5.43 (PL 82 302A). See also Augustine, *In evangelium Iohannis* 18.3 (PL 35 1537).   [c] Isidore, *Etymologiae* 8.5.44 (PL 82 302A).
[d] Irenaeus, *Adversus haereses* 2.10.1 (PG 7 735A).   [e] Matt 11:27.

from Arius, because the latter said that the [three] beings are unequal but similar, while the former two maintained that they are both unequal and dissimilar. Thus reports Epiphanius in his accounts of the heresies,[a] as does Eusebius in his *History of the Church*, book 10, chapter 25.[b] Also differing from Arius, who distinguished among the [three] substances, certain Donatists[90] posit a Son who is of the same substance although not equal to the Father, as Augustine reports in Sermon 31 [from the collection] *On the Words of the Apostle*.[c] In addition the Metangismonites said that the Father and the Son were two vessels, and that "the smaller vessel was inside the larger vessel."[d]

Err, 38v

Other [heretics] divided God into three parts. [The Arian] Maximinus feared[91] that the Father would be [only] part of God, and that each of the persons would be one-third of the Trinity.[e] As Hilary relates in books 4 and 6 of *On the Trinity*, prior to Maximinus, Manichaeus[92] also asserted that the Son was "a portion of the Father's substance."[f] Likewise, in Hilary's view, Hieracas[93] was splitting "a lamp from a lamp, and dividing the torch of divinity into two parts,"[g] as though he were cutting a lamp-wick.

Sabellius, adhering to the unity of God, was unacquainted with [God's] modes of communication and dispensation. He claimed that the Father himself was the Son, and that the Father himself had suffered death. Therefore he is

---

[a] Epiphanius, *Panarion* 3.1, introductory summary (PG 42 338C). See also Isidore, *Etymologiae* 8.5.39 (PL 82 301C).   [b] Rufinus, *Historia ecclesiastica* 1.25 (PL 21 497A). Servetus refers to Rufinus's Book 1 as Book 10 of Eusebius's *Historia ecclesiastica*, which Rufinus translated, condensed, and extended.   [c] Augustine, *Sermones* 183.9 (PL 38 991). Sermon 183 was published as Sermon 31 in *De verbis apostoli*, a medieval collection of Augustine's sermons. See also Augustine, *Epistulae* 185.1.1 (PL 33 792-793); Isidore, *Etymologiae* 8.5.51 (PL 82 302C).   [d] Isidore, *Etymologiae* 8.5.47 (PL 82 302B).   [e] *Sentences* 1.19.7 (PL 192 575), quoting Augustine, *Contra Maximinum* 2.10.1 (PL 42 764).   [f] Hilary, *De Trinitate* 4.12, 6.5, 6.10 (PL 10 105A, 160B, 164A-B).   [g] Hilary, *De Trinitate* 4.12, 6.5 (PL 10 105A-B, 160C).

Book 1

called a patripassian, as were Noetus and Praxeas.[94] Nestorius claimed that Jesus is [two beings,] "one the Son of God, and the other the son of a man."[a] But since our sophists argue that these [**38**] monstrosities arose among heretics, and outside the Church, I shall pursue these matters no further, even though they are innumerable.

Err, 38v

I now turn my attention to the sophists themselves and their Church, demonstrating in particular that they are actually Nestorians. For in reality they profess two sons, even though, like Nestorius himself, they would deny it. For as is apparent from the disputations [with the Nestorians] as related by Maxentius of Constantinople,[b] and as Liberatus instructs us in his account of Nestorius's beliefs as reported by Cyril,[c] Nestorius never admitted [that he believed in] two sons,[95] but defended himself by means of various artful tricks and evasions, just as today's sophists do. Just read [Maxentius and Liberatus], and you will clearly see that these sophists of ours are actually Nestorians and detestable in the eyes of God.

Err, 38v

[*Trinitarians Believe in Two (or More) Sons*]

Athanasius, preeminent among the trinitarians, makes out in his dialogues[96] that there are two sons, because [he writes that] there are truly two who were born and two who were begotten.[d] And in *On the Arian and Catholic Confession* he teaches that the Son of man should be understood as the human being whose body was assumed [by God] and not the actual Son of God. He says that the Son of man was filled with the Son of God.[e] Thus, not only does he

---

[a] Isidore, *Etymologiae* on Sabellius and Noëtus: 8.5.41-42 (PL 82 301C-302A); on Nestorius: 8.5.64 (PL 82 304A). On Nestorius, see A.R1.95.
[b] Maxentius, *Dialogi* (PG 86a 125A-B).   [c] Liberatus, *Breviarium causae* (PL 68 986C-D).   [d] [Athanasius], *De nominibus sanctissimae Trinitatis* (PL 62 265C-D); *De fide sua* (PL 62 292C-D); *De assumptione hominis* (PL 62 264A).   [e] [Athanasius], *De ariana et catholica confessione* (PL 62 303D-304A).

grant that there are two sons, one the Son of man, the other the Son of God, but also that there are two sons of God: one a metaphorical son, the other a natural one. For [according to Athanasius] this entire human being, Christ, is now the Son of God by means of the figure of speech [*communicatio*] *idiomatum*, while prior [to the incarnation], there was another being who was the real, although incorporeal, Son of God. Consequently, there are two Sons of God.

Similarly, in his dialogue *On the Assumption of Man*, Athanasius maintains that the "assumed" man, whom others refer to as "a human nature," is, *according to the flesh, the first born son among many brothers*, and thus he is called the Son of man.[a] For if the human being who is assumed is a man and is begotten, then he is a son. Nevertheless, this sophist concludes that there is one son because there is just one composite person. Athanasius teaches about a composite person in his letter to Epictetus, denying that the man and the Word make a single substance.[b]

Jerome, in his letter to Pope Damasus[97] known as *The Exposition of the Faith*, and John of Damascus, in book 3 of *On the Orthodox Faith*, say that in Christ there are "two perfect and complete substances, the substance of God and the substance of a human being."[c] The word "son" is a substantive noun [that is, a noun denoting substance].[d] Consequently each substance is a Son. As John of Damascus says, "God wholly assumed everything that makes up our [human] nature, with all its [39] attributes and all its properties intact."[e] Therefore, he took upon himself the whole Son.

---

[a] [Athanasius], *De assumptione hominis* (PL 62 258C, 262D-264A), referring to Rom 1:3, 8:29   [b] Athanasius, *Epistola ad Epictetum* 4 (PG 26 1055B).   [c] *Sentences* 3.2.1 (PL 192 759), quoting Pelagius, *Libellus fidei ad Innocentum Papam* (not Jerome; see A.R1.97). Following this, Peter Lombard quotes something similar from John of Damascus, *De fide orthodoxa* 3.4 (PG 94 998A).   [d] See A.R1.63.   [e] *Sentences* 3.2.1 (PL 192 759), quoting John of Damascus, *De fide orthodoxa* 3.6 (PG 94 1006B).

Book 1

Augustine, too, both denies and affirms that there are two sons. For in book 2 of *On the Trinity* he says that "the Son of man is assumed" while the one who assumes him is the Son of God.[a] The seed of Abraham is assumed, and this "seed of Abraham" is a son of Abraham.[b] Therefore, it is a son of Abraham who is assumed. In book 13 of *On the Trinity* [Augustine] says that "the Word is the true Son of God, and the flesh the true Son of man."[c] In his *Enchiridion*[d] [Augustine] says that the Word is "God, born of God; the man, however, is born of Mary."[98] And in *Against Felicianus* he says that in Christ "the Son of God is one thing and the Son of man another, just as in a man the soul is one thing and the body another." Then, a little later [in the same work] he says, "Mary gave birth. She did not give birth to the Son of God; she gave birth to [Christ]," the Son of man.[e]

I look with horror upon such blasphemy. [To claim] that Mary did not give birth to the Son of God! Therefore, I decline to cite any more evidence, since anyone can already clearly see, right before their eyes, [that these people are claiming] that there are two [sons] who were begotten and two [sons] who were born.

I know that they claim, by means of the figure of speech known as [*communicatio*] *idiomatum*, that the Son is said to have been born of Mary. And by means of this same figure of speech they say that the man [Jesus] is the Son of God. But these figures of speech do not make it any less true that, by actual begetting, there are two who were begotten, and two sons. In fact, there are three. For if this human being who was assumed is the son of Mary, and if this Deity is the Son of God, and if both of them together form a unity, then there is now a third son, who is a composite formed from the other two.

---

[a] Augustine, *De Trinitate* 2.11 (PL 42 851).   [b] Gal 3:16.   [c] Augustine, *De Trinitate* 13.24 (PL 42 1033).   [d] Augustine, *Enchiridion* 38 (PL 40 251).   [e] [Augustine], *Contra Felicianum* 11 (PL 42 1167).

The sophists deny that the Word and the man are a single substance, fearing that this substance might seem to be a fourth person in their Trinity, thus creating a quaternity in the divine. Athanasius makes this argument in the above-mentioned letter to Epictetus.[a] In order to avoid the appearance of a quaternity, Augustine, in his Tractates 27 and 99 on the Gospel of John and also in his letter to Honoratus, says that [the Son] is one composite person.[b] For if the man [Jesus] is a person, then he is a fourth person.

[*The Trinity Contains Four (or More) Persons*]

Err, 39r

Having shown that [the sophists] really [believe in] three sons, I shall now show in another way that there is a quaternity in [their conception of] divinity. Joachim [of Fiore] alleged that Peter Lombard made a quaternity in the divine. But he himself made God a collectivity, as [Pope Innocent III] claimed in the chapter "We Condemn" in *On the Supreme Trinity and the Catholic Faith*.[99] According to Peter Lombard and all the rest [of the sophists], the [divine] essence is a nature that neither begets like the Father, nor is begotten like the Son, nor proceeds like the Holy Spirit. Rather [the essence] is "a kind of supreme being."[c] From this [Joachim] inferred **[40]** a fourth image [of the divine] and, therefore, a quaternity.

Let me add another argument to that of Joachim. In the view of all trinitarians, the Trinity itself is not a person. For as Augustine says in book 5 and book 8 of *On the Trinity*: "The Father is not the Trinity, nor is the Son the Trinity, nor is the Holy Spirit the Trinity," rather together

---

[a] Athanasius, *Epistola ad Epictetum* 2 (PG 26 1054A).   [b] Augustine, *In evangelium Iohannis* 27.4, 99.1(PL 35 1617, 1886); *Epistulae* 140.12 (PL 33 543).   [c] *Sentences* 1.5.5 (PL 192 536). The phrase "a kind of supreme being" (*quaedam summa res*) is found, in a somewhat different context, in Augustine, *De doctrina Christiana* 1.5 (PL 34 21).

Book 1

they form the Trinity.[a] Therefore they are collectively called the Trinity. Furthermore, in books 2 and 3 of *Against Maximinus*, Augustine says that the Trinity is "three joined together."[b] Therefore, God, who is the Trinity, is a collective God; and the essence, which is the Trinity, is a kind of collectivity. But if [the Trinity] is only one being, it must be a fourth being.

Confused about this, Augustine (in Book 7 of *On the Trinity*), and the rest of the sophists who came after him, say that the essence is not predicated of persons as a material substance, as when we say "three statues are made of a single [metal], gold"; nor as [human] nature is predicated of temperaments, as when we say that "three men are all of one nature; nor as genus is predicated of species; nor as species is predicated of individuals; nor as a container is of its contents; nor as the greater is predicated of lesser things"; nor as the whole is of its parts; nor as a sum is of numbers.[c] Rather, [the essence] is an illusion predicated on illusions.

When God is spoken of as threefold, or triune, the assertion is open to question. For in *Etymologies* Isidore says that God is "triune, multiple, and numerable, because the Trinity is a unity of three."[d] In Tractate 6 on the Gospel of John, Augustine says "[I have said] God three times [but not three gods]."[e] Thus the question arises, does this number grow from a unity into a triplicity? There can be no number unless there is more than one unity; therefore, [according to the sophists] in God there are many unities.[100]

---

[a] Augustine, *De Trinitate* 5.11 (PL 42 918) and preface to book 8 (PL 42 947). [b] Augustine, *Contra Maximinum* 1.10, 2.10.2 (PL 42 751, 765). On the numbering of the books in *Contra Maximinum*, see A.R1.38. [c] *Sentences* 1.19.12 (PL 192 576), referring to Augustine, *De Trinitate* 7.11 (PL 42 943-945). [d] *Sentences* 1.24.10 (PL 192 587), referring to Isidore, *Etymologiae* 7.4.1 (PL 82 271A). [e] Augustine, *In evangelium Iohannis* 6.2 (PL 35 1425).

To ask whether the Father begot [a Son] once, as if in an instant of time, and then ceased begetting, or whether he is continuously begetting the Son, is an empty exercise. For [the sophists] would have us believe that this begetting has neither a beginning nor an end, but is always in the process of occurring.[101] According to them, the second being is continuously born and begotten — just as in the case of the procession of the third being, which they say is continuously being breathed into existence.

[*The Procession of the Holy Spirit is Incomprehensible*]

Err, 39v But now we come to another, far more trenchant question: What is the difference between to proceed and to be begotten? Why is the third being not said to be begotten, and why is it not called a Son, like the second? Why is the [41] second being not said to be breathed forth as the third one is? For there is equal reason [to describe either of them in either way], since both are incorporeal, alike, and co-equal. Gregory [of Rimini] says that it is impossible for him to understand this question, although he professes to believe [these things].[a] As if true faith were possible without comprehension and understanding!

About this distinction between proceeding and begetting, see what the scholastics say [in their commentaries] on *Sentences*, book 1, distinction 13. Spurred on by the three sons of Beelzebub, they spew forth the devil's own prodigious monstrosities and demonic illusions, accompanied by their own "relations" and "formalities."[b]

Athanasius, in books 2 and 3 of *On the Holy Spirit*,[102] says that it is not possible to give a reason why the Son is not called the Holy Spirit or the Holy Spirit the Son.[c] After

---

[a] Gregory of Rimini, *Super primum et secundum sententiarum* 1.13.1.
[b] See, for example, Duns Scotus, *Reportata super primum sententiarum*, dist. 13.   [c] Athanasius does not say this in *De sancto spiritu*. For an explanation of Servetus's reasons for making this claim, see A.R1.102.

Book 1

Athanasius, Augustine busied himself with this question in numerous places (books 2, 9, and 15 of *On the Trinity*;[a] book 3 of *Against Maximinus*;[b] question 10 of *To Orosius*;[c] and tractate 99 on the Gospel of John[d]). He finally admitted that he did not know "the difference between begetting and procession."[e]

In John 3 the Holy Spirit is said to be [both] begotten and born. *That which is begotten of the Spirit is Spirit; that which is born of the Spirit is Spirit.*[f] Thus, in dialogue 3, Athanasius understands these words to mean that the Holy Spirit is born from God.[g] And in his book *On the Profession of the Catholic Rule*, he approves the idea that the Paraclete Spirit is God, since it is begotten by and born of God.[h] The Son is also clearly said to proceed in John 8.[i]

Therefore, just as the Spirit proceeds, so it is born, and just as the Son is born, so he proceeds. God is called the *Father of spirits*, the *Father of lights*, the *Father of glory*,[j] and the Father of the Holy Spirit who is born of God. If, without either a "real distinction" or a metaphysical begetting, God is called the Father of the Holy Spirit, then he may also be called the Father of the Word. I shall [later] present an even stronger argument for why the Son is present in the

Err, 39v

---

[a] Augustine, *De Trinitate* 2.5, 9.1, 15.45-48 (PL 42 848, 959-961, 1092-1096). Most of the citations listed here can be found in *Sentences* 1.13.3-4 (PL 192 555-556). [b] Augustine, *Contra Maximinum* 2.14.1 (PL 42 770-771). What Servetus called book 3 of *Against Maximinus* is book 2 in modern editions; see A.R1.38. [c] The work called *To Orosius* here is not Augustine, *Ad Orosium contra Priscillianistas et Origenistas*. Instead it is [Augustine], *Dialogus quaestionum LXV sub titulo Orosii percontantis et Augustini respondentis* (PL 40 737). Servetus copied the misleading citation from Peter Lombard. [d] Augustine, *In evangelium Iohannis* 99.8-9 (PL 35 1890). [e] Augustine, *Contra Maximinum* 2.14.1 (PL 42 770). [f] John 3:6. These are two alternative translations of this verse; the Greek word includes both meanings, "begotten" and "born." [g] [Athanasius], *De nominibus sanctissimae Trinitatis* (PL 62 266A). [h] [Athanasius], *De professione regulae catholicae* (PL 62 283D). [i] John 8:42. [j] Heb 12:9; James 1:17; Eph 1:17.

Word, based on the prefiguration of Christ [in the Old Testament],[a] without which all the sophists' talk of sonship is incomprehensible.

John of Damascus resisted making a distinction between begetting and procession because [it seemed to him] incomprehensible.[b] It is incomprehensible that three [geometrical] points should be one point, wafting variously here and there.[103] It is [also] incomprehensible that one simple essence could contain within itself three beings, the first of which [42] is continuously bringing forth the second, so that those two beings can then continuously breathe out a third from within themselves; and that "on the throne of majesty" this set of triplets would "sit on a triclinium."[c]

[*God is Indivisible and Yet Divided*]

Err, 40v   Despite all these deviations and deformities, the three beings are said to be equal and of equal power. Indeed, as Augustine says in *Against Maximinus*, the Son has the power to beget another, incorporeal son, and this other son, in turn, has the power to beget a grandson, thus creating a quaternity, and even a quintuplicity, in the Godhead.[d] The third person also has the power to beget a real son. Thus it is possible to have an infinite number of equal, invisible gods, as many as can be found in Boccaccio's entire *Genealogy* [*of the Pagan Gods*].[e] Who would think that such horrendous ideas as these could proceed from the good Spirit? Furthermore, according to Augustine, the third being can, by itself, breathe out, incarnate itself, and create another saviour.[f]

---

[a] This argument will be developed in book 3.   [b] John of Damascus, *De fide orthodoxa* 1.8 (PG 94 819A, 823A).   [c] See A.R1.57-58.
[d] Augustine, *Contra Maximinum* 2.12.3 (PL 42 768).   [e] Giovanni Boccaccio, *Genealogia deorum gentilium* (1360; first printed in 1472), an extensive dictionary of classical mythology by the author of the *Decameron*.   [f] Augustine, *Contra Maximinum* 2.17 (PL 42 783-784). See also Augustine, *De Trinitate* 5.14 (PL 42 920).

Book 1

Nevertheless [the sophists] now say that only the second being has a body, and that it alone is united as a *suppositum* to a human nature.[104] A great multitude of questions arises from this. [For instance,] how is it that only the second person creates, supports, gives voice to, and defines the limits of the dependence[105] of this connotative human being, when all of these beings exist simultaneously, each of them in each of the others, and all of them in all of the others?[a] Although everyone says, "The outward actions of the Trinity are indivisible,"[106] here God is clearly being divided — either that, or it is necessary to "Scotusize" him.[107] On the subject of this figment, the Scotist realists boast that Ockham was forced to admit their truth,[b] and accept that there are [real] "relations" [in the Trinity].[108]

Athanasius, in his little work *On the Unity of the Faith, To Theophilus*, says that the Trinity was born of Mary and that it was the Trinity that assumed a body, because the Trinity is always a unity and its actions indivisible.[c] And therefore it was the Trinity that descended to the Jordan and the Trinity who said, "*This is my son.*"[d] Augustine teaches exactly the same thing at the end of book 4 and elsewhere in *On the Trinity*.[e] If the Trinity said, "This is my son," then [Christ] must be the son of the Trinity, even though [the trinitarians] deny this. At the end of book 1 of the dialogues,[f] as well as in *On the Unity of the Faith, to Theophilus*,[g] Athanasius says that the Father, the Word, and the Spirit are all in Christ.[109]

In *On the Orthodox Faith*, book 3, chapters 6 and 7, John of Damascus also affirms, based on passages from the

Err, 40v-41r

---

[a] *Sentences* 1.19.5 (PL 192 574), based on Augustine, *De Trinitate* 6.12 (PL 42 932).   [b] Ockham, *Super sententiarum* 1.26.1.   [c] [Athanasius], *De unitate fidei* (PL 62 285C).   [d] Matt 3:17; see also Mark 1:11, Luke, 3:22.   [e] Augustine, *De Trinitate* 4.30 (PL 42 910).   [f] [Athanasius], *De unitate sanctissimae trinitatis* (PL 62 243D, 246B).   [g] [Athanasius], *De fide sua* (PL 62 297B); the citation of *De unitate fidei* is a mistake.

writings of Athanasius [43] and Cyril, that the entire Trinity — and thus the whole and complete nature of God — is united to the whole and complete nature of the human being [Jesus].[a] Since the Holy Spirit and the Father are both present as substance in the human being, it is consequently impossible to determine what proportion of each of those three beings is present in the human being. For the human being, the Son, contains hypostatically in himself the Word and the Spirit, the entire the fullness of God.

Let us now examine some further examples of [the sophists'] foolishness. If the Word had "assumed" a female, they would have called the Word the Son of God and the woman the daughter of man. This would clearly indicate that there are two children. The Son of God himself would then be a woman, or else a masculo-feminine androgyne.[110] If, in this way, angels could clothe themselves in asses' bodies, [the sophists] would have to admit that angels are asses, that angels die in asses' skins, and that angels are four-footed creatures with long ears. Following this same line of reasoning they would also have to concede that God himself is an ass,[111] that the Holy Spirit is a mule, and that the Holy Spirit would die when the mule did.[b] What an utterly dimwitted herd of cattle [these sophists are]! No wonder then that the Turks laugh more at us than they do at asses and mules.[112] For we have become *like horses and mules, which have no understanding.*[c] What great blindness!

Err, 12r

[*Contradictory Models of the Trinity*]

No one can be brought to understand that a human being was begotten by God.[113] The great Augustine, in *On [Faith and] the Creed* and in book 1 of *On the Predestination of the Saints*, says that Jesus Christ was assumed by the Son

---

[a] John of Damascus, *De fide orthodoxa* 3.6-7 (PG 94 1007B, 1011A-B).
[b] See *Restoration*, 199-200 (dialogue 1).   [c] Ps 32:9.

of God, and that Jesus Christ was [thereby] united with the Son of God.[a] In the *Enchiridion*, Augustine, deluded by his own metaphysics, was unable to comprehend that the man Jesus, because he was begotten by the Holy Spirit, ought to be called the son of the Holy Spirit.[b] For if there is a third distinct being that begets, then [this being] is a father.

The eminent Athanasius, in *On the Arian and Catholic Confession*, also maintains that Jesus Christ is united to the Son of God and that Jesus Christ is filled with the Son of God.[c] Basil the Great, in book 2 of *Against Eunomius*, twists his own words, with remarkable futility, in order to pronounce the Son "begotten" but not "something begotten."[d] That great theologian, Gregory of Nazianzus, who came after Athanasius, declares that the second being was begotten, while the third being is neither begotten nor unbegotten,[e] neither able nor unable to be born. This point of view is also adopted by Augustine and others.[f]

Err, 41v

Whether the third being proceeds from the Father [**44**] and the Son, or from the Father alone, as the Greeks contend,[114] is a bitterly-contested question, which I shall easily deal with later.[g] I wonder why they do not also debate the question of whether the second [being] proceeds from the third, since "things may be the causes of each other."[h] For, in Isaiah 48, Christ says, "*The Lord [God] and his Spirit have sent me.*"[i] Therefore the Son is sent by the Spirit.

Err, 41v

---

[a] Augustine, *De fide et symbolo* 5, 8 (PL 40 184, 186); *De praedestinatione* 1.31 (PL 44 982). Where Servetus used the word "assume" (*assumere*), Augustine had *suscipere*, meaning to take up, raise, and acknowledge, as a child is claimed by its father. [b] Augustine, *Enchiridion* 38 (PL 40 251-252). [c] [Athanasius], *De ariana et catholica confessione* (PL 62 302C, 303D-304A). [d] Basil, *Contra Eunomium* 2.8 (PG 29 586B-587B).
[e] Gregory of Nazianzus, *Orationes* 31.7 (PG 36 139C-D). [f] *Sentences* 1.13.5 (PL 192 556), quoting Augustine, *De Trinitate* 15.47 (PL 42 1094-1095). [Augustine], *Dialogus quaestionum XLV* 2 (PL 40 734).
[g] *Restoration*, 189 (book 5). [h] De Oria, *De enunciatione* 2.2.6, quoting Aristotle, *Metaphysics* 5.2 (1013b 9-10) and *Physics* 2.3 (195a 9-10).
[i] Isa 48:16.

This is the way Ambrose explains [this passage] in book 3 of *On the Holy Spirit*.^a The Son, who comes from the Father, was sent by the Holy Spirit. In accordance with the divine nature, the Son comes from the Father; therefore, in accordance with the divine nature, he is sent by the Holy Spirit. Following the same line of thought, in book 2 of *On the Trinity*, Augustine says that the Son was sent by the Holy Spirit, just as he was by the Father.[b] Hilary, in his explanation of the passage *The Spirit of the Lord is upon me*[c] in book 8 of *On the Trinity*, says that the spirit of the Father, in all its divinity, is upon the Son. The Son is thus truly said to have been begotten by the Holy Spirit. He was fully anointed by the Holy Spirit, he is completely filled with the Holy Spirit, and the Spirit of the Lord is said to be upon him.[d]

[Then we might ask:] can the Father and the Son be described as the two original sources of the third being, or collectively as one breather [of spirit], or one original source because they are one essence, and whether, if such is the case, this essence is the original source of the [divine] breathing.[e] These are unintelligible questions. For [the sophists] would like the fourth image, which they call the essence, to be entirely superfluous. But if the essence does not breathe, then the Father and the Son do not breathe together as one.

[The sophists] do not know whether the Holy Spirit ought to be called "light from light" or "light from lights."[115] They would not dare to concede that it is the substance, or essence, of God that breathes out the Spirit or begets that which is begotten, for fear of speaking of the substance or essence in relative terms. For Augustine, the foremost instructor in this sort of sophistry, in book 5, chapter 7 of

---

^a *Sentences* 1.15.4 (PL 192 560), quoting Ambrose, *De spiritu sancto* 3.7-8 (PL 16 810C-811B). ^b *Sentences* 1.15.4 (PL 192 560), quoting Augustine, *De Trinitate* 2.8 (PL 42 849-850). ^c Luke 4:18, quoting Isa 61:1. ^d Hilary, *De Trinitate* 8.23-25 (PL 10 253A-254B). ^e This question is discussed in Duns Scotus, *Ordinatio* 1.12.1.

On the Trinity, promulgates this rule: "What is spoken of relatively does not indicate substance."[a] Why then do they admit that God begot the Son? And that God begot God?

Now, if God is spoken of relatively, that does not indicate substance, and [therefore] God is not a substance. As they say, God begot, but did not beget a substance; therefore, he begot a property. But what they assert is contradictory: "Essence did not beget essence," but "God did beget God."[b] **[45]** Substance begot substance and substance did not beget substance. Nature begot nature, light begot light, wisdom begot wisdom, reason begot reason, spirit begot spirit, love begot love, and will begot will. [God] begot and did not beget. Although the Father was Wisdom and Reason, and begot them, the Father was not the *sophos logos* [the Word of Wisdom], because he begot it.[116]

Read the questions Augustine raises in books 6 and 7 of *On the Trinity*.[c] If one says "God from God," then why not "essence from essence"? If one says "wisdom from wisdom," then why not "reason from reason"? If "person from person" means that there are two persons, why doesn't "wisdom from wisdom" mean that there are two wisdoms? [Why doesn't] "light from light" mean that there are two lights? [And why doesn't] "love from loves" mean that there are three loves?

They say that it is of great importance whether "notions" are common or whether they, instead, are constitutive of persons;[117] whether the acceptance of terms is complete or incomplete, and whether the distribution [of the terms of a syllogism] is complete or incomplete. Everything both is and is not everything else. In regard to the subject with which we are dealing, all syllogisms are doomed to failure. Although A is B and A is C, nevertheless it cannot be concluded that B is C, when A is the essence, B the Father, and C the Son.[118]

Err, 42r

---

[a] *Sentences* 1.5.1 (PL 192 535), quoting Augustine, *De Trinitate* 5.8 (PL 42 916).   [b] *Sentences* 1.4.1, 1.5.5 (PL 192 534, 536).   [c] Augustine, *De Trinitate* 6.2, 7.3 (PL 42 924, 936).

Thus I prove that God is not the Trinity, based on Augustine's argument in *On the Trinity*, book 5: No one person is the Trinity; each person is God; therefore God is not the Trinity.[a] If you prefer a conclusion in terms of a universal negative,[b] the logic is as follows: Every god is a person; no person is the Trinity; therefore, there is no god who is the Trinity. Every divine essence is either the Father, or the Son, or the Holy Spirit; but neither the Father, nor the Son, nor the Holy Spirit is the Trinity; therefore there is no divine essence that is the Trinity. Regarding the particular properties of these three persons, there are countless other unresolvable syllogisms.[119]

Err, 42r   There is a lengthy discussion of "persons" in book 1 of [Peter Lombard's] *Sentences*, from distinction 25 up to distinction 35.[120] [In their discussion of *Sentences*,] Scotus and Ockham, the leaders of the [realist and nominalist] schools, seek to establish the foundations of our faith upon various notions, relations, formalities, and quiddities,[121] things that neither Christ nor his apostles ever contemplated.[122] In this chaos of confusion, in this deadly chimaera,[123] there is no [**46**] order, only everlasting horror.

[*Unanswerable Questions*]

Err, 42r-v   Why should I even bother to mention those dreadful subterfuges of the Lombard, whom the sophists venerate as their Master? Indeed, in book 1, distinction 32 of *Sentences*, he proposes questions from Augustine, about matters that neither of them understood. The first question is: Why is the Holy Spirit called the love by which the Father loves, but the Son is not the wisdom by which the Father is wise? What is the logical reason for saying, "The Father loves

---

[a] No person is the Trinity: Augustine, *De Trinitate* 5.12 (PL 42 918-919). Each of the persons of the Trinity is God: Augustine, *De Trinitate* 5.9 (PL 42 917).   [b] In Aristotelian logic a universal negative is a statement of the form "no A is B."

Book 1

with the love that proceeds from him," but not, "He is wise with the wisdom" that proceeds from him?ᵃ

Similarly, the question arises whether the Son, who, properly speaking, is wisdom itself, is wise in and of himself, or is he wise through the Father? For one is "wisdom which is begotten," and the other "wisdom which is not begotten."ᵇ And, furthermore, through which person, then, will the Holy Spirit be wise? Through whom do he and the Son love? Further on, in distinction 33, in the section beginning, "But perhaps [you might ask]," is Hilary's unresolveable question: "What is the reason for saying that properties cannot be in the persons [of the Trinity] without defining them, while saying that they are in the [divine] essence in such a way that they do not define it?"ᶜ

Who, I ask you, other than someone who is completely senseless, could stand to listen to such *disputes about words*ᵈ without laughing? In neither the Talmud nor the Quran are there such horrible blasphemies. But we have become so accustomed to hearing them that we find nothing extraordinary in them. Future generations, however, will find them astonishing. Indeed, they are even more astonishing than the demonic inventions that Irenaeus attributes to the Valentinians.¹²⁴

Therefore, may the Lord Jesus Christ, the true Son of God, our saviour and liberator, deliver us from these monstrosities. Amen.

Err, 42v

ᵃ *Sentences* 1.32.3 (PL 192 608), referring to Augustine, *De Trinitate* 7.1 (PL 42 933). Augustine was discussing the meaning of 1 Cor 1:24 ("Christ the power of God and the wisdom of God"): "Does this mean that God is the Father of his own wisdom and power, so that he is wise with the same wisdom which he has begotten and powerful with the same power which he has begotten?"   ᵇ *Sentences* 1.32.4 (PL 192 608).
ᶜ *Sentences* 1.33.8 (PL 192 612), referring to Hilary, *De Trinitate* 2.9-11 (PL 10 58A-59B). The passage continues: "I answer you this time with Hilary ... I don't know."   ᵈ 1 Tim 6:4.

DE TRINITATE
DIVINA LIBER SECVN-
dus, quorundam locorum expo-
sitionem continens.

SVperiore libro, post tria de Christo axiomata, tria in eũ pharisæorũ, & totidẽ sophistarũ argumenta, plurima sunt à nobis in mediũ ꝓducta, ac trinitariorũ sophistarũ mõstra ferè oĩa patefacta. Hoc iã secundo libro, odorẽ illũ cælestem sequuti, locos aliquot enarrabimus, vt sensim nobis aperiant scripturę de Christo. Si qua verò supererit aliquando difficultas, in sequentibus penitus tolletur. Nõ enim possunt omnia in quouis loco cõmodè exponi, in re hac præsertim tã ardua, & tanta tenebrarum nostri seculi confusione.

Primus erit locus euangelij Ioãnis, In principio erat λο- *Primus* γίς. Propriè significat λογές internã rationem, & externũ *locus.* sermonẽ. Quoquo modo est repræsentatio certa. Repræsentatio erat, idealis ratio, seu relucẽtia Christi i mẽte diuina, sicut i nobis, tã interna ratio, quã externus sermo, est relucẽtia, seu repræsentatio rei alicuius. Omnis logos est repræsentatio quędam, & lucida repræsentatio, sicut erat lux & logos. Omnis itẽ sapiẽtia est naturalis relucẽtia rei ꝓpositæ. At ꝗ ita, vt erat Christus princeps omniũ propositus i mẽte diuina, ita naturaliter & hypostaticè relucebat. Hic sapiẽtia ipsa Dei olim dicta est ἀπαύγασμα, relucẽtia: et Christus ipse, q ibi relucebat, ab apostolo hodie dicitur ἀπαύγασμα, relucẽtia gloriosa. Qualiter aũt relucẽtia ipsa ꝓdierit, visibilis apparuerit, & sine aliqua dei mutatiõe caro facta fuerit, postmodũ ostẽdemus. Fuit verè fulgor diuinus, homine ab æterno referẽs, & eũ mũdo proferens. Cũ Ioãne verè

On the Divine Trinity

Book 2

An explanation
of some Bible passages

[47] In the preceding book, after presenting three propositions about Christ, three arguments about him by the Pharisees, and as many by the sophists, we presented many other arguments, and exposed nearly all the monstrosities of the sophistic trinitarians. Now, in book 2, following that heavenly trail, we will discuss a number of passages, so that what the scriptures have to say about Christ may gradually be revealed to us. Any difficulty that might remain will be thoroughly dealt with in the following books. For amid the great confusion of this dark time, not everything about any particular passage can be neatly explained, especially when dealing with such a difficult subject.

Passage 1
[John 1:1: In the beginning was the Word, and the Word was with God, and the Word was God.]

The first passage is from the Gospel of John: *In the beginning was the* λόγος (*logos*, word). The word λόγος properly signifies both inner thought and outward speech. In both cases, it means an accurate representation. It was a representation, an ideal thought or radiant reflection[1] of Christ in the divine mind. In the same way, our inner thoughts, like our outward speech, are the reflection or representation of some thing. The entire *logos* is a representation, and a luminous one, since it *was the light*^a as well as the *logos*. Likewise, all wisdom is a natural reflection of something set before it. And thus, since Christ was the first thing set forth in the divine mind, he was naturally and hypostatically reflected. Hence in an earlier age the wisdom of God was called ἀπαύγασμα (*apaugasma*, radiant reflection),[2] and Christ himself, who was reflected there, is called by the apostle [Paul] ἀπαύγασμα, the glorious reflection.[3] We will presently show how that reflection was produced, appeared visibly, and, without any alteration in God, was made flesh. This truly was the divine radiance, which brought forth a man from eternity, and revealed him to the world.

Err, 47r

In accordance with the precise meaning of the word λέγω (*lego*), which is: "I say, I speak," we can rightfully say, along with John [48], that the λόγος was the utterance — the externally perceptible word, or speech — of an ideal thought at the beginning of the world. Likewise, the rest of Scripture sets forth the Word — because *God said, God spoke* — not with *empty words*,[b] but with speech made visible. This was because God, through this speech, through this Word, wished to manifest himself to the world, and to appear outwardly.

Err, 48r

The older apostolic tradition understands the Word to be a disposition of God, a clear and visible outward dispensation. Irenaeus and Tertullian call this οἰκονομία (*oikonomia*, economy), disposition, or dispensation.[c] The Word by which God was made manifest was, according to the divine disposition, in God himself, as the visible essence, the oracle in the cloud[d] — so that, by God's great artistry, whoever hears the Word will also see it. This was the Word in substantial form, the oracle in the fire,[e] a visible divinity, God personified. This was called *Elohim*, God seen with a human

---

[a] John 1:4, 9. [b] Eph 5:6. [c] See A.R1.47. [d] Matt 17:5, Mark 9:7, Luke 9:35. [e] For example, Ex 3:2, Acts 2:3-4.

face: a fountain of light and the *fountain of life*,[a] Christ *with God*.[b] From this oracle, this Word, and from God personified in the person of Christ, the spirit came forth, as if from the mouth of Christ, giving life to all things and breathing the breath of life into Adam. Adam was made, body and soul, in the image of Christ, and the person of Christ was present in God when [God] said, "*Let us make man in our image and our likeness.*"[c]

Err, 91r

The uttered Word of God is God himself speaking from eternity, appearing in the darkness of the cloud. After the utterance, once the shadow of darkness is removed, God is seen in the flesh of Christ. The man Jesus Christ is the Word of God, the voice of God that *proceeds* in substance *from the mouth of God*.[d] Imagine your own voice issuing from your mouth as a cloud, overshadowing a woman, becoming *fructifying dew*,[e] falling into her womb, and making her pregnant. In this way Christ was begotten in substance in Mary by the utterance of God.

Err, 48r-v

In Revelation 19, John clearly teaches that the man Jesus Christ is truly the Word [49] of God. For he is the one whom [John] saw *sitting on a white horse*,[f] and *whose name is the Word of God*.[g] Indeed he is the Word because he *proceeds from the mouth of God*.[h] John saw *the word of life* and *touched it with* his *hands* when he saw and touched the body of Christ,[i] in which *deity dwelt in bodily form*.[j] Irenaeus too proclaims that Jesus, born of Mary, whose body hung on the cross, was the Word of God after *the Word became flesh*.[k] This body is called the *bread of life*[l] and the heavenly flesh.[m] Rejecting the [*communicatio*] *idiomatum* (sharing of attributes) of the sophists, we maintain that the

Err, 48v

---

[a] Ps 36:9. [b] John 1:2. [c] Gen 1:26. [d] Matt 4:4. [e] Isa 45:8, 55:10.
[f] Rev 19:11. [g] Rev 19:13. [h] Matt 4:4. [i] 1 John 1:1. [j] Col 2:9.
[k] John 1:14. Irenaeus, *Adversus haereses*, 4.24.2 (PG 7 1050A-B), 5.18.1, 5.18.3 (PG 8 1172B-1173A, 1174A-B). [l] John 6:35, 48.
[m] See A.R1.29.

body of Christ, the very flesh of Christ, is the Word of God. For that which *proceeds from the mouth of God*[a] is the Word of God, the speech of God.

The Word of God is the seed of the begetting of Christ, which sprouted and bore fruit [in the womb of Mary].[b] The prophets teach us that the seed has sprouted.[c] This is summed up in the mystery of regeneration by the parable of [the sower]:[d] *the seed is the Word of God*,[e] just as the seed of the sower is the word of the preacher of the gospel. The word of the Gospel of Christ, sown in our heart, produces in us, by the power of the Spirit of God, a new person — the image of Christ begotten by the Holy Spirit by means of the Word of God. The Word truly begets in us an image of that utterance which was the Word that begot Christ.

In this regard it should be noted that the phrase, *the Word became flesh*,[f] is full of meaning — more than can be discussed at this time. First of all, God wanted to reveal himself in the flesh, in order to glorify the flesh. The entire mystery of the Word was the glorification of the man who was to come, just as the man [Jesus] was already *glorified* in God [*before the world was made*] (John 17).[g] Everything that God had previously performed by his Word or with his own voice, is now done by Christ in the flesh, to whom is *given* sovereignty and *power over all*.[h] The answers that Moses received from the oracle [of God], now come from the mouth of Christ. *I will put my words in his mouth, and he will speak* in my name (Deut 18).[i] *I do not speak for myself alone*, Christ said, *but speak as the Father taught me*.[j] He is said to be the Word [50] of the Father because he conveys and makes known the mind of the Father. Indeed, he is the way that the Father can be seen, tasted, touched, and

Err, 49r-v

---

[a] Matt 4:4. [b] See Mark 4:27. [c] For example, Isa 11:1, 55:10, 61:11; Zech 6:12. [d] Matt 13:3-8, 18-23; Luke 8:5-15. [e] Luke 8:11. [f] John 1:14. [g] John 17:5. [h] John 17:2. [i] Deut 18:18. [j] John 14:10, 8:28.

smelled. He is also to be understood as the *Word made flesh*, since he is begotten in the flesh by the Word uttered *in the beginning*.[a]

God thundered [4] *from on high* and his voice became *fire, cloud,* and *rain*.[b] *The Word made flesh* is understood as a person, because that face, that person, *Elohim* who created everything, existed in the flesh. This face of Christ is the face of God, which in earlier times was seen by many. The Word is made flesh in substance, for that bright cloud of the oracle, which was the glory of the Lord, became flesh in substance as the dew of the begetting of Christ.[c] And the essence of the flesh is the same as that of the Word. Indeed, the essence of being is formative light, as you will see.[d] *Err*, 16r-v

Likewise, the passage under discussion contains the meaning of the incarnation with respect to the Spirit. Just as the Word of God is made a man, so the Spirit of God is the spirit of that man, hypostatically and in substance. This will be revealed at length later, along with other mysteries of Christ.[e] Great and sublime is this mystery of Christ, which, in the time of the apostles, was not spoken of *rashly by the crowd*.[f]

Entreated by many to argue against Ebion and Cerinthus,[g] John fasted and prayed until he produced *In the beginning was the Word*.[h] It was enough for salvation to believe that Jesus was the anointed one, the Messiah, the Son of God, the Saviour. This faith alone justified ordinary people, even if they did not fully understand the divinity of Christ.

Therefore, since [the mystery of the incarnation] was known only to a few and because there was a scarcity of copies of the scriptures and general ignorance of the sacred language, as the metaphysical sophists invaded Christianity

---

[a] John 1:1, 1:14. [b] For example, 2 Sam 22:12-14 (cloud, fire, thunder); Ps 18:13 (thunder); Ps 29:7 (fire); Jer 51:16 (rain). [c] Isa 45:8, 55:10. [d] *Restoration*, 147 (book 4). [e] *Restoration*, 165 (book 5). [f] Acts 19:36. [g] Irenaeus, *Adversus haereses* 1.26.1-3, 3.11.1 (PG 7 686A-687A, 7a 879C-880A). [h] Jerome, prologue to *In evangelium Matthaei* (PL 26 18B-19B).

and cut God to pieces, the genuine [apostolic] tradition soon died out. Accounts are easily gathered from passages in Irenaeus, showing how barren knowledge of this [mystery] was in that age.[a] With each passing day this [knowledge] was being [further] corrupted, as can be seen from Tertullian.[b] Around the same time, Clement of Alexandria, in book 1 of *Stromata*, already laments that "in [preserving] the tradition of the blessed doctrine, few were like the [apostolic] fathers," and that many things had already been lost.[c] Later, in book 6, **[51]** he says that "knowledge derived from the apostles had managed to reach only a few."[d]

Faithful reader, even if you do not achieve an understanding of the manner of Christ's begetting and of his divinity in all its fullness, nevertheless always believe that he is the Messiah, your saviour, begotten by God. This is all you need to believe, in order to live in Christ.

By praying fervently, as passionately as I could, through the grace of the Anointed One, who alone is set before us as a standard, I obtained knowledge of his truth — although I am by no means perfect, nor have I comprehended it perfectly. As this concerns our present subject, the mystery of Christ — the light and the *logos*, that luminous representation — I will now properly explain the Word as set forth in John.

In the beginning was the Word, that is, the reflection of Christ, the word that represented Christ, the word that was uttered in the begetting of Christ. This reflection of Christ was *the Word with God*, existing in God himself, shining brightly in the cloud, and *was God* himself. For the sophists, however, saying "the Word was with God" is the same as saying that the second invisible being was sitting with the

Err, 50r

---

[a] Irenaeus tells how information from the time of the apostles came to the church of his time in *Adversus haereses* 3.3-4 (PG 7 849A-855A).
[b] Tertullian, *Adversus Marcionem* 1.21 (PL 2 270B).   [c] Clement of Alexandria, *Stromata* 1 prologue (PG 8 702A-703B).   [d] Clement of Alexandria, *Stromata* 6.7 (PG 9 283B).

first, metaphysically, in the second corner of the triclinium, while the third being was in the third corner.[a] They want the second being to be with the first being, but not with the divine essence, for this would have established a distinction between the second being and the essence. Therefore, either the divine essence is something other than God, or John was wrong to say that *the Word was with God*. Here I speak of essence in the manner of the sophists, as a fourth likeness containing the other three. In actuality the Word was the very essence of God, or a manifestation of the very essence of God. There was not in God any other subsistence, or hypostasis, than the Word, in that *bright cloud* in which God was at that time seen to subsist.[b] And in that [cloud] the face and person of Christ were reflected.

Err, 50v

Err, 115v

All things were made through the Word of God[c] means, according to the [sophists'] metaphysics, that the first being created everything by means of a second being — which is absurd and ridiculous. The scriptures actually teach that *all things were made through* the Word of God, because *God said, "Let there be," and it was.*[d] *By the Word of the Lord the heavens were made, for he spoke, and it came to be.*[e] Irenaeus plainly shows this in book 1, chapter 19, and book 2, chapters 2 and 56.[f] **[52]** Before him, Justin, or some other older disciple of the apostles,[5] had explained this in a similar fashion, as cited by Irenaeus, in book 4, chapter 52.[g]

Err, 50v

The Scriptures also tell us that the utterance of God was the calling of Christ.[6] God called him *from the beginning*, and by that calling brought him into being. In Isaiah 41: [*The Lord* was] *calling* [*his*] *generation from the beginning*.

Err, 50v-51r

---

[a] See A.R1.57.　[b] Matt 17:5.　[c] John 1:3.　[d] See Gen 1:3, 6, 9, etc.
[e] Ps 33:6, 9.　[f] Irenaeus, *Adversus haereses* 1.22.1, 2.2.4, 2.30.9 (PG 7 669A-B, 714B-715A, 822A-B). The chapter numbers are different from those cited by Servetus because Servetus used Erasmus's Basel edition of Irenaeus (1526), which uses numbering different from what has become standard.　[g] Irenaeus, *Adversus haereses* 4.32.1 (PG 7 1070B-1071A).

Err, 50v-51r

From the rising of the sun, he called my name.[a] And in chapter 46: [*I will accomplish all my purpose*] *calling a bird from the east, the man of my counsel from a far country: I have spoken, and I will bring him forth.*[b] And in chapter 49: *The Lord called me from the womb, and he pronounced my name.*[c] Hence, in book 2, chapter 48, Irenaeus says[d] that the generation of the Son of God is called "naming."[7]

Err, 51r

Because of this calling or naming, some say that the name of Christ was begotten from the beginning. In support of this they often cite Psalm 71: *Before the sun,* ינון שמו (*yinon shemo,* his name shall beget sons), [that is] *before the sun his name* will be begotten, or *will be continued in his sons.*[e] The literal meaning [of this text] refers to Solomon: he *will be continued in his sons in the presence of the sun, while the sun endures;* by begetting, his name will be propagated.[8] The true meaning of this passage is the propagation of the sonship of Christ among his followers.

Err, 51r

Thus "before the sun" does not mean at a time prior to the sun, but "in the presence of the sun," [that is,] *while the sun endures.* The Hebrew word ליפני (*lipne,* before) can take either meaning. It could be said of Christ that, *while the sun endures,* his name is continued, or will be continued, in his [spiritual] sons. In the future, [the Psalmist] says, he *will be continued in his sons.* And the origin of his sonship was [also] *before the sun* existed, since from the beginning his sonship was in the seed of the Word.

Passage 2

[Colossians 1:15: He is the image of the invisible God, the firstborn of all creation.]

Err, 51r

From what we have just said, we gather that Christ is the firstborn. We now add an explanation of the Apostle's words

---

[a] Isa 41:4, 25.   [b] Isa 46:11.   [c] Isa 49:1.   [d] Irenaeus, *Adversus haereses* 2.28.6 (PG 7 809A).   [e] Ps 72:17 (Pagnini).

in Colossians 1 and more fully investigate in what sense Jesus Christ is said to be the *firstborn of all creatures*. The metaphysicians assign this firstborn status to the second being. They say that his begetting cannot be described,[a] citing Isaiah 53: *who can describe his generation?*[b] But this does violence to the words of Isaiah. For what he actually says is this: *He was rejected by men, a man of sorrows, like a lamb led to slaughter, and like a sheep that is silent before the shearer; who can describe his generation?* — that is, his progeny — *for he was cut off from the land of the living*.[c] [53] In Acts 8, Philip teaches that all of this refers to Jesus.[d]

Err, 51r

As the Hebrew word דור (*dor*, generation) teaches, Isaiah does not speak of the generation of Christ by the Father, but of an evil generation of murderous Jews,[g] and [prefiguratively] of that good Christian progeny, to which Christ gave birth by his death. This will be the new heavenly progeny: so great, so excellent, and so plentiful that it cannot be described. This is similar to what we have quoted above [at the end of Passage 1]: *while the sun endures*, [Christ's] *name will be propagated in his sons*.[e] And since the Hebrew word means the propagation of sons, we can say with Isaiah, *who can describe* Christ's *generation* [of progeny]? Clearly, no one — until now.

How Christ was begotten is unknown to the world. He is that Melchizedek, of unknown ancestry (Hebrews 7).[f] *No one knew where he was from* (John 7).[g] Melchizedek is said to resemble the Son of God[h] — not the imaginary son, but the Son of man. In God there is no metaphysical begetting of a distinct being. Such a thing could not [even] be called begetting. The Word is said to be uttered, whereas a human being is begotten. The utterance of the Word in the generation of Christ by the Father is eternal; the begetting of the flesh in the mother takes place in time. Whatever happens

Err, 51r-v

---

[a] *Sentences* 1.2.6 (PL 192 528).   [b] Isa 53:8, quoted in Acts 8:33.
[c] Isa 53:3, 7, 8 (Pagnini).   [d] Acts 8:35.   [e] Ps 72:17 (Pagnini).
[f] Heb 7:3.   [g] John 7:27.   [h] Heb 7:3.

to a human being, takes place in time. Those things that are of God take place forever in the eternal present.[10]

Err, 52v-53r

Now direct your attention to this, in order to understand what it means for Christ to be the firstborn. For we gravely err when, judging according to the flesh, we suppose that there is past and future when it comes to God. God accomplishes everything without any interval of time. There is no "was" in him; instead we always find "is." Nothing is past to him; everything is present: for *to God, all things are alive.*[a] *To his eyes all things are laid bare and in plain sight.*[b] *He summons things that do not* [now] *exist as though they did.*[c] *To him a thousand years* are as a moment, and a moment of *one day is as a thousand years.*[d]

Err, 53r

The prophets teach that there are no distinctions of time in God. They often "substitute one time for another," make known "future events as if they were past,"[e] and consider all things in relation to the present. The reckoning of time is not necessary for God, but it arose because [time] is necessary for human beings. To measure it the *heavenly lights* were set in place so that there would be fixed *seasons, days, and years.*[f] Therefore he who made time, had no time [**54**] before time, nor did he who established the beginning, have a beginning before the beginning. This is firm and solid reasoning. For God, who created time, in no way made himself subject to time. Numenius has a strong argument for this: "Whatever is understood as changing in the past or in the future has an element of incompletion: for the future is not yet, and the past is no more. But in God, because he is the first being and the highest agency, nothing is lacking."[11] Therefore, in the presence of [God], there is no variation in time.

Err, 80v-81r

Many people err in dealing with this subject. For they argue that the passage of time causes change in an unchangeable God, saying, "Before a thing existed, [God] willed it to exist in the future; and now, since it exists already, he does

---

[a] Luke 20:38. [b] Heb 4:13. [c] Rom 4:17. [d] 2 Pet 3:8, quoting Ps 90:4.
[e] Pagnini, *Hebraicas institutiones* 4.6.8. [f] Gen 1:14.

not will it to exist in the future." Thus, with the "fixed point" in this proposition being "this thing will be," they imply that God had first to will it, and then not to will it. Hence, there are some who, having based knowledge of the future on God's past, improperly conclude that God's will is in bondage,[a] and that there is a fated necessity in everything.

My answer to all this is that, for God, predestination is indistinguishable from what exists. "Did will," "is going to will," the future and the past, are not found in God. For him, something happens and ceases happening just as he wills it. And just as he freely wills and can do things, so he gives to humanity free will and ability — within certain limits. God does this with divine craftsmanship, just as there is a divine skill in human beings. The divine mind is reflected in humankind. Certainly Adam, Christ, and the angels possessed free will. Whatever was or is, free will is obvious proof that predestination is not fate, nor binding by necessity.

Therefore they are deceived who believe that, because of the preordination of God, everything happens out of necessity. They measure and limit the power of God by [human] capacity. Applying such necessity to God is odious, as it includes both time and privation. Those who think that everything occurs out of necessity, do not understand that God is above time, above all necessity. They do not consider that the dispositions of God are [**55**] beyond their understanding. If the past "was," and now "is not," then once God has preordained something, his hands are tied. For not only does the bondage of God's will ensue, but also a limitation of his power. Unfortunately, in their dialogues Lucian[12] and Valla[13] reason according to the perceptions of the flesh. To this day most people continue in this error.[14]

A single argument suffices to refute necessity and the bondage of the will: that it is possible to speak of that which neither is, nor was, nor will be. Christ could have asked for

Err, 80v-81r

Err, 81r

---

[a] Perhaps a reference to Martin Luther's *De servo arbitrio* (*The Bondage of the Will*).

legions from the Father, but did not.[a] David could have killed Saul, but did not.[b] Paul could have accepted wages, but did not.[c] There are others who could have done many things that they did not, as Ecclesiasticus says.[d] Therefore there is an ability to choose freely, granted to humanity by God; but those who believe that God's predestination is bound to necessity are utterly unable to see it. God *could have saved* Christ *from death* (Hebrews 5).[e] Thus Christ says, "*Abba, Father, [all things are] possible for you*" (Mark 14).[f] Where, then, is the inevitability of predestination? If [the Crucifixion], so notably preordained and so often foretold, could have turned out otherwise, why not other actions as well?

God can make it possible for one who has fallen *to stand*.[g] He can make *a camel go through the eye of a needle*.[h] *From these stones God is able to* make human beings.[i] He *is able to do more* for us *than anything we can ask for or imagine* (Ephesians 3).[j] It was in the power of Ananias not to sell the land; and once it was sold it was in his power to keep the whole price, says Peter.[k] Yet because he abused his power, he was justly punished. Otherwise, if he had been compelled by necessity, then [his punishment] would have been an injustice.[l] For, according to the scriptures, necessity provides an excuse.[m] Whenever we so wish, we can do good (Mark 14).[n] This is the gift of God, that it is in our power to act according to our own free will.

Paul teaches that people are under no necessity of acting, but have the power of their own wills (1 Corinthians 7,

---

[a] Matt 26:53. [b] 1 Sam 24:3-7. [c] 1 Cor 9:17-18. [d] Ecclus 31:10. [e] Heb 5:7. [f] Mark 14:36. [g] Rom 14:4. [h] Matt 19:24; Mark 10:25; Luke 18:25. [i] Matt 3:9. [j] Eph 3:20. [k] Acts 5:4. The story of the pretended donation of Ananias and Sapphira to the church is told in Acts 5:1-11. [l] See Erasmus, *De libero arbitrio*, C4v. [m] 4 Macc 5:13, 8:22. [n] Mark 14:7: "For you always have the poor with you, and you can show kindness to them whenever you wish; but you will not always have me."

2 Corinthians 9 and Philemon).[a] He teaches us that we should *not abuse power*;[b] therefore we have power. *He gives power* to those who come to Christ (John 1).[c] **[56]** For this reason, unbelievers, and those who *blaspheme against the [Holy] Spirit*,[d] will be punished more severely than Sodom, for they could have believed, and would not, abusing the power they had been given. *God, in his kindness, leads* us *to repentance*, offers the *opportunity to repent*. By resisting [God], we are *accumulating wrath* (Romans 2 and Wisdom 12).[e] He *stretches out* his *hand*, that we might come to our senses, but *we would not* (Proverbs 1, Matthew 23, and Revelation 2 and 3).[f] I admit that some are not given the means to come to Christ. To this Paul answers that such is the will of God.[g] Nevertheless, *the just judgement of God*[h] will be on them, as we shall show later.[i]

Now let us provide an adequate explanation of this question. We say that all eternity is to God like the present moment, and that God, in this moment of eternity, before he created the world and in the very utterance of creation, begot in Mary a son from his own substance. Later we will clearly show that the way in which the substance of God acts is by revealing and uttering what was earlier a plan in his mind.[j]

Casting off the veil of ordinary time, consider the hour in which the body of Christ was begotten and conceived as being eternally present to God before the beginning of the world. Having granted this, you will also admit that God from eternity uttered the Word in substance, and in its utterance begot in Mary a son from his own substance. Therefore

Err, 53v-54r

---

[a] 1 Cor 7:37; 2 Cor 9:7; Phlm 1:14.   [b] 1 Cor 9:18: "What then is my reward? Just this: that in my proclamation I may make the gospel free of charge, so as not to make full use of my rights in the gospel." Latin Bibles of Servetus's day use the phrase *non abutar potestate mea in Evangelio* (not to abuse my power in the Gospel).   [c] John 1:12.   [d] Mark 3:29; Luke 12:10.   [e] Rom 2:4-5; Wisd of Sol 12:10.   [f] Prov 1:24; Matt 23:37; Rev 2:21, 3:19.   [g] Rom 9:14-16.   [h] Rom 2:5.   [i] See *Restoration*, 238 (dialogue 1).   [j] See *Restoration*, 137-149 (book 4).

the man Christ is the firstborn, and begotten from eternity, since that utterance, created out of eternity, was itself the begetting of Christ's flesh. If you ask once again, "What kind of thing was this utterance of God?" we shall clearly explain it in what follows.[a] In accordance with a definite plan, God expressed, displayed, manifested, and communicated himself to the world. For now, it is enough to say that the begetting of this man by God, which was brought to completion in substance in Mary, had its beginning in substance from eternity.

Not only that, but this very generation is the cause of the generation of all other things, since it was the beginning of everything. Until the proper time, God kept within himself the Word of the begetting of Christ, [57] using images to indicate many things for the greater expression of the glory of Christ. What wonderful artistry there is in this begetting! God made everything for the glory of Christ and begot him to be the head.[b] Just now [I told you] about Christ being the firstborn so that you might comprehend the greatest truth. In what follows you will plainly see that he existed in substance before all else, and possessed eternal substance.

A second reason that Christ is called the firstborn, is that "firstborn" is a name of dignity and of abundant blessing: as David is called firstborn in Psalm 88;[c] and in 1 Chronicles 5, Joseph is called firstborn, even the *firstborn of Israel*.[d] Thirdly, according to the flesh Christ is the *first fruits* and *firstborn of creation*.[e] For our flesh is of the second [lump of potter's clay], the lump of sin, but the flesh of Christ is of that purer first lump, which was before sin.[f] For this reason, therefore, his flesh is prior to ours, and he is the firstborn of humanity, just as he is its first fruits. Furthermore, by being set apart by the mystery of the Word, he possesses another, more divine reason for his birthright.

---

[a] In book 3. [b] See Eph 4:15. [c] Ps 89:27. [d] 1 Chr 5:1-2. [e] 1 Cor 15:20; Col 1:15. [f] Rom 9:21.

Passage 3

[Psalm 2:7: The Lord said to me, "You are my son, today I have begotten you."]

Many people think that David's verse, "*You are my son, today I have begotten you*" (Psalm 2), refers to his birthright. They explain that it means "before the world I have begotten you" and claim that it was the second being who was actually begotten here. Augustine explains this verse of the psalm in a different way, and says that the begetting of the Son is always happening and that the word "today" means a continuous generation, as if the Son of God were a kind of temporary being, who is born daily.[a]

This is sheer foolishness! For the passage is not about generation, but regeneration, as Paul shows in Acts 13: Christ is risen again, as *it is written in the Psalm, "You are my son, today I have begotten you."*[b] Here Paul clearly teaches that the word "today" refers to the day of the resurrection of Christ, and rightly so. He also says in Romans, chapter 1, that Jesus Christ is *revealed as the powerful Son of God*[c] because he was resurrected from the dead. The glorious and immortal revelation of the Son happens on this day. If he had not been resurrected, no one would have believed him to be the Son of [58] God.

Then Christ was glorified, made a son anew, and, on account of [his resurrection], a new spirit was given to us, causing us to rise again like Christ — the spirit of υἱοθεσίας (*huiothesias*, adoption), the spirit of sonship, which makes us sons by raising us up. The sonship of Christ, or the idea of a son, is imprinted in us by the power of the resurrection, and given and revealed by this new spirit. Hence Paul, in the passage cited, says that Jesus Christ was then *revealed as*

Err, 54v

Err, 55v

---

[a] Augustine, *Enarrationes in psalmos* 2.6 (PL 36 71). [b] Acts 13:33.
[c] Rom 1:4.

Err, 54v   *the Son of God by the Spirit of holiness.*[a] And it was at that time, as well, that *all authority in heaven and on earth was given* to Christ (Matthew 28).[b]

Err, 55r   Indeed, it is said that the Son is revealed with power and strength. In Psalm 2 David reflected on the power and strength of Christ's resurrection, saying, *Ask of me, and I will make the nations your heritage, and the ends of the earth your possession and you shall break them with a rod of iron.*[c] Christ mentions this same rod of iron, and the power that he received at the resurrection, in Revelation 2 and 19.[d] Because of these shared words, the psalm refers to the day of resurrection. Pointing to the day [of resurrection], Christ said, "*Henceforth, from this day forward, the Son of man shall be seated at the right hand of the strength of God*" (Matthew 26, Mark 14, and Luke 22).[e] Then *the kingdom of God has come with power*, just as *the Son of God [is revealed] with power* (Mark 9 and Romans 1).[f] For in both places [the Greek phrase] ἐν δυνάμει (*en dynamei*) is used, that is, "in strength," or "with power."[g]

Err, 55r-v   In the Epistle to the Hebrews, the apostle twice cites this passage of the Psalmist to show the great power of Christ after the resurrection: how [Christ], *having become higher than the angels*,[h] was then elevated to the right hand of God and *made a high priest forever*, when [God] *said to him*, "*Today I have begotten you*" (Hebrews 1 and 5).[i] In accordance with these words, the apostle goes on to affirm the priesthood of Christ, saying, *Christ did not exalt himself to make himself the high priest, but [was appointed by God] who said to him, "You are my son, today I have begotten you."*[j] The actual transformation of Christ into a priest occurred when he offered himself as a [sacrificial] victim in the Passion.

---

[a] Rom 1:4.   [b] Matt 28:18.   [c] Ps 2:8-9.   [d] Rev 2:26-27, 19:15.
[e] Matt 26:64; Mark 14:62; Luke 22:69.   [f] Mark 9:1; Rom 1:4.
[g] See A.R1.11.   [h] Heb 1:4. See A.E1.1.   [i] Heb 1:5, 5:5-6. Ps 2:7 is quoted in Heb 1:5 and 5:5.   [j] Heb 5:5.

Thereupon, by his resurrection, he entered into the *holy of holies*.ᵃ Therefore, Christ is said to be begotten today, because today he is made the mighty Son of glory, as though he were brought into being today.

Err, 81v

This is the sense conveyed by the Targum: *You are my son,* **[59]** "it is as if I had created you this day."¹⁵ He who is reborn today is said to be begotten today: a *new man*,ᵇ a new son, and a newly created king, *born anew* with full power. In baptism we are reborn in his likeness, and, being *raised with him*, we are said to be *born anew* (John 3 and Colossians 2).ᶜ On the day of our baptism God says to us, "*You are my son, today I have begotten you.*"

Err, 55v

The meaning [of this psalm] is made clearer by its historical context. For this and the following psalm were composed when princes conspired with Absalom against David.¹⁶ After he is restored to his kingship, David says, "*I know that today I am made king over Israel*" (2 Samuel 19).ᵈ Similarly, when we escape a great danger we are accustomed to say, "Today I am born [anew]." Above all we say it on the day when we attain a new rank. Someone who yesterday was not so great is born today, a son and a king.

Err, 56r

Today immortal sonship is given to [Christ]. Today is born an incorruptible Son, the image of his incorruptible Father, although previously he would not have been called the Son of glory. Truly, indeed, he who was not the Son yesterday, is now the Son. Truly the Son of God was dead for three days, was made a son anew, and was brought from non-being back to being. When his body was restored, Christ became a new son, and thus a son newly born. The entire generation of Christ, those who were created from the beginning of the world and had fallen victim to death, are

---

ᵃ Heb 9:3,12.   ᵇ Eph 2:15.   ᶜ John 3:3; Col 2:12. Erasmus's New Testament, like some modern translations, has not "anew" but "from above."   ᵈ 2 Sam 19:22.

restored on this day. On this day, everything is renewed; on this day, the new kingdom of Christ is established. For Christ can truly say with David, *"Today I am made king."*ᵃ

Err, 56v   Now would be a good time to hear the answers to the Christians made by the Jew, David Kimhi, in his commentary on this psalm. For the sophists used such benighted arguments that he laughed at them as though they were asses and madmen. They sought to compel [Kimhi] to believe in a mathematical and invisible Son by explaining that *I have begotten you today* means before the creation of the world. To them he shrewdly replied, "If in those eternities there were two distinct incorporeal beings together, similar to one another and equal, they were twins, not father and son."ᵇ And **[60]** likewise, if a third being of a similar kind were now added to those two equal beings, you would be justified in calling them a triple [monster] like Geryon.ᶜ

The sophists used to say that the actual generation [of the Word] from God is like [the emanation of] rays from the sun.¹⁷ [Kimhi] was horrified by such a monstrous [view of] God, particularly since this would argue separation, change, and dissimilarity in Godᵈ — just as there is separation, change, and dissimilarity between the sun and the ray. [Kimhi] also clearly recognized that the sophists were wrong about the word "today," since in Hebrew a demonstrative pronoun is used here, indicating that a certain day is meant: *You are my Son, on this day I have begotten you.*ᵉ The Targum also observed this usage.ᶠ

Err, 56v   Likewise the sophists erred by refusing to acknowledge the literal meaning given by the Jews. What could be more mad than to deny that *I will be a father to him, and he shall be a son to me*ᵍ is a literal reference to Solomon? This is made

---

ᵃ 2 Sam 19:22.   ᵇ Kimhi, *Commentarium*, 17.   ᶜ Geryon was a three-headed, three-bodied, winged giant killed by Hercules in his tenth labour.   ᵈ Kimhi, *Commentarium*, 17.   ᵉ Kimhi, *Commentarium*, 15.   ᶠ See A.R2.15.   ᵍ 2 Sam 7:14; 1 Chr 17:13.

abundantly clear in 1 Chronicles 22 and 28.[a] If it were otherwise, neither Solomon nor David nor anyone else could be called a type of Christ. For although *the testimony of Jesus Christ is the spirit of prophecy*,[b] there is another, literal sense.

We grant to the Jew that there is a literal sense [to the scriptures]. Nevertheless, we caution him that beneath [the literal sense] lies the mystery of the coming Messiah, which even [the Jews] are willing to allow,[c] because at times the wording seems to be out of the ordinary or exaggerated. For example, the king's *possessions* extend to *the ends of the earth*,[d] he *crushes the kings of the earth with a rod of iron*,[e] his sceptre is eternal,[f] he *sits upon the throne* of God[g] as king and priest,[h] and so on. In a way, these things are being said about kings, but they are more lofty than is appropriate for them.

Thus it is readily apparent that the spirit [of the words] points elsewhere — especially since words are used that do not apply to [earthly kings]. For instance, in Psalm 109, which is quoted by Christ against the Jews in Matthew 22,[i] three things are evident: that the true Messiah is a priest as well as a son of David; that his priesthood and his throne are for ever;[j] and that he is called the Lord by kings and by his own ancestors.[k] For this reason we ought to argue with the Jews as Christ did, in order that they might comprehend the true mystery that underlies [the psalm]. For they themselves **[61]** all admit that nothing written in the sacred tongue [Hebrew] is without mystery.[l]

Err, 56v

---

[a] 1 Chr 22:10, 28:6.   [b] Rev 19:10.   [c] Kimhi, *Commentarium*, 15. "There were at one time those who explained this Psalm, in the manner of our rabbis of blessed memory, as being about Gog and Magog and the King Messiah."   [d] Ps 2:8.   [e] Ps 2:2, 9.   [f] Ps 45:6: "Your throne, O God, endures for ever and ever. Your royal sceptre is a sceptre of equity." [g] 2 Chr 9:8.   [h] Ps 110:4. See also Gen 14:18.   [i] Matt 22:41-46, quoting Ps 110:1.   [j] Ps 110:4: "You are a priest for ever."   [k] Ps 110:1: "The Lord said to my lord…" interpreted in Matt 22:41-46 to mean that David calls the Messiah "Lord."   [l] See, for example, Maimonides, introduction to *Guide for the Perplexed*.

Err, 57r From what has been said it follows that, typologically speaking, the Son of man is a real man. The true sonship of the man Jesus Christ was once foreshadowed in the sonship of another man: Solomon, called the son [of David]. However, to infer, typologically, the sonship of an invisible being from the sonship of the man Solomon is [to infer] the [monstrous] sonship of a Chimaera,[a] unknown to Scripture. Such a thing cannot be deduced by typological reasoning, or by any other way of representing similitude. Neither can it be established from the truth of the resurrection of the Son, nor from the revelation of his sonship, by which Jesus himself, and not that invisible being, was revealed as the true son of God. In chapter 28 [of 1 Chronicles], God says of the true Solomon, Christ, "*I have chosen him to be my son*" before all others.[b] No other being is chosen from on high before all others, other than the man Jesus Christ who is truly the chosen Son, the most highly beloved from all eternity.

Passage 4

[Genesis 49:10: The sceptre shall not depart from Judah, nor the ruler's staff from between his feet, until Shiloh comes; and to him shall be a gathering of the peoples.]

Having arrived at the conflicts between the rabbis and the sophists, I should add another passage, in which the incredible delusions of both of these groups are constantly on display. For anyone familiar with the subject, it is certainly terrible how that perfidious Jew, known as Baal Nizzahon [Master of Polemic],[18] in discussing Genesis 49, reproaches Christianity, when he himself fails to grasp the true meaning of the passage.[19]

---

[a] See A.R1.123. [b] 1 Chr 28:6.

Here is the passage, as it is written in Hebrew:

לֹאיסור שבט מיהודה ומחקק מבין רגליו
עד כייבא שילוה ולו יקהת עמים

This translates as: *the sceptre shall not depart from Judah, nor the ruler's staff from between his feet, until Shiloh comes;*[20] *and to him shall be a gathering of the peoples.*[a]

This verse ought to be divided by punctuation marks, as is readily granted by anyone who knows the difference between the Hebrew punctuation marks *atnach* and *zakef*.[21] All agree that this sceptre is to be understood as the sceptre of David's [royal authority]. What is said about Shiloh, however, was fulfilled in Joshua 18, where almost the same words are used. *The whole congregation of the people of Israel had their assembly at Shiloh*,[b] until the relocation of the Ark [of the Covenant].[c] It was at Shiloh that the people, now wealthy, first rested. This accords with the meaning of the word שילה *Shiloh*: repose and riches, such as the Israelites came to possess, when the entire country **[62]** had been distributed to them by lot. Therefore, Shiloh came before the time of David, and, when Shiloh ceased to exist in the days of Samuel, the reign of David began.

God rejected Shiloh and chose David (Psalm 77),[d] just as he rejected the synagogue and chose Christ, from whom the sceptre will never be taken away. Here [in the psalm] you can see that the mystery and loftiness of its speech are applicable to Christ alone. What Jacob actually meant was that *the sceptre must never be taken away from Judah*, which is confirmed by 2 Samuel 7, Psalm 88, and Jeremiah 33.[e] By all of these [passages] the Jews are clearly refuted. If, indeed, the sceptre is not to be taken

---

[a] The word that Servetus, like the KJV, renders as "gathering," is "expectation" in the Septuagint and the Vulgate, and "obedience" in the RSV and in much modern scholarship.   [b] Josh 18:1.   [c] 1 Sam 4:3-4.
[d] Ps 78:56-72.   [e] 2 Sam 7:16; Ps 89:3-4, 29, 36; Jer 33:14-17.

from Judah, where is it now, if not in Christ? Thus there is in this passage [of Genesis] an unmistakable prophecy about Christ and the everlasting sceptre that became his after the rejection of the synagogue.

This does not, however, rule out taking the word Shiloh literally, which Jacob's very next words clearly confirm: *binding his foal to the vine and his ass's colt to the choice vine, he shall wash his garments in wine and his cloak in the blood of grapes; his eyes shall be red from wine, and his teeth white from milk.*[a] All this came to pass at Shiloh. So fruitful did the promised land appear to Joshua upon his arrival, that one could tether his ass to a single vine and load it up with grapes. So plentiful was the wine that the clothes of the harvesters became stained with grape juice, and their eyes became ruddy from the excellence of the wine they drank. There was also such an abundance of milk, that their teeth were whitened by its frequent consumption. Thus says the good father Jacob, bestowing his worldly blessing on a carnal people.

Jacob nevertheless praises the tribe of Judah above the other tribes,[b] and he says the sceptre will abide with it: therefore that tribe held onto the kingdom most steadfastly, when the other tribes lacked the strength. For this reason, the sceptre never passed from [Judah] to another tribe. For a time Shiloh was also praised, because a double portion [of the Israelite inheritance] was allotted as the birthright of Joseph [due to Jacob having blessed both of Joseph's sons, Ephraim and Manasseh] (1 Chronicles 5 and Genesis 48).[c] Of Joseph's stock was Joshua, who established the tabernacle in Shiloh. But, as Psalm 77 says, God spurned the tabernacle of Joseph, that is, Shiloh.[d]

---

[a] Gen 49:11-12. [b] Gen 49:8. [c] Gen 48:5; 1 Chr 5:1-2. [d] Ps 78:60.

Passage 5
[Psalm 95:7-8: Today, if you hear his voice, do not harden your hearts]

The fifth passage [I shall discuss] returns to the psalmist and the word "today," which refers to the day of resurrection: *Today, if you* **[63]** *hear his voice* (Psalm 94). David sang this psalm, and a great many others, at the restoration of his kingdom, which was a type of the resurrection of Christ. He then sang *a new song*[a] for the renewal of his kingdom. The word "today" refers to the day of Christ's resurrection, which we also understand as the day of our own regeneration. *Rejoicing with great joy*,[b] this day the Prophet calls everyone to Christ.

In the Epistle to the Hebrews, chapters 3 and 4, the Apostle teaches us something similar by repeating the same word, "today."[c] [He says that] today it is given to us to enter the rest of the Lord, just as today Jesus entered into his rest. Today, the true sabbath is fulfilled for us. Today Christ, finding rest from all that he had suffered for us, gained the eternal rest of heaven, and prepared the same rest for us. Since we are resurrected with Christ, let us this day forever put aside the works of the flesh, and, every day, let us call this present day "today."[d]

The Apostle speaks about this in the passage I have just cited: *We have been made sharers in Christ, if we hold on to the original [shared] substance*[22] *firmly to the end, because it is said, "Today, if you hear his voice."*[e] Many call *our original substance* faith, by which we at first stood firm. This is certainly correct. But we should not neglect what he adds [from the psalm], because he says, *Today if you hear his voice* and also *They will not enter my rest.*[23] The Apostle teaches that "rest" was formerly to be understood as being about

---

[a] Ps 98:1.   [b] 1 Kg 1:40.   [c] Heb 3:7, 3:13. 3:15, 4:7.   [d] Heb 4:7-10.
[e] Heb 3:14-15.

the beginning of the world, but now is to be taken as referring to the end.[24]

[John] Chrysostom makes this abundantly clear in his thirteenth homily on the Gospel of John,[a] commenting on the verse, *grace for grace*.[b] He teaches that there was an old grace created [by God] for the Jews, and another, new grace, which he made for us — just as he made a new rest for us. Chrysostom teaches that one glory was given then, and another glory now, and cites Paul: we are to cross over *from one degree of glory to another* (2 Corinthians 3),[c] from righteousness to righteousness (Philippians 3),[d] *through faith for faith* (Romans 1),[e] from written law to spiritual law,[f] from *the spirit of slavery* to the spirit of liberty (Romans 8).[g] [Chrysostom] talked of a twofold adoption, a twofold covenant, a twofold sanctification, a twofold justification, a twofold temple, a twofold sacrifice, a twofold baptism, a twofold [64] circumcision, and two of all the rest [of the graces, bestowed] formerly as types, now in reality. The Apostle calls the former "the beginning," the latter "the end."

To make us sharers in the substance of God, Christ fulfilled and completed all things from the beginning to the end.[h] Thus the Apostle wishes us to pay close attention to the essence of this entire process, which he calls the hypostasis, to hold it in firm faith, and to contemplate with the living spirit the substance of the matter. The essence, the foundation, and the hypostasis of this is that we should redirect the entire process of the Law [from the law of Moses] back to its goal, Christ, in whose substance and glory we are made sharers.

Err, 95v Indeed, we take the part [of the psalm] that speaks of rest to refer to Christ, understanding that this present day

---

[a] John Chrysostom, *Evangelium secundum Ioannem,* 53r-54r (PG 59 91-93). In PG this is the first part of homily 14.   [b] John 1:16.
[c] 2 Cor 3:18.   [d] Phil 3:9.   [e] Rom 1:17.   [f] Rom 8:2.   [g] Rom 8:15.
[h] Heb 3:14.

is always the day of Christ's and our own resurrection, and that we rightly call the day [of resurrection] "today." In this, the consummation of all the ages, "today" is the seventh day from the beginning of the world, the day on which *God rested from all his works*[a] of the law. On this day, rising with Christ, we ought to put aside the works of the flesh. The unbelieving Jews are not allowed into this rest, which we, believing in the Son of God, enter today. Making no distinction between one day and another, we keep a continual, true, and spiritual sabbath, a sabbath of sabbaths, since our eternal priest is forever at rest in the tabernacle of heaven and forever reposes in us. This is the true and continual *sabbath*, which *remains for the people of God*,[b] as the Apostle says, the continuous rest of the spirit and sanctification, of which the [Hebrew] sabbath was a sign.

Err, 95v

Err, 96r

For this reason, the Apostle says that we are made sharers in Christ's rest. For this continual and perpetual rest, which he has with the Father, we now continuously enjoy by means of the spirit given by him. God did not present the rest of the spirit to our forefathers, [who lived] before the resurrection of Christ, in this way. But he will present it to you today, as you believe in him today, and rise up again with him today. Today, I say, *if today you hear his voice*. But the voice of God, to which you must attend, is that **[65]** voice from heaven [which says,] "*This is my son*."[c]

Today, therefore, O Christian reader, *do not harden your heart*,[d] but believe in the risen Son of God. For some other incorporeal being could not really die and rise again. Only that body that truly died and rose again was truly begotten by God and is truly the Son of God. This you must believe, and you must have faith in this for your salvation: that he was begotten by God for your salvation; that he is risen again; and that today he is made the Son of glory.

---

[a] Heb 4:4, quoting Gen 2:3.　[b] Heb 4:9.　[c] Luke 9:35.　[d] Heb 3:8, 3:15, 4:7, quoting Ps 95:8.

Passage 6

[Psalm 110:1: The Lord says to my lord, "Sit at my right hand, until I make your enemies your footstool."]

Err, 20v   The sixth passage is from Psalm 109: *The Lord says to my lord: "Sit at my right hand."* The sophists deduce from this a metaphysical equality between their incorporeal beings, because the same word, "Lord," is used for both: *the Lord says to my lord*.[a] But perhaps we ought forgive those who, not knowing the original language of sacred scripture, are unaware of their own ignorance.

Err, 20v   But, reader, if you know Hebrew, you will discover that the Prophet says: נאם יהוה לאדני "Jehovah said to Adon." The passage is especially noteworthy, in that it distinguishes between the Father [Jehovah] and the Son [Adon]. The same distinction is made in Psalm 96: [*the mountains melt like wax*] *before* Jehovah, *before* [*the lord of all the earth*] Adon.[b] Here Christ is that Adon, that is, the master or lord, whom the *angels worship* (Hebrews 1).[c] He is Adon, to whom the queen, the Church, bows (Psalm 44).[d] Christ is Adon, whom Malachi foretold in chapter 3,[e] and he who sits at the right hand of God, according to Psalm 109. This was said of Christ at the resurrection: and then *he sat at the right hand of God* the Father (Mark 16).[f]

Similar language occurs frequently [in Scripture]. From 1 Samuel 25: *The Lord will make my lord a house,* [*because*] *my lord is fighting the battles of the Lord. The Lord has done to my lord* [*according to all the good that he has spoken concerning you*]. *The Lord has done well to my lord*.[g] Jehovah always comes first, Adon second. Likewise in Genesis 24:

---

[a] Augustine, *De Trinitate* 2.19 (PL 42 857).   [b] Ps 97:5.   [c] Heb 1:6.
[d] Ps 45:11. Psalm 45 is a royal wedding psalm; the queen is instructed to bow to the king.   [e] Mal 3:1.   [f] Mark 16:19.   [g] 1 Sam 25:28, 30, 31.

Blessed be the Lord, the God of my lord. The Lord has led me to [the house of] the brother of my lord.[a]

Besides, according to the ancient literal, or historical, meaning, this psalm is attributed to Solomon, when the living David turned over the kingdom to him (1 Chronicles 29).[b] It was then, in accordance with the revelation of God, as he was turning over the kingdom to Solomon **[66]** in his lifetime, that David sang, "*God said to my lord.*" Singing [under the influence of God's] spirit, David foresees Christ, recognizing Christ in Solomon. According to the literal sense, David suggests one person, while the spirit points toward another.

For *the testimony of Jesus* Christ, as we have said, *is the spirit of prophecy.*[c] The prophets are to be read in this way: if you see one thing here with your eyes, you can perceive another, more sublime, with the spirit. Accordingly, the *word of God* is called a *double-edged sword* (Hebrews 4).[d] Indeed, sometimes the wording is twofold, so that there is a more powerful meaning, a truly multiple sense. David calls Solomon "Lord," as the type of Christ, of course as a foreshadowing. In actuality he is calling Christ "Lord." With this argument, as I said earlier, Christ appealed to the Jews, in order that they might understand the mystery, and the divinity, of the Messiah (Matthew 22).[e] In 1 Chronicles 29, in the literal sense it is said that *Solomon sat on the throne of* God;[f] so that it may rightly be said of him, as the one who holds the place of Christ, "*Sit at my right hand.*" *Solomon* sits there *on the throne of* God, through the power of God, *at the right hand of God*, by hyperbole and as a foreshadowing of Christ. Sacred language is full of such uses of hyperbole, which cannot be fully verified according to a literal sense, only in accordance with the mystery of Christ.

---

[a] Gen 24:27. [b] 1 Chr 29:23. [c] Rev 19:10. [d] Heb 4:12. [e] Matt 22:41-46. See Mark 12:35-36. [f] 1 Chr 29:23.

In addition, the words that come next, *until I make your enemies your footstool*, literally refer to Solomon, as do the words, *under the soles of your feet*, from 1 Kings 5.[a] The remaining words of the psalm also literally apply to Solomon, as indicated by the passage that immediately follows. He is, in fact, the one to whom *the people made free-will offerings*.[b] He is called *a priest after the order of Melchizedek*,[c] who, of course, was at once king and priest.[d] Consequently Solomon functioned to a certain extent as a priest, in the building and dedication of the temple, as a foreshadowing and type of the true king and priest, Christ.[e] Like Melchizedek, Solomon acted as a priest by offering sacrifice and blessing the people (1 Kings 8).[f] [67] Furthermore, Solomon is said to have *drunk from the brook by the way*,[g] that is, from the stream of Gihon, when they anointed him king at Gihon. He was drinking water while elsewhere Adonijah was becoming intoxicated (1 Kings 1).[h] Therefore he raised up his head, and the other was cast out of his kingship.

We will speak more later about the name "Jehovah."[i] For the moment it suffices to point out that the prophets did not apply the name [Jehovah] to Christ's earthly activity, as they did the names *Elohim* and *Adon*. To be sure there are still some unlearned people who persist in deducing [the existence of] those co-equal, incorporeal beings, by claiming that the name Jehovah was attributed to Christ by Thomas when he said, "*My Lord and my God!*" (John 20).[j] However, [such people] have no knowledge of the Hebrew language, in which the possessive "my" is never attached to the name "Jehovah." The tetragrammaton [יהוה], or the

Err, 97v-98r

---

[a] 1 Kg 5:3. [b] Ps 110:3. [c] Ps 110:4. [d] Gen 14:18. [e] In his annotations to the Pagnini Bible, Servetus said that Psalm 110 is about "Solomon, whom David calls 'Lord' as a type of Christ." [f] 1 Kg 8:55, 62. [g] Ps 110:7. [h] 1 Kg 1:25, 41. [i] *Restoration*, 125-128 (book 4). [j] John 20:28.

name "Jehovah," is never used where we read "my lord" [*Adonai*]. Therefore Thomas neither used nor could possibly have used the name [Jehovah], but rather said *Adon* or *El*. Those who discuss sacred scripture without knowing the sacred language will fall into dangerous errors.

Passage 7

[Psalm 110:3: Your people make freewill offerings in the day of your strength, in the beauties of holiness, from the womb, from the dawn. To you is given the dew of your youth.]

Fittingly, the seventh passage is from the same psalm, which reads in the Vulgate: *Dominion is with you in the day of your power, in the splendours of holiness. From the womb I have begotten you before the morning star.*[25]

Err, 75r-v

The unlearned are deluded in their exposition of this passage, understanding neither the Greek translation nor the truth of the Hebrew original. They render the word meaning "rule of the people" as "beginning," although in the Greek translation αρχη should not be taken as meaning "beginning," but rather "dominion" or "rule of the people," which the true meaning of the Hebrew original clearly teaches.[26]

Exodus describes how the princes and the people made their offerings freely to build and adorn the sanctuary (Exodus 25, 35, and 36),[a] as they did at the dedication of the altar (Numbers 7).[b] Something similar to this is being spoken of in the text that we are now considering. In terms of actual historical events, here David speaks of the spontaneous generosity of the people in the construction of the temple and the adornment of the sanctuary. This generosity, or freewill offering, took place at the time of the establishment of the rule of Solomon, as related in 1 Chronicles 29.[c]

Err, 75v

---

[a] Ex 25:1-9, 35:21-22, 36:2-3.   [b] Num 7:3.   [c] 1 Chr 29:6-9.

Err, 75v By means of this typology drawn from history, inspired by the spirit, David foretold the people's future freewill offering to Christ, given in greater [68] splendour of holiness. Indeed, the people themselves will be the offerings.

In Hebrew the passage reads:

עמך נדבת ביוֹם חילך בהדריקדש
מרחם משחר לך טל ילדתיך:

That is, *Your people make freewill offerings in the day of your strength, in the beauties of holiness, from the womb, from the dawn. To you is given the dew of your youth.*[27] This is the way that the Hebrew is punctuated, and this is the true meaning [of the passage].

Those freewill offerings of the people were made on the day of the strength or the power of Solomon. For on that day the powerful reign of Solomon was strengthened and consolidated, as was the reign of Christ at the resurrection. On the same day, Solomon, the type of Christ, was once again made king, and was for the second time anointed as king in chapter 29 [of 1 Chronicles],[a] just as the kingdom of God came with power once again on the day of Christ's resurrection. In addition, it says that these offerings were made in the beauties of holiness, because they were made to beautify and decorate the holy temple, just as we sanctify and decorate our temple in offering ourselves to our own Solomon.

[The psalm] says *from the womb* and *from the dawn*, that is, children from the womb and from the beginning of the day were offering gifts. Later it goes on to say, *To you is given the dew of your youth*. For this offering was made to the youthful Solomon, in the youthful beginning of his reign.[b]

In the same way, according to the spirit, the freewill offering of the peoples was made to Christ at the commencement of his reign, with far greater splendour of holiness

---

[a] 1 Chr 29:23. [b] Most of the text of this paragraph is taken from Servetus's note to Ps 110:3 in the Pagnini Bible.

and beauty: not by children of flesh, but by children [born anew] of the spirit, from the dawn of the day of Christ's resurrection. They were offering their gifts and themselves to the true Solomon, as can be seen from the Acts of the Apostles.[a]

Moreover, [the Psalmist] speaks of *freewill offerings*, to distinguish them from votive offerings, as נדב *nadab* differs from נדר *nadar* (Leviticus 7, 22, 23; Numbers 15, 29; Deuteronomy 12).[b] The people belong to Christ voluntarily, bound by no vows. The same word *nadab* is used of sacred rituals similar to this freewill offering in various places throughout scripture, for example, Psalm 46 and 53; Ezra 1; Ezekiel 44, 45, 46, and 48.[28] David speaks of the same kinds of offerings in Psalm 71, where tribute is offered to Solomon **[69]** by various kings.[c] It makes no difference that gold from Arabia or Ethiopia was not similarly offered to Christ. For the prophets are accustomed to prophesy using terms from the Law or from history. The literal offering pertains to history. But the spiritual offering and spiritual sacrifices apply to Christ. For Solomon it sufficed to be be given worldly tribute and to be offered gold from Arabia and Tarshish (1 Kings 4 and 10, 2 Chronicles 9).[d]   *Err*, 75v-76r

What is meant by "in the splendours of holiness" is made clear by David himself in Psalms 28 and 95 as well as in 1 Chronicles 16.[e] There the beautiful and glorious holy place [the temple] is called "the beauty of holiness" and "glory of holiness." [In the passage we are discussing] the plural, "beauties" or "splendours," is used to emphasize the manifold splendour of the glory. Psalm 67 stresses the same thing.   *Err*, 76r

---

[a] Possibly a reference to the early Christians collecting money to be distributed to the poor by the apostles who held meetings at the Portico of Solomon at the Temple in Jerusalem (Acts 4:34-37).   [b] Lev 7:16, 22:18, 23:38; Num 15:3, 29:39; Deut 12:6. All of these mention both votive offerings and freewill offerings.   [c] Ps 72:10.   [d] 1 Kg 4:21, 10:10-22; 2 Chr 9:9-21.   [e] Ps 29:2, 96:9; 1 Chr 16:29.

*In your temple at Jerusalem kings shall offer gifts to you.*ᵃ And even though no such gifts were offered by kings to Christ in the earthly Jerusalem and in that temple, Christ requires more from us. On this subject [Christ] instructs us about the temple of his own body.ᵇ And [Jesus], speaking of the Queen of Sheba, who offered her gifts to Solomon, says, *"Behold, someone greater than Solomon is here."*ᶜ Christ does not ask for what is ours, but for ourselves.

Passage 8

[Isaiah 7:14: Behold a virgin, pregnant and giving birth to a son, and she shall call his name Immanuel.]

The eighth passage is from Isaiah 7: *Behold a virgin, pregnant and giving birth to a son, and* you, mother, *shall call his name Immanuel.*²⁹ *He shall eat butter and honey so that he may know how to reject evil and choose good. For before the child knows how to reject evil and choose good, the land which you detest will be relieved of the presence of its two kings,* Rezin and Pekah.ᵈ

According to history, a sign was given to the frightened [king of Judah] Ahaz so that he might understand that two of his enemies, Rezin and Pekah, would soon be destroyed and the kingdom of Judah freed from them. At that time Ahaz was greatly afraid of those two kings, because he had already suffered much from them (2 Chronicles 28), which Isaiah had earlier prophesied (chapters 3 and 4). And later he was even more afraid when, with the entire kingdom of Judah already nearly destroyed, he saw them approaching the city of Jerusalem.³⁰ And it was then that this sign was

---

ᵃ Ps 68:29. ᵇ John 2:19-22. ᶜ In Matt 12:38-42, Jesus compares his listeners unfavourably to the people of Nineveh and the Queen of Sheba.
ᵈ Isa 7:14-16 (Pagnini).

given to him, suited to the age [70] and also containing the mystery of Christ.

When read in literal terms, Isaiah is pointing to Abijah, daughter of Zechariah, then the wife of King Ahaz,[31] whom he also calls a prophetess because she had foretold that a divine name was to be assigned to her son. Mothers are wont to adorn their sons with imposing names, which is why Isaiah directed his words ["you shall call his name Immanuel"] to the mother. Thus, while the son was rightly called Hezekiah, that is, "the strength of God," [Isaiah] says that [his mother] rightly called him Immanuel, "God with us." Hezekiah was called Immanuel, just as Solomon is called Lemuel ["belonging to God"] in Proverbs 31,[a] because God was then amongst them. Solomon's mother calls him Lemuel, just as Hezekiah's mother calls her son Immanuel.[32]

This Abijah, as a young virgin girl, conceived Hezekiah as if by a great miracle. According to the Books of Kings, Ahaz was at most eleven years old when he fathered Hezekiah.[33] The prophetess accordingly gave a divine name to her son, as if he had been conceived in the womb of a virgin, as a type of Jesus Christ. By a kind of hyperbole and figurative use of speech, he can be said to have been begotten in a virgin, especially since the Hebrew word [*almah*, often rendered "virgin"] means a young woman. Or she may have been called a virgin because of her extreme youth.[34] Unlike Mary, the mother of Jesus, Abijah did not conceive without the seed of a man. Nevertheless Isaiah teaches that a kind of miracle was prefigured in the begetting of Hezekiah, who is therefore called "The Strength of God" and "God with us." For in [Hezekiah's] time, God, with great strength, was with the people against all their enemies, especially the Assyrians. By this miraculous sign, Isaiah points to the greater miracle of the true virgin [Mary].

---

[a] Prov 31:1, 4.

What history teaches us should not be neglected, although the whole truth is not contained in it. Hence in [Isaiah] chapter 9, it is appropriately written about this same Hezekiah, *every battle of the warrior involves a clash and clothing stained with blood*;[a] but that battle will be miraculously waged with fire and a devouring flame cast down upon the Assyrians by an angel.[35] In the same way, Christ, by means of a fiery sword, destroys his enemies, and the Antichrist himself, in the figure of the Assyrian (Isaiah 11).[b] As in the resurrection of Christ on the third day, so, too, on the third day [**71**] the prayers of Hezekiah brought about the miraculous liberation of his people,[36] and *on the third day* Hezekiah, as if rising from the dead, went *up to the house of the Lord* (Hosea 6 and 2 Kings 20).[c] He was there acting as the truest type of Jesus Christ. In short, everything Isaiah says about Christ, from the beginning to chapter 40, has its type in the story of Hezekiah. In chapter 40 he begins to speak of Cyrus, who also, as the type of Jesus Christ, was a liberator from captivity. For this reason Cyrus was also called Christ [the anointed one],[d] just as [Hezekiah and Solomon were respectively called] Immanuel and Lemuel.

But turn your attention now to how artfully, in the aforementioned chapter 7, Isaiah says הרה וילדת (*harah weyoledet*), *pregnant and giving birth*, or *conceiving and giving birth*, so that the words extend into the past and the future like a *double-edged sword*.[e] For Hezekiah was already born at the time [of the defeat of Rezin and Pekah], as Isaiah relates in the following chapter, repeating precisely the same words: *I went*, he says, *to the prophetess, who conceived and gave birth to a son*,[f] in whose childhood the plundering of Damascus and Samaria occurred.[37]

But why did [Isaiah] say, *he shall eat butter and honey in order to know how to reject evil and choose good*? The prophet

---

[a] Isa 9:5. [b] Isa 11:11-16. [c] Hos 6:2; 2 Kg 20:1-5. [d] Isa 45:1.
[e] Heb 4:12. [f] Isa 8:3.

relates in the same passage that, despite their lack of cattle and the destruction of their beehives, they *will eat butter and honey*.[a] After the terrible devastation wrought by their enemies, God soon gave such abundance that even the children, eating butter and honey, were able to see the goodness of God, and to learn to choose good and reject evil. This is what Hezekiah, then a small child, came to know. Butter and honey, indeed, is children's food, which is why [Isaiah] uses these words when talking about the child. But Isaiah is also showing [the return of Judah's] fruitfulness, for which, as it was given so quickly, God was greatly to be praised. [King] Ahaz was blind to this. Not thinking of the great benefits God [had showered on them], which caused butter and honey to so greatly abound after the destruction of their flocks and beehives by the enemy, he chose evil and rejected good. A similar prophecy of future prosperity appears in Isaiah 37.[b]

The prophet adds another portent: **[72]** *For before the child knows how to reject evil and choose good, the land which you*, Ahaz, *detest will be abandoned by those two kings*, Rezin and Pekah. For both were killed before this child [Hezekiah] reached an age adult enough to know [the difference between] good and evil. This [prophecy] came to pass a little later (2 Kings 15 and 16).[c]

Therefore, Ahaz, accept this sign that God will preserve the kingdom for your son: *behold* a girl, *a young woman*, miraculously *conceiving and giving birth to a son*, whom you, mother, justly *call Immanuel*, through whom God will perform miracles among the people, and who will save the people; and who, even as a child, because of the fertility that God will give so quickly, will come to know the right path of God and will *reject evil*. And there is one more thing, [writes Isaiah]: before the child reaches that age, those two

---

[a] Isa 7:18, 21.   [b] Isa 37:30-32.   [c] 2 Kg 15:30, 15:37, 16:5-9.

kings, whom you dread, will be destroyed. Thus all these things are fulfilled to the letter, and just as they are set forth.

We must not neglect the meanings that ancient history provides, through which the mysteries of Christ are splendidly illuminated. For it was Christ alone who was actually conceived and borne by a virgin. He alone is the true Hezekiah, the true Immanuel, *Mighty God, Everlasting Father, Prince of Peace.*[a]

Passage 9

[John 3:13: *No one has ascended into heaven but he who came down from heaven, the Son of man, who is in heaven.*]

The ninth passage, from chapter 3 of John, must now be explained. *No one has ascended into heaven but he who has come down from heaven, the Son of man, who is in heaven.*[38] It is truly amazing that Christ, while living on earth, is said to be in heaven and to have already ascended into heaven, and descended as well. But even though in the previous book we have already spoken of how Christ came down from heaven,[b] we will show it again, this time more fully. For the heavenly Word, made flesh on earth, produces the substance of that flesh, as it is said that the flesh itself is from heaven.[c] That flesh possesses within itself true divine substance from heaven.

I thus show that Christ has already truly ascended into heaven. The ascent of this man towards God follows from the incarnation of the Word. The Word, coming down from heaven to earth, in turn exalts the earth to heaven, making us all citizens of heaven. Christ, we say, has already ascended to *the bosom of the Father,*[d] and heaven was then

Err, 45v

---

[a] Isa 9:6.   [b] In the second objection of the Pharisees (*Restoration*, 17-18).
[c] John 6:51.   [d] John 1:18.

for him the *inaccessible light*^a [73] where the Father dwells. He, who brought the word of heaven to us, was then truly already in heaven. At that time he alone had ascended into heaven. Neither the soul of Abraham nor the souls of the patriarchs had at that time been received into heaven. Therefore, he spoke truly when he said, "*No one [has ascended into heaven]*." He was the only one in heaven when we had not yet been *born from above*,^b as [Jesus] says. But when we are *born from above*, having become heavenly humans, dwelling in heaven, we are then said to ascend into heaven.

We are also said to come down from heaven, and to be born from heaven. And we are exalted into heaven by the spirit given to us, coming down from heaven.[39] Therefore what Christ says is always true: that *no one* is said to have *ascended into heaven but he who came down from heaven*, was born from heaven, and is exalted into heaven by the Holy Spirit descending from heaven. It was formerly applicable to him alone, and to us only after our own regeneration from above. Thus, through Christ, what is heavenly is united to earthly things, and heavenly things descend to us, so that earth is exalted to heaven. Therefore, not only Christ himself, but the also the saints, are born from heaven and come down from heaven. But only he has come down both by natural procreation and through the *whole fullness of deity*.^c

Passage 10

[*Colossians 2:9: For in him the whole fullness of deity dwells bodily.*]

The tenth passage is from Paul's Epistle to the Colossians: in Christ the whole fullness of the Law and *the whole fullness of deity dwells bodily*. The whole fullness of the Law is

---

^a 1 Tim 6:16.   ^b John 3:3,7.   ^c Col 2:9.

in Christ. For the shadows of the Law[a] prefigured various mysteries, all of which were fulfilled in this body — really and bodily fulfilled. Likewise the fullness of deity, together with the fullness of the Law, is fully in Christ, and is bodily visible and tangible in a corporeal way. Christ's own body is the very same fullness in which all things achieve fulfillment, come together in unity, are summed up, and are reconciled: God and humanity, heaven and earth, Jew and Gentile, circumcised and uncircumcised, king and priest, the law and the prophets. Christ's own body is itself the body of deity and his flesh is divine flesh, the flesh of God and the blood of God. The very flesh [74] of Christ is heavenly, begotten of the substance of God. The body that was in the tomb possessed its substantial form from the substance of the light of God, and its higher elements from the substance of the Word of God, as I shall discuss later.[b] In his flesh he is called deity in bodily form, something that could not come to pass in the shadow of the Law — since body is rightly considered to be the opposite of shadow.

Paul's use of the word "dwells" shows the kind of divinity that is in Christ. The rabbis call divinity שכינה (*shekinah*), from the word שכן (*shakan*), which means "to dwell." Therefore the divinity of Christ is God dwelling in him. In Christ there is not some portion of God, but the whole fullness of God, the whole fullness of the Word and the Spirit. By means of the same term, the dwelling place of God, the tabernacle, the place in which God lived, was called in the Law [Torah] משכן (*mishkan*), the house of God. Christ is the house of God, because Paul specifies that *God was in Christ reconciling the world to himself* (2 Corinthians 5).[c]

The divinity of Christ is God in Christ, since his form contained the divinity that [once] was in the tabernacle. Based on the logic of his divinity, and consideration of the Law,

---

[a] See A.RIn.1. [b] *Restoration*, 194 (book 5). [c] 2 Cor 5:19.

Paul teaches us clearly that the divinity of the tabernacle, and of the angels seen there, was the foreshadowing of that truth which is in the body of Christ. *These are*, he says, *only a shadow of what is to come; but the body belongs to Christ.*[a] There [in the tabernacle] divinity was prefigured, without a real body; here [in Christ] is the true body of divinity. True divinity, which was prefigured in those foreshadowings, is bodily in Christ, in the very body and the very flesh of Christ. The whole deity of the Father and of the angels is in Christ. The whole fullness of God, the whole of God the Father, with all of his characteristics, his entire substance and power, along with the fullness and splendour of deity, lives fully in this body.

The entire hypostasis, nature, and essence of God; the whole vision, adoration, and worship of God; all that God has exists substantially and bodily in Christ, as Christ is truly ὁμοούσιος (*homoousios*), truly consubstantial, with God the Father. God subsists in and is visible in Christ alone. Aside from Christ there is no face, person, or hypostasis of God. [75] The scriptures teach in various places about the splendour of his face, by which the heavens themselves are illuminated and will be illuminated in ages to come.[b] That light itself, the light which is God, is visible only in the face of Jesus Christ. All the deity and glory of the Father is in him to such a degree that the angels regard his face with wonder. And from it they learn the future and see it in him. Not only is God present in him, but all the power of God is given to him. *All things were made through*[c] Christ by his spirit and power. *All things were made through* Christ in his person. *All things were made through* Christ in his substance. All things are through Christ, all things are seen through Christ, and all things essentially exist in him.

Err, 112r-v

---

[a] Col 2:17. [b] See Matt 17:2, 2 Cor 4:6, Rev 22:4-5. [c] John 1:3; Rom 1:20.

Passage 11

[John 14:10-11: I am in the Father and the Father is in me.]

The eleventh passage is: *I am in the Father and the Father is in me* (John 14). At the beginning of book 3 of *On the Trinity*, Hilary says that "human intelligence cannot grasp"[a] the way in which those three beings are "each in the others."[b] Augustine endorses this in the book *On the Faith, to Peter*[c] and at the end of book 6 of *On the Trinity*,[d] and he adds [in book 9] that these beings are "entirely contained in each other."[e] In book 3 of *On the Holy Spirit*, Athanasius pretends by means of invisible phantoms that those beings are all in each other.[f]

It is astonishing that [these writers] have allowed themselves to become so distracted that they do not pay heed to the easily understandable interpretation given by Christ himself. For, in the same chapter, Christ says to the apostles: *the Father is in me, and I am in you; I am in my Father, and you are in me.*[g] Christ is in the Father, his substance is incorporated in him. The Father is in him, just as [Scripture] says that God was in Christ, and that the whole deity was in him, bodily and spiritually. *God was in Christ, reconciling the world to himself* (2 Corinthians 5).[h] Thus, as Peter teaches,

---

[a] *Sentences* 1.19.5 (PL 192 574), based on Hilary, *De Trinitate* 3.1 (PL 10 76A).   [b] See A.E1.20.   [c] *Sentences* 1.19.5 (PL 192 574), based on [Augustine], *De fide ad Petrum* 4 (PL 40 754): "The whole Father is in the Son and the Holy Spirit, and the whole Son is in the Father and the Holy Spirit, and the whole Holy Spirit is in the Father and the Son."
[d] Augustine, *De Trinitate* 6.12 (PL 42 932). "So they are each in the others and all in each, and each in all and all in all, and they are all one."
[e] Augustine, *De Trinitate* 9.8 (PL 42 965).   [f] Athanasius, *De sancto spiritu* 4, 5 (PG 26 630C, 634A): "The Son is everywhere, because he is in the Father and the Father is in him ... The Spirit is not outside the Word, but because he is in the Word, he is in God through the Word."
[g] John 14:10, 20.   [h] 2 Cor 5:19.

Book 2

God was with him (Acts 10).ᵃ The works that this man did, the Father did in him: *The Father who dwells in me performs the works*.ᵇ Hence Christ says that he did *what he saw his Father doing*.ᶜ Just as an artist makes with his hand what he sees being fashioned in his mind, so Christ [performs his works].[40] Similarly, Christ says that those Jews [who wanted to kill him] were doing what they saw the devil inside themselves doing. For the devil was acting in them and depicting the ideal form of evil, just as God depicts the ideal form of good in Christ.ᵈ

In *Tractates on the Gospel of John* [**76**] 18, 19, and 20 and at the beginning of book 2 of *On the Trinity*,ᵉ Augustine gives a ridiculous exposition of this passage concerning the actions of the Father in Christ by means of a threefold sophistical distinction, lest it be said that the Father is in the man. To prevent an intermingling of substances, the sophists want the Son alone to be in the man, not the Father or the Holy Spirit.[41] Who but someone deluded by the devil would deny that the substance of the Holy Spirit is in the man Christ?

Likewise they deny that the Father is in the man because this would be patripassianism. How ridiculous are the fancies they spin with their "sharing of attributes"! I do not say that he who was in the Son suffered, but that the Son suffered. Just as being born is a condition peculiar to the flesh, so are being beaten and crucified, dying, and rising again. These sufferings have no relevance to incorporeal beings. When the man [Jesus] died, we cannot say that his soul died, nor can we say that an angel or some other incorporeal being within him died. The death of an invisible being, which cannot experience the pangs of death, is a ridiculous

Err, 76r-v

ᵃ Acts 10:38.   ᵇ John 14:10.   ᶜ John 5:19.   ᵈ John 8:44.
ᵉ Augustine, *In evangelium Iohannis* 20.6 (PL 35 1559) and 19.16 (PL 35 1553); *De Trinitate* 2.9 (PL 42 850-851).

idea. I could never admit that something truly dies, which does not suffer the pangs of death. Those other deaths [of theirs], which are never mentioned in Scripture, are the work of fanatical men who are deluded by demons. By the same reasoning the Holy Spirit could die with the death of any other human being. God clearly would have been play-acting if he had based the redemption of the world on the death of that invisible being, who never really died. The redemption of the sophists is delusive, just as is the death of their invisible being, on whom they base their salvation. Thus, for them, the Son of God is dead, just as they say that angels [are liable to] die in asses' skins.[a]

Rest, 43

Another obvious delusion of the sophists is that for them even the sufferings of the man Christ were not real. Augustine on Psalm 21,[b] Jerome on Matthew 26,[c] and Hilary on Psalm 68,[d] all say that the man Christ was never saddened and never feared death.[42] Indeed Hilary asserts, in book 10 of *On the Trinity*, that neither wounds nor death itself tormented him or caused him to feel anguish. The flesh of Christ, he says, suffered no more in the Passion than if one were to try to wound fire or water with a sword.[e] With equal stupidity, in book 9 of *On the Trinity* [77] he both asserts that the Father is greater [than the Son] and denies that the Son is less [than the Father]; and he says that the Son suffered no more pain [in the Passion] than did the Father himself.[f]

Augustine, in his sermon *On the Faith*, anathematizes those who say or believe that the Son of God died.[g] Indeed Peter Lombard believes, based on Augustine, that the man did not die either. For in book 3, distinction 22 of his

---

[a] See *Restoration*, 43. [b] Augustine, *Enarrationes in psalmos* 21 1.1-2 (PL 36 167). [c] Jerome, *In evangelium Matthaei* 26 (Matt 26:37-38) (PL 26 197). [d] Hilary, *Tractatus super psalmos* 68.4 (PL 9 472B). [e] Hilary, *De Trinitate* 10.23 (PL 10 361A-362A). [f] Hilary, *De Trinitate* 9.56, 9.72 (PL 10 327A, 338B-339B). [g] [Augustine], *De fide ad Petrum* 87 (PL 40 777-778). The author warns that anyone who disagrees with anything in the entire book is a heretic and cursed.

Sentences, he concedes, on Augustine's authority, that Christ was human during those three days in the tomb.[a] If, however, he was really human [in the tomb], then he was truly alive [there] as a man. Who can stomach disputing about such ghoulish things? It is because of this kind of reasoning that they say that Christ was in the tomb and that [at the same time] Christ was in hell. But these things can [only] be said as a figure of speech (synecdoche), as when we say that Saint Peter is in paradise.[43] If, however, the man really died, then he necessarily ceased to exist as a man. If the Son really died, then the Son truly ceased to exist, although those things persist which were the Son's. For true death leads from being to non-being. If he truly ceased to exist as the Son, then it follows that deity itself was not really the Son.

Passage 12
[John 8:58: Before Abraham was, I am.]

The twelfth passage is: *before Abraham was, I am*. The utterance, *I am*, denotes an essential way of being. Just as form is what gives existence to something, the substantial form of the Word gives essence to this body — and this form existed from the beginning. Indeed, as I will show, Christ already existed from the beginning, in elementary essence and in the essence of his soul. The essence of the body and the soul of Christ is the divinity of the Word and of the Spirit. Christ is from the beginning, as much by reason of the body as by reason of the soul. The flesh of Christ has the beginning of its existence in the Father's utterance of the Word. Christ, in the Spirit of God, preceded all of time. The same Spirit, which was the spirit of *Elohim*, is now the Spirit of Christ.

Err, 67v

If one counted only on the Spirit, someone having an unclean spirit might be able to claim, "I was there, I saw,

---

[a] *Sentences* 3.22.2 (PL 192 803-804), based on [Augustine], *De fide ad Petrum* 11 (PL 40 757): "In the tomb, the same God lay dead according to the flesh only, and he descended into hell according to the soul only."

Err, 116r   I did it"—as if not the man, but the spirit itself were speaking. This is how Simon Magus, possessed by an evil spirit, made himself out to be "the Standing One," and claimed that he was from the beginning "the Standing One," the likeness of the person of Christ.ᵃ He had heard [about the Spirit of Christ] from the apostles, and by striving [78] to equal or excel the truth of Christ in this way, he fought against [that truth], so that those who did not believe in [Simon] would not believe in Christ either. One thing to be noted is that Simon Magus, the first of all the hereticsᵇ following the promulgation of the Gospel, and a formidable antagonist, never attacked the faith by the means used by the trinitarians, because no one at that time was acquainted with such inventions. The only question [that arose then] was about the visible person of Christ, who outwardly displayed the eternal spirit that he carried within himself.

Err, 70v   The spirit of Christ is truly eternal, and is the same spirit which, in the beginning, *breathed life* into Adam.ᶜ In Hebrews 9 the Apostle speaks about this eternal spirit of Christ, *who through the eternal spirit offered himself.*ᵈ

Err, 67v   Rightly, therefore, Christ said, "*Before Abraham was* born, *I am*. I am that eternal Word of God, which was uttered before the time of Abraham, the Word heard and seen by Abraham himself." Christ, the Word visible before the time of Abraham and uttered prior to Adam, *came forth* from the mouth of God *from of old* (Micah 5).ᵉ Not only do we say that Christ *comes forth* from God,ᶠ but that he is *in God*.ᵍ "I am the one who exists in the substance of the Word. My being is from eternity, by the utterance of the Word from

---

ᵃ The story of Simon Magus is told in Acts 8:9-24; in Irenaeus, *Adversus haereses* 1.23.1-4 (PG 7 670B-673A); and in [Clement], *Recognitiones* 2.5-16 (PG 1 1250B-1257A). The latter work is the source of the information that Simon called himself "the Standing One." *Recognitiones* 2.7 (PG 1 1251B-C).   ᵇ In *Adversus haereses* 3 prologue (PG 7 843A), Irenaeus called Simon "the father of all heretics."   ᶜ Gen 2:7.
ᵈ Heb 9:14.   ᵉ Mic 5:2.   ᶠ Matt 4:4, quoting Deut 8:3.   ᵍ Col 3:3.

eternity, spoken by the Father in eternity. At that time I was, in my essential form, the one who granted essence to other beings." He whom we see, [Christ,] is *from the beginning* (1 John 2).[a] *He is before all things*, and *all things are through him* (Colossians 1).[b]

The Son is born from God in eternity and from humanity in time. Give careful attention to this simile: Suppose that the power were granted to me to beget a son in a woman by a breath of air from my mouth. Then, having so breathed, suppose I should withdraw that I might say to her, "I have begotten a son. I am leaving a son in you, who, made a man, in the coming fullness of time will be born from you." This breath is not a real son, but by virtue of its seminal power, we say that a son was then begotten. Thus, in God, there was no begetting of an invisible son among those [three] beings, but there was a generation that came about by the utterance of the Word, which afterwards became visible flesh, and is the Son of the blessed God.

Err, 68r-v

Passage 13

[John 1:15: He who is coming after me, was made before me.]

From this it can be understood what the herald, **[79]** John the Baptist, says in chapter 1 of John: "*He who is coming after me, was made before me, for he was before me.*"[c] This is the way our translators render it. However they have done so incorrectly. For a period should be placed after the words "was made [before me]," so that ὅτι (for) begins the following sentence, thus: "*He who is coming after me, was made before me. For truly he was before me, and from his fullness we have all received* [*grace upon grace*]."[d] Especially as [in the same]

Err, 68v-69r

---

[a] 1 John 2:7, 13, 14, 24.　[b] Col 1:16, 17.　[c] John 1:15. Many modern translations use "ranks ahead of me," because *ante* (before) can also indicate being ahead in merit and/or status.　[d] John 1:15-16.

Err, 68v-69r

chapter] John soon repeats these same words: *He who is coming after me, was made before me.*[a] And, repeating it a third time, he says, "*This is he of whom I was saying, 'After me will come a man who was made before me. For truly he was before me and I myself did not know him.'*"[b] This man is said to have been made at an earlier time. Note the wording: made at an earlier time, that is to say, made in the past.

What will the sophists have to say on this point? For they do not grant that the second being was created, although the Arians did. Long before the Arians, Ignatius, Irenaeus, Tertullian, Clement of Alexandria, Asterius of Tyana,[44] Dionysius of Alexandria, and other early Church Fathers, plainly stated that the Son was made.[45] The Apostle, whose way of thinking neither Arius nor Athanasius ever grasped, teaches the very same thing in the Epistle to the Hebrews and elsewhere.[c] I would like to ask all the [sophists] this one question: Does the begetting of this man by God seem to them to be divine? If divine, this man should be called the one and only Son of God. If Jesus of Nazareth was begotten by this kind of generation, then he who was begotten and born is the Son. He can be seen to be that Melchizedek, [the circumstances of] whose begetting were unknown to men.[d] From the manner of his begetting, the Son is recognized.

Err, 69r-v

Passage 14

[*1 Peter 3:19-20: He went and preached to the spirits in prison, who were disobedient in the days of Noah.*]

Err, 70v

We have said that the spirit of Christ is eternal, something Peter also talks about in chapter 3 of his first epistle: [*He

---

[a] John 1:27. Bibles in Servetus's time said, "he who is coming after me, who was made before me." Modern versions of the verse omit "who was made before me." [b] John 1:30-31. [c] For example, Heb 5:9; 1 Cor 1:30, 15:45; Gal 4:4. In the Vulgate, these passages refer to Christ as *factus* (made). [d] Heb 7:3.

was put to death in the flesh, but] made alive in the spirit, in which he went and preached to the spirits in prison, who were disobedient in the days of Noah. I shall now elucidate this passage because it brings about an understanding of the mysteries of Christ in a wonderful way. In talking about imprisonment, Peter is referring to the days when the giants who perished in the flood,[a] together with the wicked angels, were cast into the prison of the abyss. **[80]** By doing so he weaves in another mystery concerning Christ's descent into the prisons of hell, and tells us the reason for the imprisonment of the angels.

In his writing about hell, [Peter] brings up the story of the giants as something of importance, because nowhere else [in Scripture] do we read of such a multitude of men and angels cast into the prison of hell; also, because of the similarity between those who did not believe the prophecy [about the flood] when the ark was being built, and the unbelievers [in Peter's time], when the church was being built by prophecy and baptism. Peter shows that Christ, through the eternal spirit, was once the saviour of the faithful through the [flood] water, just as he is now our saviour through baptism.

Some of [Peter's] words are quoted from Psalm 89,[b] using the Septuagint translation, the only Greek version [of the Old Testament] then in use. For the apostles wrote in Greek. In this psalm there is a reference to the time of the flood.[c]

Peter and Jude both assert that there were angels there [in hell].[d] And John, in Revelation, allots the prison of *the bottomless pit* to the [fallen] angels,[e] as does Luke in his

---

[a] Gen 6:4: "The Nephilim were on the earth in those days" [before the flood]. The meaning of *Nephilim* is not entirely clear, but often understood to be giants.   [b] 2 Pet 3:8, quoting Ps 90:4.   [c] Psalm 90 does not mention the flood in either the Vulgate or the Septuagint. However, in the Pagnini translation, Ps 90:5 includes the words *inundasti eos* (you have flooded them).   [d] 2 Pet 2:4; Jude 1:6.   [e] Rev 9:1-11, 20:1-3.

Err, 15r gospel.ᵃ The Septuagint translators of Genesis 6 use the word angels,⁴⁶ and Josephus refers to them in *The Antiquities of the Jews*.ᵇ The angels were the sons of *Elohim*, deceiver spirits, who imposed themselves on the world by mingling⁴⁷ their angelic life into the human race. These angels, seeing the beauty of women around them, powerfully stimulated the lust of the people, and made themselves human, pushing themselves into the bodies of gigantic men. For this reason, Jude says, those *angels,* wishing to procreate in envious imitation of men, *abandoned their* [heavenly] *origin,* lowering themselves from their natural origin.ᶜ

Indeed, the passions of evil spirits are exceedingly depraved, and bewitch humans with consummate artistry. Hence, it is said, Enoch was *caught up, lest* the spell of those angels *change his understanding* (Wisdom 4).ᵈ For, as Irenaeus says, Enoch "was engaged in an embassy to the angels."ᵉ He was addressing the angels and preaching to them, just as Paul made known to the angels preaching that was previously unknown to them (Ephesians 3).ᶠ Enoch himself rebuked the wicked, preaching repentance to them (Ecclesiasticus 44 and [81] Jude).ᵍ That is why, when tyrants wished to kill him, God took him up, *so that he should not see* a violent *death* (Hebrews 11).ʰ

[The angels] held their women in common, *taking from amongst them all those whom they chose as mates*.ⁱ Berossos⁴⁸ relates that they were punished for illicit sexual relations, that is, for an irregular form of marriage, which Moses

---

ᵃ In Luke 8:30-31, demons (not angels) "begged him not to command them to depart into the abyss." ᵇ Josephus, *Antiquitatum Iudaicarum* 1.3.1. ᶜ Jude 1:6. ᵈ Wisd 4:10-11 does not mention Enoch, but says that "some who pleased God ... were caught up so that evil might not change their understanding." The story of Enoch is told in Gen 5:24 and Ecclus 44:16, 49:14. ᵉ Irenaeus, *Adversus haereses* 4.16.2 (PG 7 1016B).
ᶠ In Eph 3:10, Paul preached "to the principalities and powers in the heavenly places." Principalities and powers are ranks of angelic beings.
ᵍ Ecclus 44:16; Jude 1:14-15. ʰ Heb 11:5, quoting Gen 5:24. ⁱ Gen 6:2.

also points out. It was they who filled the world with extravagance, tyranny, rapine, and injustice. Because of the size of their bodies, the ancient Hebrews called them gigantic demons.[a] The common noun, *Elohim*, is their term for angels, demons, and heroic human beings.[b]

Christ went among all those who were totally enmeshed in this great crime of the [angelic] spirits, casting them, body and spirit, into the abyss, where they are imprisoned. Hence the prison of Satan is said to be in a watery abyss (Luke 8, Revelation 20, and 2 Peter 2.)[c] The place is properly called ταρταρός, Tartarus, from the word ταρταρίξειν (*tartarixein*, horrible) because of the numbing cold and shivering chills caused by the waters there.[49] Peter and Jude rightly say that these angels were cast down into Tartarus and bound there, to be held captive until the final judgement.[d]

Therefore it is said that *the giants, and the demons who inhabit them, are oppressed beneath the waters* and *tremble*[50] (Job 26, Proverbs 9, and Isaiah 14.)[e] The passage from Job is powerful: *The giants, and those who inhabit them, are oppressed beneath the waters*, and are *naked before God in hell.*[51] The demons, who were the cause of the destruction of humanity [in the Flood], like the serpent in the beginning, were cursed because of what they did, and were rightfully cast into the abyss, together with the human beings [whom they had led astray]. Furthermore, in some way, [the demons] are now held in that prison, together with the souls of the giants, to be severely punished by means of fire at the final judgement.

The words of Peter are now more easily explained. *The spirit* of Christ πορευθεὶς (*poreutheis*, proceeded) *to those imprisoned spirits.*[f] When he got there, he proclaimed [his message] and *preached* [to them]. Just as God set out, went

---

[a] Gen 6:4. [b] See discussion of *Elohim* in *Errors*, 13v-15v. [c] Luke 8:31-33; Rev 20:10; 2 Pet 2:4. [d] 2 Pet 2:4; Jude 6. [e] Job 26:5; Prov 9:18; Isa 14:9. [f] 1 Pet 3:19.

to Egypt, *passed through* it, and having thus proceeded, *killed the firstborn* (Exodus 12),[a] so also *in the days of Noah* he went and, having thus proceeded there, preached to those [disobedient] spirits. Through the public proclamation of Noah[52] the spirit of Christ pronounced a terrible judgement on them, just as through Enoch he preached repentence to them.[b] [82] But, as Peter says, they did not obey.[c]

The stupefied spirits of the giants, and the deceiver angels, disdained to heed the voice of the herald. The word our [Latin] version renders as *praedicavit* (preached) is ἐκήρυξεν (*ekeryxen*) in Greek. This means to announce or proclaim, and is properly seen as referring to the time of Noah. For this reason, in his second epistle, Peter, retaining the same word and meaning, calls Noah himself κήρυκα (*keryka*, a herald),[d] an emissary [of peace] or the declarer of war. Thus Christ, having proceeded to those spirits, by means of his own eternal spirit, proclaimed his message through Noah.

What we have translated [in our Latin version] as *carcer* (prison) in Greek is φυλακή (*phylaki*), that is, confinement, surveillance, or detention. Just as Babylon is called φυλακή, custody, *a place of confinement for every foul spirit* (Revelation 18),[e] so the bodies of the wicked, as Job tells us, were in the custody of the evil spirits who inhabited them.[f] Those evil spirits who were held fast in the bodies of men were cast into the abyss, a stronger prison, in which they were still imprisoned when, after the Passion, Christ descended into hell and preached to them there.

Peter teaches us all this, using words that have a double meaning. His words, which are ambiguously expressed, are as follows: *being put to death in the flesh, but made alive in the spirit, in which* [spirit] *he went and preached to the spirits*

---

[a] Ex 12:23, 29. [b] Jude 1:14-15. [c] 1 Pet 3:20. [d] 2 Pet 2:5. [e] Rev 18:2. [f] Job 26:5. See A.R2.51.

in prison, who formerly did not obey, when the long-suffering of God waited in the days of Noah, when the ark was being prepared.[a]

For not only in Noah's time, but also in other periods, the spirit of Christ continued to act through the prophets, as Peter said in chapter 1 of the same letter.[b] This is the greatest glory of Christ. All the actions of God [**83**] in former times, of which we read, were the actions of Christ himself—because he alone was the presentation of the divine. He is *the King from of old, working salvation in the midst of the earth* (Psalm 73).[c] Both the person of Christ and his eternal spirit were really at work there.

However, concerning other kinds of evil spirits, it is not to be overlooked that Peter, when speaking of these spirits, [*false teachers*], observed that people's thoughts are overpowered by them.[d] God *saw that every thought of their hearts was evil continually.*[e] Paul also, when it is a question of winning the people's minds to obedience to the faith of Christ, says that it is a battle *against wicked spirits* (Ephesians 6)[f] because they *hold* minds *captive* (2 Timothy 2).[g] In this battle we must now fight against the wicked angels. They were made disobedient by evil spirits. For it is an evil spirit, *the spirit that is at work in the children of disobedience* (Ephesians 2).[h]

Err, 71v-72r

Refusing to contend so often with disobedient spirits of this sort, God, having preached repentence to them through Enoch, proclaimed their destruction through Noah, and inflicted it on them as well. For this reason God said, "*My spirit shall not* strive *in humankind for ever*" (Genesis 6).[i] Nevertheless, is it not a contradiction that God says, *My spirit is in humankind*, if they were possessed by evil spirits? I answer that the Spirit of God was put into

---

[a] 1 Pet 3:18-20.   [b] 1 Pet 1:10-11.   [c] Ps 74:12.   [d] 2 Pet 2:1-3.   [e] Gen 6:5.
[f] Eph 6:12.   [g] 2 Tim 2:26.   [h] Eph 2:2.   [i] Gen 6:3.

humanity from the beginning (Genesis 2).ᵃ The serpent that was thrust into our flesh, and our own sin, impedes [the spirit of God] at every turn, so that it cannot rule over the human mind.

There is often an internal conflict about this. For now and then, at certain moments in our lives, in order to counter the incitements of the evil spirit, the spirit of God watches over us, advises us, and establishes us in freedom. But when he sees us completely unwilling to obey him, then he *gives us over* to destruction, or a *debased mind*,ᵇ in order to more powerfully display his glory, just as he hardened the hearts of Pharaoh and the Canaanites.ᶜ Accordingly, down there in the abyss, [obedience to God] has been continuously preached to the human beings possessed by spirits, and to the evil spirits keeping a careful watch over the [human] bodies [84] in their custody. A sentence was passed on these spirits: those with intact bodies were to be suffocated [by drowning] and the wicked spirits thrust into them were to be bound [in chains] in the same abyss.ᵈ

Peter says that these [evil] angelic spirits, bound in *chains of night*, were *cast down into* a watery *hell*.ᵉ This is confirmed by the word φυλακή, which, strictly speaking, means "the keeping of a watch by night."⁵³ It is quite frequently used in sacred literature with this meaning, and even in the gospels, as, for example, in Luke 2 and 12 and Matthew 24.ᶠ This may indicate that the deluge erupted during the night, or else that [the evil angels] were subsequently immersed [in the watery abyss] by night, that is, in a time of darkness. Likewise, the last judgement *will come at night, like a thief in the night* (Matthew 24, Luke 17, 1 Thessalonians 5 and

---

ᵃ Gen 2:7.   ᵇ Rom 1:28.   ᶜ Ex 4:21 and elsewhere in Exodus; Josh 11:20.   ᵈ See 2 Pet 2:4, 5.   ᵉ 2 Pet 2:4 (Erasmus).   ᶠ Luke 2:8, 12:38; Matt 24:43; see also 2 Cor 6:5, 11:23; Heb 11:36. In the epistles and elsewhere in the gospels the word φυλακή means imprisonment, while in the three gospel passages cited by Servetus, it means watching by night.

2 Peter 3).[a] Also Psalm 89 mentions the hours of night, using the word φυλακή, a watch in the night, thus also referring to the prison-house of the soul.[b] For [at night] the soul's perceptions seem even more imprisoned [than usual] by sleep.

In the silence of the night the firstborn of the Egyptians were killed (Exodus 12).[c] In this chapter also φυλακή is used for *a watch in the night*.[d] And similar words are used several times in Wisdom, chapter 17: *confined in a prison not made of iron*, and *chains of darkness*.[e] The Babylonian princes, along with their king, Belshazzar, were slaughtered at night in the midst of their drunken revelry (Isaiah 21, Jeremiah 51, and Daniel 5).[f] Those Babylonian princes have fallen into *a perpetual sleep* along with the giants, never more to awaken (Isaiah 26), just as the giants of our own [spiritual] Babylon now *sleep a perpetual sleep*.[g] Therefore they were given a *debased mind*,[h] as God does not want to wake them from their sleep, but wishes instead that they perish in their drunkenness and whore-mongering. Thus the sentence well suits them: to be imprisoned in the night, horribly oppressed in spirit by [everlasting] sleep.

From all of this let us learn that the dread sentence pronounced against the spirits in the time of Noah has been made by Christ something for us to fear again — and not without justification. Truth to tell, God has pronounced sentence on our own beguiled spirits. For there is a place of imprisonment for demons in our Babylon, as is prophetically recalled by John [85] in chapter 18 [of Revelation].[i] For in our Babylon there truly are deceiver spirits who,

---

[a] Matt 24:43; Luke 17:26-31; 1 Thess 5:2; 2 Pet 3:10.   [b] Ps 90:4.
[c] Ex 12:29.   [d] Ex 12:42. In the Septuagint the related word προφυλακή (*prophylaki*, a guard or lookout) is used for watching by night.   [e] Wisd 17:16-17.   [f] Isa 21:5-9; Jer 51:57; Dan 5:2, 30.
[g] Isa 26:14; Jer 51:39, 57.   [h] Rom 1:28.   [i] Rev 8:2. The author is recalling, or alluding to, the words of the prophets: see Isaiah 24:10-12 and chapter 47, and Jeremiah chapter 50-51.

as formerly, call themselves spiritual and angelic, when they have not even a spark of the spirit of goodness. Here those dedicated as *sons of God* copulate with the *daughters of men*.[a] Because of this, Babylon, *the mother of wantonness and of earthly abominations*, must, as John says, once again be destroyed.[b]

Quite plainly, there is no one else to be seen in the Church of Babylon today, other than the sons of *Elohim*, mighty heroes *decked in purple*,[c] powerful demons, and false shepherds, all of them guided by *vain thoughts*,[d] whose entire spirits snore away in prison. These, like [the deceiver angels of old], devour food and drink, have many wives, and desire to possess women in common. Although they claim that it is impossible for them to be wrong, there is not a single one of them who seeks Christ. The world is so blind today that it believes that it is acceptable for the church of God to be governed by such prostitutes. Engaging in the grossest hypocrisy, they make an outward show of piety, and use our own humility and superstitiousness to impose themselves on us (2 Timothy 3 and Colossians 2).[e] Read chapter 56 of Isaiah. If you do not find that our shepherds are like the ones mentioned there, call me a liar.[f] Then read Jeremiah chapters 8 and 23, Ezekiel 22 and 34, and Micah 5.[g] If those who were supposed to be the *salt of the earth* have *lost their savour*,[h] how shall others be seasoned?

Passage 15

[1 Corinthians 8:6: Jesus Christ, through whom are all things and through whom we exist]

The next passage to be explained is one of many about the way in which God created the universe by means of Jesus

---

[a] Gen 6:4. [b] Rev 17:5. [c] Rev 17:4. [d] 1 Cor 3:20, referring to Ps 94:11. [e] 2 Tim 3:5; Col 2:8. [f] Isa 56:11. [g] Jer 8:8-10, 23:1-2; Ezek 22:26-28, 34:2-6; Mic 5:8. [h] Matt 5:13; Luke 14:34.

Christ (Ephesians 3, Colossians 1, Hebrews 1 and 2, and 1 Corinthians 8).[a] Here the man Jesus is, in his essence, the Word, through whom all things were made. By his grace the Word was spoken, and the world was created. Because of him all things exist. As the apostle says: *because of whom and through whom all things exist.*[b] Therefore it was he who was the end and the goal, *because of whom all things exist.* Furthermore, he is also the one through whom God made all things. For that very utterance [of the Word], which was the generation of Christ, was the cause of the creation of all things. It was by this same utterance of the Word, that is, the manifestation of Christ that was formed by this utterance, that all things were created simultaneously. Thus, everything really does exist through him.

However, since these things are to be more fully [86] explained in what follows,[c] it will be enough for now simply to understand that because he was *the Word made flesh,*[d] there was in him a power as mighty as the power of God, by means of which the universe was created. All that existed then is now in Christ, and has become his possession, so that he can call it his own. For he said, *"All that the Father has is mine."*[e] The power of the Word has become the power in the flesh, in the same way that the Word became flesh. *Err, 73v*

Thus, with utmost justice, Christ can claim that the universe was made by his own power. Moreover, to say "it is made by me" is the same as saying "it is made by my power." Returning to this theme, time after time, Paul says: *through the Son, through Christ, through whom, through him;*[f] that is, through the boundless power of God which is in him. In the Epistle to the Hebrews he says that all things are created and governed by Christ's *word of power.*[g] You hear that *Err, 73v-74r*

---

[a] Eph 3:9; Col 1:16; Heb 1:2, 2:10; 1 Cor 8:6. [b] Heb 2:10.
[c] *Restoration*, 205-206 (dialogue 1). [d] John 1:14. [e] John 16:15.
[f] Rom 11:36; 1 Cor 8:6; Col 1:16; Heb 1:2. [g] Heb 1:3.

Err, 74r   all things are made by the Word of the Son, lest you should understand in a metaphysical way the [relationship of] the Word with the Son.

Err, 73v   Another argument: If your spirit had preceded your flesh, you would be able to say that whatever had previously been done by your spirit, was done by you. Such, truly, was the eternal spirit in Christ, the spirit of wisdom, which formerly contained the ideal forms of things. As Irenaeus and Tertullian teach in many places, this wisdom was once both Word and Spirit,[54] because there was not a "real distinction." Wisdom itself was the Spirit, and also the mind of the living Christ. Since it made all things, all things can be truly said to be made by Christ himself.

Err, 73v–74r   Simon Magus, aping Christ, claimed that the world was made by himself, and by the power that was in him.[a] If, therefore, the eternal spirit of the wisdom of Christ, and the ideal forms of all the things that are, were within you, then, speaking as the Spirit, you could well say that you were there at [the very beginning]. You would possess a memory of these things and would yourself have been present to observe, in person, the creation, within yourself, of all things. Thus you could justly claim that everything was created by you.

The way in which I have set forth this matter allows you to say, with ample justification, that the universe was created through the strength of Christ's power. Later, you will readily understand[b] that in truth all things were made by Christ himself: that [before the world's creation] all things were, in substance, already contained in him; that it was Christ himself who created all things; and that he was [87] at that time the creator, in his own proper substance and person.

---

[a] Irenaeus, *Adversus haereses* 1.23.2 (PG 7 671B).   [b] *Restoration*, 205-206 (dialogue 1).

Passage 16

[John 10:17-18: I lay down my life in order to take it up again. I have the power to lay it down, and I have the power to take it up again.]

Once the divine strength and power of Christ have been correctly understood, we can then comprehend how true it was when he said: "*I have the power to lay down my life, and I have the power to take it up again*" (John 10). There is the substance of deity, and the same [divine] power, not only in the soul of Christ, but also in his flesh. The human being, in his entirety, possesses the life and power of God in himself. Since the entire divinity is in the human being, [Jesus says,] all the power of *the Father is in me*[a] and *is mine*.[b] Therefore, [Paul says,] *I can do all things [through him who strengthens me]*.[c] The divine power, [Jesus says,] which will awaken this body from the tomb and restore it to life, *is mine* and *is in me*. Therefore, I have the power to revive this body, *the power to lay down* this life, *and [the power] to take it up again*.

The Son has the power of life and death. That spirit of *Elohim*, which filled the whole earth, is now in Christ; and it is his breath that now sustains the whole world. The living Christ contains in himself all the life of the world. Therefore [he says] I have power in my own self, through the power of this life-giving spirit. But after I am dead, when I no longer exist, it cannot then properly be said, according to the logic of time, that I raise myself from the dead. Rather it is the Father who raises me.

Thus, you read in many places in Scripture that the Father raised his son Jesus from the dead.[d] If God truly

Err, 75r

Err, 75r

---

[a] John 10:38, 14:10-11.   [b] John 16:15: "All that the Father has is mine."
[c] Phil 4:13.   [d] Acts 2:24, 3:15, 4:10; Rom 4:24, 8:11; 1 Cor. 6:14; 2 Cor. 4:14; many others.

raised his dead son to life, he truly led him from a state of non-being to a state of being. Therefore, the Son was not alive [prior to his resurrection]. For true death takes away life and leads from being to non-being, while true resurrection leads from non-being to being. It was truly the ever-living person of the Son, that is, his divinity, which raised the body and gave it life; so that you might also claim that he restored himself to life, with the power that now exists in him.

Passage 17

Err, 77r-v

In the seventeenth section not one, but many, [biblical] passages will be elucidated, as we seek to know whether it is the human Christ who is called *the wisdom of God, the power of God*,[a] and *the glory of God*.[b] This inquiry into abstract nouns might present difficulties for Scotists,[55] but would not be a problem for the Hebrews. In Hebrew there are innumerable names ending in [88] *el* and *iah*, which mean "of God." It is an extremely common Hebraism, that when some outstanding property of God is appropriate to a particular being, it can be called by God's name, as when someone strong is called "the strength of God," someone wise "the wisdom of God," and [similarly] "the healing of God" or "the salvation of God."[c] A great tree is called the tree of God, a great general is the general of God, a great army is the army of God, and a great wind is the wind of God. Something beautiful and holy is called the beauty of holiness, the glory of holiness, or the splendour of holiness. Just as we ourselves often call some notable person the ornament, the flower, the glory, or the splendour of the nation, so too, because of his excellence, such names are also appropriate for Christ.

---

[a] 1 Cor 1:24.   [b] Heb 1:3.   [c] Often found in personal names, such as Gabriel ("strength of God"), Raphael ("healing of God"), or Isaiah ("salvation of God").

Christ said of John the Baptist, "*He was a blazing and a shining light*,"[a] and he called the apostles "*the light of the world.*"[b] In Acts 8, the people said of Simon Magus, "*This man is the power of God, which is called great.*"[c] Judith was called "*the glory of Jerusalem, the delight of Israel, and the pride of our nation.*"[d] Thus Christ is the true *burning lamp, shining* in the splendour of [God's] glory.[e] He is *the light of the world*,[f] the begotten light, *illuminating everyone*[g] and the expectation of all. The splendour of his face lights up all of the heavens, and will illuminate them *in the age to come*.[h] He is the wisdom of God, containing in himself all the wisdom of God, and *in him are hidden all the treasures of wisdom and knowledge*.[i] He is the strength of God, the one *through whom God creates all things*,[j] and does so even to the present day. It is he who possesses all the *power of God*[k] and *can do all things*.[l]

Err, 78r-v

Passage 18

[Genesis 19:24: *Then the Lord rained on Sodom and Gomorrah brimstone and fire from the Lord out of heaven.*]

The eighteenth passage is: *Then the Lord rained on Sodom and Gomorrah brimstone and fire from the Lord out of heaven* (Genesis 19). Because it says "The Lord . . . from the Lord," most take this to mean that there are two equal beings here, the Father and the Son, as if [Scripture] had said, "the Son [rained fire] from the Father."

In order for this passage to be readily comprehended, we must first of all be aware that we are dealing with a standard convention of the Hebrew language. As [for instance] it is

---

[a] John 5:35. [b] Matt 5:14. [c] Acts 8:10. [d] Judith 15:9. [e] John 5:35.
[f] John 8:12, 9:5. [g] John 1:9. [h] 2 Cor 4:6; Eph 1:21. [i] Col 2:3.
[j] Col 1:16. [k] 1 Cor 1:24. [l] Phil 4:13.

said in 1 Kings 8, *Solomon assembled* all the tribes *of Israel before King Solomon*,[a] that is, before himself. In 1 Kings 12 and 2 Chronicles 11, Rehoboam assembled his tribes *to restore the kingdom to Rehoboam*, that is, [89] to himself.[b] *Moses* spoke *to Hobab, Moses' brother-in-law*, that is, his own brother-in law, in Numbers 10.[c] Similarly, in Genesis 1, 5, and 9, *God created humanity in the image of God*[d] and said, "*I will remember the covenant between God*" — that is, myself — "and humankind."[e] God told Jacob to *make an altar to God* in Genesis 35.[f] In Exodus 16: *The Lord has heard your murmurings against the Lord*. And shortly thereafter, *the Lord said to Moses, "The Lord has given you the Sabbath."*[g] Also, in Exodus 31 and 35, God *filled* Bezalel *with the Spirit of God*.[h] It is common in Hebrew for the antecedent noun to be used instead of a pronoun.[56]

This, my first response [to the mistaken implication that there are two equal beings in God], which is based on the way the [Hebrew] language is used, is extremely clear. If only all these sophists had learned how to speak Hebrew! For only the holy language spoken by God himself contains within itself the true mysteries of God.

The second explanation of this passage is also based on the way Hebrew is commonly used. For instance, a great fire is called *fire from the Lord*,[i] a deep sleep is called *a deep sleep from the Lord*,[j] and a mighty wind is called *a wind from the Lord*.[k] These are all Hebraisms, as we said above. Similarly, we say *fire from the Lord out of heaven* because this fire is from the empyrean, from which place it is sent, just as we speak of the *fire that has been prepared for* the demons.[l]

The final, mystical explanation of this passage, in which we come to comprehend the mystery of Christ, is that the

---

[a] 1 Kg 8:1   [b] 1 Kg 12:21; 2 Chr 11:1.   [c] Num 10:29.   [d] Gen 1:27, 5:1.
[e] Gen 9:16.   [f] Gen 35:1.   [g] Ex 16:7, 28-29.   [h] Ex 31:3, 35:31.
[i] Lev 9:24; Num 16:35.   [j] 1 Sam 26:12.   [k] Num 11:31.   [l] Matt 25:41.

true Jehovah in the world of human beings was the Word, the person of Christ brought [to Mary] by an angel. At the time [of the destruction of Sodom and Gomorrah] an angel, acting in the name of Jehovah, rained down fire from the boundless and supreme Jehovah, the father of our Lord Jesus Christ.

Passage 19

In this, the nineteenth section, I shall not expound [upon a particular scriptural passage], but instead I inquire whether [before the Incarnation] the Word described by John was the real Son or a person [of the Trinity].

My answer is that the prophets always foretold a future Son. *The sun of righteousness shall rise* (Malachi 4).[a] *Let the earth open, that salvation may sprout forth* (Isaiah 45).[b] *There shall come forth a shoot from the stem of Jesse* (Isaiah 11).[c] *Their leader shall come from among them, and their prince shall come forth from their midst* (Jeremiah 30).[d] *A star shall arise out of Jacob* (Numbers 24).[e] *Out of Bethlehem a leader shall come forth* (Micah 5).[f] *You shall call his name Immanuel* (Isaiah 7).[g] *I will be his father, and he shall be my son* **[90]** (1 Chronicles 17 and 2 Samuel 7).[h] *He shall be called the Son of the Most High* (Luke 1).[i]

Do you really suppose that John was exercising his own human will when he chose to say "Word" instead of "Son"? Where does such a gross misuse of words come from? How could such great liberties be taken in conjuring up sons? You cannot show one word, not one iota, in the Bible, where scripture called the Word a son. Those who would correctly preserve the words of God, will read "Word" where "Word" is written in Scripture, and "Son" where scripture says "Son." For he who was formerly the Word is now the Son.

---

[a] Mal 4:2. [b] Isa 45:8. [c] Isa 11:1. [d] Jer 30:21. [e] Num 24:17.
[f] Mic 5:2. [g] Isa 7:14. [h] 1 Chr 17:13; 2 Sam 7:14. [i] Luke 1:32.

Err, 79v
Err, 79v
Err, 79v
Err, 93v

Indeed, generation in eternity is attributed to the Son, Jesus Christ. We say that the Son, the man Jesus, *was with God* from *the beginning*,[a] in his own person and substance. [Prior to the Incarnation] the Word was a person, a son, [only] insofar as it was the person and substance of the future Son. For the voice of prophecy [in the Old Testament] was the person of Christ with God. This Jesus Christ has been with God for all eternity, both in person and in essence, in terms of the substance of the body and the substance of the spirit. It must therefore be admitted that [before the Incarnation] the Word was a person — a son, but not [yet] the real Son.

Err, 92v-93r

Err, 110r

Passage 20

[Hebrews 2:16: He does not take on the nature of angels, but instead takes on the nature of the seed of Abraham.]

The final passage is from the Epistle to the Hebrews, chapter 2: *He does not take on the nature of angels, but instead takes on*[57] *the nature of the seed of Abraham*. Because of the nature of the Word, as a hypostasis and a person, we must grant that, when [the Son] came from heaven, he took on and clothed himself in flesh. Although we do grant that the man [Jesus] took on and was clothed in flesh, as when Job says, *You have clothed me with skin and flesh*,[b] I shall now explain this passage about [Christ's] taking on [flesh] in a different way.

Err, 95r

The apostle does not compare the seed of Abraham to just one angel, as if [the seed of Abraham] were a single human nature, but to the whole company of angels. That is to say, [Christ] did not come to liberate the angels and to take on their nature, but to liberate and take on the nature

Err, 95r

---

[a] John 1:1. [b] Job 10:11.

Book 2

of humanity. The apostle is here speaking, not of a past union with humanity, but of a present union, and about the daily taking of human beings to himself, as the verb ἐπιλαμβάνομαι (*epilambanomai*, to take on or assume) in the present tense clearly teaches us, when it is correctly interpreted. [Christ] takes on the nature of the seed of Abraham collectively. This is confirmed by a great many passages of scripture, particularly John 8, Psalm 104, and Isaiah 41, where it is made clear that he has taken them on.[a]

Exodus 19 likewise deals with assumption: *You have seen how* **[91]** *I bore you* [*on eagles' wings*], *and took you to myself.*[b] Also 1 Kings 12: *I will take you.*[c] And 2 Samuel 22: *He took me, he drew me out of many waters.*[d] In the same way our devoted high priest, Jesus Christ, does not take on the nature of angels but, liberating us from servitude to the devil, and drawing us out of death into life, takes us to his bosom, into the heavenly kingdom and the glory of God. In John 14 he says, "*I will take you to myself.*"[e] In Romans 14 [Paul tells us to] take one another in, as Christ takes us into the glory of God.[f] Similarly, in Deuteronomy 30: *He will take you, gather you,*[g] and bring you into his rest. This is the rest into which you, reader, will enter today, born today of heaven, and taken into the heavenly kingdom, if only you will hear his voice today, that heavenly voice saying, "*This is my Son.*"[h]

Woe to the sophists who equivocate with their scoffing words and outlandish figures of speech! Woe to those who imagine that they can tear God to pieces, mutilate him, and divide him up!

Err, 95r

Err, 95r-v

---

[a] John 8:58; Ps 105:6; Isa 41:8-9. [b] Ex 19:4. [c] 1 Kg 11:37 (not 1 Kg 12). [d] 2 Sam 22:17. [e] John 14:3. [f] Rom 15:7. [g] Deut 30:4. (30:4-5 in Vulgate). [h] Luke 9:35.

Appendix A

On the Errors of the Trinity

Book 1

DE TRINITA
TIS ERROBIBUS,
LIBER PRIMVS.

IN SCRV=
tandis diuia
ne Triadis,
sanctis arcaa
nis, ab homi
ne exordien
dum eo du=
xi, quia ad
Verbi spe=
culationem,
sine funda=
mento CHRISTI, ascendentes, quàm plurimos
cerno, qui parum aut nihil homini tribuunt, & ue=
rum CHRISTVM obliuioni penitus tradunt:
quibus ego ad memoriã, quis sit ille CHRISTVS,
reducere curabo.   Cæterum, quid, quantumq́; sit
CHRISTO tribuendum, iudicabit ecclesia.   Tria hæc in
   Pronomine demonstrante hominem, quem hu= homine cog=
manitatem appellant, concedam hæc tria. Primo noscenda, an
hic est IESVS CHRISTVS. Secundo, hic est teq́ de Verbo
filius Dei. Tertio, hic est Deus.   loquamur.

On the Errors of the Trinity

Book 1

[2r] In investigating the holy mysteries of the divine Triad, I have decided to begin with the man [Jesus Christ]. For I see so many embarking on speculation about the Word, without a foundation in Christ. They pay little or no attention to the human being and consign the true Christ wholly to oblivion. I intend to remind them who that [true] Christ is. Beyond this, what and how much should be attributed to Christ, the church must decide.

Rest, 5

> {*Before we can speak about the Word, three things must be understood about the man*}

Since the [masculine] demonstrative pronoun [*hic*, this] indicates that he was a man,[a] or what [theologians] call "a human nature," I submit the following three propositions: 1) this [man] is Jesus Christ; 2) this [man] is the Son of God; and 3) this [man] is God.

Rest, 5

[2v] [*First Proposition: This Man is Jesus Christ*]

> {*The name and title of the boy Jesus*}

In the first place, who would deny that this man was called Jesus? This was the name given to him as a boy, at the angel's command, on the day of his circumcision (Luke 1 and 2),[b] just as your name, for instance, is John, and his, Peter. Jesus, as Tertullian says, is a masculine proper name, while Christ is a title.[c]

Rest, 5

---

[a] See A.R1.1.   [b] Luke 1:31, 2:21.   [c] Tertullian, *Adversus Praxean* 28 (PL 2 192B). See A.R1.3.

Appendix A

Rest, 5

The Jews all admitted that he was Jesus, but when [Pilate was] asking them about *Jesus who is called Christ*,[a] they denied that he was the Christ. And they *put out of the synagogue* those who *confessed him to be the Christ*.[b] The apostles frequently argued with them about whether Jesus was the Christ. But there was never any doubt or question that he was Jesus, nor did anyone ever deny this.

{*Note in what sense they took these things, before John wrote about the Word*}

Rest, 5-6

Consider the intent of Paul's words, and the zeal with which he *testified to the Jews that Jesus was the Christ* (Acts 18).[c] With what *spiritual fervor Apollos of Alexandria*, in the same chapter, *confuted the Jews in public, showing by the scriptures that Jesus was the Messiah*![d] What Jesus do you think those "acts" are about? You don't believe, do you, that [Paul and Apollos] were thinking of a hypostasis?

Rest, 6

Therefore I have to concede that he is the Christ as well as Jesus, since I admit that he was anointed by God. For he is *your holy child, whom you have anointed* (Acts 4).[e] He is the *holy of holies*, whose anointing was predicted in Daniel 9.[f] And in Acts 10, Peter said, "*You know*," as if it were something easy to understand.[g] For what was said about Jesus was **[3r]** known to everyone: *how God anointed Jesus of Nazareth with the Holy Spirit and with power, for God was with him*, and *he is the one established by God as the judge of the living and the dead*.[h]

Rest, 6

"*Let all the house of Israel know assuredly*," [Peter] says in Acts 2, "*that God has made this man Jesus, whom you crucified, both Lord and Christ*" — that is, the anointed one.[i] Nonetheless, some use the pronouns in these scripture

---

[a] Matt 27:17, 22. [b] John 9:22. See also John 12:42, 16:2. [c] Acts 18:5. [d] Acts 18:24-25, 28. [e] Acts 4:27. [f] Dan 9:24. [g] Acts 10:36-37. [h] Acts 10:38, 42. [i] Acts 2:36. This argument is based on Tertullian, *Adversus Praxean* 28 (PL 2 192C-193A).

passages [*illo*, him; *ipse*, he; and *hunc*, this man] to indicate another being, even though John says that *whoever denies that Jesus is God's anointed is a liar*, while whoever accepts *that Jesus is the Christ is born of God* (1 John 2 and 5).[a]

Likewise Tertullian, in *Against Praxeas*, says that the word "Christ" is a noun pertaining to "a human nature."[b] And in books 3 and 4 of *Against Marcion*, having carefully investigated the term "Christ," he mentions nothing about that being which some consider to be Christ. Who, he asks, is the Son of man, if not an actual man, born of a human being, "flesh born from flesh"?[c] For the Hebrew expression "son of man," like "son of Adam," means nothing other than a man. The word ["Christ," or "the anointed one,"] conveys the same thing, for "to be anointed" can only refer to a human nature. If, therefore, as [Tertullian] says, "to be anointed is an experience of the body,"[d] who can deny that it was a man who was anointed? Rest, 6

Futhermore, in the first book of Clement's *Recognitions*,[e] Peter discloses the true meaning of the word ["anointed"]: "Because kings were commonly called Christs, [**3v**] therefore [Jesus], on account of the superior nature of his anointing, above all others, is called Christ the King." For "just as God made an angel first among angels, a beast first among beasts, and a star first among stars, so too did he make Christ first among men."[f] Likewise, the authority of the holy scriptures very clearly teaches us that it was a man who was called Christ, since even an earthly king can be called Christ[g] (1 Samuel 12 and 22, and Isaiah 45).[h] Rest, 6

---

[a] 1 John 2:22, 5:1.   [b] Tertullian, *Adversus Praxean* 29 (PL 2 194A-B).   [c] Tertullian, *Adversus Marcionem* 4.10 (PL 2 380B).   [d] Tertullian, *Adversus Marcionem* 3.15 (PL 2 342B).   [e] See A.R1.5.   [f] [Clement], *Recognitiones* 1.45 (PG 1 1233A-B).   [g] See A.R1.6.   [h] 1 Sam 12:1-5; 1 Sam 24:6; Isa 45:1. The reference to 1 Samuel 22 is a mistake for 1 Samuel 24. This was corrected in the corresponding passage in *Restoration*.

Appendix A

Rest, 6

Similarly, Matthew 1 [speaks of Mary], *of whom Jesus was born, that [man] who is called Christ*.[a] Note the [masculine] article [*ille*, that man] and note the title [Christ]. For these words, and also the [masculine] pronouns, are to be understood in the simplest way, as pointing to something perceived by the senses. Again, in Luke 1: *You shall call his name Jesus.*[b] And in chapter 3 Luke is very clearly describing Jesus the man when he says: *And Jesus was entering his thirtieth year, and was thought to be the son of Joseph.*[c]

Rest, 7

Rest, 7

Also, in Acts 13: *God, as he promised, brought forth Jesus from the seed of David.*[d] In the same passage in Acts, and also in John 1, John [the Baptist] says, "Do not *suppose that I am* the Christ."[e] How ridiculous John's disavowal would have been, if the word "Christ" could not refer to a human being! Furthermore, why does Christ warn us to avoid people who call themselves Christs?[f]

Rest, 7

[If the word "Christ" could not refer to a human being] Christ's question and Peter's response in Matthew 16 would have been meaningless, when Christ said, "*Who do people say that I, the Son of man, am?*"[g] and Peter replied, "*You are the Christ, you are* [4r] *the Son of the living God.*"[h] Nor was he [only] the living Word of God, for [in that case] in speaking to the human being, [Peter] ought to have said, "Christ is in you; the Son of God is in you," and not "*you are* [Christ]." And when *he charged [the disciples] to tell no one that he himself was the Christ,*[i] tell me, what was he indicating by means of that pronoun [*ipse*, he himself]? For it is as clear as day that he was referring to himself and was talking about himself. Does it not embarrass you to claim that he was nameless, and that the apostles had preached about him for such a long time without ever calling him by his own name? On your own authority, you impose on him

---

[a] Matt 1:16. [b] Luke 1:31. [c] Luke 3:23. [d] Acts 13:23. [e] Acts 13:25; John 1:20. [f] Matt 24:23-24; Mark 13:21-22; Luke 21:8. [g] Matt 16:13,15. See A.R1.7. [h] Matt 16:16. [i] Matt 16:20.

a new and unsuitable name, one that the apostles never heard of, calling him merely "a human nature."

{*Christ. Messiah.*}

By the way, do not be misled by the Greek title χριστὸς (*christos*, Christ). Instead consider the [equivalent] Hebrew word מָשִׁיחַ (Messiah) or the Latin word *unctus* (anointed). Then see if you, who admit that we [human beings] can be anointed, dare to admit that [Jesus] was anointed. I would not be so insistent on proving this point, which is basically very clear, except that I see that the minds of certain people have been led astray. The testimony of Christ is very clear. In John 8, he calls himself a human being: *"You seek to kill me, a human being who has told you the truth."*[a] And in 1 Timothy 2: *the mediator between God and humanity, the human being, Christ Jesus.*[b]

Rest, 7

Rest, 7

You may disregard the word *homo* (human being), which, if you accept the [doctrine of] *communicatio idiomatum* [sharing of attributes], has become corrupted in meaning. Instead, consider the word [**4v**] *vir* [man][c] and listen to what Peter says in Acts 2: Christ was *a man approved [by God].*[d] In the last chapter of Luke: *Concerning Jesus of Nazareth, who was a man, a prophet, mighty [in deed and word].*[e] In John 1 [John the Baptist says], *"After me will come a man."*[f] Isaiah 53 [calls him] *the lowliest of men, a man of sorrows.*[g] Zechariah 6 [says] *Behold the man whose name is the Branch.*[h] And Acts 17 [proclaims that] *God will judge [the world] by that man*[i] — that is to say, Christ.

Do not misrepresent the law of God by means of circumlocutions. Rather, carefully consider the nature of the demonstrative pronoun, and you will recognize that [pointing to something] is the original meaning of the word "this."[j] For very often, when [Jesus] was pointed out to someone, that person accepted that *"this is the Christ"*

Rest, 8

---

[a] John 8:40.   [b] 1 Tim 2:5.   [c] See A.R1.8.   [d] Acts 2:22.   [e] Luke 24:19.
[f] John 1:30.   [g] Isa 53:3.   [h] Zech 6:12.   [i] Acts 17:31.   [j] See A.R1.9.

Appendix A

Rest, 8   and "you are Jesus."ᵃ And he spoke, asked and answered questions, felt hunger, and they saw him walking on water.ᵇ Similarly, [when he asked]: *"Whom do you seek?"* [*they answered,*] *"Jesus of Nazareth." [Jesus said to them,]"I am he."*ᶜ [And Judas said,] *"Whomever I shall kiss is the one, seize him."*ᵈ In another passage [Jesus says]: *"It is I myself, touch me and see."*ᵉ And in Acts 2, [Peter says]: *"This Jesus, whom you put to death, God raised up, of which we all are witnesses."*ᶠ What could one be pointing out by the use of such pronouns?

Rest, 8   As far as visual evidence is concerned, are we not now in a worse condition than the Samaritan woman in John 4, who said, *"Come and see the man who told me all that I ever did. Can this be the Christ?"*ᵍ It is no wonder that the woman, on the basis of [her experience of] Christ, should have spoken in this way. For when she asked about the Messiah **[5r]** to come, *he who is called the Christ*, he answered, *"I who am speaking to you am he."*ʰ I — I, not that [incorporeal] being, but I who am speaking.

Rest, 8   Furthermore, about what man do you understand the following [words] of the Apostle: *As by one man's trespass, so by the grace of one man, Jesus Christ.* Or these: *As by a man came death, by a man has come also the resurrection of the dead.*ⁱ For scripture does not use the word "man" connotatively. In 1 Corinthians 15 [Paul] calls him not only a man,

Rest, 199   but Adam as well.ʲ Do we, nevertheless, prefer a connotative man and a sophistical *suppositum* as the foundation [of our faith]? Away, I implore you, with all these sophistical subtleties, and you will see *a great light*.ᵏ

The foundations of the church are the words of Christ, which are plain and of the utmost simplicity. Therefore let

---

ᵃ There are numerous instances in the Gospels of "you are Christ." However, "you are Jesus" is not found.   ᵇ See A.R1.10.   ᶜ John 18:4-5.   ᵈ Matt 26:48; Mark 14:44.   ᵉ Luke 24:39.   ᶠ Acts 2:32, 36.   ᵍ John 4:29.   ʰ John 4:25-26.   ⁱ Rom 5:15; 1 Cor 15:21.   ʲ 1 Cor 15:45.   ᵏ Isa 9:2.

us imitate the apostles, who proclaimed Christ in words that were not *fashioned by* human *artifice* (2 Peter 1).[a] *The words of* God *are pure words*,[b] to be received with simplicity. As the Apostle attests in 1 Corinthians, chapters 1 and 2, *the testimony of* Christ is *not proclaimed in lofty words*,[c] but plainly and as if we were *little children*,[d] and as if *knowing nothing other than Jesus Christ, and him crucified*.[e]

Likewise, [if Christ were not a human being] how could you speak of our brotherhood with Christ? Who is the one who is exalted *above his fellows*?[f] What kind of comparison between Christ and Moses is the Apostle making in Hebrews 3, when he says that [Christ] is *worthy of greater glory than Moses*, [5v] since *Moses was [faithful] as a servant, but Christ truly as a son*?[g] Why, in chapters 1 and 2 of the Epistle to the Hebrews, is the Apostle so insistent in declaring that Christ was exalted even above the angels?[h] For [if Christ were not a human being] it would be a trivial exercise to prove that the second nature of God is more exalted than the angels.[1] Nor can [the Apostle's] deliberately chosen words be forced to serve that interpretation. For the Apostle is quoting the words of the prophet David, who marveled at the greatness of Christ's glory because, although he was a human being, all things were made subject to him (Psalm 8).[i]

Again, in John chapter 20: [*Jesus*] *performed miracles in order that we might believe that Jesus is the Christ, the Son of God*.[j] Note what [John] considers essential about Jesus: that we believe that this Jesus, who was the only-begotten son of God the Father, was the anointed one. How could that unknown second being be recognized by the miracles? Rather, the one whom they saw performing miracles was understood [to be the anointed one], as Nicodemus

Rest, 8

---

[a] 2 Pet 1:16. [b] Ps 12:6. [c] 1 Cor 2:1. See also 1 Cor 1:17. [d] 1 Thes 2:7. [e] 1 Cor 2:2. [f] Ps 45:7. [g] Heb 3:3-6. [h] Hebrews chapter 1; Heb 2:7. [i] Ps 8:6. [j] John 20:30-31.

Appendix A

Rest, 8

acknowledges in John 3.[a] These outward signs do not reveal the inner nature of these philosophical beings. Similarly, in John 5, Christ himself attests that the works which he performs are sufficient to reveal that he was sent by the Father.[b] And similarly in John 1, Nathanael concludes that [Jesus] is *the Son of God* who was sent to be *king of Israel*, because [Jesus] says about him, *"I saw you under the fig tree."*[c] In Matthew 14 [the disciples] come to the same conclusion, because he chased the wind away.[d] And in John 6, because of the miracles he performed, Peter concludes, *"We have come to know that you* [6r] *are the Christ, the Son of the living God."*[e]

{Second proposition} [This Man is the Son of God]

Rest, 9

These conclusions [reached by those who witnessed Christ's miracles] also clearly prove my second proposition: that this man, whom I call Christ, is the Son of God. For based on the miracles that he performed, [the witnesses] concluded that he was the Son of God. And, once it has been proven that he is Jesus Christ, it logically follows that anyone who denies that he is the Son denies Jesus Christ. For scripture proclaims nothing else but that Jesus Christ is the Son of God.

Rest, 9

Besides, he is specifically identified as the Son in many scriptural passages, and thus, in relation to him, God is called the Father — truly the Father, I say, because [Jesus] was begotten by [God], who assumed the role of a human father. For [Jesus] was not in fact born of the seed of Joseph, as Carpocrates, Cerinthus, and Photinus falsely and impiously claimed.[2] Instead, in place of human seed, the almighty power of the Word of God overshadowed Mary, and the Holy Spirit acted within her. Chapter 1 of Luke continues: *Therefore the child to be born will be holy, and will*

---

[a] John 3:2.   [b] John 5:36-37.   [c] John 1:47-50.   [d] Matt 14:32-33. See also Luke 8:23-25.   [e] John 6:69.

be called the Son of God.ᵃ Consider carefully the word "therefore." Note the logical conclusion. And note the reason why [the man Jesus] ought to be called the Son of God.

Finally, Daniel reveals to us the nature of the sonship in the man Jesus Christ, calling him *a stone not cut by [human] hands*.ᵇ This same kind of sonship is also presented in Matthew 1, where it is said that [Mary] was made *pregnant by the Holy Spirit*, and *what was conceived in her came from the Holy Spirit*.ᶜ Pray tell, who is [**6v**] that child who was begotten and conceived in her, who comes from the Holy Spirit? From this [Matthew] concludes that *the son* whom *she will bear* will be the saviour *Immanuel*.ᵈ

Rest, 9

Note what Luke says: *The son whom you will conceive and bear will be called the Son of the Most High*. He further says, *He will be great, and God will give him the throne [of his father David]*.ᵉ Can it be, then, that it is the second person who will become great, and will receive from God *the throne of his father David*? Why did [the angel] not say, "He will be called the son of the first person," and "The first person will give him the throne"? Instead what he says is "*the Son of God, the Most High*" and "*God will give him the throne*."

Rest, 9

Some [theologians], labouring to distort the angel's words, misrepresent the the word "holy" in this passage,ᶠ as if Christ, the firstborn, was not worthy [to be called holy]. This [misrepresentation] is particularly [apparent] since, in the next chapter, Luke reveals why [the angel] said "holy."ᵍ It was because *every firstborn* will be called *holy* to God (Exodus 13 and 34, Numbers 8).ʰ Similarly, in Acts 4 the apostles use the expression, "*your holy son Jesus*."ⁱ

Rest, 9-10

Furthermore, [these theologians] wish to speak of the power of God in philosophical terms. If only they could comprehend what the Word of God actually is! They do not show how this [power] could act in place of the seed of

---

ᵃ Luke 1:35. ᵇ Dan 2:34. ᶜ Matt 1:18, 20. ᵈ Matt 1:21, 23, following Isa 7:14. ᵉ Luke 1:31, 32. ᶠ Luke 1:35. ᵍ Luke 2:23. ʰ Ex 13:2, 13:12, 34:19; Num 8:16-17. ⁱ Acts 4:27, 30.

Appendix A

Rest, 11

a man — nor do they make clear what it is that *will be called the Son of God*, begotten by this power that took the place of [a man's] seed. For Luke does not say that this power is to be called the Son.[a] Rather, he who was begotten by *the power [of the Most High] will therefore be called the Son of God*,[b] **[7r]** because the power of God functioned in place of a man's seed.

Nor do [these theologians] take into account how great and how profound are the mysteries of this word and seed, about which it is said, according to the parable, that *the seed* of the sower *is the word of God*.[c] Because just as by the word of God Christ is begotten and born, so by the word of God we are born again — *born again*, Peter says, *by the word of the living God*. And he calls this the *everlasting seed*.[d] This *gives us birth by the word of truth*.[e]

Therefore [the theologians] philosophized wrongly when they denied that the Son was a human being, in order to make a Son out of the Word. Yet the truth of the matter is different from this. John considered it more appropriate to say "the Word" rather than "the Son." Indeed, it is because of the action of the Word, that the flesh is called the Son.[f] I will speak [more] about the Word later.[g] For now let us preserve for Jesus Christ the *honour and glory* that are his.[h] For in so doing we shall come to understand the Word as well.

Rest, 11

Furthermore, the very nature of the word ["son"] teaches us that the Son should be called a human being. For just as being anointed is characteristic of a body, so too being born is a characteristic of flesh. Therefore, as Tertullian says, "it was flesh that was born, and the Son of God will be flesh."[i] Again, who was that little child so often mentioned in Matthew 2,

---

[a] See A.R1.11. [b] Luke 1:35. [c] Luke 8:11; see Luke 8:5-15. [d] 1 Pet 1:23. [e] James 1:18. [f] See John 1:14. [g] In book 3. [h] See Rom 16:27; Heb 2:9; 2 Pet 1:17; Rev 5:12, 13. [i] Tertullian, *Adversus Praxean* 27 (PL 2 190C). Tertullian did not endorse this sentiment, but attributed it to his opponent, the patripassian preacher Praxeas.

whom Joseph accepted [as his own], led away [into Egypt], and brought home again?[a] Do you mean to say that "child" is the name of a hypostasis? Ask yourself whether that child was *the son called out of Egypt*.[b]

Now, tell me whether he, the one you call "a human nature," was a man or a mule.[c] For if he was a human being, and was begotten and born, then he must have had a procreator. [**7v**] Tell me, then, by whom was he begotten? Clearly, he will be the son of the one who begot him. Tell me whether he was begotten by his father Joseph or by some other father. You will not find any other father but God. Otherwise you will have to claim that [the Son] was an apparition, and not flesh. For if he was flesh, that flesh was born from some father. Therefore he is someone's son. And I do not believe that you can avoid this [conclusion], unless you make one son out of two, or engage in philosophical speculation about imaginary sonships, which were unknown to Christ himself. But it is no wonder that you say that you profess two sons (not to mention two *supposita*). For you profess two nativities of two beings, which are vastly different from each other. *Rest*, 11

Similarly, if one grants that there are two begettings of two beings, then one cannot deny that two male children were begotten and born. However much sophistry you use — [however you try to explain] the nature of sonship so as to make these two one mass, one aggregate, or one connotative *suppositum* — you are mistaken if you believe that this [aggregate] is only one son, and that this is in keeping with the plain truth of scripture. For you have before your eyes two male children who were begotten and born. Who would ever make a distinction between male children and sons? *Rest*, 12

[The writers of] the scriptures never gave any thought to such craftiness. Rather, they speak very simply about Jesus, the only Son of God. Nor does scripture mention *Rest*, 12

---

[a] Matt 2:13-15.   [b] Matt 2:15, quoting Hos 11:1.   [c] See A.R1.20.

Appendix A

any other being, any other nature, besides the human being who was begotten and born. Thus Ignatius, speaking of one and the same being, says: "Jesus Christ **[8r]** the Son of God, who was truly born from God and from the Virgin,"[a] — from God before [the beginning of] the world, but later from Mary without the seed of a man. Precisely how this happened will be discussed below.[b] For now, I only desire that old women, bleary-eyed men, and barbers[3] should come to recognize that Christ is the Son of God. This is the root and foundation [of Christian faith]. I will later speak at greater length about the Word.[c] For Christ proclaimed, even to women, that he was the Messiah. Consider, I implore you, how could an old woman possibly comprehend that metaphysical son, when so many arch-heretics, even the most subtle, have fallen into error?

Rest, 12

Furthermore, in the first chapter of the Gospel of John, God says to John [the Baptist], "*He upon whom you see the Spirit* of God *descend and remain, he is* the one." [John the Baptist says,] "*And I have seen and have borne witness that this is the Son of God.*"[d] Please note the very plain language, spoken without any circumlocution. For according to [the sophists'] way of thinking, John [the Baptist] must have been deceived when he said that the man whom he saw was the Son of God. Nor is it credible that [John] himself could ever have conceived of that other [metaphysical] being, or that God had given him a sign by which he might recognize it. Or will you claim that the voice from heaven was lying when it said, "*He upon whom you see [the Spirit descend], he is the one*"? And it must also have been lying when, as [the Holy Spirit] descended in the presence of everyone, it said, "*This is my son*" or "*You are my son*" (Matthew 3, Luke 3).[e] **[8v]** If by the pronoun "this" it was indicating some other

Rest, 12-13

---

[a] [Ignatius], *Ad Trallios* 9 (PG 5 787C-790A).   [b] In book 3.
[c] In book 3.   [d] John 1:33-34.   [e] Matt 3:17; Luke 3:22; see also Mark 1:11.

hidden being, then its testimony would not have been clear, and it would have been misleading the people.

Likewise, in John 9, when [the man who had been blind] asked who the Son of God was, Jesus replied, "*You have seen him, and it is he who is speaking to you.*"[a] How could he have said it more clearly? Also, the centurion, when he saw with his own eyes [Christ on the cross], said, "*Truly this man was the Son of God.*"[b] Now consider that the pronouns [in these statements] point to a being perceivable by the senses. I do not believe that the centurion was a sophist nor that he would have spoken in terms of *communicatio idiomatum* [sharing of attributes]. *Rest*, 13

Again, hear the words of Paul, who, as soon as he had recovered his sight, entered *the synagogue* and *preached about Jesus, because he was the Son of God* (Acts 9).[c] One cannot find here any mention of the hypostasis of the Word. Actually, it was revealed by John after the fact, to support the doctrine [that the man Jesus is the Son of God]. Thus, [John] does not oppose our view, but approves of it. *Rest*, 13

Consider also whether the High Priest had in mind a second hypostasis when he asked, "*Are you the son of the blessed God?*" and Jesus replied, "*I am*" (Mark 14)[d] or "*You say that I am the Son of God*" (Luke 22).[e] Similarly, in Luke 11, [Martha says,] "*I believe that you are the Christ, the Son of God.*"[f] People must judge for themselves how these clearest of words have been perversely distorted by that sophistical doctrine, *communicatio idiomatum*. As for me, I understand the words of Christ in the simplest way possible, and will not permit any violence to be done to them. I refuse to allow you to drag scripture into the **[9r]** fictions you are concocting. Instead, [scripture], preserved intact, should draw you in. I refuse to allow you to cast doubt upon the obvious truth of the Gospel with your flights of fancy. *Rest*, 13

---

[a] John 9:37. [b] Mark 15:39; Matt 27:54. [c] Acts 9:20. [d] Mark 14:61-62. [e] Luke 22:70. [f] John (not Luke) 11:27.

Appendix A

Rest, 13   If you should say that nothing more appears to be attributed to Christ than to the rest of us, since even we are called children of God, I answer that, on the contrary, our being called children of God is proof that he is the true Son. For human beings are called children because of their likeness to the man [Christ]. Nevertheless the difference [between us and Christ] is great, as will become apparent when we come to understand the mystery of the Word.[a] And if we are called children [of God], it is because of the gifts and grace that have been given to us through [Christ]. Therefore he himself, as the one responsible for our being children [of God], is called "son" in a far superior way. And when Christ is mentioned [in Scripture], the [definite] article is used: it is said, "*This is the Son of God*."[b] He is not to be called by the generic term "a son," as we might be, but is to be denoted in a certain special and significant way.[4]

Rest, 13   [Christ] is the natural-born son [of God], but no one else is a child [of God] by direct descent. Others are not born the children of God; they become God's children. *By faith in Jesus Christ we are made children of God* (Galatians 3, John 1).[c] Therefore we are called *children by adoption* (Romans 8, Ephesians 1).[d] But to claim that Christ was adopted in a similar manner is the impiety of the Bonosians.[5] For we do not read of such an adoption of Christ, but rather of his true begetting by God the Father. He is not merely a son, but the *true son* [*of God*] (Wisdom 2).[e] [9v] And in Romans 8 he is called not merely a son in the ordinary sense of the word, but [God's] *very own son*.[f]

Rest, 13   And, just as properly as earthly fathers are called the fathers of their own children, God is said to be the father of Jesus Christ. Otherwise God cannot be called the specially efficient and productive cause of this particular effect.[g]

---

[a] In book 3.   [b] John 1:34; Acts 9:20.   [c] Gal 3:26; John 1:12.
[d] Rom 8:15, 23; Eph 1:5. See also Gal 4:5.   [e] Wisd of Sol 2:18.
[f] Rom 8:32.   [g] See A.R1.15.

For if he should choose to have his very own offspring, and acts on his own to beget him, just as an earthly father does, then why does he not deserve to be called a father just as properly [as any other father]? *"Can it be that I, who give procreation to others, shall myself be barren?" says the Lord* (Isaiah 66).[a] By no means! Rather, he is called the Father, because all paternal family relationships in heaven and on earth are named after him (Ephesians 3).[b]

Rest, 14

[The name Father is] all the more fitting, because [God] not only begot [Christ], but he endowed him with the fullness of divinity, so that in this the Son would be like the Father. And there is yet another reason why God is even more properly called a father than mortal men are: he participates in the begetting of others' [sons], while other [fathers] contribute nothing to the begetting of his Son. Therefore, if [God] is more properly called the Father, then Christ, beyond all others, is most appropriately called the Son.

Rest, 14

{*Third proposition*} [*This Man is God*]

Thirdly, I have declared this to be true: Christ is God. Indeed, he is said to be God in appearance, because, as the Apostle says, he was *in the form of God*.[c] And according to Tertullian, he was found to be God because of his power, just as he was found to be a human being because of his flesh.[d] For "Christ," if I may be allowed to speak in the manner of Paul, means someone made divine *according to* **[10r]** *the inner man*,[e] as the result of an inner anointing, which is performed by God. In terms of the flesh he is a human being, and in terms of the spirit he is God. For *what is born of the Spirit is spirit*, and *God is spirit*.[f] And so [it is written] in Isaiah 9: *Unto us a child is born; his name will be called mighty God*.[g]

Rest, 14-15

---

[a] Isa 66:9.   [b] Eph 3:15.   [c] Phil 2:6.   [d] Tertullian, *Adversus Praxean* 21 (PL 2 181B): "He is the Son of man through his flesh, just as he is also the Son of God through his spirit."   [e] Rom 7:22.   [f] John 3:6, 4:24.   [g] Isa 9:6.

Appendix A

Rest, 15

Clearly observe that both the name and the might of God are attributed to the newborn child, to whom is *given all power in heaven and on earth*.[a] In John 20, Thomas addresses [Christ] as "*my God, my Lord*."[b] In Romans 9, Christ is said to be *God*, who is *to be* praised and *blessed* in *all things*.[c] And his divinity is demonstrated in many other passages. For he was *exalted* so that he might receive divinity, and *a name which is above every name*.[d]

Rest, 15

They should beware, therefore, those who would strive to abase him to such a degree that they want him to be called just "a human nature," as if he were some lowly being. They confer so much imperfection on him that they not only deny that he is their Lord, but even deny that he was the king of the Jews, anointed by God. And they deny that he is the reconciler and the mediator. Indeed, they strip him of those things that are his by nature, denying that he was the son of Mary, and finally even denying that he was a man.

{*They deny that the man is a human being, and admit that God could be an ass* [e]}

Who would not shed tears at such a total rejection of Christ? For Moses, an earthly man, had previously been called a mediator between the people and God,[6] yet [the sophists] would deny that *the second man, from heaven, and heavenly*,[f] is the mediator. They want all of these names to belong to a hypostasis. [**10v**] To defend this idea, the currently prevailing school has devised *communicatio idiomatum*, that is, [the doctrine] that [Christ's] human nature shares attributes with God. Thus they impose a new definition on the term "human," so that it becomes equivalent to the phrase "supporting a human nature." And then, by means of *communicatio idiomatum*, they will allow that God is a human being.

Rest, 15

---

[a] Matt 28:18. [b] John 20:28. [c] Rom 9:5. See A.R1.19. [d] Phil 2:9.
[e] See A.R1.20. [f] 1 Cor 15:47. The first man, "from the earth, earthy," was Adam.

They would base this entire doctrine on John 1, *the Word was made flesh*.[a] But you will soon find out how far removed they are from what John intended. For the moment, focus your attention on this alone: if Christ himself were to be asked, would such a sophistical notion [as *communicatio idiomatum*] ever come out of his mouth? As Peter says, we ought to speak *as if* we are *speaking the words of God*.[b] Now that Christ has directed us to call upon him as our teacher,[c] we should expect to be informed [about the nature of Christ] by what he himself said.

Think about this: if Christ or his disciple Paul were once again preaching to us, could they endure such human fabrications and seductive verbal trickery, and how could they stand the fact that the universal and catholic faith is now dependent on these things? Are [such inventions] *founded on solid rock*, or are they rather *built on sand*?[d] How then shall *every tongue profess Christ*,[e] if those artificial and sophistical words are to be found in only one tongue, [Latin]? How would [the sophists] be in a position to judge other nations' thinking about [the Christian] faith? If you would like to find out whether [what the the sophists say] is grounded in the scriptures, see if the word **[11r]** *homo* (human being) as used in the Bible bears the definition that they have imposed on it, and whether, where the Latin word [*homo*] is used to render Greek or Hebrew words, it is permissible to substitute the entire expression "supporting a human nature."

Rest, 15

Are they not making Christ into a great sophist, and even a sophist teacher, by claiming that the prophets, the apostles, and the evangelists used the word "Christ" to signify the second person, connoting "that which can support a human nature"? What would they say if, throughout the Bible,

Rest, 15-16

---

[a] John 1:14. [b] 1 Pet 4:11. [c] Matt 23:10. [d] Matt 7:24-27; Luke 6:47-49.
[e] Phil 2:11.

Appendix A

Rest, 16

instead of the word "Christ," the word "anointed" [which means the same thing] had been used? Would they, speaking in the simplest way, claim that it was a second person who was anointed, and had received *the holy spirit and power*,[a] as is said about the true Christ in Acts 10? Or could the second being say, "*All things have been delivered to me by my father*"?[b] Furthermore, was the Father speaking about him sophistically when he said, "*Behold my child, whom I have chosen, my beloved, I will put my spirit upon him*" (Isaiah 42)?[c] You will find that [these words, quoted] in Matthew 12, refer not to [a second being], but to the man Jesus.

Rest, 16

But what exactly is *communicatio praedicatorum* [sharing of properties]?[d] For the attribute "supporting a human nature" was not, prior [to this theological speculation], applicable to a human being. How, then, does a human being share his properties with God, if they do not actually belong to him?

Therefore, having rejected this sophistical quibbling, with pure hearts we acknowledge the true Christ, who

Rest, 16

is completely filled with divinity. But because his **[11v]** divinity depends on the mystery of the Word, for now let us say, roughly speaking, that God is able to share *the fullness of deity*[e] with a human being, and to give him *a name which is above every name*.[f] If, indeed, we grant that Moses was *made a god to Pharaoh*,[g] then, in a far more powerful and superior way, Christ became the God, Lord, and Teacher of Thomas and of us all.[h] Because God was in him in a unique way, and because through him we have [access to] a merciful God, he is expressly *called Immanuel, that is, God with us*.[i] What is more, in Isaiah 9 he himself is called [by the Hebrew word] *El* [God].[j]

---

[a] Acts 10:38. [b] Matt 11:27; Luke 10:22. [c] Matt 12:18, quoting Isa 42:1. [d] See A.R1.22. [e] Col 2:9. [f] Phil 2:9. [g] Ex 7:1. See A.R1.25. [h] John 20:28. [i] Matt 1:23, quoting Isa 7:14. [j] Isa 9:6.

Furthermore, if God has given us the privilege *that we should be called sons of God* (1 John 3),^a with Christ this privilege will be even greater, so that not only is he called the Son of God, but he is called — and is — our God as well. For *worthy is the lamb who was slain* to receive divinity, that is, *to receive power, riches, wisdom, strength, honour, glory, and blessing* (Revelation 5).^b And there is in him another manifold *fullness of deity*,^c as well as his other *unsearchable riches*,^d about which we will speak below.^e

Rest, 16

These are all attributes that God shares with the man [Jesus Christ]. However, the man gives God no new property, for what new property can a human being bestow on God? What is given is either a worthless, inconsequential thing; or a perfecting [of God], and thus God would have previously lacked perfection; or an imperfection. And so you are claiming that the idea of imperfection [**12r**] is now compatible with God, which is monstrous. Moreover, when God gives something to a human being, this does not detract from God, but rather elevates the human being. There is no change in God; the only alteration is in the human being.

Now, if a pronoun [such as "this"] points to Christ, I grant that "this" is our God, the *blessed God*,^f the *mighty God*.^g But if the pronoun indicates the invisible God, I recoil in horror from granting — as the utterly shameless sophists do, with their *uncircumcised lips*^h — that "this" is mortal; that "this" is a human being, hungry and thirsty; that "this" is an ass; that "this" has long ears.ⁱ Nor would it do any good if you were to cry out against them, "You would confound heaven with earth."^j For they will say brazenly,[7] "These are the words of God," as if refined by fire.^k

---

^a 1 John 3:1.   ^b Rev 5:12. See A.R1.24.   ^c Col 2:9.   ^d Eph 3:8.
^e *Errors*, 111v-112r (book 7).   ^f Rom 9:5.   ^g Isa 9:6.   ^h Ex 6:12, 30.
ⁱ See A.R1.20.   ^j A reference to Juvenal, *Satires* 2.25, and Livy, *History of Rome* 4.3; discussed in Erasmus, *Adagia* 1.3.81; in *Opera omnia*, II-1:384.   ^k See Ps 12:6.

Appendix A

{*Let no unclean word proceed from your mouth.*^a}

There is no more effective argument against such people than to remind them of the teaching of the apostles Peter and Paul. In 2 Timothy 1: *Keep to the form of sound words, which you have heard from me.*^b 1 Peter 4: *If any speak, let them speak as if they were using the words of God.*^c 1 Timothy 4: *Anyone who* follows *a different teaching, and does not accept the sound teaching of Christ, which is in accordance with piety,* is puffed up [with *pride*] *and knows nothing.*^d Compare this with the piety of the teaching that [the sophists] have learned from Paul, which concedes that God has long ears and is an ass. It is no wonder that the Turks call us ass-worshippers,[8] since we are not ashamed to call God an ass.

Rest, 43

[**12v**]   {*Three objections of the Pharisees refuted*}

[*The First Objection of the Pharisees*]

Rest, 16

You may contend that if Christ is God in the way [I have described], there will be more than one god. In these circumstances, it is my intent that Christ alone shall be my master, and that he alone will speak in my defence. For all of the difficulties may be settled by his words.

{*The words of Christ are especially to be heeded*}

Rest, 16

To this objection of the Pharisees, the Master himself replies in John 10, "[*Is it not written in your law that*] *'I said, you are gods'?*"^e Here Christ clearly says that he is God, not by nature, but in appearance; not by means of his nature, but through [God's] grace. For when he was accused of *making* himself *out to be God*, he answered [that he spoke] about God in the same way that the Prophet [David] spoke of gods, attributing to himself that same conception of deity.^f

---

^a Eph 4:29.   ^b 2 Tim 1:13.   ^c 1 Pet 4:11.   ^d 1 Tim 6:3-4 (not 1 Tim 4).
^e John 10:34, quoting Ps 82:6.   ^f John 10:35-36.

Since he goes on to say, "*If he called them gods, to whom the word of God was spoken,*" how much more ought the Son of man, *whom the Father sanctifies*, be called not just the Son, but God as well.[a] That he is God, therefore, is given to him as a special privilege, because the Father sanctifies him. He was anointed by grace and exalted. Because *he humbled himself*,[b] he was exalted *above his fellows*[c] and he was given *a name which is above every name.*[d] And, as Peter says, *he received honour and glory from God the Father.*[e] All these things [were received] through [God's] grace. For Scripture clearly shows that, by nature, only the Father can be called God.

By saying, "God and Christ," "Christ and God,"[f] [Scripture] links them together, showing that Christ is a being distinct from God. Similarly, when it is said that God is the father of Jesus Christ,[g] a distinction is being made between God and **[13r]** Christ, like that between a father and a son. And furthermore, [Scripture] says *the Christ of God*,[h] *the God of our Lord Jesus Christ*,[i] and *the head of Christ is God.*[j] And Christ [cries out] to God, "*my God, my God.*"[k] It is the common usage of Scripture to call the Father God, and Christ the Lord and Master.

Also, in John chapter 17, Christ himself says, "*that they may know you, the only true God, and Jesus Christ whom you have sent.*"[l] Although I would, indeed, say that Christ is the true God, nevertheless, this passage in truth makes a distinction between [the Son] and the Father. And in 1 John 5, John said of Christ [that he is the true God][9] in order to differentiate him from idols, and those falsely considered to be gods.[m] Similarly, in 1 Timothy and in Colossians, only

Rest, 17

---

[a] John 10:35-36.   [b] Phil 2:8.   [c] Ps 45:7.   [d] Phil 2:9.   [e] 2 Pet 1:17.
[f] For example, Gal 1:1 ("through Jesus Christ and God the Father") and 1:3 ("from God our Father and the Lord Jesus Christ").   [g] For example, 2 Cor 1:3; 1 Pet 1:3.   [h] Luke 9:20.   [i] Eph 1:17.   [j] 1 Cor 11:3.
[k] Matt 27:46; Mark 15:34.   [l] John 17:3.   [m] 1 John 5:20-21.

Appendix A

the Father is called *the invisible God*.[a] Besides, when Christ is called good, he assigns the quality of goodness to the Father [alone] (Matthew 19).[b]

No one should be amazed when I introduce passages of scripture that have been cited by heretics for their own purposes. For, although the scriptures have been misused by heretics, they have not on that account lost their soundness, so that they cannot ever be used again. For, just as you do, I also interpret [these passages] as referring to the human being [Jesus Christ]. Nor do I introduce them for the same purpose [that the heretics have in mind]. What if I say that Jesus Christ is indeed the great God, and at the same time, I say what he, speaking with the utmost simplicity, said, "The Father is greater than I"?[c] Does that make me an Arian? For since Arius foolishly thought the Son **[13v]** unlike the Father, and completely incapable of containing the glory of Christ, he introduced a new creature, superior to a human being. Nevertheless, without [introducing] this [new creature], and without making any distinction [in the Godhead], he could just have granted [what Jesus had said], "The Father is greater than I." But in his desire to philosophize about a plurality of separate beings, he fell into the most shameful of errors.

{*God is not the name of a "nature"*}

Do not be deceived by the word "God," whose meaning you do not understand. Nor are you capable of understanding it, until you know what [the word] *Elohim* means. If you are familiar with Hebrew, I will soon make [the word's meaning] perfectly clear to you. For you must bear in mind that everything that was written about Christ took place in Judaea. And in all languages, with the exception of Hebrew, there is a paucity of names for the divine. Therefore we are deceived, because we do not know how to distinguish between God and God.

---

[a] 1 Tim 1:17; Col 1:15.   [b] Matt 19:17. See also Mark 10:18; Luke 18:19.   [c] John 14:28.

Thus, according to the meaning of the word *Elohim*, Christ was made our God. This is no more than to say that, after the Father gave him the kingdom, all judgement, and all power, he became our *Lord, our judge, and our king*.[a] Thomas indicates this plainly enough, when he says, "*My Lord, my God*."[b] And Isaiah says, *He shall be called the mighty God*.[c] Also pay careful attention when Scripture calls King Cyrus — who was the type of the true Christ — *Elohim*, the God of Israel: *I will give you hidden treasures, so that you may know that I am the Lord, who calls you by your name, the God of Israel* (Isaiah 45).[d]

Similarly, if [**14r**] we grant that Moses was *established as a god to Pharaoh* in Exodus 7,[e] why do we deny [the divinity] of the true Christ? For Christ far surpasses Moses (Hebrews 3).[f] Such comparisons are really too trifling to use to prove the exaltedness of Christ. But you compel me to resort to them, since you hold such an unworthy view regarding his humanity. Nor do you bear in mind that God, in a way that is beyond our ability to explain, is able to raise up a human being and to place him at his right hand, above every other kind of exaltation. However, even this is insufficient for a correct understanding of Christ. For this you must wait until you come to understand the mysteries of the Word.[g] Then you will know that Christ himself is God, and has been so from eternity.

Moreover, if you pay careful attention to the Hebrew word used when Christ is called God, you will learn from the Old Testament the kind of deity that is in Christ. By doing so, you can observe the distinction between יהוה (*Yahweh*), the proper name of God, and אלהים, אדני, אל (*El, Adonai, Elohim*), and other similar words assigned to God as attributes. I will demonstrate below[h] that, in John 20, [when] Thomas [said, "*My Lord and my God!*" he] was

---

[a] Isa 33:22. [b] John 20:28. [c] Isa 9:6. [d] Isa 45:3. See A.R1.18.
[e] Ex 7:1. [f] Heb 3:3-6. [g] In book 3. [h] *Errors*, 98r (book 5).

Appendix A

addressing Christ as *Adonai* [Lord] and *Elohim* [God], and not as *Yahweh*.

Likewise, in Hebrews 1, [when] the Apostle [says "God" he] means *Elohim*.[a] The Greek philosophers were amazingly misled by their ignorance [of Hebrew idioms]. Indeed, according to tradition, it is Solomon who is here called *Elohim*, for this passage [in Hebrews 1] is actually taken from Psalm 44.[10] Nor does the Apostle place the entire force of his argument on the one word *Elohim*, but also says that his *throne* **[14v]** and his kingdom are *for ever and ever*. For with [this reference to] the word *Elohim* alone, he would not have proved Christ greater than the angels, nor greater than the other rulers who are likewise called gods by the Prophet [David]. Indeed, angels are [implicitly] called *Elohim* by the Apostle himself, when in the very same chapter he says [quoting Psalms], *Worship him, all you angels*.[b] And [in the next chapter he also quotes Psalms]: *You have made him a little lower than the angels*.[c] In both cases *Elohim* is [the Hebrew word] used.

Nor should I here neglect to mention — although it might seem to undermine my argument — that they are mistaken who would say that [Christ] is lower than God, rather than the angels. For this [way of thinking] is far from the intent of the Prophet, as well as from the Apostle's own thinking, which is concerned only with angels.[d] Nor is it my concern here to inquire into the natures [of these beings]. However, I will preserve this Hebrew usage, because among the Hebrew people, great beings are called "gods" and "angels," and because they use the same words when speaking either of angels or of extraordinary human beings. Peter calls "angels" those who in Genesis 6 are called *Elohim*,[e]

---

[a] Heb 1:8, quoting Ps 45:6, "Your throne, O God, is for ever and ever."
[b] Heb 1:6, quoting Ps 97:7.   [c] Heb 2:7, quoting Ps 8:5. The word used is *Elohim*, which can be translated as "God" or "gods" as well as "angels."
[d] See A.E1.1   [e] 2 Pet 2:4; Gen 6:2, 4.

or [more precisely] sons of *Elohim*. So too, in Job 1 and 38, the heavenly angels are called the sons of *Elohim*.[a] And similarly, אלים (*elim*) is used of angels and mighty men (Psalm 88 and Job 41).[b]

This comparison [between Christ and the angels] is made so that the letter may serve the spirit. For, as I will discuss below, David, in those adversities from which he was freed, is a type of the passion and resurrection of Christ, and is said to be a little lower than the gods [*Elohim*],[c] because he endures calamities that gods and the powerful are not accustomed to suffer. [15r] And that is also our understanding of Christ at the time of the passion. If you pay close attention to what Paul says, you will find that [the text] supports nothing other than the meaning expressed by the Psalmist: it is to be understood that [Christ] was made lower *because he suffered death by crucifixion*,[d] and he was *made lower than the angels* when, deprived of his angelic glory, he suffered so ignominiously.

The apostles — following, I believe, the Greek translation [of the Old Testament, the Septuagint] — when they wished to indicate a great being, were accustomed to use the word "angels." [For example, Paul says,] *Though I speak with the tongues of men and of angels*[e] and *we shall judge angels*,[f] that is, those who are greater than us. [In Psalm 78] manna is *the bread of angels*,[g] that is, marvelous bread; [and Revelation says] *in the sight of the angels*,[h] that is, in the sight of great leaders. The Chaldean version[i] also uses this translation throughout. In the above-mentioned Psalm 8, both in Greek and in Chaldean, *Elohim* is rendered as "angels." And the apostles were accustomed to quote the Greek translation [the Septuagint], where [the word "angels"] is used in this way.

---

[a] Job 1:6, 38:7.   [b] Ps 89:6; Job 41:25 (41:16 in V).   [c] Ps 8:5.
[d] Heb 2:9.   [e] 1 Cor 13:1.   [f] 1 Cor 6:3.   [g] Ps 78:25.   [h] Rev 14:10.
[i] The Targums, translation of the Hebrew scriptures into Aramaic. Servetus found this in Agostino Giustiniani's *Psalterium*.

Appendix A

{*The Aldine edition [of the Septuagint] is not [the version] of the 70 translators*[11]}

Rest, 80   Consequently, what Peter says about the [sinful] angels also becomes clear, for the Septuagint translators called [*Elohim*] "angels" in Genesis 6.[a] When their story is told [in 2 Peter 2], one ought to keep in mind the scriptural account [in Genesis 6]. Peter also says, in book 1 of the *Recognitions of Clement*, that there once were "men who led the life of angels."[b] The Epistle of Jude also calls these notorious creatures angels, who *left their own dwelling* to prowl the surface of the earth.[c] **[15v]** And it is these who are called wanderers in Ecclesiasticus 16.[d] Indeed, Cain, along with his progeny (whom the Hebrews called great demons), was himself *a fugitive on* the face of *the earth*.[e] But I will discuss these words of Peter at greater length in book 3.[f] For now, it suffices to have shown [the true meaning of] the word *Elohim*, lest anyone should try to argue against me based on passages from the Epistle to the Hebrews.

In fact, so far from rejecting those names for divinity [*El, Adonai, Elohim*], I claim that they are well suited to Christ, because of his excellence. Thus, in order to convey the difference [between Christ and] other gods, [scripture] adds that [he is called] God of *all the earth, great* God, *terrible*,[g] *mighty, wonderful*,[h] and *blessed above all things*.[i] Due to the paucity of [Greek] names for divinity, the Apostles could only express this [concept] to Greek speakers by using the word θεὸς (*theos*, god). But they rarely employed the word. All this ought to be weighed carefully. The Greek-speaking writers [of the New Testament] would not have caused us so much trouble if they had possessed a good knowledge of Hebrew.

---

[a] 2 Pet 2:4; Gen 6:2.   [b] [Clement], *Recognitiones* 1.29 (PG 1 1223A).   [c] Jude 1:6.   [d] Ecclus 16:8-9.   [e] Gen 4:12,14.   [f] *Errors*, 71v-72v (book 3).   [g] Ps 47:2.   [h] Isa 9:6.   [i] Rom 9:5.

{All of their arguments are turned back upon them}

The argument [previously] made about the plurality of gods[a] can be turned on its head. For if [those who make this argument] take into account Christ's reply [to the Jews when they accused him of blasphemy],[b] they are forced to concede that those three beings are gods, and gods by nature. Either Christ is not God by nature, or, when pressed regarding his divinity, he did not properly address the question. [He said, *"If he called them gods to whom the word of God came ... do you say of him whom the Father consecrated and sent into the world, 'You are blaspheming,' because I said, 'I am the Son of God'?"*[c]]

Therefore their own argument works against them. If they are *gods [to whom the word of God came]* in the same way in which [Christ] is the Son is God, then let them contrive for themselves as many gods by nature as they wish. But for us, as for Paul, *there is but one God, who is the Father,* **[16r]** *and one Lord Jesus Christ,* who is the Son (1 Corinthians 8).[d] Also adding strength to my argument: it must be granted that Christ is God based upon the divinity that is shared with him by the Father.[e] Therefore, since the basis of their divinity is one and the same, [Christ], together with the Father, is one God.

{The Second Objection of the Pharisees}

Nevertheless you may demand to know how Christ can be said to have *come down from heaven,* and to have come *into the world,*[f] sent by the Father. In the previous discussion I have already indicated that those who rely on arguments of this kind appear to be resorting to the weapons of the Pharisees, and, like them, to be carnally minded.[g] For in John 6 the Pharisees murmured, *"Is he not the son of Joseph,*

Rest, 17

---

[a] See *Errors,* 12r. [b] John 10:33. [c] John 10:35-36. [d] 1 Cor 8:6.
[e] See John 10:38, "The Father is in me and I in him." [f] John 6:38.
[g] See John 8:15; Rom 8:6-8.

Appendix A

<small>*Rest*, 17</small>

whose father and mother we know? How then does he say, 'I have come down from heaven'?" [a]

The Master was unwilling to disclose the truth to them; but later, explaining the matter to the disciples, he said, *"What then if you shall see the Son of man ascending up to where he was before? It is the Spirit who gives life; the flesh profits nothing; these words are spirit and life."* [b] Christ was not here speaking of that second being of theirs, but of himself, when he said, *"I have come down from heaven."* [c] Therefore your way of thinking works against you.

I therefore say that it was the Word of God that came down from heaven, as is written in the Book of Wisdom: *Your almighty Word, O Lord, leaped down from heaven.* [d]

<small>*Rest*, 50 S</small>

For *God thundered from on high,* **[16v]** *and spoke forth from heaven,* [e] and this Word became his Son on earth. And during the discourse on the bread of heaven, Christ reveals who he is.[f] For what was the *bread that came down from heaven,*[g] if not the *Word of God,* by which *man lives,* rather than *by* material *bread alone?*[h] And, as he himself bears witness, this Word, this bread, is Christ himself, his very own flesh, and the very body of Christ.[i] However, since discussion of these things presupposes [an understanding of] the mystery of the Word, it must be postponed to subsequent books [in this work].[j] In the meantime you should nonetheless have understood *"from heaven,"* that is, *from on high,* because, as [Christ] himself proclaims, *"You are from below, I am from on high"* (John 8).[k] Furthermore, you should have been able to understand Christ's words in their spiritual sense, for Christ, in the spirit of God, came before all time, and was in heaven, just as he remains *with* us *even to the end of the world.*[l] For this reason alone, because his words were

<small>*Rest*, 18</small>

---

[a] John 6:42. [b] John 6:62-63. [c] John 6:38. [d] Wisd of Sol 18:15.
[e] Ps 18:13. [f] John 6:32-58. [g] John 6:50. [h] Matt 4:4 and Luke 4:4, quoting Deut 8:3. [i] John 6:52-56. [j] In books 2 and 3. [k] John 8:23.
[l] Matt 28:20.

heavenly, you must grant that he himself was from heaven. For *the baptism* [of Jesus] *by John was from heaven*,[a] and *the second man was from heaven, and heavenly.*[b]

Rest, 18

To say that [Christ] was sent by the Father seems to present no great difficulty. For even John is said to have been sent by God: *There was a man sent by God, whose name was John* (John 1).[c] Similarly, Moses and the prophets are spoken of as having been sent by God. In John 17, speaking to the Father about the apostles, Christ says, *"As you sent me into the world, so do I send them into* [**17r**] *the world."*[d] And in John 20: *"As the Father sent me, so I send you."*[e]

Rest, 18

I am forced to resort to these parallels, not because they are similar in every way, but only so that I may persuade you that it was a human being who was sent; something which, led astray by your philosophy, you make every effort to deny. For it is highly illogical to say that the second being, which is itself the nature of God, was dispatched like a passive object. It is true that Christ's remarkable mission, and his coming forth from the Father, are firmly rooted in God. This I will reveal to you when I disclose the mystery of the Word.[f] Similarly, what is so wondrous in saying that Christ "came into the world"? For the same thing applies to others, [that is, to] *every person who comes into this world* (John 1).[g] And [consider] Luke 19: *Blessed is the king who comes in the name of the Lord.*[h] What king do you think is intended?

Rest, 18

Furthermore, keep in mind that those who are acted on by the spirit of God are not of this world (John 17 and 1 John 2).[i] They are said to enter the world, as if they were going into the homes of publicans.[j] They are said to enter into that earthly tabernacle, our body, and to be clothed in flesh, as when one clothes oneself in a garment.[k] And one

---

[a] Matt 21:25; Mark 11:30; Luke 20:4.   [b] 1 Cor 15:47. The "second man" is Christ, the second Adam.   [c] John 1:6.   [d] John 17:18.   [e] John 20:21.
[f] In book 3.   [g] John 1:9.   [h] Luke 19:38, referring to Ps 118:26.
[i] John 17:14,16; 1 John 2:15-16.   [j] See Luke 19:2-7.   [k] 2 Cor 5:1-4.

Appendix A

who speaks in the spirit envisions himself as being beyond the world. Peter said that he was bound in *this tabernacle*[a] as if it were something placed over him. Certainly he was speaking *according to the inner man*.[b]

{The Third Objection of the Pharisees}

Rest, 19

You may also object: how it is that Christ, in Philippians 2, *did not consider it theft to be* [**17v**] *equal to God*?[c] These words of Paul are so obscure, and so variously interpreted, that by themselves they could not conclusively prove anything to anyone; especially since it is obvious that Paul is here speaking simply about [the man] Jesus Christ.

To begin with, some interpret this passage to mean that the second person, without robbery, considered itself to be equal to the first. They twist this impious interpretation even further, applying it to "philosophical natures," claiming that [the second person] did not consider it theft to be what it was by nature.

Others interpret this passage as meaning that [Christ] did not consider [committing] theft in order to be equal to God. That is, he did not consider the theft of equality with God; he never intended to usurp for himself equality with God. This way of understanding [the passage] better accords with [the Pauline text] than the first, because Paul never gave a thought to such natures and because [the first interpretation] is contrary to the thinking of Paul, who was concerned only with the restraint and humility of Christ.

Likewise, the nature of the word "but" [as in "*but emptied himself*"] — which, as lawyers say, is taken adversarially — is incompatible with [these interpretations]. The meaning of [this passage] must be: He did not exalt himself, but

---

[a] 2 Pet 1:13.   [b] Rom 7:22. See also Eph 3:16.   [c] Phil 2:6-7: "[Christ], though he was in the form of God, did not consider it theft to be equal to God, but emptied himself, taking the form of a servant."

humbled himself; he did not consider [committing theft to be equal to God], but abased himself, emptied himself, and submitted himself.

But I am wasting effort needlessly on these [interpretations] (all of which are false), when the true resolution lies in the words of the Master. For it is found in [Christ's reply to] the charge made by the Pharisees who, in John 5, attack him for *making himself out to be equal to God*.[a] And in his reply Christ does not deny this equality, **[18r]** but says that *whatever the Father does, the Son* shall *likewise do*.[b] Thus, *like the Father, the Son raises the dead and gives them life, makes lepers clean;* gives sight to *the blind;* and heals *the deaf,* the paralyzed, those possessed by demons, and others.[c] And, finally, *the Father has given all judgement* and all power *to the Son, so that all might honour the Son even as they honour the Father.*[d]

Rest, 19

See how Christ is made equal to God, because all things that the Father has are his. See how the μορφή (*morphe,* form), that is, the appearance of the Deity,[e] shone in him as he performed his great miracles. And this is what Paul says: he *was established in the form* and appearance *of God*.[f]

Rest, 19

With these things in mind, let us now turn our attention to the humility of Christ, which Paul sets before us as the exemplary model for all humility. So great was [Christ's] humility that the more he was endowed with power, the more he made himself obedient and abased himself. For there are many good men who become tyrants, if they win a political office, or come into some other kind of good fortune. But this was not the case with Christ. For Christ did not consider using his great equality to God to commit theft.

Rest, 19

[Christ] refused to use [his power] like a thief. First of all, he declined [to participate in] a theft [of power] when *he realized that* [the people] *were going to take him by force and*

Rest, 20

---

[a] John 5:18. [b] John 5:19. [c] John 5:21; Matt 11:5; Luke 7:22.
[d] John 5:22-23. [e] See A.R1.36. [f] Phil 2:6. See A.R1.40.

Appendix A

Rest, 20   *make him a king* (John 6).[a] Instead he conducted himself in a humble manner, since he did not want his *kingdom* to be *of this world*.[b] And [in Philippians 2] Paul is referring to [Christ's] preaching in [John] chapters 5 and 6.[c] **[18v]** Secondly, [Christ] *did not consider* committing *theft* [of power] in order to violently defend himself against the Jews by taking command of *twelve legions of angels*.[d] He chose, instead, to suffer humbly.

Rest, 20   This, then, is the equality that he possessed, being *in the form of God*: the equality of power with God, which he had in himself, because of the power given to him to be equal to God (John 5).[e] For he was shown to be God because of his power, just as [he was seen to be] a man because of his flesh. *Everything the Father has is* his,[f] and *all things* brought about by the Word of God *are made through him*, since he himself is the Word of God.[g]

Rest, 20   In Luke 22 [Christ] said this about his equality of power [with God]: *The Son of man will be seated at the right hand of the power of God*.[h] In Acts 7 Stephen sees him [*standing*] *at the right hand of God*.[i] And in Ephesians 1 — speaking not of that [metaphysical] being, but of Christ — Paul proclaims this equality [with God] and exaltation to the right hand of God, saying that he was established *above all rule, authority, power, and dominion, and every name that is named, not only in this world, but indeed even in the world to come*. Finally, *all things have been placed under his feet*, and [God] *has given him to the church to be the head over all things, he who fulfills everything in all things*.[j]

Rest, 20   Similarly, his equality of power with God is noted in Daniel 7: *Behold, the Son of man came up to the Ancient of Days, and* all kingly *power was given to him*.[k] Jeremiah, in chapter 30, marvels at him: *Who* is it who thus *approaches*

---

[a] John 6:15.   [b] John 18:36.   [c] John 5:18-23, 24-30; 6:32-58.
[d] Matt 26:53.   [e] See John 5:18-23, 24-30.   [f] John 16:15.   [g] John 1:3. See also Col 1:16.   [h] Luke 22:69.   [i] Acts 7:55-56.   [j] Eph 1:21-23.
[k] Dan 7:13-14.

and draws near to **[19r]** God,[a] so that he approaches equality with [God]? And it is the plain truth that although Joseph was established as Pharaoh's equal, strictly speaking, he might very well have said, "The Pharaoh is greater than I am."[b]

Rest, 20

{*Here the [Pharisees'] charge is refuted in many ways*}

Furthermore, Paul did not say that there are two beings and one nature, or that the second person is equal in essence to the first. For if Paul thought that this second person considered itself to be equal in nature to the first, without the commission of theft, why did he not say that it was equal to the first person, rather than to God? For [Paul says] *The Word of God is living*,[c] and by this he indicates [that the Word is] something distinct from God. Besides, for what purpose did he insert [into his letter] this passage about theft? Paul must have been speaking foolishly [if he meant] that there could possibly be any suspicion of theft in one who is the very same being and has the very same nature. Who cannot see that the word "considered" is thoroughly human? Who cannot also see that it is impious to impute the consideration of robbery to those [divine] beings?

Again, listen to what [Paul] says: *Being established in the form of God*.[d] How could he have said that the second person had the appearance of deity, if it is the very same deity and nature — and if it is God, just as properly, completely, and as much by nature, as the first person? Paul must have been speaking foolishly, and he who said, *"The Father is greater than I"*[e] must have been lying. For without any disparagement [of Christ], one can grant here that [the Father] has seniority because of his relation to the Son, which is established by the word "Father" and the pronoun "I" [used] in relation to it. Moreover, if there is metaphysical

---

[a] Jer 30:21. [b] See Gen 41:40-44. [c] Heb 4:12. [d] Phil 2:6. [e] John 14:28.

[19v] equality, one would have to grant that the first person is the father of God and is equal to the Son, just as readily and properly as [one would have to grant] the converse, [that the second person is the son of God and is equal to the Father]. Scripture, however, abhors such an idea.

You should ponder the implications of Paul's words, *wherefore God highly exalted him*,[a] for the reference here is to the one who considered [committing theft]. Or could it be that the second person was so exceedingly exalted because it had so humbled itself? To say that a nature of God humbles itself is, I think, ridiculous indeed. Besides, as I have just said, by taking into account Paul's purpose [to show the modesty and humility of Christ], we can overcome the blindness of Theophylact [who equated the form of God with the nature or substance of God].[12] For [in Philippians 2] Paul is not concerned with the nature of Christ, but with his appearance. How, then, can equivalency of natures be deduced from this?

Likewise, when one reads the adverb "equally" here, one should keep in mind the Greek word ἴσα. For the word "equally" does not describe nature, but disposition. And [Christ], who promises that he can do all the things that the Father does, was able to elevate himself to an equality with God in terms of power.

Rest, 21

The true and infallible explanation is that [Christ], *established as the appearance of God*, and having the power of God, *did not think of being equal to God as theft*. He did not consider using the power of God to commit theft. For it would truly have been theft if, by the use of violence, he had renounced the work for which his Father had intended him, or if he had seized for himself a royal tyranny over the world. And this is the real meaning of the word ἁρπαγμός (*harpagmos*, theft). For [20r] Christ was never interested in theft. He never took anything from anyone by violence.

---

[a] Phil 2:9.

The Greek article τὸ makes this idea clear, as [Paul] says, "he who was equally God." [That is to say,] he did not consider [using] his equality to God to commit theft. Nor is the [adverb] "equally" of utmost importance for Paul, as some groundlessly believe. Instead, he infers [equality] as the logical consequence of the appearance of deity. For he says that [Christ], who was *established as the appearance of God*, did not consider τὸ εἶναι ἴσα θεῷ — *did not consider being equal [to God]*— did not consider this equality (which, of course, he possessed, having been *established in the form of God*) — to be theft.[a]

It is clear from [John] chapter 5 that this is the sense [that Paul intended]. It is not possible that [Paul] means some other kind of equality, different from that [in John 5]. For when [Christ's] equality with God is being debated, Christ does not deny it.[b] On the contrary, he shows that he in fact possesses [this equality], not by using it to commit theft, like a tyrant or a giant, but rather by conducting himself humbly, in keeping with his subservient human condition, *becoming obedient unto death*.[c]

When [Paul] says that [Christ] assumed the *form* or appearance *of a servant*,[d] he does so in order to distinguish [this form] from the form of God, about which he had just spoken. For in both places [the word] μορφή (*morphe*, form) is used, and he uses this word pointedly, in order to assert the superiority of humility. For although [Christ] was powerful in either appearance, he used the humbler of the two. He did not use the appearance and the strength of God, but [appeared] as an ordinary human being. It is said that he was *found in the guise of a human being*.[e] **[20v]** As the Psalmist says, "*You shall die like human beings, even though you are gods*" (Psalm 81).[f] And Samson, who because of his surpassing strength seemed not human but superhuman, said, "*I shall* then *be weak, like other men*" (Judges 16).[g]

Rest, 21

Rest, 21-22

---

[a] Phil 2:6. See A.R1.41.   [b] John 5:18-23.   [c] Phil 2:8.   [d] Phil 2:7.
[e] Phil 2:8.   [f] Ps 82:6-7.   [g] Judg 16:7, 17.

Appendix A

Rest, 22

You have now seen all of the scriptural passages that speak about [Christ's] equality [with God]. These passages are quite irrelevant to the [theological] battles of our time. The debate about the equality or inequality of natures was unknown to the apostles.

{*Ignorance of the [Hebrew] names for the divine has misled philosophers*}

Rest, 65

Some philosophize about an equality of nature [in divinity], because the same word [*dominus*, lord] is used [twice] in Psalm 109: *The Lord said to my lord* [*"Sit at my right hand."*]ᵃ But they should be pardoned, for, not knowing the original language of the sacred scriptures, they are unaware of their own ignorance. However, if you know Hebrew, you will discover that the Prophet actually says נאס יהוה לאדני (Yahweh said to Adon). Moreover, in Malachi 3, Christ is clearly referred to as "Adon."ᵇ And the prophecy about being seated at the right hand [of God] is fulfilled in Christ in the last chapter of Mark, as is also demonstrated in the tenth chapter of Hebrews.ᶜ Nevertheless philosophers depict other seating arrangements in the worlds to come. Besides, as is well-known from the words of Christ, he never attempted to apply the name יהוה (*Yahweh*) to himself. [If he had], the Jews would have had a ready answer for him.[13]

{*There is not a single letter in the Gospel that speaks about a mathematical son*}

To sum it all up, in order that you may know where my thoughts are tending, I maintain that, with the exception of the single passage about the Word in John,ᵈ all of scripture, from first to last, speaks of **[21r]** the human being, Christ himself. The Word, as used by John, designates not what is,

---

ᵃ Ps 110:1.   ᵇ Mal 3:1.   ᶜ Mark 16:19 and Heb 10:12, referring to Ps 110:1.   ᵈ John 1:1-18.

but what was. The error lies in not understanding what that [Word] once was, and how it then became flesh. Do not let your imaginings lead you astray, but store this up deep in your heart: in the whole of scripture it is the human being Christ himself who is speaking. May your thoughts always be directed toward him. May God grant you a joyous spirit to listen. Then, setting aside every false claim, artificial distinction, and equivocation, I will restore the scriptures for you in the clearest possible form and place God himself before your eyes, so that you may always gaze upon the face of Christ.

{*The Holy Spirit*}

Philosophers have invented a third absolute being, really and truly distinct from the other two, which they call the third person, or the Holy Spirit. In this way they have devised an imaginary trinity — three beings in one nature. In reality, however, in the guise and in the name of unity, they are foisting upon us three beings, three gods, or one god in three parts.

On the [same subject], listen to the opinion of more recent [writers], for example, John Mair, *On the First Book of Sentences*, distinction 4, in the solution of argument 6.[a] For such [philosophers] see no difficulty in saying that there are three beings — taking these words in their absolute sense — which are absolutely, **[21v]** simply, truly, and in reality different or distinct [from one another], so that one [of them] can be born from a second, and yet another blown forth from the first two, while all three of them are enclosed in one enormous jar. Nevertheless, because I do not wish to misrepresent these persons, I will call them the first being, the second being, and the third being. For in the scriptures I cannot find any better name for them. I will speak later of what is meant by the term "persons."[b]

Rest, 29

---

[a] Mair, *In Primum sententiarum* 4.6.   [b] See *Errors*, 36v.

Appendix A

Rest, 29

Granting the existence of these three [beings], whom it is their custom to call "persons," by arguing from lesser to greater,[a] [these theologians] absolutely admit that there are several beings, several entities, several essences, several substances, and several *ousias* (substances).[b] Consequently, since they take the word "God" in an absolute sense, they will have several gods. But if this is the case, why should we reproach the tritheists,[c] who say that there are three gods? For the [theologians themselves] also labour to construct three gods, or one god in three parts. These three gods of theirs form one composite *ousia*. And even though some of them refuse to use words such as "composite," they nevertheless use the word "constitute," and say that God is constituted out of three beings.

Rest, 31-32

Clearly, then, we [Christians] are all tritheists, and we have a tripartite God. We have thus all become atheists, that is, a people without God. For as soon as we try to think about God, our thoughts are diverted to three images, so that no conception of unity is able to endure in our minds. But what does it mean to be without God, other than not to be able to think about God? A confused jumble of three beings is constantly looming before our minds and hampering our understanding, driving us to madness [**22r**] whenever we think about God.

See how valiantly [the philosophers] strive to defend [the concept of] one God! For even if they have admitted, absolutely and in every way, a plurality of beings and entities, and consequently many absolute Gods, nevertheless, for them there is still one connotative God.[d] For, as can be seen in the work [of John Mair] to which I have just referred,[e] they say that these words, according to the way in which they use, or, rather, abuse them, ought not to be taken in their absolute sense, but rather in some kind of artificial,

---

[a] See A.R1.64. [b] See also *Restoration*, 25. [c] See A.R1.67.
[d] See A.R1.66. [e] Mair, *In primum sententiarum* 4.6.

sophistical, and connotative way. They seem to be living in some other world when they dream up such things! For the kingdom of heaven knows nothing about such nonsense.

Scripture speaks about the Holy Spirit in another way, unknown to [the philosophers]. But because this subject requires a deeper investigation, I shall postpone the discussion of it to later books.[a] For scripture deals with this subject in a mysterious and nearly incomprehensible way, especially for those who are not accustomed to the unusual manner in which it speaks about [the Holy Spirit].

By the term "holy spirit" [Scripture] sometimes means God himself, sometimes an angel, sometimes the spirit of a man, sometimes a kind of inspiration, or the breath of divinity on the mind, a mental impulse, or respiration; although a distinction between breath and Spirit is sometimes observed. And some would have "the holy spirit" understood as nothing but correct human understanding and reasoning. Among the Hebrews, רוח (*ruach*, wind, breath, or spirit) means simply **[22v]** a breathing or blowing, which is spoken of without distinction as either wind or spirit, whereas among the Greeks, πνεῦμα (*pneuma*, breath or spirit) is used for any kind of spirit or mental impulse whatsoever. It presents no difficulty that this spirit is called holy, for all stirrings of the mind, when they concern the religion of Christ, are called holy, and are sacred to God. For *no one can say that Jesus is the Lord, except by the Holy Spirit*.[b]

[*Some Passages from Scripture*]

It remains to discuss several scriptural texts, on the basis of which the *moderni*[14] think they can philosophize the three beings. For instance: *There are three who bear witness in heaven, the Father, the Word, and the Holy Spirit, and these three are one* (1 John 5).[c] But first, in order to provide a more

Rest, 22

---

[a] In books 4 and 7.   [b] 1 Cor 12:3.   [c] 1 John 5:7-8. See A.R1.43.

Appendix A

satisfactory response, I will address two other passages of scripture, which [the *moderni*] also use in proving their case: *I and the Father are one* (John 10)^a and *The Father is in me and I am in the Father* (John 14).^b

Rest, 25

Augustine makes use of [John 10], saying "because [John] says 'one'" to counter Arius, and saying "because [John] says 'are'" to counter Sabellius.^c Thus, when countering Sabellius, [Augustine] concludes that there are two beings, while, when countering Arius, he concludes that they have one nature. I think, however, that these words possess a simpler meaning, for it is Christ who is speaking, and he says "we are" because he is both God and man.

As Tertullian says in *Against Praxeas*, Christ said *unum* ["one" in the neuter gender], and not *unus* ["one" in the masculine gender].[15] **[23r]** For "[the masculine word] *unus* appears to mean something singular in number," as if it were denoting the singularity of one and the same being. But "'one' in the neuter form [as used by John] pertains not to singularity, but to unanimity" or agreement, "so that the two [God and Christ] are thought of as existing in one [divine] power."^d And this is what the early Church Fathers correctly called one *ousia* (substance), because there is only one [divine] power that was bestowed on the Son by the Father.

Nevertheless, the later [Church Fathers] have unfortunately made a mockery of the word *homoousia*[16] — just as they have with "hypostasis" and "persons" — claiming that the word *ousia* means "nature." This is not only contrary to the proper meaning of the word [*ousia*], but also runs counter to all of the passages of scripture in which the word is found. For in John 17, and in the last chapter of Matthew,

---

^a John 10:30.   ^b John 14:10-11.   ^c *Sentences* 1.31.9 (PL 192 606), quoting Augustine, *In evangelium Iohannis* 36.9, 71.2 (PL 35 1668, 1821).   ^d Tertullian, *Adversus Praxean* 22 (PL 2 183C-184B). In his quotation of Tertullian, Servetus has changed the word *unitatem* (unity) to *unanimitatem* (unanimity) and added *concordiam* (agreement).

and everywhere that Christ speaks about the power given to him by the Father, the word *ousia* is used,[17] which to the Greeks does not mean "nature," but abilities, works, prosperity, wealth, and power, all of which Christ has in abundant measure. And he and the Father share one power, one accord, and one will.

Rest, 25

The meaning of the Latin word *unum*, like the Greek word ἕν (one), embraces unanimity of purpose, similarity, and sharing the same wisdom. But to understand the word *unum* in scripture as meaning "one nature" is metaphysical rather than Christian. Indeed, except when [philosophizing about] Scripture, the Greeks have never understood the word ἕν as meaning "one nature." If then you ask why the Greek [Church Fathers] understand the word in this way, consider the answer that Basil the Great provides in book 4 of *Against Eunomius*.[a] Here he does not argue according to the proper meaning of the word ἕν, but instead **[23v]** resorts to syllogistic reasoning in order to philosophize.[18]

Accordingly, we ought to accept an interpretation of the word [ἕν] either based on its proper meaning or guided by other passages of scripture. In the scriptures, however, you will never find [the word] *unum* being used to convey the metaphysical unity of nature. Quite the opposite, as is clear from the words of Christ himself, who, in John 17, reveals himself as a faithful teacher. For he prays to the Father on behalf of the Apostles "*that they may all be one, as you, Father, are in me and I in you, that they also may be one in us,*" and "*that they may be one, even as we are one.*"[b] Frequently repeating the word [*unum*], he prays that [his disciples] may be one. Does it then follow that we, who are one in a similar way, constitute one nature? We are certainly one, in that we are all in concord, *preserving the unity of the Spirit in the bond of peace.*[c] See also Jeremiah 32: *I will give*

---

[a] [Basil], *Contra Eunomium* 4 (PG 29 679C).   [b] John 17:21, 22.
[c] Eph 4:3.

them one heart, and one way.[a] Also, in Acts 4, [we read] that *the multitude of believers were of one heart and of one soul.*[b] And in book 8 of *Against Celsus*, Origen expressly says that the passage ["*I and the Father are one*"] should be understood in accordance with [Acts 4]. He says that the Father and the Son are one, for, "although it is apparent that they are two beings in substance, they are one in agreement, harmony, and oneness of will."[c]

{*Erasmus also interprets it this way in his Annotations.*[19]}

A similar interpretation appears in Cyprian's letter to Magnus.[d] In Galatians 3 Paul argues that we are all one in the unity of faith.[e] And in 1 Corinthians 6 [he says] *Whoever* [24r] *is joined to the Lord is one spirit* with him.[f] However, [Paul] never gave a thought to the idea of one nature. Indeed, even if [Christ] had said, "I and the Father are not two, but one," you could not conclude anything from that. For although a man and a woman are *not two, but one flesh,*[g] nevertheless one nature cannot be philosophized from this.

You may say that the passage from John 17[h] does not necessarily mean likeness in every respect, and that the apostles cannot be called one as appropriately as are the Son and the Father. In this you are correct: it is not a likeness in every respect. But you say there is no [likeness], when there is some. Without a doubt they are not alike in every respect, for only [the Son] is *in the bosom of the Father,*[i] and is one power with the Father, that is, the same deity and ruling power. That is why he is said, particularly by those who are familiar with the mystery of the Word, to be one with the Father in a far superior way. But it does not necessarily

---

[a] Jer 32:39.   [b] Acts 4:32.   [c] Origen, *Contra Celsum* 8.12 (PG 11 1534B-C). See A.R1.51.   [d] Cyprian, *Ad Magnum* 5 (PL 3 1188B).
[e] Gal 3:28.   [f] 1 Cor 6:17.   [g] Matt 19:6, quoting Gen 2:24. See also Mark 10:8.   [h] John 17:21, 22.   [i] John 1:18.

follow that you can conclude from this that there is a mathematical unity of natures, for that is something very different, a mere philosophical flight of fancy, and one which is never expressed in sacred literature. Besides, it would have been absurd and irrelevant for Christ to say *"they may all be one, even as we are one,"* if [God and Christ] were one nature, and we were [merely] in harmony.

Furthermore, you will grasp Christ's meaning from a different perspective if you do not take his words ["*I and the Father are one*"] in a raw and undigested form, but instead note the arrangement [of these words] and his reason for saying them. For Christ also says [in John 10] that he is one with the Father [in an argument intended] to prove **[24v]** that *no one* can *snatch* his *sheep from* his *hand*, because *the Father gave them to* him.[a] And if *no one is able to snatch them from the Father's hand*, then it follows that *no one will* be able to *snatch them from* his *hand*, because he and the Father are one power, and he tends [his flock] by acting in unanimity with the Father.[b]

This [explanation] reveals [the meaning of] another passage: *The Father is in me and I am in the Father* (John 14).[c] In discussing this passage, however, [the theologians] become incoherent. For in book 4 of *On The Trinity*, Hilary says, "Human intelligence cannot grasp the meaning of the words."[d] And yet he concludes that the [three] beings are mutually contained in each other, saying that "each is in the others,"[20] the first in the third, the third in the second, and vice versa. But it is amazing that he allows himself to become so distracted that he pays no heed to the explanation

Rest, 75

---

[a] John 10:27-29.   [b] John 10:30. In Augustine, *Collatio cum Maximino* 6 (PL 42 712), this argument was used by the Arian, Maximinus.
[c] John 14:10-11.   [d] *Sentences* 1.19.5 (PL 192 574), quoting Hilary, *De Trinitate* 3.1 (PL 10 76A). Servetus, following an early printed edition of *Sentences*, cited book 4, but corrected it to book 3 in *Restoration*. The error was corrected in *Sentences* after the 1528 edition.

Appendix A

Rest, 75

of the Master. It does no good to call Christ master of anything but empty words, if one disregards what he has to say. For in that same chapter, John 14, Christ says to the apostles, "*I am in the Father, you are in me, and I am in you.*"[a] However, the apostles are not forcibly crammed, as the theologians would have it, into one nature with Christ. Adding further strength to my argument, in [John 14 and 15], Christ makes it clear who he is, when he says that he is in us as long as we heed his words,[b] and that he is in the Father, because he loves him and *keeps his commandments.*[c] Even more significantly, in the same chapter [John 14] and also in John 10, [Christ] implies that he is in the Father because he does the works of the Father, saying, "*Believe me because of the works* **[25r]** *themselves, so that you may know and believe that the Father is in me, and I am in the Father.*"[d]

Hilary should have considered the kind of logical reasoning the Master used. How is Christ is implying, from these works, the metaphysics of natures, or of several beings dwelling together in a single nature? In chapters 10 and 17 [of John], Christ reveals who he is. And it is said that he is in the Father in very much the same way as he had said that he was one with the Father. For he says, "*As you, Father, are in me and I in you, may they also be one in us*," and "*That the love with which you loved me may be in them, and I in them.*"[e] In John 6 [it says that] Christ *abides in us, and we in him*.[f] In Ephesians 3, [Paul] concludes that Christ lives in us because of faith and love.[g] 1 John 2 points out that *we are in him* because of love.[h] And in [John] 3 it says: *Whoever keeps his commandments abides in him, and he in them.*[i]

From this, [Christ's] basic meaning is easy to comprehend. First, the Father bears witness, for [as Christ says] "*The Father who sent me bears witness to me.*"[j] He does indeed

---

[a] John 14:20. [b] John 14:21, 23. [c] John 15:10. See also John 14:15.
[d] John 14:11, John 10:38. [e] John 17:21, 26. See also John 10:30, 38.
[f] John 6:56. [g] Eph 3:17. [h] 1 John 2:5. [i] 1 John 3:24. [j] John 8:18.

bear witness by saying, "*This is my beloved Son.*"[a] Secondly, the Word bears witness, because the words of Christ himself, when he bears witness about who he is, clearly reveal him to be from God. It is above all from Christ's own words that we recognize how great he is, even though, in today's world, there are those who would render them trifling and ineffectual. However, by the spirit that has been given [to us], they will be recognized as living [words].

Thirdly, the Holy Spirit testifies. [25v] I am saying nothing [for the present] about this testimony, as I will explain it in the next book. And there you will see what else is meant by the term "paraclete."[b] But for now I will simply say, as Christ makes clear in John 14 and 15, "*While I am among you,* the speech that you hear, that is, *the words which I say to you,* bear witness."[c] Later, when, as it says in the final chapter of Luke, *you are clothed with power from on high,*[d] "*you [also] will bear witness.*"[e] Also, in Acts 1, [Christ] commanded [the apostles] to bear witness when they *receive the power* from *the Spirit coming upon* them.[f] This is the testimony of the Holy Spirit. In the same way Paul calls the testimony of his *conscience the testimony of the Holy Spirit* (Romans 9).[g]

And these three are one, as has been clearly shown above.[h] As the *Glossa Ordinaria* explains, "They are one, that is, bearing witness to the same thing."[21] John's intention is to show the power of the truth by the agreement of witnesses who do not waver or vary in their testimony. For they would be disqualified by anything objectionable [in their testimony], just as usually happens in court when there is conflicting testimony. In addition, a gloss[22] on Matthew 17 says, "Behold Moses and Elijah conversing with Jesus. For the Law and the Prophets and Jesus speak as one and are in

---

[a] Mark 9:7; Matt 3:16-17, 17:5; Luke 9:35. [b] *Errors,* 60v-61v. [c] John 14:25, 15:11. [d] Luke 24:49. [e] John 15:27. [f] Acts 1:8. [g] Rom 9:1. [h] 1 John 5:7-8.

harmony."[a] Thus *there are three who bear witness*[b] to the Word: Christ himself; Moses, that is, the law given by the Father; and Elijah, that is, the spirit of the prophets. *For the testimony of Jesus is the spirit of prophecy* (Revelation 19).[c] *And these three are one*, and among them there is the utmost harmony and agreement.

[26r] This explanation may be obtained from the words of the Master, who in John 5 cites three witnesses. The first is the witness of the Spirit, for John [the Baptist] bore witness to the descent of the Spirit.[d] The second is [Christ's] own witness, for the works he accomplished bear witness. Third, he cites the testimony of the Father, bearing witness.[e] And these three [testimonies] are consistent.

We are now able to turn [the sophists'] argument back against them, by showing that John's statement[f] cannot be taken to mean what they think it does, because [their interpretation] is totally opposed to John's purpose and way of thinking. For it is evident that [this passage] is not concerned with the nature of those three beings, but is about the reliability and the unity of their testimony.

Moreover, consider the objective to which this testimony is leading; and think about where John's evidence is heading. For it is not his intention to derive one "ideal form" from another, or to prove that the second being is the daughter of the first.[23] Rather, he sets about proving that Jesus of Nazareth, whom his *eyes have seen* and whom his *hands have touched*,[g] is the Son of God, and not the son of Joseph. And it is to this belief that he is exhorting us, as though we are strictly bound to assent to it. For whoever does not believe in this way is not a Christian. And whoever does not believe in this way is not firmly grounded *on that rock: "You are the Christ, the Son of the living God"* (Matthew 16).[h]

Rest, 23

---

[a] Theophylact, *In quatuor evangelia* 17.9 (PG 123 330C). [b] 1 John 5:7-8.
[c] Rev 19:10. [d] John 5:33, referring to John 1:32. [e] John 5:36-37.
[f] 1 John 5:7-8. [g] 1 John 1:1. [h] Matt 16:16, 18.

{Peter was the first stone, because he believed more firmly and earlier [than others] that Jesus was the Son of God}

Indeed, this is the rock after which Peter was named, the rock upon which Peter was the first building stone laid. This rock, the foundation of the Church, is the belief that Jesus Christ is the Son of God. This is *the cornerstone upon which the whole* [**26v**] *structure grows, building up the body of Christ, which is the church*.[a] But you might say that *Christ himself is the cornerstone.*[b] Then what, pray tell, is Christ in us, unless we believe that he is the Son of God? For *Christ dwells in* our *hearts through faith* (Ephesians 3).[c] It does no good to say that Christ is, in and of himself, the rock, if you take away the very thing that establishes us upon that rock.

Rest, 23

The second authoritative biblical passage which, according to Peter Lombard (*Sentences*, book 1, distinction 2), "most clearly provides support for [the doctrine of] the Trinity" is in Romans, chapter 11.[d] *From him* — by the agency of the first [being] — *through him and in him are all things*.[e] Augustine, in book 2, chapter 6 of *On the Trinity*, explains [the passage] in terms of the three beings: "From him, by means of the first [being]; through him, by means of the second; in him, by means of the third."[24] However, I do not believe that Paul, if he had been questioned about this matter, would ever have philosophized in this way, for it would have been contrary to his usual manner [of thinking], and irrelevant to what he is doing here. For here Paul is simply marvelling at the loftiness of God the Father, and the only philosophy that can be drawn from this passage [Romans 11] is contained in the little phrase, "*through him.*"

---

[a] Combination of Eph 2:20-21, Eph 4:12, and Col 1:24.   [b] Eph 2:20.
[c] Eph 3:17.   [d] *Sentences* 1.2.8 (PL 192 529). The PL edition of *Sentences* incorrectly says Romans 8.   [e] Rom 11:36.

Appendix A

{Irenaeus interprets "through the Word" as meaning "through [God] himself"}

Paul elsewhere says *"through the Word,"*[a] and here [in Romans 11] says *"through him."* From this it may be gathered that everything that God accomplished by means of the Word, he accomplished by means of himself. Irenaeus also testifies to this.[b] Accordingly, the next book will show that this passage, as Irenaeus explains it, runs counter to [what the later theologians say].[c] Here, Paul intends only to direct our attention to the many and various dispositions of God and the greatness **[27r]** of his power, just as [he does] when he says that [God the Father] *is over all, through all, and in all* (Ephesians 4).[d] This is all the more true, since in 1 Corinthians 8 the Apostle does not include the third person in the same triple formula: *There is one God, the Father, from whom are all things, and we exist in him; and one Lord, Jesus Christ, through whom are all things, and we exist through him.*[e] Behold these three [phrases]— *from him, through him, and in him* — [in a passage] where he says nothing about the third person. And in Colossians 1 the Apostle is speaking only about the Son when he says, *All things were created through him and in him.*[f]

Jerome philosophizes the three beings from [the parable of] the *three measures of meal*.[g] But it is an extremely silly argument, and smacks of a kind of Platonism, to philosophize numbers of beings based upon parables and the numbers in them.[25] If we are permitted to engage in this sort of philosophizing, why condemn Marcus and Colorbasus and others like them,[26] who, from the parables, and based on the letters and numbers in sacred scripture, philosophize about Triads, Tetrads, and Ogdoads? In like fashion they theorize about the Demiurge, the Bythos, the Pleroma, and

---

[a] Rom 10:17. [b] Irenaeus, *Adversus haereses* 4.20.4 (PG 7 1034A-B).
[c] *Errors*, 50v (book 2). [d] Eph 4:6. [e] 1 Cor 8:6. [f] Col 1:16.
[g] Jerome, *In evangelium Matthaei* 2 (Matt 13:33) (PL 26 91B).

even about their various Aeons.[27] [Jerome's three beings] seem to differ from these in name only. And just as [the Gnostics] claim that beings arise one after another out of the "laughter and tears" of the Aeons,[28] so we are now claiming that the first being produces the second by a process of self-reflection and that these two, by the love they share, breathe out the third. Where in the scriptures, I ask you, [**27v**] have you read of such monstrous notions as these? And we, outdoing them, add something even more horrible: [the notion] that these three beings — so different from one another — are one and the same being.

In addition [Peter] Lombard says, "Almost every single syllable of the New Testament agrees in implying the Trinity."[a] To me, however, not only all the syllables, but all the letters, and *the mouths of babes and sucklings,*[b] even *the very stones cry out*[c] that *there is one God the Father* and *his Christ, the Lord Jesus.*[d] *For there is one God, and one mediator between God and humanity, the man Christ Jesus* (1 Timothy 2).[e] And *for us there is one God, who is the Father, and one Lord, Jesus Christ* (1 Corinthians 8).[f] Even John, to whom the heavens opened in the Apocalypse, saw only God the Father *and his Christ*. And there only God *and the Lamb* are praised.[g] Likewise Stephen, to whom *the heavens* were also *opened, beheld the glory of God, and Jesus standing at his right hand,*[h] yet he did not see any third person. In Matthew 23 [Jesus says] "*You have one Father,*" and "*one Teacher, Christ.*"[i] And in John 8 [he says,] "*It is not I alone [who judge], but I and the Father [who sent me].*"[j]

Rest, 28

These words of Christ, spoken with such great emphasis, always go straight to my heart: "*I am not alone*," he says, "*because the Father is with me.*"[k] And [he also says,] "*They

Rest, 28

---

[a] *Sentences* 1.2.8 (PL 192 529).   [b] Matt 21:16, quoting Ps 8:2.
[c] Luke 19:40.   [d] 1 Cor 8:6; Rev 11:15.   [e] 1 Tim 2:5.   [f] 1 Cor 8:6.
[g] Rev 21:22, 22:3.   [h] Acts 7:55-56.   [i] Matt 23:9-10.   [j] John 8:16.
[k] John 16:32.

Appendix A

Rest, 28

have not known the Father, nor me" (John 16)[a] and "[*This is eternal life*] *that they may know you, the only true God, and Jesus Christ, whom you have sent*" (John 17).[b] **[28r]** He did not command us to invoke the name of the third being, but to pray only to the Father and to himself, and to the Father in his name.[c] Likewise, when he said, "*No one knows the Father but the Son, nor the Son, but the Father*,"[d] was the third being sleeping, or unacquainted with them? And in 1 John 1, although John wants us to be in *fellowship with the Father and with his Son, Jesus Christ*,[e] he says nothing of fellowship with the third being.

Rest, 28

In 1 John 5, Paul says, "*I charge you, before God and the Lord Jesus Christ and the elect angels, to watch over these things without hasty judgement.*"[f] Note that Paul's solemn admonition was made before God, Christ, and the angels,

Rest, 29

and not before the third being. Similarly, in Revelation 3, Christ says, "*I will confess his name before my Father and before the angels.*"[g] What a grievous affront to the third being, for Christ to say "before the angels" and not "before [the third being]"! In like manner, in Mark 8, Luke 9, and Luke 12, [Christ] mentions only himself, the Father, and the angels.[h] And in Revelation 1, John wishes us *grace and peace from almighty God, from the seven Spirits who are before his throne, and from Jesus Christ, who is the faithful witness*,[i] yet he asks for nothing on our behalf from the third being. Also, in all of his letters, Paul says, "*God the Father and the Lord Jesus Christ*," or "*from God the Father and the Lord Jesus Christ.*"[j]

[28v] The scriptures often mention the existence of God the Father, and the Son, and [people] seeing and worshipping

---

[a] John 16:3. [b] John 17:3. [c] John 14:13-14, 15:16, 16:23-26. [d] Matt 11:27. [e] 1 John 1:3. [f] 1 Tim 5:21 (not 1 John). Servetus corrected this in *Restoration*. [g] Rev 3:5. [h] Mark 8:38; Luke 9:26, 12:8. [i] Rev 1:4, 5.
[j] This formula is often used at the beginning of an epistle, and occasionally at the end as well. See Rom 1:7; 1 Cor 1:3; 2 Cor 1:2; Gal 1:3; Eph 1:2, 6:23; Phil 1:2; Col 1:2; 1 Thes 1:1; 2 Thes 1:1, 1:2, 2:16; 1 Tim 1:2; 2 Tim 1:2; Titus 1:4; Phlm 1:3.

them, but they do not mention the Holy Spirit except when discussing an action, as though it were a kind of accidental predication.[29] This is worth noting. For, [in Scripture,] it appears that the [name] Holy Spirit designates not a separate being, but the activity of God — that is to say, a certain kind of energy or the inspiration of the power of God.

Following others, [Peter] Lombard makes his case for the triad of beings using this text from Exodus 3: *The God of Abraham, the God of Isaac, the God of Jacob.*[a] This might be tolerable if they were speaking of the Trinity as it should be understood, although this passage is not a proof of it.[30]   *Rest*, 25

However, a proof [of the Trinity] is found in Matthew 28: *Baptize in the name of the Father, and the Son, and the Holy Spirit.*[b] [*Baptize*] *in the name of the Father*, because he is the original, true, and primary source of *every gift* (James 1).[c] [*Baptize*] *in the name of* Jesus Christ, because *through him we have received the reconciliation*[d] provided by this gift: *nor is there any other name under heaven by which we must be saved* (Acts 2).[e] And [*baptize*] *in the name of the Holy Spirit*, since all who are *baptized in the name* [*of Jesus Christ*] *receive the gift of the Holy Spirit.*[f] [Saying "in the name of the Holy Spirit"] is like saying "in the name of the grandeur of Caesar," or "in the name of the glory of God."   *Rest*, 24

In Clement's *Recognitions*, Peter does not talk of three equal beings, but rather about a triple invocation of the divine name.[g] For these are three wondrous dispositions of God, in each of which divinity **[29r]** blazes forth. This is the soundest way to understand the meaning of the Trinity. For the Father is the whole substance [of the divine] and the one God, from whom those degrees [of divinity], and their personifications, descend.   *Rest*, 24

---

[a] Ex 3:6. [b] Matt 28:19. [c] James 1:17. [d] Rom 5:11. [e] Acts 4:12 (not Acts 2). Servetus corrected this in *Restoration*. [f] Acts 2:38.
[g] [Clement], *Recognitiones* 3.67, 6.9 (PG 1 1311D, 1352B-C).

Appendix A

{*In our time they say that the [divine] essence is "communicated" to the three beings*}

Rest, 24

There are three [persons], not by some distinction of beings in God, but because, through the οἰκονομίαν (*oikonomia*, economy) of God, there are various forms of deity.[a] For the same divinity that is in the Father is communicated to the Son, Jesus Christ, and to our spirit, which is the *temple of the living God*.[b] Both the Son and our sanctified spirit "share in the substance of the Father," and are "members" [of the deity], "pledges" [of his love], and "instruments" [of his will],[c] although the appearance of deity differs in each of them. This is why they are said to be "distinct persons," that is, the multiform aspects of deity, having different likenesses and appearances. The most ancient apostolic traditions do not differ from this way of thinking. On the contrary, they endorse it.

Rest, 26

Now, the fact that those three beings are not being spoken of [in Exodus 3] is shown by the following passage: when God speaks to Jacob, he says, "*I am the God of your father Abraham and of Isaac*" (Genesis 28 and 32).[d] Now you cannot possibly infer from this that there are two philosophical beings. Furthermore, when [God] spoke to Isaac, he said, "*I am the God of your father Abraham*" (Genesis 26).[e] If we are to understand [Exodus 3] as referring to those three beings, how can *the God of Abraham, the God of Isaac, and the God of Jacob* be called the father of Jesus Christ in Acts 3?[f] Can it be that this imaginary Trinity is to be called the father of Jesus Christ? If so, then just as the first [being] begot the man [Jesus], so also did the second, and thus we will [have to] grant **[29v]** that the Son of God is the father of Jesus Christ.

---

[a] See A.R1.47.   [b] 2 Cor 6:16.   [c] Tertullian, *Adversus Praxean* 3 (PL 2 158C-159A).   [d] Gen 28:13, 32:9.   [e] Gen 26:24.   [f] Acts 3:13.

Having excluded this [absurd interpretation], we must understand that [in Exodus 3] God was seeking to dissuade the Jews from believing in a plurality of gods. For the Jews were prone to [worship] a multiplicity [of gods] (just as we ourselves are today) and they were accustomed to multiplying their gods according to the number of their cities: *According to the number of your cities were your gods, O Judah* (Jeremiah 2 and 11).[a] To prevent them from multiplying their gods according to the number of ages or generations of men, and lest they believe that there was one God of Abraham, another God of Isaac, and another God of Jacob, God proclaimed that he was the same God of them all.

Rest, 26

[God] makes this clear in the words immediately preceding, when he says, "*I am the God of your fathers.*"[b] This was his customary way of speaking: "*I am the God who led you out of the land of Egypt*"[c] and "*out of Ur of the Chaldeans.*"[d] And in Exodus 6 he says that it was he who appeared to [the patriarchs]: "*I am God, who appeared to Abraham, Isaac, and Jacob.*"[e] Also, in Isaiah 48, [God says], "*I am he, I am the first, I am the last.*"[f]

Rest, 26

A second interpretation, which is consistent [with the explanation I have just given], can be found in the words of the Teacher himself. For [God] spoke of himself as the "God of Abraham, Isaac, and Jacob" in order to show that he is God, not only of those who are now alive, but even of those who have died. With these words Christ proves the resurrection [of the dead]. For if God is the God of those who have died, it follows that they are all still living (Luke 20).[g] Therefore, **[30r]** you should carefully consider how much meaning lies hidden in the words of the [Old Testament], even when the literal meaning seems obvious. Here the Teacher provides us with a wonderful lesson [in biblical

Rest, 26-27

---

[a] Jer 2:28, 11:13.   [b] Acts 7:32, quoting Ex 3:6.   [c] Ex 20:2; Ps 81:10.   [d] Gen 15:7.   [e] Ex 6:2-3.   [f] Isa 48:12.   [g] Luke 20:37-38. See also Matt 22:32; Mark 12:26-27.

Appendix A

interpretation]. If you keep this in mind, I will shortly be able to clearly demonstrate to you [the nature of] Christ, based upon the [Old Testament].

[*The Holy Spirit is Not a Separate Being*]

Besides, if you think about it in the right way, the argument [that Exodus 3 describes the Trinity] can be refuted on the basis of [the theologians'] own interpretations. The actions of the Holy Spirit [in Exodus 3] do not indicate a third being. Fire appears [to Moses] in this passage,[a] and fire is said to be a special characteristic of the Holy Spirit, as is the appearance of a dove (Matthew 3 and Luke 3).[b] But listen to the voice [from heaven]: "*You are my beloved son.*"[c] "*I am the God of your fathers.*"[d] These are not words that a separate third being would utter. Similarly, just as it is written, *the Holy Spirit spoke*,[e] so too [it is written that] God spoke through the *mouths of* saints and *prophets* (Acts 3 and Hebrews 1).[f] Therefore those things that characterize the activity of the Holy Spirit cannot be attributed, as accidents, to a separate being, but only to God himself, because *God is spirit.*[g] Also [God says], *I who sanctify you am holy.*[h]

Nor is the name Paraclete [or advocate] exclusive to this third being of theirs, for Christ himself is called a paraclete (1 John 2).[i] And while [the Gospel of John] speaks of *another paraclete* than Christ, even there Christ is described as a paraclete.[j] [John] says "another" because at that time, when they were hearing him daily, [his disciples] were being comforted by the Word itself, [that is,] by Christ, and he was defending them. [After Christ's ascension] they would have as defender, not the [physical] presence of the Word,

---

[a] Ex 3:2. [b] Matt 3:16; Luke 3:22. See also Mark 1:10. The appearance of the Holy Spirit as fire or a dove is discussed in *Sentences* 16.2 (PL 192 562-563), quoting Augustine, *De Trinitate* 2.10 (PL 42 851). [c] Matt 3:17; Luke 3:22. See also Mark 1:11. [d] Acts 7:32. [e] Acts 1:16, 28:25. [f] Acts 3:18; Heb 1:1. [g] John 4:24. [h] Lev 21:8. [i] 1 John 2:1. [j] John 14:15-19.

[30v] but the Spirit, and they would be comforted by the Spirit, when the truth was revealed to them.

In addition, Paul says that it is God, not the third being, who *has anointed us* (2 Corinthians 1).[a] And [when Paul says] "*the spirit of God abides in you*"[b] he means nothing other than "*the anointing which you have received from him abides in you.*"[c] And this is what teaches you all things (1 Corinthians 2).[d] "To *receive the* Holy *Spirit*"[e] means nothing other than "*you will receive power* when the heavenly messenger *comes upon you from on high*" (Luke 24 and Acts 1).[f] Power of this sort is not a separate being. This is proved in Mark 5 and Luke 8, where Jesus *knows in himself that the power has gone out of him*.[g] Tell me, if you can, what that entity or being is, which is said to have gone out of him, and then I will have to speak, just as you do, of another heavenly power.

Besides, the Holy Spirit cannot be described as a third being in an absolute sense, but is only called a being in an accidental sense. The proof of this is that the Holy Spirit is said to increase and decrease. In Numbers 11, *the Lord said to Moses, "I will take away some of your spirit"* and then, taking some of the spirit which was in Moses, he gave it to seventy men.[h] And in 2 Kings 2 [Elisha says to Elijah], "*Let me have a double portion of your spirit.*"[i] Likewise, in John 3 it is written: *for* God *does not give the Spirit by measure.*[j] And in Daniel 6, *the spirit of God was greater* in Daniel than in the others.[k]

Furthermore, why is it that the apostles were so often *filled with the Holy Spirit*? (Acts 2 and 4).[l] Could it be that the third being visited them many times, physically [31r] uniting itself with them [on each occasion]? Actually, [being filled with the Holy Spirit] means only that the apostles burned

---

[a] 2 Cor 1:21.   [b] Rom 8:9-11; 1 Cor 3:16.   [c] 1 John 2:27.   [d] 1 Cor 2:9-10.   [e] Acts 8:15,17,19.   [f] Luke 24:49; Acts 1:8.   [g] Mark 5:30; Luke 8:46.   [h] Num 11:16-17.   [i] 2 Kg 2:9.   [j] John 3:34.   [k] Dan 6:3.   [l] Acts 2:4, 4:8, 31.

with eagerness to be heard, and, aflame with the utmost fervour of faith and love, debated with and admonished the Pharisees. To say that John [the Baptist] *was filled with the Holy Spirit while yet in the womb*[a] means nothing more than that *the infant*, by divine power, *leapt in his mother's womb* (Luke 1).[b] You cannot infer from this that the third being was united with [the infant] in this way. For [the Spirit] is greater than [anything] carnal and profane. Otherwise you might conclude, with equal justice, that the spirit of Elijah was united with [John the Baptist], because he is said to have come with *the spirit and power of Elijah*.[c]

Besides, what does it mean *"to grieve the Holy Spirit"*[d] and that *"the spirits of prophets are subject to the prophets"*?[e] Can the third being suffer such affliction?

Now, "to give the spirit" means exactly what it says: *I will give them a new heart and a new spirit*[f] and *[the Lord] gives us understanding*.[g] And, as John says, *[the Son of God] has given us understanding that we may know him*,[h] just as Solomon *was given a wise heart*[i] and *the spirit of wisdom, the spirit of counsel, the spirit of knowledge and piety*.[j] Later I will discuss why, on the basis of passages such as these, God's holy spirit is truly said to be in us. For now, keep in mind that [spirit] is a special attribute of God, and that, by antonomasia,[31] it is appropriate [to call God] the Wise, as well as the Mighty, the Just, and the Merciful. Therefore God, by sharing these gifts with us, is said to bestow his spirit upon us. Indeed, such virtues are usually **[31v]** called exemplary virtues. For, just as the ἰδέα (ideal form) of [these virtues] shines forth in God, so too their shining in us is said to be an exemplar of God, or his holy spirit, in us. And this is so, not only because such gifts are bestowed on us, but because [God] alone gives us the breath of life and is said to give us his spirit (Ezekiel 37).[k]

---

[a] Luke 1:15. [b] Luke 1:41. [c] Luke 1:17. [d] Eph 4:30. [e] 1 Cor 14:32. [f] Ezek 11:19. See also Ezek 18:31, 36:26. [g] 2 Tim 2:7. [h] 1 John 5:20. [i] 1 Kg 3:12. [j] Isa 11:2. [k] Ezek 37:5. On the relationship between breath and spirit, see *Errors*, 22r-v. See also Job 33:4.

Furthermore, that the Holy Spirit is not a distinct being is proven by the use of the expressions *the spirit of Christ* and *the spirit of the Son* in 1 Peter 1 and Galatians 4.[a] Similarly, in Romans 8: *The Spirit of God dwells in you. But if anyone does not have the Spirit of Christ, he does not belong to him. But if the Spirit of him* — that is, the Father — *who raised Jesus,*[b] etc.[32] On the basis of [this passage], Hilary says in book 7 of *On the Trinity* that the Holy Spirit sometimes means the Father, sometimes the Son, and sometimes the third being.[c] Consequently the names of these three beings become confused with one another.

Many claim that there are other ways by which the Trinity can be deduced, whether by syllogistic proof or by demonstration. For instance, in book 3, chapter 2 of *On The Trinity*, Richard [of St. Victor], by means of a "clear proof," concludes "based on the special nature of love," that "it is impossible for there not to be a plurality" in God. For if there is love, it is for another[d] — that is, [the love of the Father] for the Son. And if there is love, then this love itself must be something, hence the third person.

Similarly, Henry of Ghent, in quodlibet 6, question 2, [**32r**] concludes by means of the intrinsic middle[33] that, because begetting occurs here below, there must, of necessity, be begettings amongst the gods. For [according to Henry] there is only speculative knowledge in the Father, and only practical knowledge in the Son. But in neither of them is there ardent love, as there is in the third person.[e] Consequently one [of the persons of the Trinity] can do nothing without another, unless they copulate and beget amongst themselves.

---

[a] 1 Pet 1:11; Gal 4:6. [b] Rom 8:9-11. [c] *Sentences* 1.34.2 (PL 192 614), based on Hilary, *De Trinitate* 8.25 (PL 10 254A-255A). Servetus, following Peter Lombard, cited book 7. [d] Richard of St. Victor, *De Trinitate* 3.2 (PL 196 916C). [e] Henry of Ghent, *Quodlibeta theologica* 6.2 (solutio). Henry calls the Holy Spirit "enticing and affectionate" (*incentivum et affectativum*) love.

I am setting aside a great many other arguments of this kind which I have examined. Instead of resolving every difficulty that these philosophers raise, you should use as your guiding rule the legal opinion laid down in the paragraph beginning, "The Praetor says," in the section entitled "On Injuries" in the *Digest of Roman Law*: "those things that have been deemed worthy of particular notice, if they are not expressly mentioned, are to be understood as being disregarded."[a] But you must decide whether this article of faith [the Trinity] — since it is the principal foundation of the entire [Christian] faith, upon which our knowledge of God and Christ depends — ought to be deemed worthy of particular notice. And, based on your reading of the scriptures, [you must determine] whether it is expressly mentioned, when not a single word can be found in the entire Bible about the Trinity, neither about its persons, its essence, the unity of the *suppositum*, the single nature made up of several beings, nor the other *empty babblings* and *disputes about words*,[b] which Paul says belong to *false knowledge*.[c]

[*Other Objections to the Trinity*]

[*The Trinity is Contrary to Reason*]

Rest, 29

It now remains for me to demonstrate, by means of reasoned argument and authoritive texts, that these three beings cannot coexist in one God.

Rest, 29

First of all, I could attack this imaginary triad by using the sixteen arguments [showing the logical inconsistencies in the idea of the Trinity] raised by Robert Holkot [**32v**] in distinction 5 of book 1 of his *Sentences*.[d] He does not give an adequate response to any of the objections he raises, nor can he offer anything but a sophistical response. Indeed, he grants that this article [of faith] is entirely contrary to

---

[a] *Corpus Juris Civilis* 47.10.15.26.   [b] 2 Tim 2:16; 1 Tim 6:4.
[c] 1 Tim 6:20.   [d] See A.R1.59.

natural reason. See also "preludes" in Pierre d'Ailly's [*Questions,*] book 1, question 5.^a

[*The Trinity is Inconceivable*]

But for now I will demonstrate my proposition in another way. I will prove not only that these three beings cannot exist in one God, but also that they are unimaginable, and that to think about them is utterly impossible. For in order to have an idea of the Trinity, it would be necessary to have separate ideas of each of the three beings, so that it would be possible to have an idea of one of them without having an idea of any of the others. Everyone denies [that this is possible]. *Rest*, 30-31

You may say that someone might have an idea of the Trinity by having an idea of God "connotatively" as those three beings. O what a solid structure these sophists have erected! How, I ask, can you wish us to be required to believe in things about which even your Aristotle was never certain?[34] Can it be right for our faith to rely with such great certainty on these uncertain connotations? How do you know? Who revealed these connotations to you? Indeed, as I will very clearly show elsewhere in this work, there are no such variations in the intellect, although they might be found in the words of Nicander.[35] In any event, since there is absolutely no certainty [where connotations are concerned], [Christian] faith cannot be based upon them. *Rest*, 31

Again, according to your wisdom, how can anything be connoted by the term "white," unless it can be conveyed absolutely by another abstract term, [**33r**] "whiteness"?[36] And this also applies to other concrete terms that connote a particular thing. Or will you say that only a "disposition" is connoted here? Furthermore, [we must bear in mind] the rule of Porphyry: "From any essential commonality, a concept may be abstracted, which has an absolute and irreducible meaning."^b *Rest*, 31

---

^a See A.R1.60.   ^b See A.R1.71.

Appendix A

Rest, 31

I would then ask: according to their rules, is the Trinity unknown to Christ and the angels? Do they suppose that, in the mind of Christ and in the minds of the angels, there are three conceptions of three beings, so that they distinctly perceive three gods? In Matthew 18, Christ says that *angels see the face of* his *Father*.[a] They do not see other contrivances. Similarly, [while on earth] Christ saw nothing in himself other than the Father;[b] nor does he now [in heaven] see anything else but him.

Rest, 31

Dream as much as you want, [but when you do,] direct your gaze at those mental images, and you will discover that the Trinity cannot be understood without three mental images. For "observing mental images is necessary for understanding" ([Aristotle] *On the Soul* 3).[c] Although you deny it in your words, in your mind you are worshipping a quaternity [of gods]. For you have four pictures [in your mind], and the fourth is a mental image representing the essence [of the divine]. For "observing a mental image is necessary for understanding" the essence. And once you have come to realize this, you will clearly understand what I am about to say elsewhere about the formation of ideas [in the mind]. But if you pay attention, you can recognize even now that your Trinity is nothing but a tumult of false appearances in your imagination, which holds you spellbound.

Rest, 32

[33v] But if you say that all [Christians] proclaim as though with a single voice, "it is enough to believe,"[d] even though [what we are asked to believe] is incomprehensible, you are only exposing your own foolishness. For you are accepting an incomprehensible thing without satisfactory scriptural testimony. As [scripture] says, they *understand neither what they are saying nor what they are affirming* and [*like irrational beasts*] *they blaspheme those things about which they have no understanding.*[e]

---

[a] Matt 18:10. [b] See John 5:19. [c] See A.R1.72. [d] See A.R1.73.
[e] 1 Tim 1:7; 2 Pet 2:12.

This is all the more [absurd], since you yourselves profess that what you understand is itself the object of faith. But if you have this faith, tell me: what is the extent of your understanding? What is it that you think you understand? Can it be that you consider your own mental confusion to be an adequate object of faith?[a]

Besides, "nothing can be in the intellect unless it"— or something similar or analogous to it — "has first been [perceived by] the senses" (*Posterior Analytics*, book 1 and *On the Soul*, book 3).[b] But neither close at hand nor from a distance have you ever had the sensory perception of three beings that together constitute a single nature. Nor can you make one category of being equivalent to another. For two, three, or more beings coexisting as one nature cannot be found. And consequently, no basis can be found in sensory perception by means of which the mind could, using syllogistic reasoning, reach such a conclusion. Indeed, [the mind] is wearied and confused by [the Trinity], because it struggles to envision it, while lacking a basis in sense perception — which is like laying the foundation of a building in the air.

Next, let us imagine that there is a separate person of the Father, as my adversaries readily admit [we can], since **[34r]** they make a formal distinction between the persons and the essence [of the Trinity]. Then, I ask, since it is agreed that any being has its own essence and its own nature, how can I imagine a multiplicity of beings without a multiplicity of essences? Or that a new being can be added without a new essence? Could you ever perceive this [Trinity], or anything like it, by sensory perception? Certainly not. Therefore you cannot hope to perceive any such thing in your mind.

[*God is One*]

We are taught to avoid such plurality, not only by reason, but by countless authorities and also by all the testimonies

---

[a] See A.R1.74.   [b] See A.R1.75.

Appendix A

Rest, 33   provided by the pagan philosophers, poets, and sibyls[37] cited by Lactantius Firmianus,[a] that you might thereby recognize what a laughingstock you would be if you attempted to sell these [pagans] your three beings in exchange for one god. But this perhaps might seem to be going too far afield.

Rest, 33   I can, however, demonstrate the [same] thing from the sacred scriptures, from the Old as well as the New Testament. In Matthew 19 [Jesus says,] "*There is one who is good, God.*"[b] And in Mark 10: "*No one is good but one, God.*"[c] Thus, are they not content with unity in name only, who fail to acknowledge the One Itself, and, by means of their artificial word "essence," turn to a plurality of beings? And lest anyone take offense, note that it is the Son who is speaking here. From [these words of Jesus] it is clear that the entire basis of the unity of God is to be found in the Father alone. Nothing else exists [in the divine] but God the Father and Jesus Christ the Son. This is [shown by] 1 Corinthians 8, a crucial text: *There is* **[34v]** *one God, who is the Father, and one Lord Jesus Christ.*[d] See also Ephesians 4: *There is one God and Father.*[e]

    I do not understand this madness that prevents people from seeing that, in the scriptures, the entire rationale for the unity of God is always presented in reference to the

Rest, 33   Father. *For there is one God, and one mediator between God and humanity, the man Jesus Christ* (1 Timothy 2).[f] Also note that [Paul] so often speaks about the one God and his Christ, and that he says that *God is the father of Jesus Christ*,[g] and that Jesus Christ is the mediator,[h] and that *through him we have access to* God.[i] Do you think it should instead be understood that the first being is the

---

[a] Lactantius Firmianus, *Divinae institutiones* 1.5-6 (PL 6 129-148).
[b] Matt 19:17.   [c] Mark 10:18.   [d] 1 Cor 8:6.   [e] Eph 4:6.   [f] 1 Tim 2:5.
[g] For example, Rom 15:6; 2 Cor 1:3, 2 Cor 11:31; Eph 1:3; Col 1:3.
[h] In addition to 1 Tim 2:5, see Heb 8:6, 9:15, 12:24.   [i] Eph 2:18.

father of the second, and that it is through the second being that we have access to the first?

Likewise, when Ignatius, Irenaeus, and the other early Church Fathers argue against heretics that almighty God, the God of the Old Testament, the God of the Law and the Prophets, is also the God of the New Testament and the father of Jesus Christ,[a] do you think it should be understood that they were preaching about three separate beings? Similarly, Tertullian, even though he sometimes seems to contradict himself, nevertheless proclaims many of the clearest truths drawn from apostolic tradition.[b] Christ is also proclaimed very clearly, even to the uneducated, in Clement's *Recognitions*, which, although an apocryphal book, is still quite old, [35r] and in which you will find many traces of ancient simplicity.[c] However, lest I should seem to be building [my case] on an uncertain foundation, I will omit [any further discussion of this apocryphal work].

Rest, 33

I will, however, mention the words of Ignatius [in his epistle] to the Philippians. "If anyone," he writes, "preaches that the God of the Law and the Prophets is one, but denies that Christ is his son, then he is a liar." And "If anyone professes faith in Jesus Christ, while denying that the God of the Law and the Prophets is the father of Christ, then he is not established in the truth."[d] Also in the Epistle to the Tarsians, [Ignatius] clearly says of Christ that "he is not God over all things, but [God's] son."[e] Indeed, as Justin, a disciple of the apostles, [is quoted by Irenaeus as saying], "Faith could not have been placed in Christ himself, if

Rest, 33-34

---

[a] Irenaeus, *Adversus haereses* 4.2.2 (PG 7 977A-B). [Ignatius], *Ad Philadelphios* 5-6 (PG 5 830A-B). Origen, *De principiis* 2.4.1 (PG 11 198C).   [b] Tertullian, *Adversus Marcionem* 3.1 (PL 2 322C-D).
[c] [Clement], *Recognitiones* 2.40 (PG 1 1267B), 7.23 (PG 1 1364C).
[d] [Ignatius], *Ad Philadelphios* 6 (PG 5 830 B). The quotation is from the epistle to the Philadelphians, not Philippians; Servetus corrected this in *Restoration*.   [e] [Ignatius], *Ad Tarsenses* 5 (PG 5 891B).

Appendix A

he had said that some being was God, apart from the creator, maker, and father of all things."[a]

Consider what Irenaeus says in book 1, chapter 28 [of *Against Heresies*]: it was the heresy of Cerdo[38] that יהוה (*Yahweh*), who was "proclaimed to be God in the Law and the Prophets, is not the father of Jesus Christ."[b] Look at this passage, and also at the next chapter,[c] and ask yourself why [Irenaeus's] ways of speaking are not found among our trinitarians.[39] This way of thinking [about God] is the only valid one. Consider that Irenaeus's entire book is on this subject, yet never mentions [the trinitarians'] nonsense.

Rest, 34

Rest, 34

The Old Testament often instructs us that we should profess a unity, not a plurality [in God]. **[35v]** For example, in Exodus 20: *I am your God, and you shall have no other gods apart from me.*[d] Also in Deuteronomy 6: *Hear, O Israel, Yahweh is our God, and Yahweh is one.*[e] [In this passage] I decided to change [the word "Lord" (*dominus*) to "*Yahweh*"] because those who do not know the proper meaning of the [Hebrew] word are most shamefully deceived.[40] Also: *Know therefore today, and ponder it in your heart, that* God *is God in heaven above and on earth below; there is no other* apart from him (Deuteronomy 4).[f] And in countless other places, the God of Israel, the one God, is said to be one.

{*Nevertheless, they do not want to say that he is one, but say that he has three partners*}

[To the theologians] all these things appear easy to answer. However they merely adorn their speech with impressive-sounding words, while not convincing our minds, when they say that there are many beings, yet only one essence. As if anything whatsoever does not have its

---

[a] Irenaeus, *Adversus haereses* 4.6.2 (PG 7 987B).   [b] Irenaeus, *Adversus haereses* 1.27.1 (PG 7 687B-C). Chapters 28 and 29, in the edition that Servetus was using, are entirely contained within PG chapter 27.
[c] Irenaeus, *Adversus haereses* 1.27.2 (PG 7 688A-689A).   [d] Ex 20:2-3.
[e] Deut 6:4.   [f] Deut 4:39.

own essence! Indeed, as I will show later,[a] it is more coherent [to say] that one being can have several essences, than that many beings should have but one essence. I have often asked them to explain the difference between beings and natures. However, I have never been able to find any explanation, except that רז״ל [our teachers of blessed memory][b] use [these terms] in this way.

Furthermore, the position they defend, since it is unsupported by evidence from the scriptures, can be seen to be illegitimate, for it is well established [in scripture] that there is one God. And I find no mention of these beings whom they call persons. Nor does scripture say anything about the essence, nor anything at all about all their other doctrines, *empty babblings and disputes about words.*[c] *O Timothy*, [Paul admonishes] *avoid strange new expressions, professing which, some have erred concerning the faith.*[d] And elsewhere [Paul says]: *Do not be carried away by strange and* [36r] *outlandish questions.*[e] And again, in 2 Timothy 2, Paul charges us not to be led astray by *disputes about words.*[f]

It is now clear from their own words that their argument is based merely on wordplay. For, by allowing that there are three beings, whom they call "persons," it may also be proved by the argument from convertibles[g] that they are thus granting that there are three entities, and consequently that there are three substances. Therefore, if [the word] "God" has an absolute meaning, it clearly follows that [the theologians] are really tritheists, and consequently are actually opposing both the scriptures and the unity of God. And since they sophistically defend a connotative God, they are therefore hateful to God (Wisdom 37).[h]

Rest, 30

---

[a] *Errors*, 102r-v (book 5). [b] The Hebrew is unclear in the original; we follow E.M. Wilbur in interpreting it as shown. This is a well-known abbreviation for a Hebrew phrase meaning "our teachers of blessed memory" (Wilbur, *Two Treatises*, 56 n.1). [c] 2 Tim 2:16; 1 Tim 6:4. [d] 1 Tim 6:20-21. [e] Heb 13:9. [f] 2 Tim 2:14. [g] See A.R1.69. [h] Ecclus 37:23: "He who speaks sophistically is hateful."

Consider, if you will, another "solid foundation": while granting that there are three beings, they deny that there are three entities and three substances. Their explanation for this is that since those nouns [*entia* (entities) and *substantia* (substance)] end in *-tia*, they must be "essentials" [*essentia*, or qualities belonging to the divine essence]. O world of wonders! That merely to suit the requirements of word endings, God has become a laughingstock to us! And that based on the grammatical exigencies of one word, and not those of another, we ought to confess a plurality in God! Are we to insist that the Hebrews, the Greeks, and speakers of other languages have nouns ending in *-tia*, so that there may be a consistent rule for mocking God in every language? Are not these the *disputes about words*[a] that Paul abhors? If you should ask them how they lay such utterly empty [theological] foundations, they will reply that they learned to do so by following the usage of their teachers. Nor does it bother them if they *nullify the word of God*, if only they can preserve [**36v**] *the leaven of* their *tradition*.[b]

Furthermore, hear what scripture has to say about persons, so that you may discover how closely what [the theologians] say actually conforms to scripture. For, in scripture, the outward appearance and presentation of a human being is called a "person," as when we say, "this person is beautiful." And this is the way in which we understand Romans 2, Colossians 3, Acts 10, and 1 Peter 1, when they say that *God is no respecter of persons*,[c] because he does not care about outward differences — whether someone is *male or female, slave or free, Jew or Greek*.[d] And it is thus that we understand 1 Samuel 17, James 2, Leviticus 19, and Deuteronomy 1, where it says that we should *not take into consideration the person of the poor or the countenance of the mighty*.[e] See also 2 Corinthians 1, 2, 3, 4, 8,

---

[a] 1 Tim 6:4. [b] Matt 15:6, 16:6. [c] Rom 2:11; Col 3:25; Acts 10:34; 1 Pet 1:17. [d] Gal 3:28. [e] Lev 19:15. Similar ideas are expressed in 1 Sam 16:7 (not 1 Sam 17); James 2:1-7; Deut 1:17.

10, and 11, where the Greek πρόσωπον (*prosopon*, person) is [variously] translated into Latin as *vultus, persona, aspectus*, and *facies*.[a] Outside of scripture, the meaning of the word *persona* in Latin is so well known, that some devil must have instigated them to invent those mathematical persons of theirs, and to foist upon us imaginary and metaphysical beings in place of persons.

For one person of the Deity shone forth in Christ, another in the manifestations and utterances of God the Father, and another in the sending forth of the Spirit. Thus, in the Gospel, we know of three persons, that is, [three kinds of] divine manifestation.

According to Tertullian, when [Jesus] speaks about "*another Paraclete*"[b] he does not name a substance, but a person, because he meant here another aspect, appearance, or disposition of the deity.[c] **[37r]** For scripture pays attention to modes of presentation and not to metaphysical natures. Examine in the original sources what [Christian] tradition once thought about persons, and how the whole thing has been distorted by the pernicious [ideas] of our times. As for the monstrosity they have created out of the [term] "hypostasis," I shall later have more to say when I speak about the Word.[d]

Furthermore, consider the passage mentioned above, as quoted in Mark 12: *Hear, O Israel*, your *God is one, and there is no other apart from him.*[e] And the second commandment is about your neighbour. *On these two commandments*, says Matthew 22, *depend the whole Law and the Prophets.*[f]

---

[a] 2 Cor 1:11, 2:10, 3:7, 3:13, 3:18, 4:6, 8:24, 10:1, 10:7, 11:20. In the Vulgate, 2 Cor 1:11 and 2:10 use *persona*, 3:7 has both *facies* and *vultus*, and the other verses use *facies*. In his translation of the New Testament, Erasmus used *conspectus* (not *aspectus*) in 2 Cor 2:10, 8:24, and 10:7. All of these words refer to appearance or facial expression.   [b] John 14:16.
[c] Tertullian, *Adversus Praxean* 9 (PL 2 164B).   [d] *Errors*, 95v-96v (book 4), 114r-116v (book 7).   [e] Mark 12:29, quoting Deut 6:4; Mark 12:32, quoting Deut 4:35.   [f] Matt 22:39-40.

Appendix A

Therefore, in none of the commandments of the Law, is belief in an imaginary Trinity required. For there is only one who said, "*I am, I am [the Lord], and apart from me there is no saviour*" (Isaiah 43).[a] And, *I am the Lord, and there is no other, there is no God beside me*, there is no Lord apart from me, *I am the Lord, and there is no other* (Isaiah 45).[b] The Hebrews are supported by so many authorities that they are right to wonder that such a splitting up [of God] into gods was introduced into the New Testament. They think our testament is schismatic, since they see that their own God is so abhorrent to us.

Rest, 34

[*The Man Jesus Is the Son of God*]

If we must debate with [the Jews], we ought to adopt the apostolic practice, which is to point out to them that this Jesus whom they saw is the Christ, and the Son of God. This is also what we are taught by the Teacher, who attempted to persuade the Jews in this way. In John 8 he says that [**37v**] (*Yahweh*), "*whom you claim to be your God, is my Father.*"[c] See how clearly, and in a way that was intelligible to [Jewish thinking], he was speaking to them about his God. *This is why they wanted to kill him: because he had said that God was his father* (John 5).[d] And [they also said] that *he deserved to die, because he made himself out to be the Son of God*.[e] Why do you not consider what [the Jews] meant when they said these things? Christ does not deny their meaning. Rather he confirms it, when he answers, "*You say that I am* the Son of God."[f]

Furthermore, if Paul were in Damascus today, attempting to persuade the Jews that *this man is the Son of God*,[g] what do you think he would be indicating by the pronoun [*hunc*, this man]?[h] What kind of argument do you believe

---

[a] Isa 43:11. [b] Isa 45:5-6. [c] John 8:54. [d] John 5:18. [e] John 19:7.
[f] Luke 22:70. [g] Acts 9:20. [h] See A.R1.1.

would persuade the Jews whom you see now awaiting the Messiah? They are like the [Samaritan] woman who was awaiting the Messiah, and she was persuaded by the words of Christ.^a

Some people, however, think themselves so grand that they do not even deign to gaze upon this man. For they consider it a degrading and contemptible thing for the Son of God to be called a human being. They make the Son of God out to be something far more exalted, and they claim that the Son must be of the same nature as the Father, or, as they say, of the same "ultimate species."^b Thus, from the outset, they reject the [divine] sonship of a human being as blasphemy.

Rest, 14

But let the Teacher himself answer on my behalf. In John chapter 10 he shows that he is the Son of God by comparing himself to other human beings. For "even though [God] *called* other human beings *gods, you claim* [**38r**] that I am *blaspheming because I said, 'I am the Son of God,'*^c when *the Father has sanctified* me *above* all my *fellows*."^d

Rest, 14

Behold clearly that he who was sanctified is to be called the Son of God. He is the one who *will be called holy, the Son of God*.^e He is the one whom the apostles call *"your holy son Jesus."*^f It is evident that [the theologians' concept of] "ultimate species" is fallacious even in the case of brute animals, and they make up out of their own heads whatever they need [to complete their argument]. If only they would draw a little nearer to God! They are trying to look at him from too great a distance.

They should also harmonize the Old Testament with the New. For when speaking of the Messiah the Hebrew scriptures very often [use the words] *glorified, honoured, crowned, glorious, comely, illustrious, noble, glory, praise, loveliness,*

---

^a John 4:25-26.   ^b See A.R1.17   ^c John 10:35-36, referring to Ps 82:6.
^d Heb 1:9, referring to Ps 45:7.   ^e Luke 1:35.   ^f Acts 4:27, 30.

beauty, magnificence, and *honour*.[a] All of these [words] are also used frequently in the New Testament in reference to Jesus Christ, the Son of God. However, [the theologians] assign none of these [words] to the human being, nor do they concern themselves with the Messiah of the Old Testament. They attribute everything to the second being by means of *communicatio idiomatum*, [and so can] say that there are not two kings, nor two who are glorified.

[*The Trinity Leads to Heresy*]

Rest, 36-37 Now let us consider the monstrous ideas brought to life by this controversy about the Trinity. For we need only bring them into the light in order to refute all of these philosophers. Once the philosophy of three beings had entered the world, the tritheists said, "there are three gods."[b] **[38v]** Even though they deny it with their lips, this is what our [trinitarians] profess.

Rest, 37 The Arians severed the second being from the substance of the first, as if it were a lesser being.[c] Macedonius denied that the third being is God,[d] and claimed that [the Holy Spirit] is the servant of the Father and the Son.[e] See how, having once gone astray at the outset, these desperate men are tossed about on the high seas, forever "bringing in a greater question [in order to resolve] a lesser one."[f] Whoever dreams up a new God always heaps new blasphemies upon him.

---

[a] For example, from the Vulgate: Isa 55:5 (*glorificavit*, glorified); Ecclus 42:21 (*decoravit*, honoured); Ecclus 45:9 (*coronavit*, crowned); Isa 43:4 (*gloriosus*, glorious); Song of Sol 1:15 (*decorus*, comely); Isa 62:2 (*inclytus*, illustrious); 1 Sam 9:6 (*nobilis*, noble); Isa 4:2 and 40:5 (*gloria*, glory); Isa 12:2 and Jer. 17:14 (*laus*, praise); Ps 21:5 [20:6 in V] (*decor*, loveliness); Ps 96:6 [95:6 in V] (*pulchritudo*, beauty and *magnificentia*, magnificence); Ps. 8:5 [8:6 in V] (*honor*, honour). [b] Isidore, *Etymologiae* 8.5.68 (PL 82 304C). [c] Isidore, *Etymologiae* 8.5.43 (PL 82 302A). See also *Sentences* 1.28.4 (PL 192 598). [d] Isidore, *Etymologiae* 8.5.44 (PL 82 302A). [e] Sozomenus, *Historia ecclesiastica* 4.27 (PG 67 1199B). [f] Irenaeus, *Adversus Haereses* 2.10.1 (PG 7 735A). See A.R1.88.

In addition, the Aëtians and Eunomians say that these beings are unlike each other.[a] The Origenists rave that "the Son cannot see the Father, nor can the Holy Spirit see the Son."[b] [The Arian] Maximinus feared that the Father would be [only] part of God, and that each of the persons would be one-third of the Trinity.[c] And the Metangismonites said that the second being was contained within the first, "like a smaller vessel inside a larger vessel."[d]

Rest, 37-38

The Nestorians claim that Jesus is [two beings], one the Son of God and the other the son of a man,[e] which is what, in actual fact, our [current theologians] are professing. For as is apparent from the disputations [with the Nestorians], as related by Maxentius of Constantinople, Nestorius never admitted [that he believed in] two sons, but defended himself with various sophistical tricks,[f] extremely similar to the ones [used by our latter-day sophists]. Read [Maxentius], and you will clearly see [that our modern theologians are actually] Nestorians.

Rest, 38

The Eutychians, on the other hand, claimed that in Christ there is only a divine nature,[g] as if he were a phantom who glided down from heaven, which is what the Marcionites also said.[h] The Monarchians, such as Praxeas and Victorinus,[i] said that "Jesus is God the Father **[39r]** Almighty," and that "he is seated at his own right hand."[j] A little later, the Sabellians, who are also known as patripassians because they believed that the Father suffered [on the Cross], proceeded to confuse the person and titles

---

[a] Isidore, *Etymologiae* 8.5.39 (PL 82 301C). See A.R1.89. [b] Isidore, *Etymologiae* 8.5.40 (PL 82 301C). [c] *Sentences* 1.19.7 (PL 192 575), quoting Augustine, *Contra Maximinum* 2.10.1 (PL 42 764). See A.R1.91. [d] Isidore, *Etymologiae* 8.5.47 (PL 82 302B). [e] Isidore, *Etymologiae* 8.5.64 (PL 82 304A). [f] Maxentius, *Dialogi* (PG 86a 25A-B). See A.R1.95. [g] Isidore, *Etymologiae* 8.5.65 (PL 82 304A). [h] Tertullian, *Adversus Marcionem* 3.8-11 (PL 2 331C-336C). [i] See A.R1.94. [j] [Tertullian], *Adversus omnes haereses* 8 (PL 2 74A).

of Christ with those of the Father.[a] Finally, the Alogi, unable to comprehend the mystery of the Word, said that John was speaking falsely when he said *the Word was God*.[b]

[*The Trinity Contains Four (or More) Persons*]

Rest, 39-40   In more recent times, as is related in the decretal [*On the Supreme Trinity and the Catholic Faith*], Joachim [of Fiore] alleged that the Master [of Sentences, Peter Lombard,] made a quaternity in the Divine. According to Master Lombard, the [divine] essence is a nature that neither begets like the Father, nor is begotten like the Son, nor proceeds like the Holy Spirit. Rather [the essence] is "a kind of supreme being."[c] From this it appears to be a fourth image [of the divine].

{*The chapter entitled "We Condemn" in On the Supreme Trinity*}

Rest, 39-40   Joachim was willing to grant that "no one substance, essence, or nature" is by itself those three beings. Rather he said they are one "collectively," just as "many human beings [constitute] one people." Thus, although [Joachim] argued correctly that there is a fourth image [present in the conception of the Trinity], he came to a foolish conclusion.[d]

{*The fourth image is the essence*}

Many others spew out other kinds of errors. For, as [the philosophers] say, "When you accept one inconsistent proposition, many others necessarily follow,"[e] and *the last error will be worse than the first*.[f] Not only among the heretics, but in our own church as well, countless monstrosities have sprung up, countless [questions] have

---

[a] Isidore, *Etymologiae* 8.5.41-42 (PL 82 302A).   [b] According to Isidore, *Etymologiae* 8.5.26 (PL 82 300B), the Alogi rejected John's gospel.
[c] *Sentences* 1.5.5 (PL 192 536). The phrase "a kind of supreme being" (*quaedam summa res*) is found, in a somewhat different context, in Augustine, *De doctrina Christiana* 1.5 (PL 34 21).   [d] See A.R1.99.
[e] See A.R1.87.   [f] Matt 27:64.

arisen — questions that are not merely dubious, inextricable, and knotty, **[39v]** but also extremely absurd. For, as the Teacher himself says, "*He who walks in darkness does not know where he is going.*"[a]

[*The Procession of the Holy Spirit is Incomprehensible*]

Of these [countless] questions, the first that arises is this: What is the difference between to proceed and to be begotten?[b] And why is the third being not called a son, and why is it not said to be begotten like the second? In his discussion of the subject in distinction 13 of *On the First Book of Sentences*, Gregory [of Rimini] says that it is impossible for him to understand [this question], although he professes to believe [these things].[c] But, having been caught in such an awkward predicament, God knows what kind of faith he could have had. Likewise, Augustine, John of Damascus, and all the rest recoil in horror at this question.[d] However I can resolve this question in just a few words, by saying that although flesh is physically begotten, this is by no means true of spirit. For to say that the Word is begotten is utter nonsense and a gross abuse of language. This will emerge very clearly once I have explained how the Holy Spirit may be said to "proceed."[e]

Rest, 40-41

[*God Is Indivisible, Yet Divided*]

Furthermore, [theologians] say "essence from essence,"[f] although "essence does not beget."[g] It is only the [Gnostic] Demiurge that begets. Therefore, they ought to say instead that [the Father] had a kind of spiritual wife, or that he

---

[a] John 12:35.   [b] *Sentences* 1.13.4 (PL 192 555), quoting Augustine, *Contra Maximinum* 2.14.1 (PL 42 770).   [c] Gregory of Rimini, *Super primum et secundum sententiarum* 1.13.1.   [d] Augustine: see note b. John of Damascus: *De fide orthodoxa* 1.8 (PG 94 819A). See also *Sentences* 1.13.3-4 (PL 192 555-556).   [e] *Errors*, 62r (book 2).
[f] *Sentences* 1.5.6, 1.5.11 (PL 192 536, 539), referring to Augustine, *De Trinitate* 7.3, 15.23, 15.24 (PL 42 936, 1076, 1078).   [g] *Sentences* 1.5.1, 1.5.5 (PL 192 535, 536).

Appendix A

alone, being masculo-feminine or a hermaphrodite,[a] was simultaneously both a father and a mother. For, by the definition of the word ["father"], there cannot be a father without a mother. And thus they go even farther than Ptolemaeus the Valentinian, since they fragment their fantasies, wrapping them up in God himself in a convoluted way, whereas he, [at least,] lays things out clearly and distinctly.[b]

They even say that **[40r]** the first being continuously begets[c] — not from something else or from nothing, but from itself — [a son] who is the same as itself.[d] They claim that he begot not once, as Valentinus held, but rather that, by copulating with his spiritual wife, he is constantly impregnating, forever giving birth, and that he cannot cease from such intercourse, for he is compelled to do this continuously. And they assert that this spiritual Bythos is said to be produced day after day, even though it is of the same nature as the eternal Demiurge.[41] I use Valentinian terminology, because between [our theologians' ideas and those of the Valentinians] there exists only a verbal distinction.

Furthermore, [the Valentinians] say that the third Pleroma is naturally produced from these two Aeons,[42] while [our theologians say that] the third being receives the [divine] essence by proceeding, just as the second does by being born. And they always go on to insist that these three spirits, or three beings, which are so different in their origins and so dissimilar in form, are one and the same being. Thus this one is not that, and that one is not the other, yet all are one!

---

[a] Irenaeus, *Adversus haereses* 1.11.5 (PG 7 570A). See also 1.1.1 (PG 7 447A-B); 1.2.4 (PG 7 458A-459A); 1.18.2 (PG 646B); 1.30.3 (PG 7 695C). [b] See Irenaeus, *Adversus haereses* 1.8.5 (PG 7 531B-537A), which contains an exegesis of John 1 by Ptolemaeus. [c] See A.R1.101.
[d] *Sentences* 1.5.4 (PL 192 536), quoting Augustine, *De fide et symbolo* 3.4 (PL 40 183).

This is so monstrous a notion, that I would rather, like Valentinus, unleash a hundred ogdoads of demons, than so trample upon and diminish the nature of God, the Best and Greatest,[43] dividing him up into three different beings, dissimilar in form. For however much they attempt to disguise this division by using a variety of impressive-sounding terms, were it not that you have become accustomed to speaking about these beings with such great piety, you would easily conclude — if you would only open your eyes — that to present God in such a variety of forms is the greatest blasphemy of all.

Despite all these [40v] deviations, [Augustine] says, in *Against Donatus*, that the three beings are equal and of equal power. For according to Augustine, the Son has the power to spew out a son for himself and a grandson for the Father. According to this logic, this third spirit has the power to impregnate a chimaera, and to blow out offspring! Nevertheless, [Augustine] says, the Son has never begotten, [not because he could not, but] "because it was not fitting for him to do so."[a]

Rest, 42

They also say that, although the third being belongs to us, the second is actually not ours, but the Father's.[b] [They claim] that the second being is united to a human nature hypostatically, that is, like an ass.[c] And they say that the other two [beings] are not in Christ.[d] But I would then like to know why, when the Teacher himself is speaking, he does not say that the Son, or the second person, is in him, but rather, "*the Father who abides in me*" or "*the Father is*

---

[a] *Sentences* 1.7.2 (PL 192 541), quoting Augustine, *Contra Maximinum* 2.12.3 (PL 42 768). Servetus mistakenly identified the work as *Against Donatus*. He corrected this in *Restoration*. [b] *Sentences* 1.18.10-11 (PL 192 572). [c] See A.R1.20. For a different approach to the question of whether God could be an ass, see A.R1.111. [d] *Sentences* 3.1.2 (PL 192 758), quoting [Augustine], *Liber seu diffinitio ecclesiasticorum dogmatum* 2 (PL 42 1213).

in me.[a] Similarly, when it is said that the spirit of God is in him, why do we not say that the second being, rather than the third, was contained within him?

Rest, 42   I cannot understand where all this *empty babbling*[b] comes from, [such as the idea] that only the second person supports, gives voice to, and assumes [the nature of a human being] as a unified *suppositum*, and defines the limits of its dependence,[c] especially when [the sophists] glue the [three] persons so firmly together that they act as one. For they say, "The outward actions of the Trinity are indivisible."[d] But they themselves can neither explain nor comprehend how this human nature depends, as a *suppositum*, only upon the second being and not on the others, and [how it is] that only the second being is united to the flesh [of a human being]. For here God is clearly being divided — either that or it is necessary to [41r] "Scotusize" him.[e] On this subject, the realists claim that Ockham was forced to admit their truth, and to imagine [real] "relations" [in the Trinity].[f] But God is Truth, and both [the realists and the nominalists] are liars. For Christ says that whoever testifies on his own behalf is lying.[g]

> {*All of their speculations about God, unless proved by Scripture, are false, because everyone is a liar.*[h]}

Furthermore, what if the second person had "assumed" Mary, just as it "assumed" Christ? The sophists would then have to grant that Christ is Mary, that Christ gave birth to the Son of God, that Christ is his own mother, and that Christ is therefore both a man and a woman. Please contain your laughter — if you can! For them to admit this, they must have foreheads of iron, unable to blush.

---

[a] John 14:10-11.   [b] 2 Tim 2:16.   [c] See A.R1.105.   [d] *Sentences* 3.1.4 (PL 192 758). See A.R1.106.   [e] See A.R1.107.   [f] See A.R1.108.   [g] John 5:31.   [h] Rom 3:4.

[Contradictory Models of the Trinity]

They say that there is a great difference between [the terms] "constitution" and "composition." For they apply the word "constitution" to the divine, maintaining that the Son is "constituted" from the essence, but not "composed" of it.[a]

Moreover, just as they allege that there are two different births of two different beings in Christ,[b] so they also maintain that there are two exhalations of the third being. First of all, by means of some chimerical and fantastic process, [the third being] flows out from within the first two. Secondly, they claim that, by means of another transformation, it is exhaled by the other two into the outer world over the course of time. In addition, they also assert that both it and the second being are made or produced continuously.[c] Behold the imaginary emissions of the Aeons that are continuously produced, begotten, born, and coming into existence. And strangely, they somehow would like the fourth image [the Trinity], notwithstanding its congenital deformities, **[41v]** to be the simplest image of them all. For the two produced beings — along with another being, which begets but is not begotten — are supposed to constitute one single superfluous nature, which is neither begotten nor begetting, neither breathed out nor capable of breathing.

In addition, there is much dispute over which names belong to the human nature, and which to the second being. First of all, they assign the name "son" not to the man, but to the second being.[d] And consequently, when Jesus Christ is

---

[a] "Constituted": *Sentences* 3.6.3 (PL 192 769), quoting Hilary, *De Trinitate* 10.57 (PL 10 389A). "Composed" or "composite": *Sentences* 3.7.6 (PL 192 773), quoting John of Damascus, *De fide orthodoxa* 3.3 (PG 94 987B-990A). [b] *Sentences* 3.8.2 (PL 192 775), quoting John of Damascus, *De fide orthodoxa* 3.7 (PG 94 1010C). [c] Holy Spirit produced continuously: *Sentences* 1.14.1-2 (PL 192 557). Son produced continuously: *Sentences* 1.9.11 (PL 192 548). [d] *Sentences* 3.7.4 (PL 192 772).

Appendix A

called the Son of God, the words "Jesus" and "Christ" both fly away [to attach themselves to the second being]. Finally they contend that [the title] "Son of man" is used, not of a human being, but of the [second] being.[a] Indeed, they deny that the man himself is a human being.[b] Thus the human nature remains nameless.

Rest, 43

Furthermore, Basil the Great, in book 2 of *Against Eunomius*, contends, with remarkable futility, that [Christ] should be called "begotten" but not "something begotten," a son but not a child.[c] And that great theologian, [Gregory of] Nazianzus, maintains, in his theology, that the third spirit is neither begotten nor unbegotten.[d] This point of view is also adopted by Augustine and others.[e]

Rest, 43-44

Whether the third person proceeds from the Father and the Son, or as the Greeks claim, only from the Father,[f] is an old, bitterly contested, and futile question, which I shall easily deal with later.[g] Indeed I wonder why they do not also debate the question of whether the second [person] proceeds from the third, just as the third does from the second, since "things may be the causes of each other."[h] For it is written in Isaiah 48, *and now the Lord [God] and his spirit have sent me*.[i] **[42r]** Therefore the Son is sent by the Spirit. And it is also said that he was *conceived of the Holy Spirit*,[j] and that *the Spirit of God was upon* him.[k]

Rest, 44

Furthermore, [one may ask] whether these questions are intelligible: Can the Father and the Son be described

---

[a] *Sentences* 3.22.4 (PL 192 804), quoting Augustine, *Contra Maximinum* 2.20.3 (PL 42 789). [b] *Sentences* 3.7.10 (PL 192 774), quoting Cassiodorus, *Expositio psalmorum*, Ps 56 (PL 70 400C). [c] Basil, *Contra Eunomium* 2.8 (PG 29 586B-587B). [d] Gregory of Nazianzus, *Orationes* 31.7 (PG 36 139C-D). [e] *Sentences* 1.13.5 (PL 192 556), quoting Augustine, *De Trinitate* 15.47 (PL 42 1094-1095) and [Augustine], *Dialogus quaestionum LXV* 2 (PL 40 734). [f] See A.R1.114. [g] *Errors*, 62r (book 2). [h] De Oria, *De enunciatione* 2.2.6, quoting Aristotle, *Metaphysics* 5.2 (1013b 9-10) and *Physics* 2.3 (195a 9-10). [i] Isa 48:16. [j] Matt 1:20. This wording also appears in the Apostles' Creed. [k] Luke 4:18, quoting Isa 61:1.

collectively as one breather [of spirit]? Can they be called one original source because they are one essence? And, if such is the case, is this essence the original source of the [divine] breathing? For [the sophists], at least the *moderni*,[a] would like the fourth image, which they call the essence, to be entirely superfluous.

Rest, 44

Now, it matters a great deal [to the *moderni*] whether "notions" are "common," or "constitutive of persons."[b] Similarly, it matters very much [to them] whether or not something is called a *suppositum* — so much so that the whole kingdom of heaven would appear to depend upon it. For they deny that the man, Jesus Christ, is a *suppositum*. There is a lengthy discussion [in book 1 of Peter Lombard's *Sentences*], from distinction 25 until distinction 35,[c] which Ockham pursues at length in his own distinction 26.[d] And they seek to establish the foundations of our faith upon various notions, relations, formalities, quiddities,[e] and sonships — which Paul never even contemplated — *founded on sand* and not *on solid rock*.[f] And not considering the majesty of faith solidly established, they appear to be taking it lightly.

Rest, 45

{*Having rejected Christ, the sophists have chosen this sort of teacher for themselves*}

[*Unanswerable Questions*]

I now ask you to note the "solidity" that the Lombard Rabbi exhibits in book 1, distinction 32 of *Sentences*, in the section beginning "Moreover." This deals with a very trenchant question, one which befits the most "solidly" established majesty of God: What is the logical reason for saying that the Father loves by the love that proceeds from him, but not that he is wise by the wisdom that [**42v**] that

Rest, 46

---

[a] See A.E1.14. [b] See A.R1.117. [c] See A.R1.120. [d] Ockham, *Super sententiarum* 1.26. [e] See A.R1.121. [f] Matt 7:24-27; Luke 6:47-49.

Appendix A

Rest, 46

proceeds from him? And, completely terrified by this difficulty, [Peter Lombard] wavers, not knowing where to turn.[a] Similarly, in distinction 33, in the section beginning "If perhaps," there is another difficult question, which is nevertheless absurd: "What is the reason for saying that properties cannot be in the persons [of the Trinity] without defining them, while saying that they are in the [divine] essence in such a way that they do not define it?"[b]

[The Trinity Makes Christianity a Laughingstock]

Rest, 46

What Turk, Scythian, or barbarian, I ask you, could bear these *disputes about words*,[c] as Paul calls them, without laughing? But to pursue each one [of these disputes] would be superfluous here, although there are among them many other monstrous fictions dealing with the subject of the Incarnation, going far beyond scriptural language, and quite foreign to it. Ask yourself this: do these questions really capture the apostolic way of thinking? See for yourself if this is the teaching of our Teacher, Christ. Even though nowadays we have become accustomed to these [questions], future generations will find them astonishing. Indeed, they are even more astonishing than the Valentinian doctrines that Irenaeus reports. There is not a single letter in the entire Bible that even remotely suggests fantasies such as these.

Yet the cruelest thing is that this tradition of the Trinity has provided the Muslims with God only knows how many opportunities for laughter. The Jews, too, shudder at the thought of believing in these figments of our imaginations, and mock our stupidity along with the Trinity. Also, it is because of the blasphemies [inherent in the doctrine of the

---

[a] *Sentences* 1.32.9 (PL 192 610): "I admit that this question is difficult for me ... it disturbs my weak understanding." [b] *Sentences* 1.33.8 (PL 192 612). The passage actually starts with *Sed forte* ("But perhaps"), not *Si forte* ("If perhaps"); Servetus corrected this in *Restoration*.
[c] 1 Tim 6:4.

Trinity] that [the Jews] do not believe that this man [Jesus] is the **[43r]** Messiah who was promised in the Law. Not only do the Muslims and the Jews [laugh at us], but even the beasts of the field would mock us[44] if they could comprehend our fanciful ideas. For *all the Lord's works praise* the one God.[a]

[*The Witness of the Quran*]

Listen, as well, to what Muhammad has to say. For greater trust is to be placed in one truth spoken by an enemy, than in a hundred of our own lies. For he says in his Quran that Christ was the greatest of the prophets, the spirit of God, the power of God, the breath of God, the very soul of God, and the Word born of a perpetual virgin by the breath of God — and that it is because of the malice of the Jews toward [Christ] that they are in their current state of wretchedness and misfortune. He says, moreover, that the Apostles and Evangelists as well as the first Christians were the very best of men, who wrote the truth and believed neither in the doctrine of the Trinity nor in the idea of three Persons in the Divine Being, and that it was men from later times who added these things.[45]

Rest, 35

[*Greek Philosophy vs. Scripture Truth*]

Thus this raging pestilence was superimposed [on the scriptural account], and *new gods* were added, *who have come but recently, gods whom our forefathers never worshipped*.[b] This philosophical plague was inflicted on us by the Greeks, for it is they, above all others, who are most devoted to philosophy. And we, hanging upon every word they speak, have been turned into philosophers as well.

Perhaps some will consider it a sin if I propose that [the philosophers] could possibly have gone astray. But to prove this, I need only show that they have never understood

---

[a] Ps 145:10. [b] Deut 32:17.

Appendix A

the passages of scripture [**43v**] that they have brought forward [as proof-texts of their doctrine of the Trinity]. If they could only compare the clarity that existed [in apostolic times] with their own confused obscurity, they would realize how deservedly Paul called *the church of God the support and pillar of the truth*.[a] [Paul's words] mean nothing other than that what is said in the Gospel is true. And this is the message of the Gospel: that Jesus Christ is the Son of God. For, as I have said, and will say at greater length below,[b] the mainstay and foundation of the truth — the foundation upon which the church is built — is the belief that Jesus Christ is the Son of God. And it is because of this foundation that Paul calls [the church] *the pillar of the truth*.

Therefore, it cannot be said that our church lacks a foundation. Indeed, this respect for the solid truth is called *the rock, the pillar*, and *the church of God*.[c] For a church can still be a church when it has ceased to be the Church of God; and Peter[d] might still be present in it though the rock [on which the church is built][e] no longer remains. Matters such as these might seem too trivial to be worth mentioning, except that there are those with *teeth of iron*,[f] who are content if they can only sink their teeth into and tear away a single passage of scripture. But I would prefer that they pay just as careful attention to all the other passages in the scriptures.

Furthermore, I ask you, what good does it do [these philosophers], that Christ said to the apostles: "*I am with you always, even unto the end of the world*"?[g] For Christ has remained with the apostles, and with all who shared their [faith], and so shall remain [**44r**] *until the end of the world*. But we do not share [the faith of the apostles], because if we did, we would continue to be faithful to their teaching (1 John 2).[h]

---

[a] 1 Tim 3:15. [b] *Errors*, 82v-84v (book 3). [c] See, for example, Matt 7:24-25 (rock); Acts 20:28 (church); 1 Tim 3:15 (pillar). [d] That is, the Pope. [e] See Matt 16:18. [f] Dan 7:19. [g] Matt 28:20. [h] 1 John 2:3-6.

{All the promises of the Law were made with the stipulation [that we must keep his commandments]. This is apparent from John 15 and Psalm 88.[a]}

Pay attention to what follows and you will then understand the stipulation [that Christ attached to his promise]: "*Preach the gospel, and teach [them] to observe all I have commanded you, and behold, I am with you.*"[b] Where, I ask you, are those who preach Christ now? Where are [those who keep] his commandments? Especially the [injunction] to believe that he is the Son of God, so that Christ can be truly with them. At the end of book 3, I will demonstrate to you that you do not know what this gospel is, which [Christ] directed [his disciples] to preach.[c] Indeed, I will prove to you that you are not actually a Christian.

You believe that the Church is a mathematical body, holding the spirit of God imprisoned, bound by the hair,[d] even though none of you know either Christ or his spirit. [Jesus] said, "As often as you are *gathered in my name [I am there]*."[e] But how can those who do not know Christ be gathered in the name of Christ? And how shall the Holy Spirit be in that congregation, if they are all full of the spirit of *fornication and theft*?[f] Beware, therefore, lest, by merely repeating the words, "The church cannot err," you stand in the way of a true knowledge of Christ, and are defending the error of being ignorant of him.

May the Lord give you understanding, so that you may devote yourself to the simplicity that is to be found in the scriptures. *If you seek* Christ *with all your heart*,[g] he will unfailingly bestow his grace upon you.

---

[a] John 15:10; Ps 89:30-32.   [b] Mark 16:15; Matt 28:20.   [c] *Errors*, 83r-v.
[d] See Song of Sol 7:5.   [e] Matt 18:20.   [f] Mark 7:21. See also Gal 5:18-21.
[g] Deut 4:29; Jer 29:13.

Appendix B

Servetus's Introduction, Selected Marginal Notes and Chapter Headings for the Pagnini Bible

Servetus's Introduction, Selected Marginal Notes and Chapter Headings for the Pagnini Bible

This appendix consists of translations of Servetus's editorial introduction to the 1542 edition of Santes Pagnini's *Holy Bible*, and a selection of the marginal notes and chapter headings that he contributed to its apparatus. Servetus's introduction briefly explains his principles of interpreting scripture, in particular the prophetic works of the Old Testament. The marginal notes (here paired with translations of the corresponding Bible texts), as well as the chapter headings that he modified, demonstrate these principles in action. This supplementary material is particularly relevant to book 2 of *The Restoration of Christianity*, which consists of twenty case studies in Servetus's interpretation of the Bible. But it is important for the study of book 1 as well. For book 1 also contains in-depth analyses of several crucial biblical passages, including the well-known hymn in Philippians 2 and the notorious Johannine Comma in 1 John 5.

The first edition of Pagnini's Bible, with a translation of the Old Testament based upon a fresh reading of the Hebrew text, was issued in several printings, in Lyons and elsewhere, during 1527-28. This was the first Bible to be issued with verse numbers. Verse numbers were not included in the subsequent editions: an unauthorized edition published in Cologne in 1541 by Melchior von Neuss, and the official second edition, edited by Servetus (under his pseudonym of Michel de Villeneuve) and published in Lyons the following year. However, these editions did include some new apparatus: chapter headings and marginal notes.

Appendix B

Most of the chapter headings in the von Neuss edition were copied from a Vulgate Bible that was issued during 1526-30 by von Neuss's colleague Franz Birckmann in Cologne. These were adapted to the Pagnini Bible, largely by employing Pagnini's idiosyncratic spellings of proper names. The headings for the psalms, however, were composed by Pagnini himself for his psalter of 1530. Servetus followed in the footsteps of von Neuss's editor, largely adopting the headings from the 1541 edition. But he did make some changes to the headings in certain sections of the Bible. When making the headings for the psalms, Servetus clearly consulted Pagnini's psalter, for he corrected some variances introduced in the 1541 edition. More importantly, he made changes to a good portion of the headings in the prophetic books, dropping some phrases, adding others, and changing words, in order to highlight his own biblical interpretation and remove anti-Jewish rhetoric.

The marginal notes in the von Neuss edition are cross-references, not interpretive prose. This is also the case with most of the marginal notes in Servetus's edition. But he treated the Psalms and prophetic books differently, providing notes ranging from single words to paragraph-length explanations. Unlike the chapter headings, Servetus's marginal notes are not modified from pre-existing text. The fact that many of these notes were later redacted by the Inquisition is an indication of the presence in this edition of a more unorthodox mind that that of Santes Pagnini, a Dominican friar. Moreover, the content of the notes is fully consistent with the views put forth by Servetus in his prefatory editorial essay, as well as those contained in his theological works.

We cannot be sure that even the main text of the 1542 Bible is entirely the work of Santes Pagnini. There are many variances between the Bible text in the 1542 edition and the earliest editions of 1527-28. Servetus, who is known to have been in possession of Pagnini's papers, containing "very learned annotations,"[1] may have been executing Pagnini's instructions in altering the Bible text. And, in addition, he could easily have received oral instructions from Pagnini prior to the Hebrew scholar's death in Lyons in 1541. In the absence of the papers used by Servetus, or any other record of Pagnini's wishes, we cannot know how much of this Bible was newly translated by Servetus.

---

[1] Joannes Nicolaus Victorius, prefatory epistle to Pagnini Bible (1542).

But knowing Servetus's character, and his record in modifying and adding to the apparatus of Ptolemy's *Geography*,[2] we may be confident that there is a fair amount of Servetus to be found in the 1542 Pagnini Bible.

In contrast to the success of Servetus's *Geography*, which later authors eagerly mined, his revisions of Pagnini's Bible, being theologically suspect, had no influence on subsequent editions. In 1557 Robert Estienne published his *Sacra Biblia Latina*, which featured Estienne's own revision of Pagnini. *Biblia Sacra Variarum Translationem* (1616, reprinted 1747), an Old Testament with four translations in parallel columns, reverted to the original 1527-28 version for its Pagnini text.

In the compass of an appendix it is not possible to include all of the marginal notes that are contained in the 1542 edition of Pagnini's *Holy Bible*. Following the example of Ángel Alcalá in volume 2-2 of Servetus's *Obras Completas*,[3] we focus our attention on the notes that, in some copies, were crossed out by the Catholic authorities. There are redacted and unredacted copies readily available to us, so this is a straightforward task. We have made our own selection of these, then added a number of other annotations that drew the attention of previous biographers and scholars of Servetus and his works: the anonymous source of the annotations in the *Impartial History*,[4] Robert Willis,[5] and Louis Newman.[6] We have also included some annotations bearing on the parts of *Restoration* that are featured in this volume. All told we have selected 70 of these little comments — most, and likely all, composed by Servetus. Unfortunately we cannot provide more than a very small sample of Servetus's modified chapter headings. Here we show each heading as it was in the 1541 von Neuss edition, side by side with the corresponding heading in the 1542 Servetus edition. There are twenty of these pairs of headings.

---

[2] Hughes, "Michael Servetus's Britain."
[3] Alcalá, *Obras Completas* vol. 2-2, 493-509.
[4] *Impartial History*, 46-58. The translations of Servetus's notes are taken from "An addition to the foregoing letters concerning Servetus, being an account of his notes upon a Bible printed at Lyons in 1542," in Michel de la Roche, *Memoirs of Literature*, vol. 4 (1712; second edition, London, 1722), quoting an anonymous informant.
[5] Willis, *Servetus and Calvin*, 147-154.
[6] Newman, *Jewish Influence in Christian Reform Movements*, 540-547.

Appendix B

Introduction to the 1542 Edition of the Pagnini Bible

Michel de Villeneuve's greeting to the reader

In the prologue to Ecclesiasticus, the wise Jesus, son of Sirach, pointed out that Hebrew words weaken and lose meaning when translated into another language. Considering it carefully, we must allow that the lively spirit, emphases, connections, antitheses, allusions, and other things of this kind, cannot be precisely preserved in our versions. Accordingly, in the past and to this day, most of those who have laboured over the interpretation of the Bible have never captured its whole meaning. Especially since those who remain uninformed about the deeds performed by the Hebrews may easily disregard the historical and literal meaning [of Biblical texts], which is a reliable record of things to come. Thus they foolishly, and in vain, hunt everywhere for mystical meanings.

For this reason, Christian reader, I would like to ask you, again and again, first to learn Hebrew, and then to go on diligently to study Hebrew history before you undertake a reading of the prophets. For each prophet, according to the literal sense, was focused on his own time in history. This prophecy also foreshadowed the future, and, inspired by the Spirit, contained the mysteries of Christ. For, as Paul says, *all these things happened to them as types,*[a] and *the testimony of Jesus Christ,* as John says, *is the spirit of prophecy.*[b] Yet there was once another, literal sense conveyed by the prophets, as in the events recounted by history. Some may deny the existence of the truly literal meaning, because it does not always seem pertinent. Although I am willing to concede this point, we must carefully consider that the Hebrew language is full of exaggeration, and that there are other, greater mysteries contained in its texts. Likewise we must consider that if a literal sense is not indicated, nevertheless there is some sort of shadow of future truth, like the truth that is applicable only to Christ shining out in the foreshadowing [of Christ] in David. For

---

[a] 1 Cor 10:11. [b] Rev 19:10.

events in the life of Christ are foretold in stories of David taken from the psalms. Therefore David is said to be a type of Christ. It is said that Solomon also was a foreshadowing [of Christ]: "*I will be a father to him.*"[a] And about the Israelite people it is said, "*Out of Egypt I have called my son.*"[b] However this truly applies to Christ alone, so that we may say that the literal prophetic meaning is also about Christ. Moreover, this book is said to be written, with an inward and an outward meaning. The face of scripture is twofold, like a *double-edged sword*.[c]

The power of scripture is fruitful. Beneath the ancient *letter that kills* it contains so much freshness of the *spirit giving life*[d] that when one sense is gathered from it, it would be a sin to omit the other — all the more so because the historical sense unaided brings the other, mystical sense to light. Thus we have attempted to elicit by means of annotations the ancient literal or historical sense, which is everywhere neglected, so that, by its type, the mystical and true meaning may be made known. The end purpose of all this, veiled by shadow and type, is Jesus Christ, whom the blind Jews do not see. Yet we are all able see him clearly, revealed to us as the face of our God. To which end, as in Pagnini's own version, we have spared no effort to follow up on all his annotations, of which he left us so many. He left not only annotations, but also an exemplar of his work in which, in countless places, there were corrections made in his own hand. Because of all this I am prepared to affirm that the text is now more sound and closer to the truth of the Hebrew original. But the Church and Hebrew scholars must be the judges in this matter. For no one else is capable of doing so.

Give thanks for any benefit you derive from this edition, first to God, the Best and Greatest, then to Hugues de la Porte, citizen of Lyons, whose labour and expense brought this book to light. Farewell.

---

[a] 1 Chr 17:13.   [b] Hosea 11:1; Matt 2:15.   [c] Heb 4:12.   [d] 2 Cor 3:6.

Appendix B

Selected Marginal Notes from the 1542 Edition of the Pagnini Bible

1. Psalm 1:1. *Blessed is the man who does not walk according to the counsel of the wicked.*

    The wicked counsel of Ahithophel[a] was the occasion of this psalm, and also the next five.

2. Psalm 2:7. *The Lord said to me, "You are my son, today I have begotten you."*[b]

    Paul says that "today" refers to the day of Christ's resurrection, just as it is said that on the day that David escaped from his enemy, on that day he was born, and on that day he was made king once more.

3. Psalm 8:5. *And you have made him a little lower than the angels, and crowned him with glory and honour.*

    That is, [lower] than "gods, or illustrious men," to whom David, through persecution, was made inferior. David, who was later crowned, was a type of Christ.

4. Psalm 11:1. *I trusted in the Lord. How can you say to my soul, that it should fly to your mountain, like a bird?*

    That is, [fly to the mountains] of the land of Judah, [as David did] in fear of Saul's siege.[c]

5. Psalm 22:16. *Dogs surrounded me, and a gang of evil-doers surrounded me. They have cut my hands and feet.*

    David, while fleeing like a four-legged beast going through rough ground, sustained cuts to his hands and feet. Hence it reads in Hebrew: "my hands and my feet are like those of a lion." But, in the same sentence, the Septuagint reads *Charu* [they cut] instead of *Chaari* [like a lion]. It is a true mystery of Christ.

---

[a] See 2 Sam 17:1-4. [b] This is passage 3 in book 2 of *Restoration*. [c] David was besieged in Keilah and fled to Ziph in the Judean mountains (1 Sam 23).

Pagnini Bible

6. Psalm 40:6. *You do not want sacrifices or offerings; you have opened my ear.*

It is better [for God] to be heeded than [to receive] an animal sacrifice. Indeed, David offered no sacrifices in the desert. Hebrews 10.[a]

7. Psalm 45:6. *Your throne, O God, is for ever and ever. The sceptre of equity is the sceptre of your kingdom.*

The throne of Solomon is called eternal to foreshadow that of Christ; and [Solomon] himself is called God, just like Cyrus and Moses.[b] But the real God is in Christ alone.

8. Psalm 45:11. *And the king will desire your beauty. Because he is your lord, also bow down to him.*[c]

Pharaoh's daughter, whom Solomon married.

9. Psalm 68:18. *You have ascended the heights, you have led the captive into captivity, you have received gifts from the people.*

That is, to the summit of the stronghold, Zion (2 Samuel 5 and 1 Chronicles 11).[d] This is where gifts were given and also where [David] captured the rebel Jebusites.

10. Psalm 69:21. *And they gave me poison for my food and they served me vinegar for my thirst.*

In the literal sense, Nabal did this (1 Samuel 25).[e] When [the young men] asked for food and drink, he gave them in return harsh words and insults. "For the testimony of Jesus Christ is the spirit of prophecy" (Revelation 19).[f]

11. Psalm 72:5. *They will fear you as long as the sun and the moon exist, throughout the generations.*

---

[a] Heb 10:5. [b] See A.R1.18 (Cyrus), A.R1.25 (Moses), A.R1.26 and A.E1.10 (Cyrus). [c] Discussed in passage 6 in book 2 of *Restoration*. Here the queen is identified with the Church. [d] 2 Sam 5:1-16; 1 Chr 11:1-9. [e] 1 Sam 25:9-12.
[f] Rev 19:10. Christ is given sour wine or vinegar during the crucifixion; see Matt 27:34; Mark 15:36; Luke 23:36; John 19:29.

Appendix B

This is hyperbole when said about Solomon, but it is the truth when said about Christ. Many things were once said about [such men as Solomon] that are more sublime than could possibly be true. Thus it is evident that the spirit of prophecy points elsewhere.[a]

12. Psalm 82:8. *Rise up, O God, judge the earth, for you have all nations as an inheritance.*

O Christ! God, far surpassing all our gods. Rise up, come.

13. Psalm 89:27. *And I will make him the first-born, high above the kings of the earth.*

With Saul having been rejected, David was [considered] the first-born of kings, just as, with Esau having been rejected, Jacob was [considered] the first-born [son].[b]

14. Psalm 95:7-8. *Today, if you obey his voice, do not harden your heart, as in contention, as on the day of temptation in the desert.*[c]

As in Meribah (contention), as in the day of Massah (proof) in the desert. See Exodus 17, Hebrews 4, Numbers 14.[d]

15. Psalm 110:1. *The Lord said to my lord, "Sit at my right hand until I make your enemies your footstool."*[e]

This refers to Solomon, whom David calls Lord, as a type of Christ, because such a great kingdom had been handed over to him. David knew that the Son of God, the Lord of the world, would descend from him. Therefore under the type of a beloved son, he calls [Solomon] Lord. And, in the passage cited, Solomon, to accord with his strength, is said to sit upon the throne of God, at the right hand of God. This is clearly a foreshadowing. Solomon quotes these words ["until the Lord put his enemies under the soles of his feet"] from 1 Kings 5.[f]

---

[a] This point is made with additional detail in connection with passage 3 in book 2 of *Restoration*. [b] 1 Sam 15:1-26 (Saul); Gen 27:37-40 (Esau). [c] This is passage 5 in book 2 of *Restoration*. [d] Ex 17:6-7; Heb 4:7; Num 14:20-23. [e] This is passage 6 in book 2 of *Restoration*. [f] 1 Kg 5:3.

16. Psalm 110:3. *Your people will come freely in the day of your strength, in the beauties of holiness, from the womb, from the dawn. To you is given the dew of your youth.*[a]

> Taking into account the punctuation, the [people] are said to have given offerings there in the splendour of holiness, from the womb, from the dawn, that is, children from the womb and from the beginning of the day, were offering gifts freely to you. Later he goes on to say, this flood of tributes was given to you, as the dew pouring over your youth. For this offering was made to the young Solomon.

17. Psalm 110:4. *The Lord has sworn, and will have no cause to regret it, "You are a priest forever, according to the order of Melchizedek."*

> [Christ] was at once king and priest. Hence Solomon sometimes also acted as a priest.

18. Song of Solomon 6:9. *My dove, my perfect one, is the one. She is the only one of her mother, she is the favourite of her parent.*

> She was the daughter of the Pharaoh, loved by Solomon above all others.

19. Isaiah 2:2. *And it will come to pass in the last days that the mountain of the house of the Lord shall be set up on the highest peak of the mountains, and shall be raised above the hills, and all nations will gather together there.*[b]

> In the time of Hezekiah, [Isaiah] predicts that there will be liberation after the latest forced migration of the Israelites.

20. Isaiah 4:2. *In that day the branch of the Lord will be beautiful and glorious, and the fruit of the land will be lofty and glorious to those Israelites who have escaped.*

> That is, Hezekiah, always considered a type of Christ by the prophet.

---

[a] This is passage 7 in book 2 of *Restoration*. Some of the text of the marginal note is incorporated into the discussion of the passage (*Restoration*, 68). [b] Isaiah 2:2 is almost identical to Micah 4:1. However, the marginal notes are different.

Appendix B

21. Isaiah 7:14. *Behold a virgin, pregnant and giving birth to a son, and you, mother, shall call his name Immanuel.*[a]

Literally, this is about Abijah, at that time about to give birth to Hezekiah, who was Immanuel and the Strength of God. The two kings, enemies of Judaea, were destroyed before his reign (2 Kings 16 and 18).[b]

22. Isaiah 8:3. *And I went to the prophetess, who conceived and gave birth to a son.*[c]

That is, Abijah, daughter of Zechariah the prophet, who gave birth to Hezekiah, 2 Kings 18 and 2 Chronicles 29.[d]

23. Isaiah 8:10. *Speak a word, and it will not stand, for God is with us.*

Because he is Immanuel (God with us) — that is, because God is with Hezekiah against the Assyrians.

24. Isaiah 9:2. *The people who walked in darkness have seen a great light. Light has shined upon those who were living in the land of the shadow of death.*

From the light that Hezekiah, a type of Christ, brought to his oppressed people, the prophet is carried away to the boundless and eternal light of Christ.

25. Isaiah 9:5. *For all who fight, fight with fury and their clothing is covered with blood. All will be burned as food for the flames.*

For every battle of the warrior involves a clash and clothing stained with blood; but that battle will be waged with fire and a devouring flame cast down upon the Assyrians by an angel.[e]

26. Isaiah 11:4. *But he will justly judge the poor, and make upright rulings for the meek of the earth. He shall strike the earth with the rod of his mouth, and with the breath of his lips he will kill the wicked.*

---

[a] This is passage 8 in book 2 of *Restoration*.   [b] 2 Kg 16 and 18 (whole chapter).
[c] Quoted in passage 8 (*Restoration*, 71). The identity of the prophetess is discussed in A.R2.31.   [d] 2 Kg 18:2; 2 Chr 29:1.   [e] This text is copied nearly word for word into passage 8 (*Restoration*, 70).

With words alone Hezekiah defeated the wicked Assyrian. By hyperbole some things are attributed to Hezekiah which actually apply only to Christ, who, just with his breath, will kill the Antichrist. 2 Thessalonians 2.[a]

27. Isaiah 16:1. *Send the lamb for the ruler of the land, from Petra of the desert to the mountain of the daughter of Zion.*
That is, lambs that were once sent in tribute to the ruler of your land, to the king of Israel, are now to be sent to the mountain of the daughter of Zion.

28. Isaiah 19:20. *For, when faced with oppression, they cried out to the Lord. He will send them a saviour, a great man, and he will free them.*
That is, Hezekiah; for when the Egyptians, having been greatly oppressed by the Assyrians, saw Hezekiah so victorious over the Assyrians, they praised the Lord, and even entered into a treaty with the Assyrians. All these things, in a more lofty sense, look to Christ.

29. Isaiah 35:5. *Then the eyes of the blind shall be uncovered and the ears of the deaf will opened.*
Liberation from the Assyrians contributed much to their knowledge of the true God.

30. Isaiah 40:3. *A voice crying in the desert, clear the way for the Lord, make straight in the wilderness the road of our Lord.*
The voice of the herald was broadcast in the empire of king Cyrus, so that any path through the desert taken by the Israelites, returning from Babylon, might be made open. This was an opportunity for the prophet to draw attention to Christ. See Jeremiah 31.[b]

31. Isaiah 40:9. *Say to the cities of Judah, "Behold your God."*
Literally, this refers to Cyrus, as in [Isaiah] chapter 45.

---

[a] 2 Thes 2:8. [b] Jeremiah 31 is a song of praise for the return of the exiles and the promise of a new covenant with Israel and Judah.

32. Isaiah 40:18. *To whom then will you liken God, and in what likeness will you depict him?*

He guides the untutored Jews in wonderful ways, so that they would not believe the future deliverance from Babylonian captivity to be due to idols, but to the creator God, who also foretells these things before they happen.

33. Isaiah 41:2. *Who awakened the righteous one from the east and called him to his service?*

The righteous man, Cyrus, who was about to execute the justice of God by destroying Babylon.

34. Isaiah 41:25. *I awakened one from the north and he will come. From the rising of the sun he will call my name.*[a] *And he will trample on rulers as if they were clay, as if he were a potter pressing down clay.*

Cyrus invoked the name of the true God (2 Chronicles 36 and Ezra 1).[b] He was from a region northeast of Jerusalem.

35. Isaiah 42:7. *I, the Lord, called you to righteousness, and I will take you by the hand and watch over you. I will give you as a covenant of the people, as the light of nations, that you will open blind eyes, that you will lead the fettered out of the dungeon, those sitting in darkness out of the prison.*

The loftiness of these words applies to Christ alone. Accordingly, such a temperament was given to Cyrus, a type of Christ, that he was gentle. He watched over the Jews as allies, drawing the nations to the light of God and leading those imprisoned by delusion into the light. Here there was a foreshadowing of future truth.

36. Isaiah 43:10. *"You are my witnesses,"* said the Lord, *"and my servant whom I have chosen."*

That is, Cyrus, who confessed that he was thus ordained by God.

---

[a] Discussed in passage 1 (*Restoration*, 52).   [b] 2 Chr 36:22-23; Ezra 1:3.

37. Isaiah 46:11. *Calling a bird from the east, the man of my counsel from a far country. I have spoken and I will being him forth.*[a]

That is, Cyrus, hastening [to fight] against Babylon.

38. Isaiah 48:16. *Approach me and hear this: from the beginning I have not spoken in secret; from the time when this thing happened, I have been there. And now the Lord God and his spirit have sent me.*

That is, I clearly foretold to you about the Assyrians from the beginning, and in my presence [the events] happened. You must understand that the Lord has now sent me again, so that through his spirit I might foretell the future about Babylon.

39. Isaiah 49:6. *And he said, it is a too little a thing that you should be my servant to raise up the tribes of Jacob, and to restore the forsaken of Israel. [Thus] I have also given you as a light to the nations, that you should be my salvation to the ends of the earth.*

God comforts the downcast prophet, saying that his prophecy will bring light to the nations. This was accomplished by Cyrus in order to invite faith in him. But all the more lofty things are about Christ. The mystical sense does not, however, exclude the literal one, although it far inferior, like a shadow.

40. Isaiah 51:4. *Listen carefully to me, my people, and hear me, my nation. For I will issue a law, and my justice will be a light for the peoples to make peace.*

The law from Cyrus, that is, Christ, to forward the rebuilding of the new Jerusalem.

41. Isaiah 53:1. *Who has believed what we have heard, and to whom has the arm of the Lord been revealed?*

An incredible thing about Cyrus, and also a great mystery, that the sublime mysteries of Christ lie hidden under the guise of lowly historical types.

---

[a] Discussed in passage 1 (*Restoration*, 52).

Appendix B

42. Isaiah 53:5. *But he was wounded because of our transgressions, he was worn down because of our iniquities.*

The prophet mourns the killing of Cyrus, driven out, as it were, for the sins of the people. They had it much worse under Cambyses, because the construction of the temple, already begun, was then halted, and the building demolished (Daniel 9).[a] God thus gave the prophet the opportunity to preach the passion of Christ, to whom alone the sublimity and truth of these words apply.

43. Isaiah 53:8. *He suffered, in prison and under judgement, and who can describe his generation?*

Time of life. For [the Hebrew word] *dor* [generation] does not mean the begetting of sons but an age, a sojourn, a period of life.[b]

44. Isaiah 60:6. *All those coming from Sheba will bring gold and frankincense and will shout praises to the Lord.*

All these things literally happened during the time of the second temple. This is proven by what is given in various histories. However, using hyperbole, much is said referring mystically to the Christian church.

45. Jeremiah 23:5. *Behold, days are coming, said the Lord, when I will raise up for David a righteous branch, and he shall reign as king and will prosper and bring righteousness and justice to the land.*

About "the Branch": literally Zerubbabel, insofar as he maintains control over the kingdom. See Zechariah.[c]

46. Jeremiah 23:6. *In his days Judah will be saved and Israel will live with confidence. And this is the name by which they will call him: "The Lord is our righteousness."*

That is, we are freed from Babylon solely by the righteousness of God. These verses refer mystically to Christ, who truly is our

---

[a] Dan 9:26-27. [b] Discussed in passage 2 (*Restoration*, 53), where Servetus seems to have changed his mind about the interpretation of the Hebrew word *dor*: "And since the Hebrew word [*dor*] means the propagation of sons, we can say with Isaiah, *who can describe* Christ's *generation* [of progeny]?" [c] Zech 6:12.

God and our righteousness. For prophetic words are a *double-edged sword*.[a]

47. Jeremiah 30:21. *And their power shall come from amongst them, and their ruler will emerge from out of their midst, and I will make him approach and come near me. For who is it who thus opened his heart, in order to be supported by me? said the Lord.*

Zerubbabel, supported only by the spirit of God, was stronger than the king of Persia (Zechariah 4).[b] He was a true type of Jesus Christ, who alone is so tightly bound to God the Father.

48. Jeremiah 50:20. *In those days, and at that time, says the Lord, iniquity shall be sought in Israel, and there will be none. And sin in Judah, and none will be found. For I will spare those who remained.*

Although they may be charged with many things, nevertheless, Cyrus, that is Christ, spares them.

49. Ezekiel 9:3. *And the glory of the God of Israel was raised up from the cherubim, upon which it was resting, to the threshold of the house.*

Here is the transfer of the glory of God from the temple of stone to the man, Jesus Christ, who is also God, and far above the cherubim.

50. Ezekiel 40:3. *And there was a man, whose appearance was beyond that of bronze, with a linen thread and a measuring stick in his hand, and he was standing in the gateway.*

Christ is the builder of the heavenly city, in high mount Zion. He outlines this in a foreshadowing.

51. Daniel 9:25. *And know and understand that from the going out of the message to return and build Jerusalem, until the arrival of the anointed leader, will be seven weeks.*

The seven weeks are from the appearance to [Daniel] of God's command concerning the restoration and building of Jerusalem, until [it was made known to] Cyrus the leader, the anointed

---

[a] Heb 4:12.   [b] Zech 4:6.

of God, who carried it out. And in sixty-two weeks the streets and walls shall be restored and built, in difficult times. And after sixty-two weeks Cyrus will be slain, and will be as nothing. And Cambyses, the successor to Cyrus, will destroy and abandon the building. However, Darius shall reconfirm the first covenant. After him will come the astonishing abomination of Antiochus, and that will put an end to the territory of the Jews.

52. Hosea 6:2. *He will bring us back to life after two days, on the third day he will raise us up, and we will live in his presence.*
After one and another day, in the time of Hezekiah, they are freed from the Assyrians by prayer.

53. Hosea 11:1. *Because Israel was a child, and I loved him, I called my son out of Egypt.*
That is, the people of Israel, a type of Jesus Christ, true Son of God. It is said to Solomon, I will be to him as a father, and he shall be to me as a son, 1 Chronicles 22 and 28.[a]

54. Joel 2:28 (Joel 3:1 in Pagnini Bible). *And afterwards, I will pour out my spirit over all flesh, and your sons and daughters will prophesy.*
In the time of Hezekiah, when Satan, prince of the Assyrians, was defeated, the spirit was given great glory and signs and wonders were seen in the sky, as in Acts 2.[b]

55. Joel 2:31 (Joel 3:4 in Pagnini Bible). *The sun shall be turned into darkness, and the moon into blood, before the great and terrible day of the Lord arrives.*
A time of great suffering for the people preceded the great day of liberation and the destruction of the Assyrians.

56. Micah 4:1. *And it will come to pass in the last days that the mountain of the house of the Lord shall be set up on the highest peak of the mountains, and shall be higher than the hills, and the peoples shall flow toward it.*[c]

---

[a] 1 Chr 22:5, 28:6.   [b] See Acts 2:17-19.   [c] Micah 4:1 is almost identical to Isaiah 2:2. However, the marginal notes are different.

The goal of all this is Christ. However, it ostensibly concerns the glory of Jerusalem after destruction of the Assyrians. From this the word of truth emerged, which also fought without a sword. For the teaching of Hezekiah and the renewed treaty, see 2 Chronicles 29 and what follows.[a]

57. Micah 4:5. *All peoples walked each in the name of its own god, but we will walk in the name of the Lord our God, for ever and ever.*
That is, all peoples who worshipped particular gods. This shows us that the Assyrian [religion] did not prevail over faith in the only true Lord.

58. Micah 4:7. *And the Lord will reign over them in Mount Zion, from this time on and forever.*
Literally, "forever" is a long period of time. It is so admitted in Hebrew. And God reigned continuously over the devout in the time of Hezekiah. But the promises were not extended to the impious, who followed that time.

59. Micah 4:13. *And I will kill, as a sacrifice to the Lord, what they value most, and dedicate their strength to the Lord of the whole earth.*
That is, whatever is precious to them will be an offering to the Lord. This killing refers to the Assyrians.

60. Micah 5:2. *And you, Bethlehem Ephrata, small as you are among Judah's clans, from you will go out for me one who will be the ruler of Israel, and his goings out are from ancient times, from the days of old.*
The birth of the type [of Christ], Hezekiah, was foreordained (and also foretold in Isaiah) to be in Bethlehem, from which David had come long ago. Thus here he says "goings out," as if several Messiahs had come from there over the course of time.

61. Micah 5:5. *When Assyria comes to our land, and when they crush our buildings underfoot, we will raise up against them seven shepherds and eight princes of men.*

---

[a] 2 Chr chapter 29-32.

Appendix B

These are the men that Hezekiah sent to Isaiah (Isaiah 37).[a] They are a type of the real disciples of Jesus Christ, who alone goes out from eternity, out of God.

62. Zechariah 3:8. *Hear now, O high priest Joshua, you and your counsellors who are with you, for they are men concerned with omens. For behold I bring my servant, the Branch.*
Behold, I bring my servant Zerubbabel, the Branch. He is the true branch of David, and sustains in himself the branch of Christ the king.

63. Zechariah 6:12. *Behold the man whose name is the Branch, and, from under him, he will sprout forth and build the temple of the Lord.*
Behold the man, that is, Zerubbabel, whom I call the Branch; it will sprout forth in him.

64. Zechariah 9:9. *Behold your king will come to you, just and saved, humble and riding on the back of an ass, the foal of an ass.*
In the humble Zerubbabel, the Branch who is to reign is revealed (Matthew 21).[b]

65. Zechariah 9:11. *As for you, Jerusalem, exult in the blood of your covenant.*
That is, the blood that you poured out in the presence of Antiochus to preserve the covenant.[c]

66. Introduction to Zechariah chapter 11.
We usually associate the destruction of the temple with the Romans. But there is another explanation — especially since the law and the prophets, up until Christ, would have literally foretold it, saying that it would be the end and the goal of all things. Indeed, after Christ, the temple of stone ceased to be the temple of God. The material thing was of no value, just a large building that Christ predicted would be destroyed. Rather, he

---

[a] Isa 37:2. [b] Matt 21:1-5. [c] 2 Macc 5:11-14.

lifted up what was essential about the temple, by transferring it to himself.[a]

67. Zechariah 11:8. *And I had three shepherds expelled in one month. I was angry with them, and they were disgusted by me.*

There were three kinds of shepherds: princes, priests, and prophets.

68. Zechariah 11:10. *And I picked up my staff [called] Pleasantness, and I broke it, rendering void my covenant, which I had made with all peoples.*

That is, the new covenant. He predicts that, just as many peoples were bound to the Israelites [by a covenant] during the time of the second temple, a new covenant, the covenant of Christ, would be provoked by the Antichrist, of whom Antiochus is a type.

69. Zechariah 11:13. *And the Lord said to me, cast into the treasury that great payment, by which I was valued by them. And I took the thirty pieces of silver, and threw them into the treasury in the House of the Lord.*

This refers to the potter, for in the potter's field the shattered pieces of the staff may be joined together.[b]

70. Zechariah 11:14. *And I cut my second staff into two pieces, setting them apart, in order to break apart the brotherhood between Judah and Israel.*

Like brothers, after the Babylonian captivity, Judah and Israel had once again agreed upon a covenant.

---

[a] Matt 24:1-2; Mark 13:1-2; Luke 21:5-7.   [b] See Matt 27:7-10.

Appendix B

Selected Chapter Headings from the 1541 and 1542 Editions of the Pagnini Bible

	1541 Edition (von Neuss)	**1542 Edition (Servetus)**
Isaiah 2	About the coming and death of Christ, and the condemnation of the Jews.	Literally, he predicts the coming of Hezekiah, and the calling to Jerusalem of the dispersed Israelites; with the Assyrians destroyed without use of the sword.
Isaiah 3	He predicts that, with Christ coming, all the strength is to be taken away from Judea.	It is predicted that Jerusalem is to be weakened until [the time of] Hezekiah.
Isaiah 9	He prophesies the birth of Christ, and his rule.	He prophesies the birth of Christ, and his rule, under the type of Hezekiah.
Isaiah 11	He predicts the birth of Christ, and his people, the cross, and the sepulchre, the conversion of the remnants of Israel, and the faith of the nations.	He predicts the birth of Christ, his victory against the Antichrist, and the conversion of the remnants of Israel.
Isaiah 40	About the coming of John the Baptist, the preaching of the apostles, and the calling of the nations.	About the coming of John the Baptist, and the redemption of Christ.
Isaiah 41	About the ascension and resurrection of Christ.	The ruin of ignorant Babylonians to be prepared by God.
Isaiah 43	[God] makes the faithful people safe; he considers the nations as idolaters; he condemns the sacrifices of the Jews.	[God] makes the faithful people safe; liberation; a new thing: baptism.

Pagnini Bible

	1541 Edition (von Neuss)	**1542 Edition (Servetus)**
Isaiah 45	About Cyrus, the type of Christ, who will free the people. About the coming of Christ, about converting the nations to faith.	About Cyrus, the type of Christ, who will free the people.
Isaiah 49	Christ, who will bring all nations to himself, addresses the church.	Christ, who will bring all nations to himself, speaks through the prophet, and about baptism.
Isaiah 50	About the condemnation of the Jew, and also the passion of Christ.	About the disapproval of the Jews, and also the passion of Christ, under the type of Isaiah.
Isaiah 51	The Jews having been condemned, the Lord calls the people, to whom he promises a glorious church, etc.	The Lord calls the people, to whom he promises a glorious church, etc.
Daniel 12	About the resurrection of the dead.	Prince Michael comes to aid the afflicted people against the Antichrist.
Hosea 3	Condemned Jews in the latter days are to be converted to the Lord.	Condemned Israelites are to be converted to the Lord.
Joel 1	He prophesies against the Jews, and laments the devastation of his land.	He prophesies against the Israelites, and laments the devastation of his land.
Joel 2	With the sound of trumpets he predicts the coming of enemies, and urges repentance; about the sending of the Holy Spirit, and the day of the passion of Christ.	With the sound of trumpets he predicts the coming of enemies, and urges repentance.

Appendix B

	1541 Edition (von Neuss)	**1542 Edition** (Servetus)
Micah 2	He makes threats to sinners, encourages them to reform, and foretells the coming of Christ.	He makes threats, encourages reform, and foretells the coming of Christ.
Micah 5	About the devastation of Jerusalem, on account of the killing of Christ; about Christ soon to be born in Bethlehem.	About Christ soon to be born in Bethlehem.
Micah 6	The Lord lectures the people about righteousness and their sins.	The Lord lectures the people about their sins, committed after so many benefits.
Zechariah 11	The temple to be destroyed by the Romans; Christ to be betrayed for thirty pieces of silver; about the shepherd who is the Antichrist.	Damage to the second temple under Antiochus. Christ to be betrayed for thirty pieces of silver; about the shepherd who is the Antichrist.
Zechariah 14	The destruction of Jerusalem by the Romans, on account of the murdered Christ; the coming of Christ and his judgement.	The destruction of Jerusalem by Antiochus; the coming of Christ and the rebirth by baptism.

Annotations

Annotations

The Restoration of Christianity

Introduction

1. 2 Corinthians 3:18 is often translated as, "But we all, with our faces unveiled, beholding the glory of the Lord…" However, Servetus, with his belief that Christ is the face of God made visible to humans, interpreted the verse as referring to the unveiled face of God.[1]

2. The shadows of the law is a common image in Christian literature. One example is Hebrews 10:1: "the law has only a shadow of the good things to come." Jerome wrote, "After the shadow of the law, you may come to know the truth of the gospel," and "There is a shadow in the old law, until the day breaks, and the shadows are driven away."[2] Erasmus referred to the Christian era as a time "after the shadows of the law were banished."[3]

3. In his 1953 biography of Servetus, Roland Bainton speculated, "Perhaps he thought of joining the Welser expedition in Venezuela," a 1534 expedition that ended in disease, violence, starvation, and cannibalism.[4] More likely Servetus was referring to a "new island" of the imagination, as Thomas More did when he located "the new island of Utopia" off the coast of South America.

---

[1] See, for example, *Restoration*, 97, 124 (book 3).
[2] Jerome, *In Isaiam prophetam* 15 (Isa 55:12-13) (PL 24 536C); *In epistolam Pauli ad Galatas* 2 (Gal 5:4) (PL 26 397B).
[3] Erasmus, *Ecclesiastes: sive de ratione concionandi*, in *Opera omnia*, V-4:222.
[4] Bainton, *Hunted Heretic*, 47, 181n.52.

Book 1

1. The Latin masculine pronouns *hic* and *ille* are often used to mean not merely "this" and "that," but "this man" or "that man" or simply "he." This is the first of several arguments in *The Restoration of Christianity* based upon Latin and Greek grammar. Servetus did not originate this kind of theological argument. Theologians had clearly been using such arguments for some time when Erasmus made fun of them in *The Praise of Folly*: "Here he finally got around to [his main thesis] that, from the rudiments of grammar, he could demonstrate a representation of the entire Trinity, more clearly than any mathematician could trace it out in the sand."[1]

2. Servetus generally used the word *veteres*, "the ancients," to mean the ante-Nicene fathers. Here he was thinking of Tertullian, whom he cited explicitly in the parallel passage in *On the Errors of the Trinity* (*Errors*, 2v).

3. Tertullian wrote that "Anointed" (i.e. Christ) "is no more a proper name than 'clothed' or 'wearing shoes,' but is something that, by circumstance, is applied to a proper name."[2]

4. Servetus cannot have read the genuine works of Justin, as they were unavailable in print before 1551, and were unfamiliar to him when Calvin confronted him with one of them at his trial in 1553. Aside from isolated quotations in the works of authors such as Irenaeus and Eusebius, the only "Justin" text available to Servetus was the pseudepigraphal *Exhortation to the Gentiles*, translated into Latin by Gianfrancesco Pico della Mirandola. In this, pseudo-Justin says that Christ "assumed man, who had been formed in the image and likeness of God."[3]

5. *Recognitions*, a work emphasizing the unity of God, was once attributed to the first-century Clement of Rome, but was probably

---

[1] Erasmus, *Moriae encomium*, 298; in *Opera omnia*, IV-3:164.
[2] Tertullian, *Adversus Praxean* 28 (PL 2 192B).
[3] [Justin], *Admonitorius gentium*, 47.

composed centuries later. Servetus knew that the attribution to Clement was doubtful. Nevertheless, he considered the work to be of value: "Christ is also proclaimed … in Clement's *Recognitions*, which, although an apocryphal book, is still quite old, and in which you will find many traces of ancient simplicity" (*Errors*, 34v; see also *Restoration*, 33). Here Servetus may have had in mind a passage in Giovanni Pico della Mirandola's *Apology*: "Clement, the disciple of the apostles … published books, which were called *Recognitions*, in which, using the voice of Peter, doctrines were expounded that appear truly apostolical."[4]

6. Kings are called "the Lord's anointed" in many places in the Old Testament in addition to those cited by Servetus.[5] In his notes to Daniel 9 in the Pagnini Bible, Servetus called the Persian king Cyrus *Christum dei,* "the anointed of God."[6]

7. "Who do people say that I am?" is a combination of two different questions from the Gospel of Matthew: "Who do people say that the Son of man is?" (Matt 16:13) and "But who do you say that I am?" (Matt 16:15).

8. Here Servetus is contrasting two words, both often translated into English as "man": *homo* (human being or humankind), and *vir* (an adult male person). He recognized that the word *homo*, in orthodox Christian doctrine, has a specialized theological meaning when applied to Christ. Therefore Bible texts that refer to Christ as *homo* might not demonstrate to all of his readers that Christ was a human being in the commonly-accepted sense of the word. For this reason, he cited texts that refer to Christ (or to Old Testament figures understood to be types of Christ) as *vir*, a word that carries fewer theological overtones.

9. The grammatical term "demonstrative pronoun" is related to the Latin verb *demonstro*, meaning "point out."

---

[4] Giovanni Pico della Mirandola, *Apologia*, 130.
[5] For example, 1 Sam 2:10, 10:1, 15:17, 26:9.
[6] Pagnini Bible (1542), marginal note to Dan 9:25.

10. Augustine wrote in *Confessions* that he understood that Christ had a human mind and soul "because he ate and drank, slept, walked about, was sometimes cheerful and at other times sad, and talked to people."[7]

11. In Luke 1:35 the angel tells Mary, "The Holy Spirit will come upon you, and the power of the Most High will overshadow you." One way of interpreting this verse is to see "Power of the Most High" as a name for the second person of the Trinity. Nicholas of Lyra, in the commentary on Luke 1:35 in the *Glossa Ordinaria*, equated the Power of God with the Son, based on 1 Corinthians 1:24: "Christ, the power of God and the wisdom of God." According to this interpretation, the second and third persons act "copulatively" (that is, by *copulatio personae*, or union of persons) in the begetting of Christ. For example, John of Damascus described the conception of Christ as a two-stage process, in which the Holy Spirit prepared the Virgin for the Power of God (that is, the Son) to beget the Word in her.[8] Servetus thought that this explanation of the Incarnation, which included the idea that the Son begot the Son, was absurd. Accordingly, he repeatedly used two words, *fortitudo* (strength) and *virtus* (power), to translate the Greek word δύναμις (*dynamis*, the root of such English words as "dynamic"). He wanted to make the point that the word δύναμις refers to an abstract quality — the power, or strength, of God — and not to "Power of God" as a name for the second person of the Trinity.

12. Servetus apparently interpreted Isaiah 48:16 as "The Lord God and his spirit sent me." Although the Latin of Isaiah 48:16, *Dominus Deus missit me, et spiritus eius*, could be read this way, modern translations, based upon their reading of the Hebrew, generally read the verse as "The Lord God has sent me and his spirit." The actual meaning of the Hebrew, however, is considered rather unclear.

13. In the corresponding section of *On the Errors of the Trinity*, the idea that the flesh is the Son of God is attributed to Tertullian

---

[7] Augustine, *Confessiones* 7.25 (PL 32 746).
[8] John of Damascus, *De fide orthodoxa* 3.2 (PG 94 986B-987A).

(*Errors*, 7r). However, Tertullian actually opposed this sentiment, which he ascribed to his opponents, the followers of the patripassian preacher, Praxeas. By dropping the citation of Tertullian from *The Restoration of Christianity*, Servetus may have been showing that he had come to realize that Tertullian did not endorse this view.

14. John does not explicitly say, "God is the father of this bread." Rather, he says that the Father sends bread down from heaven (John 6:32-33). Jesus says "I am the bread of life" (John 6:35, 48) and later says that the bread is his flesh (John 6:51).

15. According to Aristotle there are four explanations, or causes, of things: material, formal, efficient (or productive), and final. The material cause is what something is made of. The formal cause describes the form or shape by which we recognize it. The final cause is the end or rationale of a change. The efficient cause is what produces that change; for example, an artist can be viewed as the efficient cause of a sculpture. According to Aristotle, a father is the efficient cause of a child.[9]

16. Here, Servetus asserts that the very concept of fatherhood (*paternitas*) is named after God the Father. This is not the only way of interpreting Ephesians 3:15. In his commentary Jerome explained that the Latin word *paternitas*, the Biblical Greek word πατριά, and the corresponding Hebrew word *mesphath*, all mean kindred or family.[10] Consequently, Erasmus, in his translation of the New Testament, chose not to use the word *paternitas*, explaining that in his time the exclusive meaning of *paternitas* was the abstract concept "fatherhood."[11]

17. *Species specialissima*, or "ultimate species," is the lowest or most particular species, which cannot be subdivided into other species. The term was used by Aristotle, and is associated with the debate

---

[9] Aristotle, *Physics* 2.3 (194b).
[10] Jerome, *In epistolam ad Ephesios* 2 (Eph 3:15) (PL 26 488A).
[11] Erasmus, *Responsio ad annotationes Eduardi Lei,* in *Opera omnia*, IX-4:241-242. See also Erasmus, *Annotationes*, "Omnis paternitas" (Eph 3:15); in *Opera omnia*, VI-9:208-210.

on individuation in medieval scholastic literature. Among those employing this concept were Boethius, Avicenna, Bonaventure, Henry of Ghent, William of Ockham, Thomas Aquinas, John Mair, and Juan de Oria. It was also used by church fathers Gregory of Nyssa, Cyril of Alexandria, and John of Damascus to support their assertion that there is no subordination in the Trinity.

18. In Isaiah 45:3, God speaks to the Persian king Cyrus, who, because of his conquest of Babylon and his liberation of the exiled Jews, is called a Messiah. Servetus read the verse as "I am the Lord who calls you by your name, the God of Israel." Thus he interpreted it to mean that the Lord is calling Cyrus — and also Christ, for Servetus considered Cyrus a type of Christ —"the God of Israel." The passage is now usually read as, "It is I, the Lord, the God of Israel, who call you by your name."

19. Romans 9:5 is one of ten New Testament texts, purportedly proving that Christ is God, that were listed by Diego López de Zúñiga (Stunica) in his controversy with Erasmus.[12] These texts, together with Erasmus's treatment of them in his *Annotations* and in his controversial works responding to Zúñiga and others, were the focus of discussion at the 1527 Valladolid conference, which was convened by the Spanish Inquisition in order to pass judgement on Erasmus's New Testament scholarship.[13] One of those summoned to voice his opinion was Servetus's mentor, the royal chaplain Juan de Quintana. While the assembled Spanish clergy and monks did not pronounce Erasmus heretical, they nevertheless castigated him for his incautious critical interpretations, which they thought undercut the authority of church teaching.

Servetus was no doubt acquainted with Zúñiga's list, for almost all of these controversial texts are featured prominently in both *On the Errors of the Trinity* and *The Restoration of Christianity*. However, Servetus did not always adopt Erasmus's readings, as he,

---

[12] Stunica, *Annotationes contra Erasmum Roterodamum* (Alcalá de Henares, 1520). Erasmus's responses are in *Opera omnia* IX-2.
[13] Conferencia de Valladolid.

like the Church, wished to preserve proof-texts showing that Christ was fully God.

In the first three editions of his *Annotations*, Erasmus wrote, "unless 'who is God over all' has been added later, in this passage Paul has openly called Christ God." *On the Errors of the Trinity* reflects this, saying, "In Romans 9, Christ is said to be God" (*Errors*, 10r). In the 1535 *Annotations* Erasmus considered three different ways of reading the passage. 1) "From them, according to the flesh, is Christ, who is God over all, blessed forever." 2) "From them, according to the flesh, is Christ, who is over all things. God be blessed forever." 3) "From them, according to flesh, is Christ. God, who is over all, be blessed forever." The latter reading, as Erasmus observed, renders the verse ineffective as an anti-Arian proof-text.[14] Although Servetus must have been familiar with the later *Annotations*, in *The Restoration of Christianity*, he stuck to his previous interpretation: "Christ is said to be in everything and over all things, God who is to be praised." Centuries later, this remains one of the most controversial verses in the New Testament.

20. Servetus stated several times that his adversaries admit that God could be an ass.[15] This idea is part of Servetus's critique of the orthodox understanding of the dual nature of Christ, which in his view made Christ a kind of hybrid creature, like a mule. A mule is the offspring of a male donkey (also known as an ass, from the Latin *asinus*) and a female horse; so if Christ is a mule, then God, as the male parent, must be an ass.

21. According to William of Ockham, "The statement, 'the Son of God is a man,' is not true in the sense that he is a nature composed of a body and an intellective soul, but is true because he is a *suppositum* supporting such a nature."[16]

---

[14] Erasmus, *Annotationes*, "Qui est super omnia deus" (Rom 9:5), 3rd ed. (1522), 317; 5th ed. (1535), 391-392. *Opera omnia* VI-7, 224-226 gives the 1535 text, with the earlier versions given in a footnote.

[15] *Errors*, 7r, 10r, 12r (twice), 40r; *Restoration*, 15, 43.

[16] Ockham, *Summa logicae* 1.7, p. 2 col. 2.

22. *Communicatio praedicatorum* means the same thing as *communicatio idiomatum*. Although it is a rarer usage, it is more of a purely Latin term, as *idioma* is a borrowing from Greek. Servetus used *communicatio praedicatorum* here, instead of his more usual *communicatio idiomatum*, because he was about to talk about *praedicata* (properties) being shared between God and a man.

23. The Edinburgh manuscript uses the evocative idiom *pinguiore minerva* ("by means of a more thick-headed minerva") — that is to say, "by a more coarse art," Minerva being the goddess of wisdom and art. This and similar expressions mean "simply put" or "put in plainer language for the less well educated." The parallel passage from *On the Errors of the Trinity* uses *grosso modo* ("in a rough manner," *Errors*, 11v) and the final text of *The Restoration of Christianity* has *simpliciore via* ("in a simpler way," *Restoration*, 16). Elsewhere in *Errors* Servetus used the expression *rudi minerva* ("by means of a rough art," *Errors*, 60r), which is sometimes found in the writing of his time.[17] After employing a "thick-headed minerva," Servetus decided to change the wording from what might have seemed a rather arcane classical idiom to the more direct "in a simpler way" in the printed edition of *Restoration*.

Pingui minerva was already a cliché when Cicero wrote *pingui, ut aiunt, minerva* ("by a thick-headed minerva, as they say") in *On Friendship*.[18] Servetus may have encountered the formula *pinguiore minerva* in Erasmus's *Praise of Folly*. He might also have been familiar with Erasmus's discussion of the expression and its variants (e.g. *crassa minerva*) in *Adages*.[19]

24. The Greek word πλουτον (*plouton,* wealth) used in Revelation 5:12 is rendered as *divinitatem* (divinity) in the Vulgate, although the Latin word for wealth is really *divitias*. Erasmus used *divitias*

---

[17] Servetus's contemporary Juan Luis Vives used both at once: *pingui quidem et rudi Minerva* ("by means of a rough and even coarse art"). Vives, *De conscribendis epistolis* (Cologne, 1537), 13.
[18] Cicero, *De amicitia* 19.
[19] Erasmus, *Moriae encomium*, 148, 171; in *Opera omnia*, IV-3:92, 104. Erasmus, *Adagia* 1.1.37; in *Opera omnia*, II-21:152.

in his New Testament. In *On the Errors of the Trinity* Servetus accepted Erasmus's *divitias* (*Errors*, 11v), but reverted to *divinitatem* in *The Restoration of Christianity*. He may have felt that the Vulgate reading made the argument less complicated, especially as he had just claimed that he was about to put things "in a simpler way" (see A.R1.23).

25. The Pagnini Old Testament and most modern translations of Exodus 7:1 say that God made Moses "as" or "like" a god to Pharaoh, indicating that this was the role that he was to adopt in dealing with the ruler of Egypt. This quasi-deification also justified the important part played by Aaron in the negotiations: "and Aaron your brother shall be your prophet." Even without "as" or "like," it is clear that Moses was only to be a god to Pharaoh, and not to the Israelites or to anyone else. Since pharaohs, like many other ancient kings, had deity ascribed to them within their own cultures, Moses needed this bit of god-like status in order to stand up to such a divine king. He would discard it when it was no longer required. Thus Moses's divinity, as Servetus says, "is a gift of limited duration."

26. Psalm 45, a royal wedding psalm, is traditionally associated with King Solomon. The idea that Solomon is called "God" is based on the ambiguous Vulgate Latin of Psalm 45:7, which may be read as either "Your God has anointed you God," or "God, your God, has anointed you." The latter is the overwhelming consensus of modern translations based upon the Hebrew. In his commentary on this passage, Calvin, like Servetus, adopted the former reading, ascribing divinity to the king on the understanding that, because Solomon is a type of Christ, it is actually Christ who is being called God.

27. The epithets gathered by Servetus in this sentence come from four different Bible passages: Isaiah 54:5, Titus 2:13, Isaiah 9:6, and Romans 9:5.

In Isaiah 54:5, "God of the whole earth" is applied to "your redeemer, the Holy One of Israel." The Hebrew word translated as "redeemer" was originally meant to apply to Yahweh, but has been taken by many Christians as an explicit reference to Christ.

Titus 2:13 may or may not be read as saying that Christ is the great God. One rendering is: "the revelation of the glory of our great God and saviour, Jesus Christ." Another is: "the revelation (or coming) of the glory of the great God, and of our saviour Jesus Christ." Erasmus thought that the reading of this passage in the Greek was uncertain and that the latter reading was a possible one. Nevertheless, he felt that, in the larger context, this reading did not support Arianism.[20]

The word "mighty," taken from Isaiah 9:6, is actually only half of an epithet. The Latin of Isaiah 9:6 (in both the Vulgate and Pagnini's translation) turns the list of four epithets in Hebrew — wonderful counselor, mighty God (or God warrior), eternal father, and prince of peace — into six: wonderful, counselor, God, mighty, eternal father, and prince of peace. Thus the messianic king celebrated by Isaiah, who is taken to be a type of Christ (the verse leads off "For unto us a child is born") is called "God" and "mighty" rather than a name representing a warrior divinely anointed.

Romans 9:5, which has been read as calling Christ "God who is over all blessed," is discussed at length in A.R1.19.

Servetus viewed these verses as indicating the full Godhood of Christ. He was arguing with both non-Christians (Jews and Muslims) and with those trinitarian Christians whom he perceived as being tritheistic in their separation of the persons of the Father and the Son. For if Christ is "great God" and "God of the whole earth," then he is God himself, not merely a "person" or a hypostasis.

28. A reference to Duns Scotus's claim that there were relations between the persons of the Trinity and that these relations provided real, as opposed to formal, distinctions among the constituents of the Trinity. For Scotus, the unity of God was assured by the lack of any such distinction in the divine essence.

29. Some early Christian groups, including the Marcionites, Gnostics, and Docetists, believed that the humanity of Jesus was nourished in Mary, but came directly from heaven without any contribution from her substance. Tertullian, Irenaeus, and Ignatius

---

[20] Erasmus, *Annotationes*, "Dei et salvatoris" (Titus 2:13), in *Opera omnia*, VI-10:202.

argued against this idea. The doctrine was adopted by the sixteenth-century anabaptists Melchior Hofmann and Caspar Schwenckfeld, and later picked up by Mennonites and other anabaptist groups.

30. The interpretation of John 1:9 hinges on whether "coming into the world" modifies "light" (as in the NRSV: "The true light, which enlightens everyone, was coming into the world") or "everyone" (as in the KJV: "the true Light, which lighteth every man that cometh into the world"). In the Vulgate, which Servetus quoted exactly, "coming into the world" agrees grammatically with "everyone."

31. Tertullian reported that Saturnilus, a disciple of Simon Magus, said, "The substance of Christ was not a body, but only an apparition."[21] According to Epiphanius, this doctrine was promoted by Basilides, another disciple of Simon, as well as by Saturnilus.[22]

32. Aside from the catalogues of heresies of Irenaeus and Epiphanius,[23] there is very little record of either Cerinthus or the Ebionites, and what is thought to be known about them is largely speculative. There was likely no such person as Ebion. The supposed founder of this Jewish-Christian sect was probably invented to explain the name Ebionites, which comes from a Hebrew word meaning "the poor." The Egyptian Cerinthus (fl.c.100) was a Gnostic Christian with views about the humanity of Jesus that were similar to those of the Ebionites.

33. The Ignatian epistles that Servetus consulted are not the same as those included today in collections of the works of the Apostolic Fathers. Servetus knew the "long recension" of the letters of Ignatius, which modern scholars believe to contain spurious letters and later interpolations. The "short recension" — versions of seven letters now believed to reflect very early Christian thinking, possibly that of Ignatius himself — was not rediscovered and put into print until the seventeenth century. Almost all of the material used by

---

[21] Tertullian, *De praescriptionibus* 46 (PL 2 62A).
[22] Epiphanius, *Panarion* 2.23.1 (PG 41 299B and 311B).
[23] Irenaeus, *Adversus haereses* 1.26.1-3 (PG 7 686A-687A). Epiphanius, *Panarion* 2.28.1, 2.30.2, 14 (PG 41 378D-379A, 407A, 430B-C).

Servetus when he refers to Ignatius is drawn from sections of the long recension that are not found in the short recension. Accordingly virtually all of the Ignatian material he deployed, even when citing a genuine letter of Ignatius, is pseudepigraphal.

34. Philippians 2:5-11 has long been treated as a crucial proof-text supporting the orthodox trinitarian argument that the Son, in his divine aspect, is equal to God, and that it is only the human aspect of the Son, Jesus, who can rightly say, "The Father is greater than I" (John 14:28).[24] Modern scholars identify this passage as a quotation by Paul of a soteriological hymn, which provides evidence of early Christian belief, predating Paul's own message.[25]

The entire discussion of Philippians 2 in Servetus's "Third Argument of the Pharisees" is heavily influenced by Erasmus's *Annotations*. In several places Servetus quoted or paraphrased Erasmus's language. Erasmus argued that this text, along with a number of other "proofs" of Christ's divinity, did not really demonstrate anything about the nature of Christ or of God. While not disbelieving in either the Trinity or the divinity of Christ — both of which he accepted on the authority of the Church — Erasmus thought that the text was solely intended to be a moral lesson, a call to Christians to model their lives after the pattern of Jesus.[26] Because this passage was generally held to disprove Arianism, Erasmus was accused by many Catholics and Protestants of having reopened the door for this ancient heresy.[27]

A commentary on Philippians, credited to Ambrose, gave Erasmus a key to understanding this passage. (Erasmus later began to question the attribution of this commentary to Ambrose.[28] It is now believed to be the work of another author, identity unknown,

---

[24] See, for example, Augustine, *De Trinitate* 1.14-15 (PL 42 828-830).
[25] Ralph P. Martin, *A Hymn of Christ*, 3rd ed. (Downers Grove, IL: InterVarsity Press, 1997).
[26] Erasmus, *Annotationes*, "Esse se aequalem deo" (Phil 2:6); in *Opera omnia*, VI-9:290.
[27] Kirk Essary, "The radical humility of Christ in the sixteenth century: Erasmus and Calvin on Philippians 2:6-7," *Scottish Journal of Theology* 68:4 (Nov. 2015), 398-420.
[28] Erika Rummel, *Erasmus' Annotations on the New Testament* (Toronto: University of Toronto Press, 1986), 199 n. 76.

commonly referred to as Ambrosiaster). The commentary explained that Jesus Christ, in his miracle-working human incarnation — up until the time he was arrested — was in the form of God. Only when he gave himself up to the human authorities did he empty himself of his divinity and take the form of a servant.

Servetus acknowledged the importance of Erasmus's (and Ambrosiaster's) reading as a lesson in humble behaviour, and took it a step further by making it central to his own re-creation of Christian theology. In Servetus's view, Christ the preacher and miracle-worker was the face of God insofar as it can be perceived by human beings (*Restoration*, 92-93).

35. The Latin word translated here as "theft" is *rapina*, which is itself a translation of the Greek word ἁρπαγμός (*harpagmos*). This word embraces a cluster of ideas including theft, plunder, usurpation, and even rape. The KJV translates it as "robbery," while the RSV renders it "a thing to be grasped" and the NRSV as "something to be exploited." All of these words and expressions convey something of the meaning of *rapina*, but no translation into English captures the full range of meanings of either the Greek or the Latin word. Servetus encountered a similar difficulty when he was translating *harpagmos* into Latin: he found the word *rapina* insufficient to express the nuances of the Greek word. In his discussion of Philippians 2:6 in *On the Errors of the Trinity* he used the word *latrocinium* (robbery) as a synonym for *rapina* (*Errors*, 17v). He also used *usurpare* (to usurp) to describe what Christ would not consider doing (*Restoration*, 21).

36. The Greek word μορφή (*morphe*) in Philippians 2:6 is usually translated as "form" ("he was in the form of God"). *Morphe* can mean shape, figure, appearance, or type as well as form. Accordingly it has been translated into Latin as *forma* (shape, appearance, beauty); *figura* (shape, figure, beauty); *species* (appearance, beauty, type); and *effigies* (image, likeness). Servetus paired *forma* with *species* — both of which carry the meanings of "appearance" and "beauty"— in order to emphasize the idea of *morphe* as something visible. For while his more orthodox opponents understood *morphe* to mean the eternal, invisible form of the second person of the

Trinity, Servetus understood it as "the visible appearance of God" — a principal theme of book 3 of *The Restoration of Christianity*.

37. The word translated here as "appearing" is *existens* — one of many possible translations of the Greek ὑπάρχων (*hyparchon*), which means beginning, arising, or being. But *existens* can also mean "appearing." Servetus thus, once again, makes his theological point, that Jesus Christ was the appearance of God.

38. Servetus refers here to "the third book of *Against Maximinus*," although in modern editions of Augustine's *Against Maximinus* there are only two books. Servetus's citation is to volume 6 of the edition of Augustine's works prepared by Erasmus, first published in 1528-29. In this edition, *Debate with Maximinus* (*Collatio cum Maximino*) and *Against Maximinus* (*Contra Maximinum*) are presented as a single work in three books: *Debate with Maximinus* is book 1 and the two books of *Against Maximinus* are books 2 and 3.

39. In the passage cited by Servetus, and in a number of places in *On the Trinity*, Augustine consistently says that Christ the man was humbled and exalted but the Son's divine nature remains unchanged, neither humbled nor exalted.[29] When Servetus said that Augustine contradicted himself, he may have been thinking of passages in works attributed to Augustine but not actually written by him, such as *On the Faith, To Peter* and *Dialogue of 65 Questions*.[30]

40. In both the Vulgate and Erasmus's New Testament, Philippians 2:6 says that Christ "was" in the form of God (*esset in forma Dei*). Servetus preferred to use an alternatative verb, "was established" (*constitutus est*). Servetus quoted the passage nine times: six times with *constitutus*, twice with *existens* (see A.R1.37), and only once with *esset*.[31] The use of *constitutus* in Philippians 2:6 goes back to an earlier version of the Latin Bible than the Vulgate. It was employed

---

[29] See Augustine, *De Trinitate* 1.14, 1.31, 2.1 (PL 42 829, 841-842, 845-846).
[30] [Augustine], *De fide ad Petrum* 18-21 (PL 40 759-760). [Augustine], *Dialogus quaestionum LXV* 46 (PL 40 748).
[31] With *constitutus*: *Errors,* 18r, 19r, 19v, 20r (twice), *Restoration,* 21. With *existens*: *Restoration,* 19, 21. With *esset*: *Errors,* 9v.

by early Church Fathers such as Tertullian, Cyprian, and Hilary (though Hilary also used the better-known wording).

41. Servetus had his attention drawn to the Greek words τὸ and ἴσα by Erasmus's discussion of the significance of these words in his annotations to Philippians 2:6. Erasmus explained that the article τὸ in the phrase τὸ εἶναι ἴσα θεῷ (to be equal to God) indicates that the verb εἶναι (to be) is acting as a noun ("being"). Thus it refers to Christ's underlying status as God and does not show him as a separate entity with an equal status. Erasmus suggested that Paul wished to downplay Christ's actual equality to God while he humbled himself in a human form. Erasmus also explained that ἴσα is not an adjective, but a noun being used adverbially. While he translated it as an adjective ("equal") in all of the editions of his Latin New Testament, he did render τὸ εἶναι ἴσα θεῷ as "to be equally God" in his annotations.[32]

42. Servetus interpreted "to be equal to" as meaning "to be" or "to be the same as." In his view, to say that Christ is equal to God is the same as saying that Christ is God. Servetus opposed those who thought that the concept of equality implied that there are two separate beings, whose status relative to one another is being weighed. For example, John Chrysostom said, "One does not use the word 'equal' to refer to just one person. For an equal must be equal to someone."[33]

43. The passage about the threefold testimony in heaven is known as the "Johannine Comma." ("Comma," in this sense, is not a punctuation mark, but a Greek term for a short clause.) It is now generally thought to be a later interpolation in the text of 1 John 5, and is omitted or relegated to a footnote in the great majority of modern Bibles, including the most recent editions of the Vulgate. For example, 1 John 5:7-8 in the NRSV reads:

---

[32] Erasmus, *Annotationes*, "Esse se aequalem deo" (Phil 2:6); in *Opera omnia*, VI-9:288.
[33] John Chrysostom, *In epistolam ad Philippenses commentarius* 2.6.2 (Phil 2:6) (PG 62 220).

> There are three that testify: the Spirit and the water and the blood, and these three agree.

The NRSV gives the alternate version including the Comma in a footnote:

> There are three that testify in heaven: the Father, the Word, and the Holy Spirit, and these three are one. And there are three that testify on earth: the Spirit and the water and the blood, and these three agree.

The Comma cannot be found in Greek patristic literature, and was unknown to Church Fathers such as Tertullian, Cyprian, Hilary, Ambrose, Jerome, and Augustine, who would have included it in their many quotations of 1 John 5:7-8, and used it in their apologetics, if it had been available to them. Erasmus omitted it from the first two editions of his New Testament (1516 and 1519) because he did not find it in any of the Greek manuscripts that were then available to him. Under pressure from theologians who considered the Comma an indispensable refutation of Arianism, Erasmus restored it in his third edition (1522), giving as pretext his acknowledgment of a single Greek manuscript that included it, the early sixteenth-century Codex Montfortianus. Nevertheless, in a long note that he added to his annotation on the passage, he continued to cast doubt upon the authenticity of the passage and the codex that contained it. Moreover, he claimed that the text was not useful in the defence of trinitarian orthodoxy: "Suppose we accept [the Johannine Comma] as not being controversial. Since what is written about the testimony of water, blood, and spirit being one refers not to one and the same nature but to a harmony of testimony, are we to suppose that the Arians could have been so slow-witted as to not interpret the passage about the Father, the Word, and the Spirit in the same way?"[34]

Erasmus's treatment of the Johannine Comma was charged against him at the 1527 Council of Valladolid: "Erasmus in his annotations on 1 John 5 [actually in his *Apology to Zúñiga*] defends

---

[34] Erasmus, *Annotationes*, "Tres sunt qui testimonium dant in coelo" (1 John 5:7); in *Opera omnia*, VI-10:544.

corrupt codices, wantonly attacks Saint Jerome, and promotes and protects the Arian cause. For he wages inexorable combat against [the passage] 'There are three who bear witness in heaven, the Father, the Word, and the Holy Spirit, and these three are one,' rejecting anything in its support."[35]

Servetus's mentor Juan de Quintana, one of the experts called upon to hand down an opinion at Valladolid, wrote that "to claim that [the passage] about the threefold testimony in heaven is not contained in the body of the holy canon and is not written by the apostle John is erroneous." Furthermore, for Erasmus "to have removed that threefold testimony in heaven from the first edition of [his] New Testament was reckless; yet to have restored it in the latest edition of the New Testament, and not because it was from the body of sacred scripture, is not Catholic thinking and he is not therefore excused from error."[36]

The controversy surrounding Erasmus's interpretation of the Comma may have alerted Servetus to the importance of this text. Taking Erasmus's hint that the Comma was insufficient to refute heresy, he chose to accept the Comma and give it his own interpretation.

44. The names Holy Spirit, spirit, and angel are sometimes used interchangeably in the Bible, as in Isaiah 63:9-10, John 1:32 and 1:51, and Acts 8:26 and 8:29. Hebrews 1:7 (quoting Psalm 104:4) says, "he makes his angels spirits (or winds) and fiery flames his ministers." This may be combined with Acts 2:3-4 (the first Pentecost), where a mighty wind, or spirit, leads to the disciples appearing with tongues of fire. Servetus discussed this in book 5 (*Restoration*, 182-183).

45. In book 5 of *The Restoration of Christianity,* Servetus described the Holy Spirit as "a substantial mode of the divine adapted to the spirits of angels and human beings" and as having a "substantial union" or "substantial unity" with the spirit of Christ (*Restoration*,

---

[35] Conferencia de Valladolid, 17-18.
[36] Conferencia de Valladolid, 93-94.

185, 187). In the first dialogue, Servetus wrote, "That breath of air, containing the breath of God, represents symbolically the true and substantial deity of Christ's breath, which he breathed from its original source into everything, and which filled everything" (*Restoration*, 214).

46. Irenaeus wrote, "From the name 'Christ' one can infer the one who anoints, the one who is anointed, and the act of anointing itself, by which he was anointed. For he who anointed was the Father; the Son was anointed, and the Spirit was the anointing — as when the Word spoke through Isaiah, 'The Spirit of God is upon me, because he anointed me,' signifying the Father who anoints, the Son who is anointed, and the anointing, which is the Spirit."[37]

47. The word "economy" comes from the Greek word οἰκονομία, meaning the management or governance of the household. In the context of theology it refers to the activity of God in planning and ordering the world. It is one of the two main ways of presenting the Trinity, both of which can be found in orthodox Christianity: the metaphysical and the economic. The first way, favoured by many, looks into the interior of the Godhead and tries to analyze how the persons of the Trinity relate to, and interact with, each other. The economic Trinity, on the other hand, is looked at only from the outside, from the viewpoint of the human observer. One such economic portrayal, by Irenaeus, is that of the two hands of God — the Word and the Holy Spirit — exterior organs that God uses for creation and salvation.[38] The incarnation is part of the economy, and so are the sacraments. Irenaeus set forth the idea of God's plan, or dispensation, for humanity. Tertullian related the economy to the three persons, each of whom has a special (and required) role to play in the economy of God. Thus, Servetus cited Irenaeus and Tertullian to argue that the Trinity is an account of the external activity of God, not an internal or structural description of God.

---

[37] Irenaeus, *Adversus haereses* 3.18.3 (PG 7 934B).
[38] Irenaeus, *Adversus haereses* 4.20.1, 4.38.3, 5.28.4 (PG 7 1032A-B, 1107C-1108C, 1200B-C).

48. Servetus quoted approvingly from Hilary's *On the Trinity*, "infinity in the eternal, the appearance [of God] in the image, and the benefit in the gift," then accused Augustine of obscuring Hilary's meaning. When Augustine quoted this passage, he took it from a variant edition of Hilary's *On the Trinity*. Instead of "infinity in the eternal," this edition has "eternity in the Father."[39] The version of Hilary that Servetus used is now generally considered to contain the original reading.

Peter Lombard, who was seen by Servetus as a member of the "sophist crowd," quoted the variant text of Hilary used by Augustine. Servetus must have enjoyed Peter Lombard's comments on the challenge of interpreting this obscure bit of Hilary: "[The words] are of such great profundity that the human mind can barely comprehend them, and then, even when they are explained, only up to a certain point. What Augustine wrote about [this passage in Hilary] contains a great deal of difficulty and ambiguity."[40]

49. The sermon referenced here is not sermon 56 in modern editions of Augustine's sermons, but is the fifty-sixth item in the collection *De verbis Domini*, a collection of Augustine's sermons included in volume 10 of Augustine's collected works published in Basel, 1531-32. This sermon 56 is identical to tractate 71 of the *Tractates on the Gospel of John*.

50. Luke 15:12-13 is from the story of the prodigal son: "the younger of them said to his father, 'Father, give me the share of property (οὐσία) that will belong to me'… He squandered his property in dissolute living." Interestingly, the KJV translates *ousia* as "substance": the younger son "wasted his substance with riotous living."

51. In the discussion of John 10:30 ("I and the Father are one") in *On the Errors of the Trinity*, Servetus cited the same passages from Origen and Cyprian, but used them to make an apparently Arian

---

[39] Augustine, *De Trinitate* 6.11 (PL 42 931), quoting Hilary, *De Trinitate* 2.1 (PL 10 51A).
[40] *Sentences* 1.31.3 (PL 192 604).

point: that the Father and Son are one in power, will, and action, but not one in substance. He quoted Origen as saying, "they are two beings in substance, but in agreement, harmony, and identity of will, they are one" (*Errors*, 23v).

By the time he wrote *The Restoration of Christianity*, Servetus was making more of an effort to differentiate his theology from Arianism. He now asserted that Christ is "truly of the same substance as God the Father." Moreover, "true Christians are one with Christ, not only through their harmony of thought, but in actual substance" (*Restoration*, 25). He still cited the passages from Origen and Cyprian, but he no longer included the quotation from Origen, as it would have undercut his new assertion about the unity of their substance.

52. Servetus delighted in pointing out the logical absurdities inherent in the doctrine of the Trinity. Here he cited Peter Lombard, Hilary, and Augustine, each apparently saying that the Trinity is the father of Jesus Christ, even though Christ is himself part of the Trinity. However, the cited passages do not entirely or unambiguously support his characterizations of them.

Servetus quoted Peter Lombard as saying, "the whole Trinity is the father of the man," using the singular genitive form of the word *homo* (*hominis*, of the man or of the human being) as if it referred to the man Jesus. The actual quotation from Peter Lombard uses the plural genitive form of *homo* (*hominum*, of men or of humanity), and is couched in more conditional language. A more accurate rendering of Peter Lombard would be, "the Trinity may be called the father of humankind."[41]

Hilary wrote, "Thus he is father to [Christ], just as he is the father of all human beings."[42] The referent for the pronoun "he" is unclear; in his discussion Hilary applies "he" variously to God as a whole, the Father, and the Son. Servetus chose to interpret it as referring to God as a whole, or the Trinity. Interestingly, the word "Trinity" is not used in book 11, and in fact is hardly used

---

[41] *Sentences* 1.26.5 (PL 192 593).
[42] Hilary, *De Trinitate* 11.14 (PL 10 408C).

at all, in Hilary's *On the Trinity*. It appears that the Trinity is to be understood, implicitly, as the subject everywhere, making Servetus's interpretation defensible.

In the passage cited, Augustine called the one God — including the Son and the Holy Spirit — "our Father." However, he cautioned, "The Trinity cannot be called father in this way, except perhaps metaphorically, in reference to creation, by the adoption of sons."[43] In his paraphrase Servetus removed the qualification.

53. Genesis 18 was given a trinitarian interpretation by Augustine, Gregory the Great, Isidore of Seville, and many other ancient and medieval writers.[44] "Abraham saw three, but worshipped only one" is an ancient trinitarian formula, used by, among others, Ambrose and Augustine.[45] It was adopted as part of the Roman Catholic liturgy, as an antiphonal response to the reading of the Genesis 18 text on Quinquagesima Sunday.

54. The word rendered here as "divine council" is *synagoga*. This is the word used for the divine council in the Vulgate, Psalm 82:1 (Ps 81:1 in the Vulgate).

55. Michael is mentioned in the two great apocalyptic books of the Bible. In the prophecy of Daniel, Michael is referred to as "one of the chief princes," "your prince," and "the great prince, the protector of your people" (Daniel 10:13, 10:21, 12:1). In Revelation 12:7-9 "Michael and his angels" fight and vanquish a great dragon, "that ancient serpent, who is called the Devil and Satan, the deceiver of the whole world."

Although the angel in Genesis 18 is not identified as Michael, this might be inferred from the wealth of Jewish and Christian (and also Muslim) traditions about Michael as a hero and/or angel. These traditions were clearly very important to Servetus. He chose

---

[43] Augustine, *De Trinitate* 5.12 (PL 42 918-919).
[44] See, for example, Augustine, *De Trinitate* 2.34 (PL 42 868); Isidore, *Allegoriae* 21 (PL 83 104A); Gregory the Great, *Homiliae* 1.18.3 (PL 76 1152A).
[45] Ambrose, *De fide* 1.13.80 (PL 16 547B 570A). Augustine, *Contra Maximinum* 2.26.7 (PL 42 809).

Annotations ⁓ *Book 1*

two Bible verses about Michael as epigraphs for *The Restoration of Christianity*: "At that time Michael the great prince will arise" (Daniel 12:1, part of a vision of "the time of the end") and "And there was war in heaven" (Revelation 12:7, the beginning of the story of the fight between Michael and the dragon).

56. The tetragrammaton יהוה (transliterated as YHWH or Yahweh, and sometimes rendered as Jehovah) is the name of God, revealed to Moses in Exodus 3:14. Observant Jews do not pronounce the name, but substitute another word such as אדני (*Adonai*, Lord) or אלהים (*Elohim*, God). Both words are plural forms and may be used as such when referring to humans, angels, or the gods of other nations, but are treated as singular when used to refer to the God of Israel.

In both Genesis 19:2 and Genesis 19:18, Lot addresses the angels as אדני (*adonai*). In the Vulgate, following the Greek of the Septuagint, *adonai* is translated into Latin as *domini* (my lords) in Genesis 19:2, but as *domine* (my lord) in Genesis 19:18. Despite the singular form of address in Genesis 19:18, the plural pronoun *eos* (them) is used. This suggested to Augustine that Genesis 19:18 was referring to something that was simultaneously both singular and plural: the Trinity. In *On the Trinity*, he asked, "Are we also meant to understand, because of the plural number [of the pronoun *eos*], that there are two persons here, even though [Lot] appeals to those same two as though they are one, one Lord God who is of one substance?"[46]

57. A *triclinium* is a couch, running round three sides of a table, on which diners reclined at meals in ancient Rome and in the medieval period; the word also referred to the dining room itself. The triclinium of the Trinity was a well-known metaphor, used by many, including Thomas Aquinas. He called the Virgin Mary "the noble triclinium of the entire Trinity."[47]

---

[46] Augustine, *De Trinitate* 2.22 (PL 42 859).
[47] Thomas Aquinas, *Expositio de Ave Maria* 1.

58. A reference to a thirteenth-century hymn by John Peckham:

> In maiestatis solio,
> Tres sedent in triclinio,
> Nam non est consolatio
> Perfecta solitario.

> (On the throne of majesty,
> three sit on a triclinium,
> for there is no perfect comfort in solitude.)

In the book from which Servetus may have taken this hymn, the accompanying commentary warns, "Deeper investigation of [the Trinity] is beyond the capacity of our minds, and it is generally considered dangerous to attempt it."[48]

59. Although Robert Holkot believed his objections to the Trinity to be unanswerable by human logic, he considered it presumptuous and foolish to attempt a logical proof of the articles of the Catholic faith. Here is a condensed version of Holkot's sixteen arguments:[49]

> 1. God is the one being than which nothing greater can be thought. But if God is three persons, then there are three beings, than which nothing greater can be thought.
>
> 2. If the three persons are distinguished from one another, the distinction must be infinite, otherwise God is finite. But if the persons are infinitely distinct from each other, then God and the devil are no more different than the Father and the Son.
>
> 3. God and the Trinity are the same in every way in which it is better to be the same than to be different. To be the same in essence and in person is better than not to be so. Therefore God and the Trinity are the same in essence.
>
> 4. If one God were three persons, God would be composed of three distinct beings.
>
> 5. The divine essence begets. Therefore it begets another god. Therefore, there are two gods, which is impossible.

---

[48] Clichtove, *Elucidatorium ecclesiasticum*, 186.
[49] Holkot, *Quaestiones* 1.5.

6. The quality of being the Father cannot be shared. The divine essence is shared by the three persons. Therefore the Father is not the divine essence.

7. Christ is a man. The divine essence is not a man. Therefore Christ is not the divine essence.

8. God the Father begets God the Son. The Son does not beget. Therefore, God begets and does not beget.

9. The Son and what the Son is are interchangeable. But the Father is what the Son is; therefore the Father is the Son.

10. If the Holy Spirit proceeds from the Father and the Son, then the Father and the Son are either a single origin for the Holy Spirit or two origins. If two, then there are two gods. If there is one origin, then it is one person.

11. If the Trinity of persons exists in the most perfect simplicity, by the same reasoning there could be four persons, and so on until there would be an infinite number of persons — all of them existing in the most perfect simplicity.

12. The Father has a son. Consequently, it is better to have a son than to not have a son, otherwise having a son would not be appropriate for God. But having a son is not appropriate for the Son. Therefore there is a perfection appropriate to the Father which is not appropriate to the Son.

13. The Son was not begotten by a created thing, therefore he was begotten by the divine substance. Therefore the divine essence begets.

14. The Trinity is one God. Therefore the Trinity is a unity. But it is neither the Father, nor the Son, nor the Holy Spirit. Therefore, there is a fourth being in the divine.

15. A person is more unified than the Trinity. Therefore, the Trinity is not perfectly one.

16. In the divine essence are many eternal, unchangeable exemplar ideas. But these ideas do not differ from each other in the way that persons do.

60. There is no work by Pierre d'Ailly called "preludes," nor is any section of his *Questions on the First, Third, and Fourth Book of Sentences* so labelled. But there is, at the spot cited by Servetus, a marginal header marking the second conclusion. Because *conclusio*

is spelled using manuscript-like Latin shorthand, looking rather like "*?clufio*," the young Servetus might have misread it as *praeludio*.[50] This garbled citation was copied into *The Restoration of Christianity* from *On the Errors of the Trinity*. Clearly the older Servetus did not double-check the reference.

61. Augustine admitted that the Trinity is not mentioned in the Bible, but said that this is because the Bible, "being suitable for children," speaks of God in language drawn from ordinary human experience. "But those things which are properly spoken only in reference to God, and which cannot be found in any created things, are seldom mentioned in Holy Scripture." The homely images in the Bible do not describe the divine nature as it really is, but must suffice, for "a purification of our minds is necessary, so that what is ineffable can be seen, although it cannot be put into words."[51] Pierre d'Ailly said, "Therefore this [article of faith] cannot be proven with clear evidence from either the New or the Old Testament."[52]

62. John Mair, also called John Major, was one of the last scholastic philosophers, teaching at Paris, and at St. Andrews in his native Scotland, in the early sixteenth century. He wrote on theology, commenting on the Gospels and on Peter Lombard's *Sentences*; on philosophy, hoping to unify realism and nominalism; on Scottish and English history; and on international law, proposing equitable treatment of the aboriginal populations of the New World. Like Erasmus, he remained a Catholic, while inspiring others, such as John Calvin and John Knox, who went on to lead Protestant reform.

63. Servetus was making a pun on the grammatical expression *substantiale nomen* (substantive noun), that is, a noun denoting a tangible object. "Person," he quipped, in addition to being a substantive noun, is a noun meaning "substance." The original meaning of the Greek word *hypostasis* is "substance," but it is used in trinitarian theology to mean "person." Thus, as Augustine said, in the "Greek

---

[50] D'Ailly, *Quaestiones* 1.5.
[51] Augustine, *De Trinitate* 1.1-3 (PL 42 819-821).
[52] D'Ailly, *Quaestiones* 1.5.

way of speaking," the word "substance" does mean "person."[53] Servetus may also have been acquainted with a discussion of this subject in Lorenzo Valla's *On Elegance in the Latin Language*.[54]

64. An argument "from lesser to greater" is one that establishes a general rule through specific instances. Arguing "from greater to lesser" applies a general rule to specific situations.

65. The primary sense of the Greek word *hypostasis* is "substance." Like the Latin word *substantia*, it is formed from roots meaning "under" and "stand," and means something that stands under or underlies. But *hypostasis*, in Greek and as adopted by Latin and other languages, has come to have a specialized meaning when applied to the Trinity. There it has a meaning intermediate between "substance" and "person."

This new definition of *hypostasis* was intended as a solution for the classic Christian dilemma of how God can be one and, at the same time, three. The early Christians expressed this using Greek words: there were three *prosopons* (persons) in one *ousia* (substance). However, in the third century, these terms proved inadequate to defend the prevailing orthodoxy against the modalist Sabellian heresy. Since the original meaning of *prosopon* (and the Latin *persona*) was a theatrical mask, the early credal formula implied that there was one God who took on three guises, negating any real separation between Father, Son, and Holy Spirit. Accordingly Origen proposed the word *hypostasis*, not as a substitute for *ousia* — as might have been expected, since the words were nearly synonymous — but to replace *prosopon*. The new formula was three *hypostases* in one *ousia*. The difficulty with this, as Jerome pointed out, was that Arians and people who understood *hypostasis* as meaning the same thing as *ousia* would think that the Christian creed proclaimed three substances, which amounted to a denial of the unity of God.[55]

Servetus rejected the formula of three persons in one substance — this was, in his view, the principal "error of the Trinity." He considered hypostasis and person alike as having the same meaning

---

[53] Augustine, *De Trinitate* 7.8 (PL 42 941). See A.R1.65.
[54] Lorenzo Valla, *Elegantiae linguae latinae* 6.34.
[55] Jerome, Epistola 15, ad Damasum (PL 22 356-357).

as substance or essence. According to him there was just one hypostasis, God, and Christ was its presentation to humankind.

66. The argument here concerns whether God is an "absolute" entity — one that can be named but not defined — or a "connotative" entity, which can be understood in terms of other, absolute entities. Servetus asserted that the passage under discussion showed that John Mair believed in three absolute beings — three gods — with one connotative essence. Mair did not actually use the word "connotative." He did, however, say that it is permissible to talk philosophically about three gods or three essences, although he cautioned that this must not be done except "among the learned." He also said that "the three beings are to be understood as transcendentals."[56] Transcendentals, properties like "oneness," "truth," and "goodness," have been taken as connotative by some scholastic philosophers, including William of Ockham (because they cannot exist by themselves, but only as properties of existence). Thus it was not a great leap for Servetus to describe John Mair as one of the "tritheists" who believe in a connotative God.

67. The word translated as "tritheists," here and elsewhere in Servetus's writing, is *tritoitae* ("tritoites"). Servetus appears to have found this word in Isidore's *Etymologies*.[57] A few manuscripts of *Etymologies*, including some early ones, used the word "tritoite," while the majority used "tritheist" in the same location. The print editions available to Servetus (1499, 1500, 1509, and 1520) all use "tritoite." Modern critical editions of *Etymologies* opt for "tritheist," as do the English translations based upon them.

68. Hilary was actually quoting an Eastern (Greek) Christian formula when he wrote, "they are three in terms of substance, but in terms of agreement they are one."[58] Hilary accepted the wording in the spirit in which it was meant, but realized that the formula would cause trouble for Western (Latin) Christians, who considered "substance" a synonym for "essence" or "nature."

---

[56] Mair, *In primum sententiarum* 4.6.
[57] Isidore, *Etymologiae* 8.5.68 (PL 82 304C).
[58] Hilary, *De synodis* 12, 32 (PL 10 490A, 505A).

69. To reason "by convertibles" is to reason by substituting one word for another that means the same thing. Here the argument requires substituting "entities" for "beings."

70. The Athanasian creed reads: "The Father is made by no one. He is not created nor is he begotten. The Son is from the Father alone. He is not made, nor is he created. Rather he is begotten. The Holy Spirit comes from the Father and the Son. He is not made, nor is he created or begotten. Rather he proceeds."

71. Porphyry was a third-century Neoplatonic philosopher who was best known for his *Isagoge*, an introduction to Aristotle's *Categories*. But "Porphyry's rule," as given by Servetus, is not actually by Porphyry at all. The text that Servetus quotes here is from Juan de Oria, *On Assertion*.[59] De Oria quoted, as Porphyry's dictum, "Genus is predicated equally of all of its species." This is a quotation from *Isagoge,* though it ultimately derives from Aristotle.[60] Servetus misidentified as "Porphyry's rule" the text in de Oria that immediately follows the quotation from *Isagoge*.

This other rule, "From any essential commonality, a concept may be abstracted," is a nominalist assertion, worded in the vocabulary of the medieval scholastics who followed William of Ockham. It can be traced back directly to Gabriel Biel, whose late-fifteenth-century *File on the Four Books of Sentences* contained the assertion, "From an essential commonality, a concept can be abstracted, quidditative and absolute."[61] Similar formulas can be found in even earlier writers: in the early fifteenth century Nicholas of Amsterdam, in his commentary on Porphyry, wrote, "A universal concept is abstracted from an essential commonality of particular things."[62] And in the fourteenth century Marsilius of Inghen, in

---

[59] De Oria, *De enunciatione* 1.2.22.
[60] Porphyry, *Isagoge* 9. Aristotle, *Topics* 4.6 (127b), and elsewhere in the same work.
[61] Gabriel Biel, *Collectorium circa quattuor libros sententiarum* 1.8.2 (c.1490), in Wilfrid Werbeck and Udo Hofmann, eds., *Collectorium circa quattuor libros sententiarum, Prologue and Book 1* (Tübingen: J. C. B. Mohr, 1973), 315.
[62] Nicholas of Amsterdam, *Exercitium veteris artis: Exercitium in Porphyrium* 12 (c.1430), in Egbert P. Bos, ed., *Commentary on the Old Logic* (Amsterdam: John Benjamins, 2016), 85.

Questions on Metaphysics, said, "By abstraction the intellect can, from communal or particular commonalities, draw a particular general concept for itself."[63]

72. The saying "observing mental images is necessary for understanding" is based on Aristotle, *On the Soul* 3.8 (432a), but Servetus did not take it directly from Aristotle's Greek, nor did he copy it from the most commonly-used Latin translation (by John Argyropoulos). Rather, the particular Latin formula used by Servetus, *intelligentem necesse est phantasmata speculari,* was first used, and given canonical form, by Thomas Aquinas, based on the 1267 translation of *On the Soul* by William of Moerbeke, which Aquinas had commissioned as the basis of his own commentary.

Servetus could have come across this common "quotation" from Aristotle in more than one secondary work. Identical or very similar versions were used by Duns Scotus and other medieval commentators on Aristotle, and it was included in the medieval anthology *Authoritative Passages from Aristotle*,[64] widely available in the early years of print. Juan de Oria, a writer Servetus is known to have consulted, used it in *On Concepts*.[65]

73. The formula "it is enough to believe" (*sufficit credere*) can be found in the works of a number of ancient and medieval writers, including Jerome, Gregory the Great, Anselm, Peter Abelard, Peter Lombard, Innocent III, Duns Scotus, and William of Ockham. For example, Ockham used this formula to say, "It is enough to believe all the truth in divine scripture implicitly."[66]

74. Augustine taught that the mind, itself a trinity of memory, understanding, and will, is an image of the divine Trinity.[67] This makes the mind, in a sense, an object of faith.

---

[63] Marsilius of Inghen, *Quaestiones in metaphysicam* 7.17 (c.1388). In Egbert P. Bos, "Thuo of Viborg and Marsilius of Inghen," in Sten Ebbesen and Russell L. Friedman, eds., *Medieval Analyses in Language and Cognition* (Copenhagen: University of Copenhagen, 1999), 536.
[64] *Auctoritates Aristotelis*, 25r.
[65] De Oria, *De conceptu* 2.0.2.
[66] Ockham, *Dialogus* 1.4.17 [1.4.20 in some editions] (Lyons, 1491).
[67] Augustine, *De Trinitate* 10.18 (PL 42 983-984).

75. The formula, *Nihil est in intellectu quin prius fuerit in sensu* (nothing can be in the intellect unless it was first perceived by the senses), or wording close to this, has often been understood as encapsulating Aristotelian thought. Aristotle did not say this exactly, but something quite similar to it is found in the two passages cited here by Servetus, and also in *On Sense and the Sensible*. *On the Soul* says, "No one can learn anything new, nor understand, without observation. Some image is needed for observation. However, images are just like objects of the senses except that they are immaterial." *Posterior Analytics* says, "Induction is impossible for those who lack senses ... For we cannot have knowledge of universals without induction, nor can we get knowledge through induction without the senses." *On Sense and the Sensible* says, "The mind cannot understand that which is outside it without the senses."[68] But in *Posterior Analytics* Aristotle made it clear that, while sensation must come first, it is not sufficient for knowledge or understanding.[69]

Although many thirteenth-century philosophers were familiar with *Nihil est in intellectu*, and treated it as a well-known formula, it is difficult to trace the origin and progress of the saying in earlier centuries.[70] It is suggestive that the twelfth century was the period when many works of Aristotle, including *On the Soul*, as well as commentaries on these works by Islamic philosophers such as Avicenna and Averroes, were being translated from Arabic into Latin. Thus the formula might have been an artifact of commentary and/or translation. If this was the case, it soon afterwards was adopted as a canonical verbal pattern. With only slight variations in wording, it was quoted by Albertus Magnus, Roger Bacon, Bonaventure, Thomas Aquinas, Henry of Ghent, Duns Scotus, William of Ockham, John Buridan, Paul of Venice, pseudo-Bede, Nicholas of Cusa, Philip Melanchthon, and many others. It appeared eight

---

[68] Aristotle, *On the Soul* 3.8 (432a); *Posterior Analytics* 1.18 (81b); *On Sense and the Sensible* 6 (445b).
[69] Aristotle, *Posterior Analytics* 1.31 (87b-88a).
[70] Paul F. Cranefield, "On the Origin of the Phrase, 'nihil est in intellectu, quod non prius fuerit in sensu,'" *Journal of the History of Medicine* 25 (January 1970), 77-80.

times in Gianfrancesco Pico della Mirandola's critique of Aristotle, *Examination of the Vanity of the Teaching of the Pagans, and of the Truth of Christian Education*,[71] a work that Servetus probably read. Based upon the exact wording of the formula as used by Servetus, and the citations that accompany it, Pico may have been Servetus's source.

76. According to Duns Scotus, distinctions between objects can be classified as real, formal, or intellectual. A real distinction is a distinction between objects that can be separated from each other. An intellectual distinction is made in the mind of an analyst, and may not necessarily describe the true nature of things. A formal distinction is weaker than a real distinction and stronger than an intellectual distinction: it describes a reality and is prior to any mental analysis, but deals only with objects that are inseparable. In his lectures on the *Sentences*, Duns Scotus proposed that there is a formal distinction between the three persons of the Trinity and the divine essence.[72]

77. Montanism, named after its founder Montanus, who flourished in the third quarter of the second century, was a charismatic movement within early Christianity that accepted new religious revelation coming from outside of the priestly hierarchy, even from women. As far as doctrine was concerned, they were less heretical than potentially heretical. As such they constituted a threat to church authority. The Montanists did not wish to be a separate group from the church universal. Tertullian's adoption of Montanism is likely one of the principal reasons that he never became a saint, as Irenaeus did.

78. Servetus, who valued the early Christian writers more than the later ones, lamented the loss of any evidence of early Christian thinking. When he wrote this, Servetus was under the impression that the writings of Justin had been lost.

---

[71] Gianfrancesco Pico della Mirandola, *Examen vanitatis* 1.5, 5.2, 5.5 (twice), 5.10, 5.11, 5.13.
[72] Duns Scotus, *Ordinatio* 1.2.2.1-4; nn. 388-410.

79. Here Servetus used *Iehoua*, a transliteration of the tetragrammaton YHWH, instead of the more familiar Latin term, *Dominus* (Lord), used in the Vulgate. See *Errors*, 35v.

80. Servetus used the Latin translation of the Quran made by Robert of Ketton in 1143, published by Theodore Bibliander at Basel in 1543 as part of a book entitled *The Lives of Muhammad, the Chief of the Saracens, and of His Successors, Their Teachings, and the Quran Itself*. Robert's translation has been criticized for favouring paraphrases over word-for-word translation. It was, however, the work of a scholar more interested in creating an elegant, readable text and a sound translation than in the polemical concerns of the ecclesiastical authorities who commissioned his work. Often when Robert deviated from a close translation it was to incorporate explanatory material that he had gleaned from Muslim commentators.[73]

The Bibliander edition of the Quran, which he titled *The Law of the Saracens, which they call Alcoran*, is divided into 124 suras, instead of the standard 114. The long suras 2 through 6 at the beginning of the Quran are each divided into several parts in Bibliander's *Alcoran*, so that suras 11 and 12, referred to here, correspond to the end of sura 4 and the beginning of sura 5 in a modern Quran. Beginning with sura 7 (*Alcoran* 17), Bibliander used the standard sura divisions, and the modern sura number may be obtained by subtracting 10.[74]

81. This paragraph, largely copied from *On the Errors of the Trinity*, is based upon material that Servetus found in Marsilio Ficino's *On the Christian Religion*.[75] To this, Servetus added a cluster of citations, referring to three named suras of the Quran. Based upon the peculiar spellings of these names ("Soretamram" for Sura Al 'Imran;

---

[73] Thomas E. Burman, *Reading the Qur'an in Latin Christendom*, 1140-1560 (Philadelphia: University of Pennsylvania Press, 2007), 29-40.

[74] For more detail on mapping the Robert/Bibliander sura numbering onto that of the standard Quran, see Hartmut Bobzin, *Der Koran im Zeitalter der Reformation* (Beirut: Franz Steiner, 1995), 225; or Hughes, "Servetus and the Quran," 68.

[75] See A.E1.45.

"Elnesa" for Al-Nisa'; and "Elmaida" for Al-Ma'idah), it seems likely that Servetus drew them from the other works included along with Robert of Ketton's translation of the Quran in Theodore Bibliander's *Lives and Teaching of Muhammad … and his Successors.*[76]

82. "A face beheld by all nations" and "came with divine power and might" are quotations from Robert of Ketton's translation of the Quran. These are some of the instances where Robert's version differs significantly from the actual text of the Quran. Quran 3:45 says that Jesus will be honoured in this age and in ages to come, but does not say anything like "a face beheld by all nations." In Quran 3:50 Jesus says, "I have come to you with a sign from your Lord," which is quite different from coming with "divine power and might."[77]

83. Saracen, a term originally used by the Romans to designate Syrians, was, beginning at the time of the Crusades, extended in meaning to apply to all Muslims.

84. In Quran 5:112-116 (Alcoran 13) it is God who prepares the heavenly table; Jesus merely asks God for it. Robert of Ketton's Latin version strengthens the language so as to make Jesus seem more than mortal. In the Quran, immediately after the passage about the heavenly table, God asks Jesus whether he ever claimed to be a god, and Jesus emphatically denies it.

85. The passage, "I swear to you by this land … and by the begetter and the begotten," in Quran 90:1-3 (Alcoran 100), in which "begetter and begotten" might also be read as "parent and child" or "father and son," has been variously interpreted. Many candidates have been proposed for the begetter/begotten pair, including Adam

---

[76] "Soretamram" is mentioned in Nicholas of Cusa, *Cribratio Alcorani*, sections 1.1 and 1.5. Chapter 15 of Ricoldo of Monte Croce, *Confutatio Alcorani* includes a number of relevant passages on Muhammad's praise of Christ, with citations of "Elnesa" and "Elmaida."

[77] Seyyed Hossein Nasr, ed., *The Study Quran: A New Translation and Commentary* (New York: Harper, Collins, 2015). All quotations from the Arabic Quran are from this source.

and his descendants, Abraham and Ishmael, and, metaphorically, the Prophet Muhammad and his spiritual community. Robert of Ketton's Latin reading, "I swear by the land in which you dwell and by the son not similar to the father," allows verse 3 to refer to God and Christ, but, ironically, only at the cost of a denial of Christ's divinity. In the margin Bibliander commented: "It is amazing that God draws back from swearing by the land and by the coequal Son, when he previously swore by demons."

86. Quran 3:47 and 19:20-21 says that Jesus was born of a virgin by the will of God, but not that he was "begotten" by God in the sense understood by Christians. Indeed, this is specifically denied in Quran 19:35: "It is not for God to take a child. When he decrees a thing, he only says to it, 'Be,' and it is."

87. The saying, "one absurdity leads to many others," in Aristotle's *Physics*,[78] was quoted by many late medieval and Renaissance writers. Servetus cited two Latin versions, one in *On the Errors of the Trinity* and the other in *The Restoration of Christianity*. The first, *uno inconvenienti dato, plura contingunt* (given one inconsistent proposition, more are produced) is close in wording to versions found in Aquinas, Duns Scotus, and the older translations of Aristotle printed in the Vatable edition of 1518.[79] It is exactly as it is found in the anthology *Authoritative Passages from Aristotle*.[80] The second, *uno absurdo dato, multa sequi* (given one absurdity, many follow) resembles the phrasing in John Argyropoulos's translation of Aristotle, and can be found, with variations, in many other writers, including Luther and Calvin, usually without attribution to Aristotle.

88. Servetus was quoting a passage in which Irenaeus articulated a rule for scriptural interpretation: that unclear or ambiguous passages must be understood in the light of clear ones, and not the other way round. Irenaeus wrote:

---

[78] Aristotle, *Physics* 1.2 (185a11) and 1.3 (186a9).
[79] *Ex physiologia Aristotelis*, ed. François Vatable (Paris, 1518).
[80] *Auctoritates Aristotelis*, 10.

> Because [the Valentinians] wished to explain ambiguous passages of scripture … they invented another God … bringing in a greater question [in order to resolve] a lesser one. But among those who have any sense, no question can be resolved by posing another question, nor can any ambiguity be resolved by another ambiguity, nor can an enigma [be resolved] by another, greater enigma. These things are solved only by what is plain, consistent, and clear.[81]

89. Aëtius of Antioch (c.313-c.366) was the founder of Anomoean (or Aëtian) sect. Aëtians denied that the Father and Son shared the same substance (*homoousios*), or even had a similar substance (*homoiousios*), thus declaring that they were dissimilar (*anomoios*) or different in substance (*heteroousios*). In his *Syntagmation*, extant because it was copied into Epiphanius's *Panarion*, Aëtius wrote that the Son was subordinate to God, and not generated by him. The disciple of Aëtius, Eunomius of Cyzicus (c.325-c.395), claimed that the Son, a creation and a product of God's will, is unlike God in essence, but like him in activity and will. He described the Holy Spirit as an activity of the Son. Like Aëtius, his thinking is preserved in the writings of his opponents, notably Basil of Caesarea and Gregory of Nyssa. The Anomeon theologians, in their organization of the Trinity into a hierarchy, were influenced by Neoplatonic thinking.

90. Donatists were North African Christians who rejected the spiritual and sacramental authority of those clergy who, under the persecution of Emperor Diocletian, recanted their faith or failed to counsel resistance and martyrdom. This rejection extended from the original *traditor* (traitor) clergy to all those who followed them via apostolic succession. Despite being declared heretical and subjected to Christian persecution and the opposition of Augustine, the Donatists' brand of Christianity persisted until the Muslim conquest. Although the theology of the majority of Donatists was the same as that of orthodox Catholic Christians, a few, as Augustine pointed out, held heterodox views about the Trinity.[82]

---

[81] Irenaeus, *Adversus haereses* 2.10.1 (PG 7 735A).
[82] See Augustine, *Epistolae* 185.1 (PL 33 792-793).

91. In *Against Maximinus*, Augustine wrote, "You [Maximinus] are afraid that the Father alone would not be the one God, but a part of the one God, who is made up of three."[83] Augustine was responding to something that Maximinus had said: "If [the Father] alone is not the one God, then he is a part."[84] Maximinus was merely noting what seemed to him to be the logical implications of the trinitarian position; Augustine added the fear.

92. Manichaeus, or Mani (216-274), a Persian, was the founder of Manichaeism: a gnostic, ascetic, and dualist religion that included elements from Zoroastrianism, Buddhism, Babylonian religion, and Christianity. Augustine embraced Manichaeism before he became a Christian.

93. Hieracas, or Hierax, of Leontopolis (fl. c.300) was an Egyptian ascetic, theologian, and Bible commentator. In addition to his view of the relationship between the Father and the Son, he taught that anything pleasurable, including sex and marriage, was forbidden by Christ; that there was no bodily resurrection, only resurrection of the soul; and that the Holy Spirit was to be identified with Melchizedek.

94. Servetus mentioned Praxeas in *On the Errors of the Trinity* as a monarchian (*Errors*, 38v-39r), and in *The Restoration of Christianity* as a Sabellian and patripassian (*Restoration*, 37). Sabellianism (or modalism) and monarchianism are beliefs that emphasize the unity of God, reducing the persons of the Trinity to modes or activities of God. Patripassianism, the belief that the Father suffered on the cross, is a corollary of the radical oneness of God. Praxeas was identified as a monarchian modalist by his enemy, Tertullian, and addressed as such in *Against Praxeas*. The name Praxeas may be a pseudonym and his theological views may have been misrepresented by Tertullian.

In *Errors*, Servetus mentioned a person named Victorinus along with Praxeas. He got the linkage of Victorinus with Praxeas from pseudo-Tertullian's *Against All Heresies*.[85] It is not known, and can

---

[83] Augustine, *Contra Maximinum* 2.10.1 (PL 42 764).
[84] Augustine, *Collatio cum Maximino* 15.10 (PL 42 728).
[85] [Tertullian], *Adversus omneis haereses*, 112 (PL 2 74A).

only be guessed, who this Victorinus is. Moreover, Victorinus's relation to the doctrine of Praxeas, as indicated by pseudo-Tertullian, is vague and ambiguous. In *Restoration* Servetus improved his argument by substituting Noetus, a better established monarchian modalist and patripassian.[86]

95. Nestorius, Patriarch of Constantinople and an opponent of Arianism, objected to Mary being called "mother of God." Because of this, his views were stigmatized as leading to the idea that there were two Christs: one the son of God, and the other the son of Mary. Joannes Maxentius was a scourge of heretics, including Nestorians, in early sixth-century Constantinople. Liberatus of Carthage was a sixth-century church historian. Liberatus's *Breviarium causae Nestorianorum et Eutychianorum* (Summary of the position of the Nestorians and Eutychians), written c. 555, quotes material prepared by Cyril of Alexandria for the Council of Ephesus in 431, in which Cyril summarized the thought of Nestorius.

96. Whenever Servetus mentioned Athanasius in *The Restoration of Christianity*, he was citing a book called *Opera omnia, quae hactenus apud Latinorum officinas reperiri potuerunt* (All of the works of Athanasius in Latin, that have been located so far), which was published in Cologne in 1548. As the title indicates, this was a rather preliminary and incomplete attempt at an edition of the complete works of Athanasius. It was by no means the first attempt to publish a collection of the works of Athanasius in Latin; editions containing varying assortments of Athanasius and pseudo-Athanasius works were published in Paris in 1520, in Lyons in 1532, and in Wittenberg in 1532 (with a preface by Martin Luther).

The Wittenberg and Cologne editions include a set of eleven short works, attributed to Athanasius but actually written in Latin, which had previously appeared in a collection published in Basel in 1528 as *Antidotum contra diversas omnium fere seculorum haereses* (Antidote against various heresies of almost every age). The same eleven items are included among the works of Athanasius in the

---

[86] Isidore, *Etymologiae* 8.5.41 (PL 82 301C-302A).

nineteenth-century *Patrologia Latina* (where they are divided into twelve items). The order of the items is different in each of these editions, and there are also some variations in the titles assigned to them. Based on the set of works that Servetus cited, the titles he used, and his references to the placement of the works within the volume, we can be confident that he was using the 1548 Cologne edition.

After it was determined in the seventeenth century that these eleven works were not really by Athanasius, they were thought to be a single work by one author, Vigilius of Thapsus. Nowadays it is believed that these works are by several unidentified, and perhaps unidentifiable, authors living in different time periods, from the fourth to the sixth centuries.[87]

Of the eleven pseudo-Athanasius works in the collection, seven are written in dialogue form. When Servetus cited the "dialogues of Athanasius," he was referring to these works. Among these are *On the Names of the Holy Trinity*, *On His Faith*, and *On the Assumption of Man*. This is not to be confused with an unrelated pseudo-Athanasian work, written in Greek and translated into Latin as *Dialogi quinque de sancta Trinitate* (Five Dialogues on the Holy Trinity). This set of five dialogues was first published in 1570 and could not have been known to Servetus.

97. Peter Lombard attributed this sentiment to Jerome, but it is actually from Pelagius's *Statement of Faith, to Pope Innocent*. In medieval manuscripts Pelagius's work was sometimes attributed to Jerome and labeled as a letter to Pope Damasus; Peter Lombard accepted this mistaken attribution. The genuine letters of Jerome to Pope Damasus discuss neither sonship nor the two natures of Christ.

98. In this passage, which Servetus, somewhat unfairly, edited down from *Enchiridion,* Augustine was not presenting a personal theological statement but was plainly quoting or paraphrasing one or more early creeds: "Thus we profess: Our Lord Jesus Christ, who

---

[87] Herbert Musurillo, review of Pseudo-Athanasii, *De Trinitate libri X-XII*, ed. Manlio Simonetti, in *Latomus* 17.1 (Jan-Mar 1958), 125-127.

although he is God from God, as a human being was born of the Holy Spirit and the Virgin Mary, and of the substances of both, that is, the divine and the human. He is the only Son of God, the Father Almighty, from whom the Holy Spirit proceeds."[88]

99. Here Servetus is citing a critique of the Trinity originally put forward by Joachim of Fiore in the twelfth century. Joachim argued that if the divine essence — described by Peter Lombard as "a kind of supreme being" — is neither the Father, nor the Son, nor the Holy Spirit, it must be a fourth person in the Trinity. In 1215 the Fourth Lateran Council rejected this argument and asserted the orthodoxy of Peter Lombard's description of the Trinity. After this Peter Lombard's *Sentences* stood as a definitive statement of Roman Catholic theology for over four hundred years.

Although Servetus admired Joachim's critique of the doctrine of the Trinity, he agreed with the council in rejecting Joachim's idea of the Trinity as a collective being, "just as many people constitute a nation."[89] This is, however, only one of several metaphors Joachim used to describe the Trinity. Other images of the Trinity — such as the psaltery, a three-sided plucked-string musical instrument with a round sound hole — emphasize much more strongly the unity of the triune God.[90]

100. The definition of numbers greater than one is found at the beginning of Euclid's treatise on number theory. He said that a number is "a multitude composed of unities."[91] Servetus could have learned this by reading Euclid or one or more of his many commentators, ancient and modern. These include Boethius, who

---

[88] Augustine, *Enchiridion* 38 (PL 40 251). See Boniface Ramsey, introduction to *The Augustine Catechism: The Enchiridion on Faith, Hope, and Love* (Hyde Park, NY: New City Press, 1999), 14.
[89] *Decretales d. papae Gregorii noni* I, title 1 (*De summa Trinitate et fide Catholica*), chapter 2 ("Damnamus"). Since Joachim's booklet, *De unitate seu essentia Trinitatis*, mentioned in the decretal, no longer exists, the decretal itself is the only source for his argument.
[90] Joachim of Fiore, *Psalterium decem cordarum* (Venice, 1527).
[91] Euclid, *Elements* 7, def. 2.

wrote *On Arithmetic* and translated Euclid's *Elements*; and Servetus's contemporary and acquaintance, Gaspar Lax. In *Arithmetica speculativa* (1515), Lax leads off with a similar set of definitions, the third of which follows on from Euclid, specifying that "a natural series of numbers is computed by the addition of unities." The orthodox trinitarian counter-argument to those who would apply Euclid to the Trinity comes from Boethius: "a repetition of unities and [their apparent] plurality does not result in a numerical difference made up of countable things."[92] A later example of this argument is provided by Bonaventure: "To the objection that a point is always simpler than a continuous [line], and that a unity is simpler than a number, it ought to be said that while this is true about a number as such, which is an aggregation of various unities, this is not the kind of number found in the trinity of divine persons. In the Trinity there is no aggregation of many unities, nor of entities or truths. Rather it is a replication of the same unity, in different persons."[93]

101. Peter Lombard discussed at length the idea that the Son is always or continuously being born, citing Gregory the Great, Hilary, Augustine, and Origen. He concluded that it was better to say *semper natus* (always born), meaning born in eternity outside of time, rather than *semper nascitur* (always being born).[94]

102. The genuine work by Athanasius that Servetus called *On the Holy Spirit* is now known as *Letters to Serapion on the Holy Spirit*. Servetus found it in the collection of works attributed to Athanasius published in Cologne in 1548; see A.R1.96.

There are now considered to be three letters to Serapion on the subject of the Holy Spirit. (At one time there were thought to be four letters, the second being divided into two parts; this is reflected in the version printed in *Patrologia Graeca*.) In the 1548 Cologne edition, the second part of letter 2 (PG letter 3) was printed as book 1; letter 3 (PG letter 4) was printed as book 2; and letter 1 was

---

[92] Boethius, *De Trinitate* 3.
[93] Bonaventure, *Quaestiones disputatae de misterio trinitatis* 3.2, reply 7.
[94] *Sentences* 1.9.10-14 (PL 192 547-549), citing, among others, Augustine, *De Trinitate* and *Enarrationes in psalmos*, and Hilary, *De Trinitate*.

printed as book 3. Thus, when Servetus referred to books 2 and 3 of *On the Holy Spirit*, he meant what we would now call letters 3 and 1.

In book 2 (letter 3/PG letter 4) Athanasius wrote, "Or you might ask: 'Is the Spirit then the Son and the Son himself the Holy Spirit?'"[95] In context, it is clear that this does not represent Athanasius's own thinking; in fact, he called those who think this way "godless."

In the 1548 edition, book 3 (letter 1) includes a marginal note: "It is not possible to give a reason why the Spirit is not called a son."[96] Servetus quoted this note almost verbatim. Of course, the note was not written by Athanasius, but was added by some later editor. It is not found in *Patrologia Graeca* or in modern critical editions.

103. Servetus further developed the line of reasoning, comparing the Trinity to three Euclidean points, in book 3 of *The Restoration of Christianity*: "These three beings, enclosed in one being, are like three [geometrical] points contained in a single point. They reduce every divine substance to something like a geometrical point. They claim that God himself is like a point many times repeated on the same plane, and that there are three points in one simple point" (*Restoration*, 119; see also *Restoration*, 129 and *Errors*, 108v). See A.R1.100, on Euclid, Boethius, and Bonaventure.

104. In scholastic philosophy, a *suppositum* is an individual, that is, a being that exists as an independent entity. According to a classic definition by Boethius, a person is further defined as a rational suppositum — so that every person is a suppositum, though not every suppositum is a person. The scholastics debated the question of whether the persons of the Trinity are supposita.[97] Duns Scotus argued that the persons of the Trinity are not supposita; only the divine essence is a suppositum. Ockham, however, thought that the essence was not a suppositum.

---

[95] Athanasius, *De sancto spiritu* 6 (PG 26 646A).
[96] Athanasius, *De sancto spiritu*, marginal note on fol. 49d of 1548 edition.
[97] See, for example, Ockham, *Quodlibeta* 4.7; Duns Scotus, *Quaestiones quodlibetales* 19.

Servetus took issue with the idea that Christ is a suppositum made up of a human nature united to the second person of the Trinity. While he agreed that Christ was a suppositum, i.e. an individual, he thought that calling Christ a human nature rather than a man denied his full humanity (see *Restoration*, 15; *Errors*, 4r, 10r); and that uniting Christ's human nature to only one person of the Trinity denied his full divinity.

105. The expression "limits the dependence" comes from Duns Scotus. Dependence is a relation, such as causality, by which things emerge from other things. To "limit dependence" is not to create independence, but to define the boundaries within which the dependent thing must exist. Duns Scotus wrote, "The Divine Word limited the dependence of its human nature, and sustained it in himself."[98]

106. "The actions of the Trinity are indivisible" or "The outward actions of the Trinity are indivisible" is a traditional saying, widely known, and taken as a principle of theology by church authorities. It was used by, among others, Innocent III, Peter Abelard, and Peter Lombard (without "outward"); by later scholastics such as Albertus Magnus, Thomas Aquinas, and Duns Scotus (with "outward"); and by Protestant theologians of Servetus's time, such as Luther, Melanchthon, and Calvin (without "outward"). It is often attributed to Augustine, who said something similar: "The works of the Trinity are inseparable."[99] However, Augustine did not originate the saying, but was quoting an already-known formula.[100]

107. To "Scotusize" is to make distinctions in the manner of Duns Scotus. In the case of the Trinity, he posited that there were "real relations" between the persons of a unified God. The word "scotusize" (*scotizare*) was in common use in the fourteenth, fifteenth, and sixteenth centuries.

---

[98] See Duns Scotus, *Ordinatio*, 3.1.1.3.
[99] Augustine, *Sermones* 213.6 (PL 38 1063) and elsewhere.
[100] For example, it was earlier used by the fourth-century anti-Arian, Eusebius of Vercelli, in *De Trinitate confessio* (PL 12 966A).

108. Nominalists, such as William of Ockham, believed that universals (categories such as rocks, horses, or people) are convenient, but arbitrary, collections of particular things that are observed to have common features. Being thus arbitrary, universals can have no underlying nature or common substance. However, in the case of the Trinity, Ockham was forced to admit the failure of philosophy and fall back on the teaching and authority of the Church. In particular, he felt that he had to allow the reality of Scotist relations, at least in the case of the Trinity: "In describing the divine, real relations are to be used. This conclusion is reached based upon the authority of saintly authors who seem expressly to specify relations in the divine."[101]

109. Here, as elsewhere when he mentioned Athanasius, Servetus was referring the 1548 edition of the works attributed to Athanasius, but mostly written by other authors (see A.R1.96). In two of the works in the collection, he read, "The Father, the Word, and the Holy Spirit are one in Christ Jesus."[102] This was the basis of his claim that "Athanasius says that the Father, the Word, and the Spirit are all in Christ." The authors, however, were not making theological statements, but merely quoting a version of the Johannine Comma (1 John 5:7-8; see A.R1.43). It consists of the familiar wording, "the Father, the Word, and the Holy Spirit are one," with the addition of "in Christ Jesus." This longer version is attested in at least one Latin manuscript of the Bible. Since it was, in the eyes of the author or authors, a quotation from the Bible, it is not surprising that Servetus found it multiple times in these works.

110. Here Servetus is comparing his opponents to the Gnostic heretics described by Irenaeus: "Some of them also believe that there is one human being, created masculo-feminine after the image and

---

[101] Ockham, *Super sententiarum* 1.26.1.
[102] The two pseudo-Athanasius works where this statement appears are *De unitate sanctissimae trinitatis* and *De fide sua*. The work that Servetus called "book 1 of the dialogues" is *De unitate sanctissimae trinitatis*, one of the pseudo-Athanasius works written in dialogue form. Servetus mistakenly cited *De unitate fidei*, a different work in the same collection, instead of *De fide sua*.

likeness of God, who is the spiritual being, and another who was formed out of the earth."[103]

111. William of Ockham considered the question of whether God, having absolute power, could have taken the form of an ass (or a stone or a tree). He concluded that, in order to redeem humankind, God might have chosen to do so.[104] Many others followed up in the discussion of this question. Some, like Giovanni Pico della Mirandola, argued that God could only assume a creature with a rational nature.[105] John Mair, on the other hand, claimed that God could assume any created thing. Faced with the syllogism — God is an ass; every ass is a stupid animal; therefore God is a stupid animal — Mair wrote: "I concede the possibility that God is an ass and that God has long ears. But I deny this: Every ass is a stupid animal. I understand 'ass' connotatively. In this eventuality, the ass would be all-knowing."[106]

Erasmus made fun of this concern of the scholastic philosophers in *The Praise of Folly*: "Here are questions which are deemed worthy of the great and so-called illumined theologians ... Could God have taken on instead the likeness of a woman? Or that of the Devil? Of an ass? A gourd? Or even a piece of flint? But then how could this gourd have preached to the people, performed miracles, or been crucified?"[107]

112. In the parallel passage in *Errors*, Servetus claimed that the Turks call Christians ass-worshippers (*Errors*, 12r; A.E1.8). Here he merely says that they laugh at Christians' asinine ideas.

113. In *On the Trinity* Augustine wrote, "They are marvelously blind if they do not notice that one cannot use the word 'begotten' except in relation to some other being."[108] With his exclamation on blindness Servetus appears to be casting Augustine's words back in his teeth.

---

[103] Irenaeus, *Adversus haereses* 1.18.2 (PG 7 646B); see also 1.11.5 (PG 7 570A), 1.1.1 (PG 7 447A-B), 1.2.4 (PG 7 458A-459A), and 1.30.3 (PG 7 695C).
[104] Ockham, *Super sententiarum* 3.1.1.
[105] Giovanni Pico della Mirandola, *Apologia* 4.
[106] John Mair, *In tertium sententiarum* 1.2.
[107] Erasmus, *Moriae encomium*, 269; in *Opera omnia*, IV-3:148.
[108] Augustine, *De Trinitate* 5.7 (PL 42 914).

114. The custom of adding *filioque*, "and the Son," to the statement in the Nicene Creed that "the Holy Spirit proceeds from the Father" originated in sixth-century Spain to counter the Arianism of the Visigoths. The addition was not officially approved by the Roman Church until the Council of Lyons in 1274. The Eastern Orthodox and other Greek churches, following the first seven ecumenical councils, do not include the "filioque" clause and consider it a heresy.

115. "Light of light" or "light from light" is one of the epithets of Christ in the Nicene Creed. Based on the *filioque* clause (see A.R1.114), the Holy Spirit might be called "light from lights" because it proceeds from the Father and the Son. For example, from a commentary on Psalms attributed to the Venerable Bede: "The Son is truly light of light, from the Father. The Holy Spirit, however, is light proceeding from lights."[109]

116. Here Servetus is pointing out the contradictions that would result from the consistent application of Augustine's rule: "what is spoken of relatively does not indicate substance." For the Trinity, with all of its parts and properties, is nothing but relationships. The rule therefore results in the absurd conclusion that the Father and the Son, being in relation with each other, not only cannot be of the same substance, but cannot be substance at all.

117. In book 5 of *On the Trinity* Augustine defined the three persons of the Trinity in terms of the "relations" among them.[110] Peter Lombard elaborated Augustine's ideas, using the word "notions" to refer to certain relations and properties in the Godhead. He identified five notions: unbegottenness; generation or paternity; birth or sonship; procession, and projection or spiration (that is, the sending forth of the Holy Spirit by the Father and the Son).[111] These notions became the focus of discussion by many theologians who followed, including Thomas Aquinas, who discussed the

---

[109] [Bede], *In psalmorum librum exegesis* 58 (PL 93 788B).
[110] Augustine, *De Trinitate* 5.12-15 (PL 42 918-921).
[111] *Sentences* 1.26.2, 1.28.1, and 1.29.4 (PL 192 591-592, 597-598, and 602).

notions in detail. He identified three of them as "constituting," or defining, persons of the Trinity: the Father is defined by paternity, the Son by sonship, and the Holy Spirit by procession. Projection, since it is shared by the Father and the Son, is "common."[112] The idea of five notions in the divine continued to be discussed by later theologians and philosophers, including Duns Scotus, William of Ockham, John Mair, and Juan de Oria.

118. The distinction between "complete" and "incomplete" distributions in syllogisms was created specifically in order to address and eliminate the contradictions and paradoxes arising out of applying classical Aristotelian logic to theology, and to the Trinity in particular. Acceptance of terms (also known as supposition) refers to the way that a word or term was to be taken in a sentence or proposition. Does it mean a particular thing, a category of things, or just the literal word itself? Mixing different kinds of supposition in the same syllogism or argument can lead to a faulty inference or a paradox.

These analytical methods, developed by practitioners of late medieval logic (*logica moderna*), were systematized by Jerónimo Pardo in *The Quintessence of Dialectic*.[113] Aside from Pardo's work, Servetus could have found discussion or critique of these logical refinements in other relatively recent books, such as Gaspar Lax, *Terms, Treatise on Syllogisms*, and *Tractate on the Oppositions of Categorical Propositions*; Juan de Oria, *On Assertion*; John Mair, *On the First Book of Sentences*; and Juan Luis Vives, *Against the Pseudo-dialecticians*.

There are ample indications within the text of *The Restoration of Christianity* that Servetus was familiar with the work of Vives, a Spanish Erasmian. Vives's *Against the Pseudo-dialecticians*, a scathing attack on *logica moderna*, mentions "complete and incomplete distribution, particularization, complete and incomplete singularization, mediate and immediate suppositions"; lists a number of paradoxes arising from syllogisms about the Trinity; and makes

---

[112] Thomas Aquinas, *Summa theologica* 1.32.3.
[113] Jerónimo Pardo, *Medulla dyalectices* (Paris, 1505).

fun of the practice of using letters (A, B, C, D, etc.) to substitute for words in syllogisms.[114] Servetus would also have digested what Erasmus had to say about the subtleties of modern dialecticians: "They parade before the unlettered masses their syllogisms, major and minor premises, conclusions, corollaries, totally lifeless suppositions, and further scholastic absurdities."[115]

There are recently discovered documents that show that Servetus was well-acquainted with, and perhaps studied under, Vives's teacher, Gaspar Lax, one of the great proponents of *logica moderna*.[116] If Servetus did study under Lax, he later rejected this intricate manner of reasoning, just as Vives did. Nor does it seem that he absorbed the subject thoroughly. For in drawing on these sources, Servetus did not always use the terminology correctly. Acceptances of terms, or suppositions, are not usually classified as "complete" or "incomplete." William of Ockham divided suppositions into proper and improper; proper suppositions into personal, simple, and material; and personal suppositions into discrete, common, determinate, confused, and confused-distributive.[117] Servetus's goal, however, was not to make an accurate and comprehensible portrayal of *logica moderna*, but to suggest, through a satirical display of arcane terminology, how far from reality such analysis was.

119. Throughout scholastic literature there is discussion of trinitarian paradoxes. Here are a few:

> The Father is God.
> The Son is God.
> Therefore the Father is the Son.[118]
>
> No Father is the Son.
> Every divine essence is the Father.
> Therefore no divine essence is the Son.[119]

---

[114] Vives, *Adversus pseudodialecticos*, D2v, B3r.
[115] Erasmus, *Moriae encomium*, 302; in *Opera omnia*, IV-3:166.
[116] Ancín and Towns, *Miguel Servet en España*, 139-151, 269-272.
[117] Ockham, *Summa logicae* 1.64, 1.70, 1.77.
[118] Peter Abelard, *Theologia Christiana* 3 (PL 178 1239B).
[119] Duns Scotus, *Quaestiones super priorem et posteriorem analyticorum* 1.22.

Every divine essence is the common property of the three persons.
The Father is a divine essence.
Therefore the Father is the common property of the three persons.[120]

120. Distinctions 25-34 in Book 1 of Peter Lombard's *Sentences* discuss the terms "person" and "hypostasis" (25 and 26); the properties distinguishing the persons (27 and 28); the persons and time (29 and 30); the equality and oneness of the Father and the Son (31); wisdom and love in the Trinity (32); and the difference between properties and persons (33 and 34).

121. Quiddities are the universal features that allow something to be classified, as opposed to the particulars that specify it exactly. Erasmus wrote, "There are countless finely-spun subtleties ... which have to do with instants, notions, relations, formalities, quiddities, thisnesses, [etc.], which no one can perceive with their eyes unless, like Lynceus, they can see, even in the blackest darkness, things that are not there."[121]

122. Erasmus wrote, "[The apostles] were able to confute both the pagan philosophers and the Jews ... But they did this by [the example of] the lives they led and the miracles [they performed], rather than by the use of syllogisms. And of course they were dealing with people who were incapable of comprehending even a single quodlibet of Scotus."[122]

123. The chimaera is a fire-breathing creature from Greek mythology composed of parts of three different animals: goat, lion, and serpent. It has come to mean any imaginary and impossible hybrid creature — and, by extension, anything impossible and imaginary. Late medieval logicians often used the chimaera as an exemplar of something nonexistent. For example, Duns Scotus, William of Sherwood, Walter Burley, Albert of Saxony, Paul of Venice, and John Mair all discussed the proposition, "Nothing and the chimaera

---

[120] Ockham, *Summa logicae* 3.1.5.
[121] Erasmus, *Moriae encomium*, 270-271; in *Opera omnia*, IV-3:144.
[122] Erasmus, *Moriae encomium* 277-278; in *Opera omnia*, IV-3:154.

are brothers."[123] In *Against the Pseudo-dialecticians*, Juan Luis Vives mocked logicians for debating propositions such as "The ass of the antichrist is the son of the chimaera."[124]

Absurd as they might seem, such discussions had a serious purpose. These philosophers were working on the problem of how to extend the classical rules of logic so that they might be made capable of handling propositions with "empty terms," that is, names that do not refer to any real entity. There was a long-established tradition of illustrating the rules of logic using certain conventional examples. Thus, instead of "Every S is P," one might say "Every human is an animal," and instead of "Some S is P" one might say "Socrates is an animal." In the same way, debating propositions such as "Nothing and the chimaera are brothers" provided a way of thinking through the logical implications of arguments involving terms about which nothing true can be said.

124. The second-century gnostic, Valentinus, propounded a mythology with a complicated genealogy of beings. Valentinianism was repudiated by, among others, Irenaeus in *Against Heresies* and Tertullian in *Against the Valentinians*. Servetus discussed Valentinianism at greater length in *On the Errors of the Trinity* (*Errors*, 27r, 39v-40r).

Valentinianism was a form of Christian gnosticism. Gnosis was one of a set of related religious phenomena that flourished in the Middle East during the Hellenistic and Roman periods, partly in response to the cultural domination of Greece and Rome and partly as a response to a hunger for individual salvation that arose in the new religions and philosophies of the mid-first millennium BCE. Other contemporary responses included apocalyptic Judaism, Zoroastrianism, Greek philosophy (notably Neoplatonism), Hermeti-

---

[123] Duns Scotus, *Quaestiones super priorem et posteriorem analyticorum* 1.12. William of Sherwood, *Syncategoremata* 8.3. Walter Burley, *De puritate artis logicae* 2.138-143. Albert of Saxony, *Quaestiones circa logicam* 5.92.1. Paul of Venice, *Logica magna* 4. John Mair, *Introductorium in Aristotelicam dialecticen, totamque logicem*, 31v.
[124] Vives, *Adversus pseudodialecticos*, B2v.

cism, Mithraism, and Pauline Christianity. Gnosticism seems never to have coalesced into an organized movement of its own; rather it mixed with some of the other phenomena to create, among other things, gnostic Christianity. This emerged in the second century CE as a major heresy, that is, a serious contender for establishing the belief system of orthodox Christianity.

Among the features that distinguished gnosticism (and gnostic Christianity) was a strong dualism, according to which there was a cosmic battle between the equally-matched forces of good and evil. The material universe, created by a malignant or incompetent god, was thought to be entirely evil. But sparks of divinity from a more transcendent god had been scattered, and those people who had these sparks implanted in them could be awakened by contact with gnosis — information that could make them children of the true, more remote God who could then break their bonds to matter and to the creator of the material universe and lead them to salvation. Christ was sent by the transcendent god as part of this plan.

There were various mythologies, some of them quite complicated, associated with different strands of gnosticism. Valentinianism is one of the most well-known, because of the detailed descriptions preserved by Irenaeus and others in their anti-gnostic polemic. The Valentinians' description of emanations from the godhead seem to many people, in Servetus's time and in our own, arbitrary, unnecessarily elaborate, and far too close to polytheism (though of a rather philosophical kind).

The origin story of the gnostics, as related in the Bible and by early Church Fathers, starts with Simon Magus. It is, however, unlikely that gnosis — an old phenomenon by the first century CE — began with this Christian rival and opponent. He may have had gnostic ideas, but so did most Christians, in varying degrees. Christianity, even in its developing orthodoxy, had picked up ideas from the salvation cults of the Middle East and from Greek philosophy. The Christianity that emerged and was codified in late antiquity was only somewhat less gnostic than the gnosticism it rejected.

Because predestination and election were central tenets of gnostic thought, Servetus criticized Calvinism as gnostic. Moreover, the theology of the Trinity reminded him of Valentinian ogdoads.

On the other hand, Servetus's theology incorporated ideas from Neoplatonism, Persian religion, and Hermeticism. When Calvin and Servetus called each other gnostic or Valentinian, they each had arguments that could be sustained. But they did not admit to themselves that they had each taken what they liked from gnosticism, before rejecting the rest.

Book 2

1. The Latin word *relucentia* means brightness, shining, or radiance as well as reflection.

2. Wisdom of Solomon 7:26: "[Wisdom] is a reflection of eternal light, a spotless mirror of the working of God, and an image of his goodness." Servetus supposed the apocryphal Wisdom of Solomon, written in Greek, to date from "an earlier age" than the Epistle to the Hebrews, attributed to Paul. They were, in fact, roughly contemporary.

3. Hebrews 1:3, "He reflects the glory of God," is the only instance of ἀπαύγασμα in the New Testament. The Latin word *relucentia*, which Servetus used here, is not the usual translation of ἀπαύγασμα. Both the Vulgate and Erasmus's New Testament use *splendor gloriae*. However, the word *relucentia* is offered as an alternative in the note to Hebrews 1:3 in Erasmus's *Annotations*.[1]

4. The 1790 Nuremberg reprint of *The Restoration of Christianity* has "innotuit" (was made known) where the 1553 edition has "intonuit" (thundered).

5. The identity of the elder quoted by Irenaeus is unknown. The nineteenth-century Servetus scholar Alexander Gordon thought Servetus's guess that it might be Justin "perfectly fair and legitimate as opinion, even though, as a critical surmise, our knowledge of Justin compels us to pronounce it most certainly mistaken."[2]

---

[1] Erasmus, *Annotationes*, "Splendor gloriae" (Heb 1:3); in *Opera omnia*, VI-10:230.
[2] Gordon, "Miguel Serveto-y-Revés."

6. Here Servetus quotes four passages from Isaiah — Isaiah 41:4, 41:25, 46:11, and 49:1 — to illustrate his statement that "the utterance of God was the calling of Christ." Comparing Servetus's version of these passages with the nearly universal Latin readings of his time, it would at first appear that Servetus is making several strategic alterations to the text in order to justify his interpretation of them as applying to the calling or naming of Christ. But these Bible texts remain controversial to this day, and quite different readings are possible, depending on which Hebrew text one adopts and how one navigates its obscurities. In at least one case, Isaiah 41:25, his reading ("he called [*vocavit*] my name," instead of the more usual "he will call [*vocabit*] my name") is closer to that of some modern scholars.[3] Servetus's familiarity with Hebrew is made much more explicit in the discussion of Psalm 72, which immediately follows.

7. Irenaeus wrote: "Thus, if anyone says to us, 'How then was the Son brought forth by the Father?' we reply that no one knows, because that bringing forth, or generation, or naming, or revelation, or whatever you like to call it, is indescribable."[4] Thus, Irenaeus does give "naming" as a synonym for "generation," although it is in the context of a list of words intended to show the inadequacy of all words.

8. Servetus offers three different Latin translations of the Hebrew verb ינון: *erit genitum* (will be begotten), *filiabitur* (will beget sons), and *propagabitur* (will be propagated). One that he does not discuss is *permanet* (continues), which is the verb used in the Vulgate. Here his reading of the Hebrew text is guided by Pagnini. The word *propagabitur* is used in the Pagnini Bible; *erit genitum* is used in Pagnini's translation of the psalm in *Psalterium sextuplex*; and *filiabitur* is used in Pagnini's *Treasury of the Holy Language*.[5]

9. This surprisingly harsh characterization of the Jews only applies, as it says here, to a single generation, and actually contradicts the

---

[3] See Joseph Blenkinsopp, *Isaiah 40-55* (New Haven: Anchor Yale, 2002), 204.
[4] Irenaeus, *Adversus haereses* 2.28.6 (PG 7 809A).
[5] Pagnini, *Thesaurus*, 1409-1410. *Psalterium sextuplex,* psalm 86.

portrayal of Jews in Matthew 27:24-25 as passing on their guilt as Christ-killers to succeeding generations. Elsewhere Servetus spreads the blame around more: "The death of Christ was repeated three times in the scriptures and Christ was murdered three times: in foreshadowing, in the body, and in spirit. Christ was killed in foreshadowing in Abel and others at the beginning of the world, Rev. 13. He was killed in the body by Jews, Matthew 27. He was killed by Papists in the worship of the spirit, Revelation 11" (*Restoration*, 459). Moreover, in chapter headings in his edition of the Pagnini Bible, Servetus removed or softened references to Jews being condemned[6] and deleted a portrayal of the Jews as Christ-killers.[7] He also said that, even if they did not accept Christ, at the final judgement, Jews and pagans could be saved by having lived up to their own standards: the Law or philosophy (*Restoration*, 335). Servetus recognized that the Jews and pagans had their own spiritual insight, as Christians did, and allowed that they were the leaven in two of the three measures of flour mentioned in the parable (*Restoration*, 460).

10. Servetus's picture of God and time, and his resolution of the problem of how to preserve free will while maintaining God's foreknowledge, may derive directly or indirectly from Augustine, *City of God*; or from Boethius, *The Consolation of Philosophy* or *On the Trinity*.[8]

11. This is a nearly word-for-word quotation from Marsilio Ficino's *Platonic Theology*. Ficino was paraphrasing an argument from Numenius's *On the Good*, which he found in Eusebius, *Preparation for the Gospel*.[9] Numenius of Apamea was a second-century Platonic-Pythagorean philosopher who influenced Plotinus and was admired by Origen. He tried to reconcile Greek, Jewish,

---

[6] See, for example, Pagnini Bible (1542), chapter headings for Isaiah 2, 43, 50, 51.
[7] Pagnini Bible (1542), chapter heading for Micah 5, Zechariah 14.
[8] Augustine, *De civitate Dei* 11.21 (PL 41 334). Boethius, *De consolatione philosophiae* 5.6; *De Trinitate* 4.
[9] Ficino, *Theologia Platonica* 3.1.3. Eusebius, *Praeparatio evangelica* 11.10 (PG 21 871).

and Christian thought. His books have been lost, but fragments of his writings have been preserved in the works of others.

12. Servetus may have had his attention drawn to the ancient satirist Lucian by Luther's disparaging remarks in his debate with Erasmus on free will.[10] In Lucian's dialogue "Jupiter Refuted," the great god is asked what makes the gods worthy of worship, when they are, like everyone else, subject to the Fates, whose decrees cannot be altered.[11] Lucian was highly regarded by Erasmus, who translated some of his dialogues, quoted him often in *Adages*, and emulated him in *The Praise of Folly* and *Colloquies*. If Servetus did not form his impression of Lucian by consulting "Jupiter Refuted" directly, he could have found this quotation in *Adages*: "Nothing can ever happen that is contrary to the law and the spun thread of the Fates."[12]

13. Servetus may have gotten his views on Lorenzo Valla secondhand. Erasmus quoted Valla in *On Free Will*: "Foresight is not the cause of the things that happen, since many things happen that are foreseen by us as well. These things do not happen because we foresee them. Rather, we foresee them because they are to come."[13]

14. In his dialogue *On Free Will*, Lorenzo Valla wrote, "God cannot avoid foreseeing what will happen," but he argued that the future is not determined by what God foresees, but by what God wills. Interpreted as predestinarian, Valla's views were approved by both Luther in *The Bondage of the Will* and Calvin in the *Institutes*.[14] In a letter to Calvin, Servetus indicated that he was well aware of Calvin's favourable attitude towards Valla (*Restoration*, 635).

15. Here Servetus is quoting from the Targum, a paraphrase of the Bible in Aramaic. The Targum reads: "You are as dear to me

---

[10] Luther, *De servo arbitrio*, A6v, B2v, G7v-G8r, H2v, S4v.
[11] *Luciani Samosatensis opera*, 201r.
[12] Erasmus, *Adagia* 3.1.39; in *Opera omnia*, II-5:60.
[13] Erasmus, *De libero arbitrio*, 46.
[14] Valla, *De libero arbitrio*, 13. Luther, *De servo arbitrio*, E4v. Calvin, *Institutes*, 2nd ed. (1539), 252-253.

as a son to a father (*abba*), pure as if this day I had created you."[15] The writers of the Targum (whom Servetus called "Chaldeus") wished to make it clear that the language was figurative in order to discourage people from taking the psalm literally, as the Christians, among others, generally did.

16. In his annotation to Psalm 2 in the Pagnini Bible, Servetus wrote, "It is said that, on the day that David escaped from his enemy, on that day he was born and on that day he was made king once more."[16] Because of the reference to conspiracies and plots, Psalm 2 could indeed be associated with the rebellion of Absalom; however, there is no explicit connection. Psalm 3, on the other hand, is headed, "A Psalm of David, when he fled from Absalom his son."

17. The metaphor of light emanating from the sun to explain the distinction of the Father from the Son was used by Justin Martyr, Tertullian, Athanasius, and Gregory Nazianzus, and is reflected in the credal formula "light from light." Lorenzo Valla discussed it in his *Dialectical Disputations*,[17] and it was mentioned in other later presentations of trinitarian theology.

18. *Sefer Nizzahon* (the *Book of Polemic*) is the name of at least two related late-medieval Ashkenazic Jewish anti-Christian works. Servetus would not have had access to either of these works, which existed only in manuscript and were not put into print until the following century (in 1644 and 1681).[18] His reference to *Sefer Nizzahon* is almost certainly drawn from the annotations in Sebastian Münster's *Hebrew Bible* (1534), which provides many references, paraphrases, and quotations of *Sefer Nizzahon*, including a long description of the extensive set of Jewish polemical arguments based on Genesis 49:10.[19] Furthermore, in an annotation to

---

[15] *Targum of Psalms* 2:7, in Giustiniani, *Psalterium*.
[16] Pagnini Bible (1542), marginal note to Ps 2:7.
[17] Lorenzo Valla, *Disputationes dialecticae* 1.8 (Cologne, 1530).
[18] See David Berger, *The Jewish-Christian Debate in the High Middle Ages: A Critical Edition of the Nizzahon Vetus* (Philadelphia, 1979).
[19] Münster, *Hebraica Biblia*, 1:50r-v.

Deuteronomy 13, Münster refers to the author of *Sefer Nizzahon* as "that perfidious Jew,"[20] a characterization borrowed by Servetus.

Servetus styles this perfidious author "Baal Nizaon." However, "Baal" is not a name, but an honorific, and "Nizaon" is the name of the book, not of the author (whose identity is unknown). Ba'al is an ancient Semitic way of saying Lord or Master, often but not exclusively applied to a god, similar to the Jewish "Adonai" or the Christian "Lord."[21] The use of an inappropriate honorific title may have been an instance of Servetus's sarcasm, as when he called Peter Lombard "Rabbi" (*Errors*, 42r).

Interestingly, the spelling used by Servetus, "Nizaon," was not the one used by Münster. Münster, and most other writers with whom Servetus was familiar — including Paul Fagius, Guillaume Postel, and Johann Reuchlin — used the spelling "Nizahon." "Nizaon" is a known, though rarer, spelling, but most uses of that spelling appear to come from after Servetus's lifetime.

19. Here is a part of what Servetus read, and felt the need to respond to, in Münster's notes in *The Hebrew Bible*:

> Let us also hear the author of Nizahon, who discusses this passage at great length, with his customary great contempt towards Christians. The Christians claim, he says, that Jesus, their Messiah, will come, according to the prophecy of Jacob, when the kingdom of the Jews ceases. In this, however, they speak falsely, since in the time of the second Temple there was no king, but rather, from the time of Zedekiah up until the time that their Jesus was born, there were merely governors set up by the kings of the Medes, Persians, and Romans.[22]

Another argument Münster drew from *Sefer Nizzahon* goes like this:

> When Christians claim that this was fulfilled in their Messiah, I ask them, how could it be proven, even out of their gospel, that Christ is born of the tribe of Judah, when their genealogy says

---

[20] Münster, *Hebraica Biblia*, 1:178v.
[21] Münster himself explains this in his *Evangelium secundam Mattheum in lingua Hebraica* (Basel, 1537), 76.
[22] Münster, *Hebraica Biblia*, 1:50v.

that he was born from the woman alone, and not from Joseph, who was of the house of David, and the whole genealogy laid out in Matthew leads not to Mary but to Joseph?[23]

Servetus deals with this question later, in dialogue 2 (*Restoration*, 263).

20. Genesis 49 contains Jacob's prophetic last words, addressed to his sons. Verses 8-12 contain the part of the address applying to Judah. Genesis 49:10 was not cited as a prophecy in the New Testament. The reading "until Shiloh comes" and the association of the name Shiloh with the Messiah emerged later. The Messianic interpretation was popular during the Reformation. The verse remains one of the most controversial in the Bible.

21. *Atnach* is a mark used to separate the first half of a verse from the second half. *Zakef* is a cantillation mark: a kind of musical notation that indicates how the text is to be sung or chanted. Here, Servetus argues, based on the position of the *atnach*, that the first half of the verse (the sceptre of Judah) should be understood as separate from the second half (the coming of Shiloh).

22. The Latin word *substantia*, translated here as "substance," is a translation of the word *hypostasis* in the Greek text of the Epistle to the Hebrews. Both words mean "to stand under" (see A.R1.65) and may be interpreted as a foundation of underlying strength. Thus, in this passage, *substantia* is most often translated as confidence, conviction, or assurance. Here, we have translated *initium substantiae nostrae*, rather awkwardly, as "the beginning of our substance" instead of the more usual "our first confidence," because Servetus's argument, in the subsequent text, will require us to deal with various levels of meaning in the words *substantia* and *hypostasis*.

23. The passage under discussion here is Hebrews 3:7-11. Servetus quotes only the first and last lines: "Today, if you hear his voice" and "They will not enter my rest." The full passage is:

---

[23] Münster, *Hebraica Biblia*, 1:50v .

Today, if you hear his voice,
do not harden your hearts as in the rebellion,
as on the day of testing in the wilderness,
where your ancestors put me to the test,
though they had seen my works for forty years.
Therefore I was angry with that generation,
and I said, "They always go astray in their hearts,
and they have not known my ways."
As in my anger I swore, "They will not enter my rest."

Hebrews 3:7-11 is a fairly accurate quotation of Psalm 95:7-11. The main difference between them is in verse 8. Where Hebrews has "as on the day of testing in the wilderness," the psalm has more detail about where this testing occurred: "as at Meribah, as on the day at Massah in the wilderness." In both the Vulgate and the Pagnini Bible, the same text is used in both places. It closely follows the version in Hebrews and does not include the reference to Meribah and Massah. However, Servetus mentions Meribah and Massah in his marginal note to Psalm 95:7-8 in the Pagnini Bible.

24. The creation story from Genesis is presented here as a type of the whole of Christian sacred history. The first six days are the period of the events narrated in the Old Testament, which Servetus calls "the beginning." The seventh day, the Sabbath, or "the end," is the Christian era, encompassing the end of the world.

25. Here Servetus quotes the version of Psalm 110:3 found in the Vulgate. The Vulgate uses Jerome's translation, known as the *Psalterium Gallicanum*, which he based upon the Greek of the Septuagint. He also made a later translation, known as the *Psalterium Hebraicum*, based directly upon a Hebrew original. The fact that his two versions of Psalm 110:3 are remarkably different from each other, and that there are many readings of the Hebrew itself, indicates that this is an unusually difficult and controversial verse. The Vulgate/Septuagint version is particularly susceptible to Christological interpretation. But versions based upon the Hebrew were also often taken to be about Christ, at least typologically, as Servetus will demonstrate.

26. The Greek word αρχη can indeed be translated as either "beginning" or "rule." In Latin the words, *principium* and *principatus*, as

Servetus points out, are similar to each other, though distinct. When he speaks of the delusion of the unlearned, Servetus may have had Augustine in mind. Augustine was not fluent in Greek and knew very little Hebrew. In his interpretation of this verse, Augustine used the Septuagint reading and rendered αρχη as "the beginning."[24]

27. Servetus based his version of Psalm 110:3 on the Hebrew text and on earlier translations made from the Hebrew. He was certainly familiar with Pagnini's translation, which is quite close to the one Servetus settled on. One difference between Servetus and Pagnini is that Pagnini says, "Your people will come willingly," while Servetus's version reads, "Your people make freewill offerings." Each of these readings can be found in other contemporary translations. Another difference is in the concluding phrase, rendered by Servetus as "the dew of your youth (*adolescentia*)," and by Pagnini as "the dew of your birth (*nativitas*)." Servetus's version agrees with Jerome's *Psalterium Hebraicum*.

28. Servetus appears to have overstated the use of the word נדב (*nadab*, freewill offering). The word *nadab* is used in Psalm 54:6; Ezra 1:4; and Ezekiel 46:12. Chapters 44, 45, and 48 of Ezekiel deal with various kinds of offerings but do not use the word *nadab*. Psalm 47:9 ("The princes of the peoples gather…") uses the word נדיבי (*nadib*), which means princes or nobles. It is possible that this word has been confused with *nadab*; one English translation, the Darby Bible (1890), interprets the word as *nadab* and translates it as "the willing-hearted among the people."

29. This quotation of Isaiah 7:14 is taken from Servetus's 1542 edition of Pagnini's *Holy Bible*. It differs from the earlier (and later) editions of Pagnini by changing "she will call his name Immanuel" to "you, mother, will call his name Immanuel." For discussion of the various editions of the Pagnini Bible, see the introduction to Appendix B.

---

[24] Augustine, *Enarrationes in psalmos* 109.12-16 (PL 37 1454-1459).

30. The story is also told in 2 Kings 15:29-16:9. Rezin, king of Syria, and Pekah, king of Samaria, formed a coalition to resist the king of Assyria, Tiglath-pileser III. Ahaz, king of Judah, declined to join the anti-Assyrian alliance. In 734 BCE Rezin and Pekah, supported by the Edomites and the Philistines, attacked Judah with the intent of replacing Ahaz with a ruler who would join their revolt. Over the next two years the Assyrians campaigned against Rezin and Pekah, capturing Damascus and indirectly saving Jerusalem. Pekah was assassinated and replaced by a pro-Assyrian ruler. Ahaz paid tribute money to Tiglath-pileser, preserving the kingdom of Judah, but acknowledging that it remained a client state.

31. Servetus's exposition of passage 8, predicting the coming of Immanuel, is meant to show that the text in Isaiah was not a prophecy of Christ, as was claimed by Christian apologists, but that the text primarily tells of an actual personage in Isaiah's time: Hezekiah, the king of Judah. This interpretation of Isaiah is more in line with the arguments of Jewish apologists, except that Servetus connects Christ with Hezekiah secondarily, through typology.

Abijah, the daughter of Zechariah and wife of King Ahaz, is mentioned in 2 Chronicles 29:1. There is nothing in the Bible to indicate that she is the same person as the prophetess in Isaiah 8:3, or the virgin (or young woman) who bears a son in Isaiah 7:14. Jewish scholar Ibn Ezra, in his commentary on Isaiah, equated the young woman of Isaiah 7:14 with the prophetess of Isaiah 8:3, and concluded that both referred to Isaiah's wife. Servetus may have been influenced in his interpretation by David Kimhi, who thought that the child mentioned in the prophecy of Isaiah was the son of Ahaz, not the son of the prophet, and definitely not Jesus. Kimhi's commentary on Isaiah was printed in the *First Rabbinic Bible*.

32. That the thirteenth king of Judah can be called Immanuel, when he is everywhere else referred to as Hezekiah, is here explained by Servetus's theory that fathers and mothers, in those days, gave their children different names. Many Old Testament figures do have two names, for example Abram/Abraham and Jacob/Israel. However, there is no certainty, according to modern scholarship, in the identification of Immanuel with Hezekiah. And there is even less

reason to suppose that Solomon was ever called Lemuel. Although there are instances in scripture of mothers, as well as fathers, getting credit for naming their children, it is not at all clear that children were ordinarily given different names by their respective parents.

33. 2 Kings 16:2, 18:2. The age of Ahaz when Hezekiah was conceived is calculated by subtracting Hezekiah's age when he was crowned (twenty-five) from Ahaz's age at death (thirty-six). Because there are problems with dating the reigns of these kings — various calculations based upon information supplied in the Bible provides inconsistent results — it is impossible to be sure of the dates and lengths of their reigns. Therefore, such calculations must be looked upon as extremely doubtful.

34. Servetus may have read the discussion of the various Hebrew words for a young woman in the notes to Isaiah 7 in Sebastian Münster's Bible: "In this passage they say *almah*, a young woman or a girl, instead of *betula*, a virgin, although it is not unusual in scripture for a virgin to be called *almah*. Thus Rebecca is referred to as *almah* before she was betrothed to Isaac. Thus Miriam, the sister of Moses, a girl six years old, is referred to as *almah*."[25]

35. This text is copied nearly word for word from the marginal note that Servetus wrote for Isaiah 9:5 in the Pagnini Bible; only the word "miraculously" has been added. A century later it appeared, without attribution, in a commentary on Isaiah by Tomaso Malvenda (1566-1628).[26] Here Servetus's note, including the non-biblical "cast down upon the Assyrians by an angel," was treated as one of seven alternative translations of Isaiah 9:5. (The other six, all without attribution, were by Robert Estienne, Santes Pagnini, Sebastian Münster, Francisco Foreiro, Johann Tremellius, and François Vatable.)

36. 2 Kings 19:32-36 tells of how Jerusalem escaped destruction by the Assyrians in 701 BCE, during the reign of Hezekiah. Hezekiah had reversed his father Ahaz's conciliatory stance towards the

---

[25] Münster, *Hebraica Biblia*, 2:371r.
[26] Tomaso Malvenda, *Commentariorum in s. scripturam* (Lyons, 1650), 5:71.

Assyrian overlords, and joined a rebellion against King Sennacherib (704-681 BCE), who had destroyed the Kingdom of Israel and scattered its people. After Judah was laid waste by the Assyrian army, Jerusalem endured a siege and was for a time under the threat of annihilation. Under these circumstances Hezekiah submitted, thus preserving a small amount of independence for his little client-kingdom. The Assyrian army was not in fact destroyed, but withdrawn after Hezekiah paid reparations.

37. According to the dating system of the biblical archaeologist William F. Albright, Hezekiah reigned 715-687 BCE.[27] If he became king at the age of twenty-five, as is claimed in 2 Kings 18:2, then he was born c. 740 BCE and would have been around seven years old during the Rezin-Pekah invasion.

38. Many modern translations of John 3:13 omit "who is in heaven" because it is not found in most Greek manuscripts. It was, however, present in the Greek and Latin texts available to Servetus. Here Servetus is arguing against theologians who cited this clause as evidence that Christ had two natures. These included Augustine and Peter Lombard (who quoted Augustine's *Against Maximinus*, but incorrectly cited *On the Trinity*).[28]

39. In the original 1553 edition of *The Restoration of Christianity*, a full line of text was inadvertently duplicated at this point (a kind of error known as dittography). The duplication was incorporated into the 1790 Nuremberg reprint. Here Servetus's text is translated it as it should have read, not as it was incorrectly printed.

40. The image of the artist is from Augustine's discussion of John 5:19: "For [the Son] does not do different things [from what the Father does], but in the same way, like a painter who makes new paintings by looking at pictures made by someone else; nor does he do the same things [as the Father], but in a different way, as when

---

[27] William F. Albright, "The Chronology of the Divided Monarchy of Israel," *Bulletin of the American Schools of Oriental Research* 100 (1945), 16-22.
[28] *Sentences* 3.22.4 (PL 192 804) quoting Augustine, *Contra Maximinum* 2.20.3 (PL 42 789-780).

the body copies out letters that the mind has imagined."[29] Servetus appears to have conflated the artist with the writer pictured by Augustine and to have turned the second part of Augustine's argument on its head, allowing for a certain modalist subordination of the Son to the Father, which Augustine was making an effort to preclude.

41. The three sermons of Augustine, *Tractates on the Gospel of John* 18-20, form a unit commenting on John 5:19. The main point of this sequence is that the works of the Father, Son, and Holy Spirit are inseparable from one another. For example, in sermon 20, Augustine wrote: "If the Father dwells in the Son, the Father performs the Son's works. That walk of a [human] body upon the sea was done by the Father, through the Son. Thus that walk is an inseparable work of the Father and the Son."[30] In sermon 19, however, Augustine said that although the works of the three persons are inseparable, only the Son is in the form of the man Christ.[31] Augustine made the same point about the inseparability of works in *On the Trinity*, only to contradict it a little further on: "The form of the man was taken on by the person of the Son, and not by that of the Father as well."[32]

42. Augustine separated the "old" (or former) man, the part of Christ subject to sin, from the rest of him. This "old" man does indeed suffer, but presumably the "new" man does not.[33] Jerome thought that Christ was sad, not because he feared death, but because of the sins and sufferings of others.[34] Hilary said that Christ did not suffer emotionally, only physically.[35]

43. A synecdoche is a figure of speech in which the whole stands for a part or a part for a whole. Synecdoche could also be used to

---

[29] Augustine, *De Trinitate* 2.3 (PL 42 846).
[30] Augustine, *In evangelium Iohannis* 20.6 (PL 35 1559).
[31] Augustine, *In evangelium Iohannis* 19.16 (PL 35 1553).
[32] Augustine, *De Trinitate* 2.9 (PL 42 850-851).
[33] Augustine, *Enarrationes in psalmos* 21 1.1-2 (PL 36 167).
[34] Jerome, *In evangelium Matthaei* 26 (Matt 26:37-38) (PL 26 197).
[35] Hilary, *Tractatus super psalmos* 68.4 (PL 9 472B).

associate a being with a place, such as Saint Peter with the gate of heaven. Augustine famously used the term "synecdoche" to explain how Christ could be said to be three days in the tomb, when it is clear from the biblical account that the passage of time between death and resurrection was somewhat less than two days. By synecdoche, he wrote, parts of days (that is, the late hours of Good Friday and the early hours of Easter Sunday) can stand for whole days.[36] A number of later writers commented on Augustine's argument. Thus the word "synecdoche" came to be associated with the image of Christ in the tomb.

44. As far as we can tell, no one but Servetus refers to "Asterius Thyensis," or, indeed, to anyone as "Thyensis." Ancients who came from Tyana, such as Apollonius, are identified as "Tyanensis" or "Thyaneus." However, there is no known Asterius of Tyana, unless it might refer to Asterius of Cappadocia (c.270-c.341), also known as Asterius the Sophist. Some of his works are partly extant, in the form of quotations by Athanasius, who argued against him. He did preach that the Son was made. But there are difficulties with this identification. Servetus says that Asterius was "long before the Arians," when Asterius of Cappadocia was, in fact, an Arian and a younger contemporary of Arius. His position on the roughly chronological list indicates that Servetus believed this person to have lived about a century before Asterius of Cappadocia. Furthermore, there is no known connection between this Asterius and Tyana. It is possible that Servetus might have conflated Asterius the Sophist with Asterius Urbanus, an anti-montanist of the late second century.

45. There are many places in patristic literature where it is said that the Son of God was made (*factus est*). However, *factus est* may also be read as "became." The presence on this list of Dionysius and Asterius, not otherwise found in Servetus's writing, suggests that Servetus may have taken this list from a secondary source. Dionysius of Alexandria later repudiated his early anti-Sabellian works.

---

[36] Augustine, *De doctrina Christiana* 3.50 (PL 34 86).

Nevertheless, they were cited by the Arians a century later in support of their own ideas.[37]

46. The printed editions of the Septuagint available in Servetus's time were the Aldine edition and the Complutensian Polyglot. The Aldine edition, published in 1518 by the firm of Aldus Manutius in Venice, narrowly beat out the Complutensian Polyglot (1520) as the first printing of this Greek version of the Old Testament. The Aldine edition also included the 1516 version of Erasmus's New Testament, making the volume the first complete printed Bible in Greek.

In both the Aldine edition and the Complutensian Polyglot, Genesis 6:2 reads "sons of God" and not "angels." The word "angels" is found in Codex Alexandrinus, an old and fairly authoritative manuscript of the Septuagint. Servetus could not possibly have read it, as it was not in any European library in his time. Nevertheless, he could have found the word "angels" in the works of the Church Fathers, which may preserve earlier readings of the text. For example, when Augustine quoted Genesis 6:2 in *City of God*, he used "angels of God."[38] In *On Idolatry*, Tertullian wrote about "those angels, forsakers of God, lovers of women."[39]

47. The 1790 Nuremberg reprint of *The Restoration of Christianity* has "comminiscentes" (devising) where the 1553 edition has "commiscentes" (mingling).

48. Berossos, a Babylonian priest, wrote a *History of Babylonia* (c.290 BCE), which is no longer extant. Fragments of his work have been preserved in a number of ancient pagan, Jewish, and Christian writers, including Pliny the Elder, Josephus, and Eusebius of Caesarea. Although the works of these authors were available in his time, Servetus got his information from the recently reprinted *Antiquities of Berossos the Chaledean Priest* by the late fifteenth-

---

[37] Dionysius of Alexandria, *Epistolae ad Sixtum Papam* 1 (PL 5 91A-B). He repudiated the idea that the Word was made in *Epistolae ad Dionysium Romanum* 2.11 (PL 5 125A).
[38] Augustine, *De civitate Dei* 15.23.3.
[39] Tertullian, *De idolatria* 9 (PL1 671B).

century charlatan Giovanni Nanni (Joannes Annius Viterbensis), which contains a collection of forged documents plus an extensive commentary.[40] The spuriousness of this work, and of the other egregious forgeries perpetrated by Nanni, was established only after the time of Servetus.

49. Tartarus was the ancient Greek hell, a dark, cold abyss below Hades in which the Titans were said to be imprisoned. It seems more likely that the adjective "tartarean," or horrible, was derived from the noun Tartarus.

50. In the Vulgate, Job 26:5, Proverbs 9:18, and Isaiah 14:9 all contain the word *gigantes* (giants), as a translation of the Hebrew word *rephaim*. The more usual meaning of *rephaim* is the ghostly dead or the departed spirits. But *rephaim* can also mean a legendary race of giant pre-Canaanites or underworld deities associated with pre-Canaanite worship. In Genesis 14:5 and 15:20 the Rephaim are mentioned as though they were a historic people or tribe, perhaps to be understood as descendants of evil angels and humans.

51. The Vulgate renders Job 26:5 as: "Behold, the giants, and those who dwell with them, groan beneath the waters." On the other hand, Pagnini's translation is: "Dead seeds, and those that abide in them, were being formed under the waters." (Sebastian Münster, in an annotation in his own Bible translation, explains that the dead seeds are "the works of God, teaching how God made the highest things out of nothing and out of the most vile things ... Observe how he brings out from dead and decayed seed budding plants and trees, as much in the water as in places near the water.") Servetus rendered the passage as: "The giants, and those who inhabit them, are oppressed beneath the waters." Thus, he agreed with Jerome, and differed from Pagnini, in translating *rephaim* as "giants." But — possibly influenced by Pagnini's "those that abide in them"— he replaced Jerome's "those who dwell with them" with "those who

---

[40] Giovanni Nanni, *Berosi sacerdotis chaldaici antiquitatum* (Antwerp, 1545), 5v-6r, 8r.

inhabit them." In Servetus's rendering, the demons possess the giants and do not merely dwell in hell alongside them.

52. Noah never speaks in the Bible; he just listens to God and obeys. But Jews, Christians, and Muslims all have traditions in which he preaches in the manner of a prophet. In *Antiquities of the Jews*, Josephus tells how Noah tried to persuade people (including the descendants of the giants) to renounce their sinful ways, and abandoned the attempt only when he feared for his life.[41] In 2 Peter 2:5 Noah is called "a herald of righteousness." In the Quran, too, he preaches to the people as a messenger of God, and is rejected.[42]

53. In a related passage in *On the Errors of the Trinity* (*Errors*, 72r) Servetus wrote, "As [Lorenzo] Valla notes here, φυλακή is 'the night watch, when thieves come and people are asleep,' and then unclean spirits rule."[43] In *The Restoration of Christianity* he dropped the quotation and the reference to Valla.

54. From Irenaeus one gathers that Wisdom and Spirit can be identified with each other, just as the Word is identified with the Son. Wisdom and the Word, however, appear to be two separate things, the two hands by which God made and sustained the world. "God did not need [angels] to accomplish what he had determined within himself to do — as if he did not have his hands. For near to him always were the Word and Wisdom, the Son and the Spirit, through whom and in whom, freely and voluntarily, he made all things."[44]

The equation of Wisdom, Word, and Spirit is clearer in Tertullian: "The power and disposition of the divine mind is also shown in the Scriptures under the name of Wisdom (*Sophia*). For what is wiser than the reason of God, or the Word? Listen therefore also to Wisdom herself, established as the second person." Also, "the Word itself [is] called Wisdom, Reason, the entire divine soul, and Spirit."[45]

---

[41] Josephus, *Antiquitatum Iudaicarum* 1.3.1.
[42] Quran 26:105-115.
[43] Valla, *In novum testamentum annotationes*, 61.
[44] Irenaeus, *Adversus haereses* 4.20.1 (PG 7 1032B).
[45] Tertullian, *Adversus Praxean* 6, 7 (PL 2 161A, 162A).

55. Here Servetus is mocking realist philosophers such as Duns Scotus for making "real distinctions" between things that cannot be separated from each other. Thus, he says, they might be compelled to make real distinctions among the power of God, the wisdom of God, the glory of God, and the other attributes of God, creating a multiplicity of really distinct persons within the Godhead.

56. Servetus might have found this observation, about the use in Hebrew of the antecedent noun instead of a pronoun (*antecedens pro relativo*), in Robert Estienne, *Annotations on the Five Books of Moses* or *Annotations on the Psalms from Hebrew Commentaries*; in Bartholomeus Westheimer, *Theological Tropes*; and in a number of other places.[46]

57. Following Erasmus, Servetus translates ἐπιλαμβάνομαι as *assumit*; the Vulgate uses a similar word, *apprehendit*. Both mean to overtake, take on, take hold of, or seize. Many modern translations interpret the word as "to help," as in the NRSV: "For it is clear that he did not come to help angels, but the descendants of Abraham." The context of Hebrews 2:16 supports the idea of Christ taking on the nature of the descendants of Abraham: "Since, therefore, the children [of Abraham] share flesh and blood, he himself likewise shared the same things … Therefore he had to become like his brothers and sisters in every respect" (Heb 2:14, 17).

---

[46] Robert Estienne, *Libri Moyse quinque cum annotationibus* (Paris, 1541), 5; *Liber psalmorum Davidis: Annotationes in eosdem ex Hebraeorum commentariis* (Paris, 1546), 42v. Bartholomeus Westheimer, *Troporum theologicorum* (Basel, 1527), 388.

Appendix A:
On the Errors of the Trinity, Book 1

1. Christ's exaltation over the angels is mentioned numerous times in Hebrews 1 and 2. However, in the Vulgate, Hebrews 2:7 (quoting Psalms 8:5) reads, "You have made him a little lower than the angels." This appears at first to be an awkward text for Servetus to have included among those that he cited to show that Christ "was exalted even above the angels."

Taking into account Servetus's familiarity with Erasmus's *Annotations on the New Testament*, the inclusion of Hebrews 2:7 among his proof-texts seems less mysterious. Erasmus was engaged in a controversy with the French humanist Jacques Lefèvre d'Etaples in the 1510s over the interpretation of the word *Elohim* in these passages. Lefèvre thought that the verse should read, "You have made him a little less than God (*Elohim*)," whereas Erasmus, based upon the readings of the majority of the Church Fathers, thought that the word *Elohim* here referred to angels. Lefèvre, thinking of the divine person of Christ within the Trinity, considered that the angel reading was a heretical assault on the divine dignity of Christ. Erasmus, on the other hand, thinking primarily of Christ's human nature, thought that these passages, like the one in Philippians 2:6-11, referred to the lowly state taken on by Christ, leading to his crucifixion. This humility, being temporary, was followed by exaltation.

Erasmus believed that there was no necessary conflict between his and Lefèvre's views and that they could be reconciled by translating the Septuagint Greek of the Hebrews passage as *"for a little while* lower than the angels," thus taking into account both the usual dignity and the temporary humiliation of Christ. The arguments deployed in this controversy, detailed in Erasmus's *Apology against Jacques Lefèvre d'Etaples*,[1] are reflected in the extensive note on Hebrews 2:7 in his *Annotations*.[2]

---

[1] Erasmus, *Apologia ad Stapulensem* (Louvain, 1517); in *Opera omnia* IX-3.
[2] Erasmus, *Annotationes*, "Minuisti eum paulo minus ab angelis" (Heb 2:7); in *Opera omnia*, VI-10, 240-270.

2. Carpocrates and Cerinthus were second-century Christian Gnostics, known for having denied the divinity of Jesus. Photinus (d.376), Bishop of Sirmium, was a modalist, who denied the pre-existence of the Son of God, saying that Christ, a mere man, only became the pre-existing Word when he was conceived in the Virgin. Servetus most likely got his information from Irenaeus and Isidore.[3] Servetus used the spelling "Fotinus," as in the 1520 edition of Isidore.[4]

3. The conjunction of bleary-eyed men and barbers derives ultimately from Horace, *Satires* 1.7.3. Servetus may have encountered it in Erasmus's *Adages*.[5]

4. There are no articles in the Latin language. Sometimes a pronoun is pressed into service as a definite article. There is no such pronoun in the Latin text of John 1:34 or Acts 9:20 (in either the Vulgate or the Erasmus translation). An article is, however, present in the Greek.

5. Bonosianism was a form of adoptionism, found in Spain and southern Gaul in the fifth through seventh centuries. Adoptionists in general believe that Jesus did not become the divine Son until after he was born and had demonstrated his preeminent goodness. The Bonosians are named after Bonosus (fl. late fourth century), Bishop of Sardica (modern Sofia, Bulgaria), who was condemned for claiming that Mary gave birth to other children after Jesus. His unorthodoxy was less than that of the later Bonosians. Servetus's information about Bonosians probably came from Isidore.[6]

6. Moses clearly plays a mediatorial role when he conveys the Law from God to the Israelites, but the Bible does not explicitly call him a mediator. In Galatians 3:19, Paul says that the Law "was ordained through angels by a mediator," though Moses is not mentioned by name. The Epistle to the Hebrews includes an extended comparison between the first covenant with Moses and the new covenant medi-

---

[3] Irenaeus, *Adversus haereses* 1.25.1, 1.26.1 (PG 7 680A, 686A-B). Isidore, *Etymologiae* 8.5.7, 8.4.37 (PL 82 298C, 301B).
[4] Isidore, *Etymologiae* (Paris, 1520), 41v.
[5] Erasmus, *Adagia* 1.6.70; in *Opera omnia*, II-2:96.
[6] Isidore, *Etymologiae* 8.5.52 (PL 82 302C).

ated by Christ; although Christ is described as "the mediator of a new covenant" (Heb 9:15), Moses is not referred to as a mediator. Outside the Bible, Moses is described as a mediator in both Jewish and Christian traditions.[7] Examples from Servetus's time include works by Jacques Lefèvre d'Étaples (1512), Johannes Faber (1528), and Haimo of Auxerre (1528).[8]

7. The expression translated here as "brazenly" is *ferrea fronte* (literally, "with a forehead of iron").[9] See also Isaiah 48:4: "your neck is an iron sinew and your forehead brass." On the advantages of having a hard forehead, see Ezekiel 3:8-9.

8. There is a history of Christians being called ass-worshippers. In the ancient world, where animal worship was a common feature of polytheistic religion, and in which the donkey, though a very useful domestic animal, was held in low esteem, ass-worship was a common smear employed against practitioners of competing religions (often found together with accusations of ritual cannibalism, what we now call the "blood libel"). It was especially applied to religions that despised worship of other animal totems. And because the Hebrew scriptures pronounce the donkey "unclean" (Ex. 13:13), not to be sacrificed and eaten, it was concluded by others that the animal was therefore sacred to the Jews. Early Christians inherited both the blood-libel and the accusation of ass-worship from the Jews. Tertullian reported that, "recently, a depraved man ... displayed a picture of [a Christian]. It had the ears of an ass, wore a toga, held a book, and had a foot with a hoof."[10] The persistence of this idea was reinforced by the pattern of a dark cross that can be seen on the skin on the backs of donkeys.

---

[7] John Lierman, *The New Testament Moses: Christian Perceptions of Moses and Israel in the Setting of Jewish Religion* (Tübingen: Mohr Siebeck, 2004), 49-50.
[8] Jacques Lefèvre d'Étaples, *Commentariorum in epistolas beatissimi Pauli apostoli* 4.3 (Paris, 1512), 123r. Johannes Faber, *Doctoris Joannis Fabri adversus Doctorem Balthasarum Pacimontanum ... orthodoxae fidei Catholica defensio* (Leipzig, 1528), 51v. Haimo of Auxerre, *Expositio in diui Pauli epistolas* 8 (Cologne, 1528), Gg vi r.
[9] The expression *ferrea fronte* is used in Augustine, *Ad Donatistas* 19 (PL 43 668) and in Pliny the Younger, *Panegyricus* 35 (often quoted in humanist literature).
[10] Tertullian, *Ad nationes* 1.14 (PL 1579B).

9. Modern scholars are divided as to whether the concluding statement in 1 John 5:20, "This is the true God and eternal life," refers to God the Father or to Christ. In Servetus's time, almost everyone (including Calvin, Luther, and Servetus himself) agreed with the Church Fathers that it referred to Christ.[11]

10. In the sixteenth century, Psalm 45 was thought to be about Solomon, who was regarded as a type of Christ. Therefore, when the king in the psalm is addressed as "God" (*Elohim*), this was taken as reference to the divinity of Christ. Today, the meaning of Psalm 45:6 seems more problematic. Does this verse, in fact, address a human king as "God"? Some believe the psalm should be read "Your divine throne…" or "God has enthroned you." It is also possible that the psalm incorporates elements from other Near Eastern cultures, in which kings were regarded as divine.

11. Servetus's assertion that the Aldine edition of the Septuagint was not that of the seventy translators must have been based upon the idea that the language in the New Testament, taken from the Septuagint by early Greek-speaking Christians, preserved older, and consequently more accurate, readings than did the relatively late, somewhat corrupted manuscripts available to the firm of Aldus Manutius. See A.R2.46.

12. This is a reference to Theophylact's commentary on Philippians 2:6, where he identifies the form of God with "nature" or "substance" (*ousia*).[12] Erasmus cited this commentary in his annotation on Philippians 2:6. In contrast to Servetus's dismissive tone, Erasmus's mention of Theophylact was appreciative.[13]

13. When the Jews accuse Jesus of making himself equal to God, Jesus speaks of himself as the Son of God, as one sent by God, and as one of whom Moses wrote, but never claims to be God, and thus the Jews are silenced (John 5:19-47).

---

[11] Calvin, *Commentarii* (*Calvini opera*, 55:376). Luther's Works, vol. 30, *The Catholic Epistles* (St. Louis: Concordia, 1967), 327.
[12] Theophylact, *Commentarius in epistolam ad Philippenses* (PG 124 1162B).
[13] Erasmus, *Annotationes*, "Esse se aequalem deo" (Phil 2:6); in *Opera omnia*, VI-9:294.

14. In general, the term *moderni* designated followers of the *via moderna*: late scholastic philosophers and theologians who were nominalists, such as William of Ockham, Robert Holkot, Gregory of Rimini, Pierre d'Ailly, and John Mair. In the early sixteenth century the term *moderni*, as used by humanists, had become a term of abuse. (The *moderni* were also disparagingly called sophists.)

To Servetus *moderni* may have meant, more specifically, the Spanish theologians who had trained at the University of Paris, which was a stronghold of late nominalist scholasticism and, particularly under John Mair, was the center of the study of late medieval logic (*logica moderna*).[14] These Spanish theologians, such as Alonso de Córdoba and Francisco de Vitoria, formed the bulk of those who met at Valladolid in 1527 to discuss and pass judgement on Erasmus's orthodoxy.[15]

When Servetus developed his arguments against these nominalists in *The Restoration of Christianity*, he dropped both mentions of the term *moderni*. By the time he wrote *Restoration* this school of thought had become less influential, and, moreover, Servetus had long been away from Spain. It is possible that, to the older Servetus, the *moderni* did not seem so much a force to be reckoned with.

15. *Unum* vs. *unus* has a long history in Latin Christian theology. Tertullian used *unum* to describe a duality within the unity of God in order to combat the monarchian or modalist heresy, which called for a more strict unity (*unus*) of the Father and Son.[16] In *On the Trinity* Hilary wrote, "*unum*, not *unus*," meaning that God is one in nature, but not one in person.[17]

Unum was picked up by the Arians to portray how God and Christ could be called one, in the sense of being in perfect accord. In Augustine's *Debate with Maximinus*, the Arian Maximinus said that "the Father and the Son were *unum* (one), *concordes* (in

---

[14] Noreña, *Studies in Spanish Renaissance Thought*, 1-19. See A.R1.118 and *Errors*, 42a.
[15] Conferencia de Valladolid, 23-24.
[16] Tertullian, *Adversus Praxean* 22 (PL 2 183C-D).
[17] Hilary, *De Trinitate* 7.31 (PL 10 226C).

agreement) and *unanimes* (unanimous)."[18] Interestingly, these are the exact words that Servetus inserted into his quotation of Tertullian's explanation of *unum* vs. *unus*. Augustine, however, saw little difference between the masculine *unus* and the neuter *unum*. According to him they both indicate the number "one." He thought that either word meant that the Father and the Son had the same substance.[19]

Servetus omitted this grammatical argument in the corresponding section of *The Restoration of Christianity*. There he wrote that Christ said "I and the Father are one" in John 10:30 "because there is one divinity, one power, one harmony of thought, and one will shared by the man and God" (*Restoration*, 25).

16. *Homoousios* (ὁμοούσιος) means "of the same substance." The word was adopted by early Christian orthodoxy as a doctrinal test. It was contrasted with a weaker word, *homoiousios* (ὁμοιούσιος), meaning "of similar substance," which was promoted by fourth-century theologians leaning toward Arianism.

17. The passages cited here (John 17:2 and Matthew 28:18) do not contain the word *ousia*, but rather *exousia*. *Exousia* is usually translated into Latin as *potestas* (authority or power). The word *ousia* occurs in the New Testament only in the story of the Prodigal Son (Luke 15:12-13), where it means "property." Servetus explained this in greater detail in *The Restoration of Christianity* (*Restoration*, 25). See A.R1.50.

18. In the 1520 edition of the works of Basil, *Against Eunomius* is in five books. Books 1-3 are actually by Basil of Caesarea, whereas books 4 and 5 are pseudepigraphal. In the cited passage, pseudo-Basil argues that it would be illogical for two beings different in substance to be perfectly united in will.

19. Erasmus provided no annotation on John 10:30. However, he did comment on its text in the midst of his long annotation on the Johannine Comma (1 John 5:7-8): "In chapter 10 of John, the Lord

---

[18] Augustine, *Collatio cum Maximino* 6 (PL 42 712).
[19] Augustine, *Contra Maximinum* 2.22.2 (PL 42 794); see also 2.20.1.

says, 'I and the Father are one.' How will the Arians be confuted by this testimony, unless you teach that the word 'one' [*unum*] is only employed in Scripture when describing things that are of the same substance? Now since we can call upon countless passages that teach that consensus and mutual benevolence are to be understood [by this word], I do not see how it can be of any use in supporting the belief of the orthodox, and in repressing the obstinacy of the heretic."[20]

20. The quotation "each is in the others" (*singulae in singulis*), which Servetus credited to Hilary, is actually from Peter Lombard. The paraphrase that follows, also not by Hilary, is based on Peter Lombard's quotation of *On the Faith, to Peter* by pseudo-Augustine.[21] In the revised discussion in *The Restoration of Christianity*, Servetus corrected himself and credited the paraphrase to Augustine, but continued to attribute Peter Lombard's formula, *singulae in singulis*, to Hilary.

21. Servetus almost certainly took this gloss at second hand from Erasmus's *Annotation* on 1 John 5:7.[22] It is not drawn from the longer marginal commentary of the *Glossa Ordinaria* but is, as Erasmus indicates, an interlinear gloss.

22. Since Servetus calls this quotation from Theophylact a gloss, he may have taken it from a secondary source. It is not, however, from the *Glossa Ordinaria*.

23. By saying "the second being is the daughter of the first" Servetus was playing upon words and grammar in an effort to reduce his opponents' theological abstractions to absurdity. The Latin word he generally used for the persons of the Trinity is *res*, meaning "thing" or, as it is translated here, "being." As this word is feminine in gender,

---

[20] Erasmus, *Annotationes*, "Tres sunt qui testimonium dant in coelo" (1 John 5:7); in *Opera omnia*, VI-10:550.
[21] *Sentences* 1.19.5 (PL 192 574), quoting [Augustine], *De fide ad Petrum* 4 (PL 40 754).
[22] Erasmus, *Annotationes*, "Tres sunt qui testimonium dant in coelo" (1 John 5:7); in *Opera omnia*, VI-10:544.

he suggests that the Father and Son should perhaps be described as the Mother and Daughter. (Modern sensibility might take issue with what Servetus deemed the essential absurdity of the idea that divine beings could be feminine.)

Theological arguments based upon grammar are weak, and this one is particularly so, because the word *res*, or "thing," could be used for any thing, animate or inanimate, male or female. Furthermore, Servetus could easily have chosen to employ a different word for "being," such as the neuter word *ens*. Perhaps he saw the weakness of this argument, for he did not retain this passage in *The Restoration of Christianity*.

24. This "quotation" is taken from Augustine, *On the Trinity*, book 1 (not book 2), as altered first by Peter Lombard, then by Servetus. Augustine actually said, "From him, from the Father; through him, through the Son; in him, in the Holy Spirit." Peter Lombard, altering the prepositions, quoted Augustine as saying, "From him, by means of the Father; through him, by means of the Son; in him, by means of the Holy Spirit."[23] Servetus, who probably did not consult Augustine directly, further modified this by substituting "first being," "second being," and "third being" for the names of the persons.

25. In his commentary on Matthew 13, Jerome used Plato's analysis of the three-part human soul — reason, will, and feeling — as an inspiration for his trinitarian reading of the parable of the three measures of meal.[24] Servetus appears to have read Erasmus's dismissive comment on this passage: "Jerome refers [this parable] to the mystery of the Trinity, delighted to philosophize about numbers."[25]

26. According to Irenaeus, Marcus "the Heresiarch" was a Gnostic teacher of the second century, a follower of Valentinus.[26] Color-

---

[23] *Sentences* 1.2.8 (PL 192 529), quoting Augustine, *De Trinitate* 1.12 (PL 42 827).
[24] Jerome, *In evangelium Matthaei* 2 (Matt 13:33) (PL 26 91B). See Plato, *Republic* 4.435.
[25] Erasmus, *Annotationes*, "In farina satis tribus" (Matt 13:33); in *Opera omnia*, VI-5:226.
[26] Irenaeus, *Adversus haereses* 1.13-17 (PG 7 577B-642A).

basus, thought to be a Gnostic Valentinian connected with Marcus, is mentioned only once by Irenaeus.[27] It has been suspected by some that the existence of a shadowy heretic by that name was born out of a misreading of that obscure passage in Irenaeus.[28] Even if an individual named Colorbasus did exist, everything that is asserted about him by the later Church Fathers is the result of speculation.

27. These are some of the principal characters and terms of Gnostic theology. Bythos (Greek for "the deep") is a name for the most basic or ultimate form of God. The Aeons, which are emanations from Bythos, together form the Pleroma (the fullness of God). Monads, dyads, tetrads, and ogdoads are groupings of Aeons. The Demiurge is an evil creator god, one of the lowest of the emanations, responsible for the fallen material universe (the *kenoma*). The Gnostics believed that the Demiurge was the God of the Hebrews and the promulgator of Jewish law.

28. According to Irenaeus, the Gnostics teach that the Demiurge, the material universe, and the souls trapped in corporeal bodies were generated by the Aeon Sophia through her passions, including her laughter and tears.[29]

29. In Aristotelian logic, "accidental predication" refers to qualities that are particular to an individual, as opposed to "essential predication," which refers to qualities that the individual inherits by virtue of its membership in a category. The term was widely used by the scholastics, including Peter Abelard, Thomas Aquinas, Duns Scotus, and William of Ockham.

30. When Peter Lombard mentioned Exodus 3:6 in *Sentences*, he was arguing against, not for, the use of this passage as a representation of the Trinity.[30] His argument, moreover, had nothing to do with the naïve idea that "the God of Abraham, the God of Isaac,

---

[27] Irenaeus, *Adversus haereses* 1.14.1 (PG 7 594A).
[28] See footnote discussion in W. Wigan Harvey, trans., *Sancti Irenaei libros quinque adversus haereses* (Cambridge, 1857), 1:127-128.
[29] Irenaeus, *Adversus haereses* 1.4.2-3 (PG 7 482B-483A).
[30] *Sentences* 1.34.5 (PL 192 616).

and the God of Jacob" was a way of referring to a threefold God. He was making an entirely different point: that it would be improper to refer to the Deity as "the God of Abraham, Isaac, and Jacob" because that would make the divine dependent upon finite human beings. Note also that Exodus 3:6 is not included among the numerous Old Testament proof-texts for the Trinity in *Sentences*.[31]

When he wrote this section of *On the Errors of the Trinity*, Servetus must have misunderstood or misremembered Peter Lombard's discussion of Exodus 3:6. When he said that Peter Lombard was "following others," he seems to have been thinking of writings that did cite Exodus 3:6 as a proof of the Trinity. (See, for example, pseudo-Jerome, *Commentary on the Gospel of Mark* and pseudo-Athanasius, *On the Unity of the Holy Trinity*[32] — thought in Servetus's time to be genuine works of major Church Fathers, but actually the work of later authors.) When Servetus reworked and corrected this material later (*Restoration*, 25-26), he argued at length against "sophists" who used Exodus 3:6 as a trinitarian proof-text, but he no longer mentioned Peter Lombard in this context.

31. Antonomasia is a figure of speech in which a description or epithet is used as a substitute for a name, e.g. "The Apostle" for "Paul."

32. Servetus found the quotation from Romans 8:9-11, contained in a long quotation from Hilary, in Peter Lombard's *Sentences*.[33] Although Servetus modified the wording of the quotation to make it match the Vulgate, he trimmed the quotation exactly as Peter Lombard did, right down to the concluding "etc."

33. The intrinsic middle, a term associated with William of Ockham, is a piece of information implicit in the premise and conclusion of an argument. For example, if the premise is "Socrates is running" and the conclusion is "A man is running," then the intrinsic middle, or hidden premise, is "Socrates is a man."

---

[31] *Sentences* 1.2.6-7 (PL 192 527-528).
[32] [Jerome], *In evangelium Marcum* (Mark 12:26) (PL 30 648C). [Athanasius], *De unitate sanctissimae Trinitatis* (PL 62 241A).
[33] *Sentences* 1.34.1 (PL 192 613), quoting Hilary, *De Trinitate* 8.21.

The intrinsic middle in Henry of Ghent's argument, as interpreted by Servetus, appears to be "human beings are created in the image of God"; thus, the production of the persons of the Trinity can be understood by analogy with the reproduction of human beings. Here Servetus substituted the sexual word *generatio* (begetting) for Henry's more abstract philosophical term *productio* (production). This substitution prepares the way for him to mock Henry's view of creation by depicting it as a sexual act in which the persons of the Trinity "copulate and beget amongst themselves."

34. Aristotle expressed uncertainly in, for example, *Metaphysics* 2.1 *Metaphysics* 3.1, and *Nicomachean Ethics* 1.3.[34] Servetus may have found the idea of Aristotle's uncertainty in a chapter entitled "Aristotle himself believed that his own teachings were uncertain" in Gianfrancesco Pico della Mirandola's anti-Aristotelean work, *Examination of the Vanity of the Teaching of the Pagans, and of the Truth of Christian Education*.[35]

35. Nicander of Colophon is known for using obscure words and inventing new ones. In the interest of stylistic variety, he avoided using the same word twice, even when referring to exactly the same thing.

36. "White" vs. "whiteness" was an example used in the discussions of many ancient Greek philosophers. Servetus was more familiar with the thinking of later philosophers such as William of Ockham, who wrote:

> A connotative term is one that signifies one thing primarily and something else secondarily. And although such a term is given its standard definition in the nominative case, it is often necessary to put one instance of this term, thus defined, in the nominative case and another in an oblique case [a case other than the nominative, such the accusative or the ablative]. Consider the term "white." For this term, having one standard definition, is in one occurrence, put in the nominative, and in another, in an oblique case. If anyone asks what the word "white" means, you could reply that it means the same thing as the phrase "something

---

[34] Aristotle, *Metaphysics* 2.1, 3.1 (993a, 995a-996a); *Nicomachean Ethics* 1.3 (1094b).
[35] Gianfranceso Pico della Mirandola, *Examen vanitatis* 4.13.

formed by whiteness" [ablative case] or "something possessing whiteness" [accusative case].[36]

37. The sibylline literature surveyed by Lactantius is not the collection of the pronouncements of the sibyls of ancient Roman legend, but rather a later set of Gnostic oracles, partly Christian, partly Jewish, partly pagan, composed in the early Christian period and ascribed to the ancient sibyls. Lactantius (and Servetus) considered these oracles to be pagan evidences of Christian truth.

38. Cerdo (fl.140) was a Gnostic Christian preacher. He believed that the God of the Old Testament and the God of the New were two distinct deities. He left no writings and did not found a sect, though he was an influence on Marcion and the Marcionites. Believing that the Old Testament God was a lower and somewhat evil deity, Marcion rejected the Old Testament and most of the New Testament, keeping only Luke and ten Pauline letters. Although Marcion's writings are no longer extant, much of his doctrine can be reconstructed from Tertullian's arguments in *Against Marcion*.

39. This appears to be a very early use of the word "trinitarian" to mean "believer in the Trinity." In a note to his translation of *On the Errors of the Trinity*, Earl Morse Wilbur claimed that this was the first time this word was used, other than to designate members of the monastic Order of the Most Holy Trinity.[37]

40. Deuteronomy 6:4 is the monotheistic credo that begins the *Shema*, a prayer that is recited twice daily by observant Jews. In this verse the name of God, *Yahweh*, is replaced by *adonai* ("the Lord") because Jews were instructed that the name Yahweh ought not be said aloud. Servetus is concerned that this oral ritual practice of Judaism, spelled out in a text also sacred to Christians, might confuse Christians and lead them to believe that Yahweh (which Christians equated to God the Father) and the Lord (understood to be Christ) are two separate beings.

---

[36] Ockham, *Summa logicae* 1.10.
[37] Wilbur, *Two Treatises*, 54-55.

41. In Valentinian thought, Bythos is unbegotten and not of the same nature as the Demiurge, which was fashioned out of psychic material by Sophia.[38] See A.E1.27.

42. There is only one Pleroma, but its thirty Aeons are divided into three groups: the Ogdoad, the Decad, and the Dodecad. The third, the Dodecad, is produced by two of the Aeons, Man and Church.[39]

43. This title, originally associated with the Roman God Jupiter in his guise as the supreme deity, was sometimes applied to God by Christians in the sixteenth century. The usage here may indicate that Servetus saw the wise pagans, whose ideas of God tended to be relatively monotheistic, as superior to trinitarians, whom he considered to be tritheists.

44. Servetus's phrase *bestiae agri illuderent* (the beasts of the field would mock) echoes Job 40:15 in the Vulgate (Job 40:20 in modern Bibles), *bestiae agri ludent* (the beasts of the field play). The Latin verb *ludo* means both "play" and "mock."

45. There are no citations of passages from the Quran here because, at the time he wrote *On the Errors of the Trinity*, Servetus had no access to a copy. The Bibliander publication of the Latin translation by Robert of Ketton, the *Alcoran*, was not printed until 1543 (see A.R1.80). Before that time Servetus had to rely on secondary sources for his information on the Quran.

There is one source that accounts for all of Servetus's assertions about the Quran in *Errors*: Marsilio Ficino's *On the Christian Religion* (1474), which was printed several times in the early sixteenth century. Servetus made use of passages such as:

> In the Quran it is admitted that Jesus of Nazareth is the greatest and highest prophet of the Hebrews.[40]
>
> [Muhammad] calls [Christ] the breath and spirit of God, the very soul of God, the power of God, the Word of God, born of a perpetual virgin by the breath of God.[41]

---

[38] Irenaeus, *Adversus haereses* 1.1.1 (PG 7 446B) and 1.5.1 (PG 7 491A).
[39] Irenaeus, *Adversus haereses* 1.2-3 (PG 7 450A-B).
[40] Ficino, *De Christiana religione* 34.
[41] Ficino, *De Christiana religione* 36.

[Muhammad] said in the Quran, "God rescued the soul of Jesus from the hands of the Jews, returning him to himself and exalting him, and ... decided to afflict the unbelieving Jews, who were deprived of every protector and guardian, with the greatest suffering in this life and the next."[42]

Muhammad strongly commended the first Christians and admitted that Christian teachings — that is, the books of the evangelists and apostles — are to be accepted based on the miraculous authority of God himself. However, after the time of the apostles these books were corrupted by the Christians.[43]

The information above supersedes what is written about this passage in Peter Hughes, "Servetus and the Quran," where it is speculated that Nicholas of Cusa's *Cribratio Alcorani* (1461) might have been the source of some of Servetus's early information about the Quran.[44]

---

[42] Ficino, *De Christiana religione* 29.
[43] Ficino, *De Christiana religione* 36.
[44] Hughes, "Servetus and the Quran," 59-60.

Bibliography

Abbreviations

The following abbreviations are used in the Bibliography.

Ante-Nicene Fathers	*Ante-Nicene Fathers: The Writings of the Fathers down to A.D. 325.* New York: Christian Literature Company, 1885-1896.
	Online edition: Christian Classics Ethereal Library, https://www.ccel.org/fathers2
Athanasius Works (1548)	*D. Athanasii ... Opera Omnia.* Cologne, 1548.
Augustine Works (1528-29)	*Operum divi Aurelii Augustini.* Basel, 1528-29.
Bibliander, *Machumetis Saracenorum*	Bibliander, Theodore (ed.). *Machumetis Saracenorum principis eiusque successorum vitae ac doctrina ipseque Alcoran.* Basel, 1543.
Collected Works of Erasmus	Collected Works of Erasmus [English translation]. University of Toronto Press. 1974–.

Nicene and Post-Nicene Fathers	*Nicene and Post-Nicene Fathers, Series I and II*. New York: Christian Literature Company, 1886-1900.
	Online edition: Christian Classics Ethereal Library, https://www.ccel.org/fathers2
Servetus Treatises (trans. Wibur)	*The Two Treatises of Servetus on the Trinity: On the Errors of the Trinity, Dialogues on the Trinity, On the Righteousness of Christ's Kingdom.* Translated by Earl Morse Wilbur. 1932; reprint, New York: Kraus Reprint Co, 1969.
Servetus Writings (trans. O'Malley)	*Michael Servetus: a Translation of his Geographical, Medical and Astrological Writings.* Translated by Charles Donald O'Malley. Philadelphia: American Philosophical Society, 1953.
Tertullian Works (1521)	*Opera Q. Septimii Florentis Tertulliani*. Basel, 1521.

Bibliography

Works by Servetus

Apologetica disceptatio pro astrologia. Paris, 1538. Republished, Berlin, 1880.

[English translation] In Servetus Writings (trans. O'Malley).

Christianismi restitutio. Vienne, 1553. Republished, Nuremberg, 1790; reprint of 1790 edition, Frankfurt: Minerva, 1966.

There are three surviving copies of the 1553 edition: in the Österreichische Nationalbibliothek in Vienna, the Bibliothèque Nationale in Paris, and the University of Edinburgh Library.

A facsimile of the Vienna copy is included in volume 6 of *Miguel Servet: Obras Completas.* Zaragoza: Larumbe, 2005.

The copy at the Bibliothèque Nationale in Paris is available online on Gallica Bibliothèque Numérique.

The Edinburgh copy includes the "Edinburgh manuscript," an alternate version of the first 16 pages of *Christianismi restitutio.* A transcription of the manuscript is found in David Wright, "The Edinburgh Manuscript Pages" (see under **Secondary Works**).

[English translation] *The Restoration of Christianity: An English Translation of Christianismi Restitutio, 1553 by Michael Servetus (1511-1553).* Translated by Christopher A. Hoffman and Marian Hillar. Lewiston, NY: Mellen Press, 2007-2010. 4 volumes.

De justicia regni Christi. See *Dialogorum de Trinitate libri duo.*

De Trinitatis erroribus libri septem. Hagenau, 1531. Facsimile reprint, Frankfurt: Minerva, 1965.

[English translation] In Servetus Treatises (trans. Wilbur).

Dialogorum de Trinitate libri duo and *De justicia regni Christi, capitula quatuor.* Hagenau, 1532.

[English translation] In Servetus Treatises (trans. Wilbur).

In Leonardum Fuchsium apologia. Lyons, 1536.

[English translation] In Servetus Writings (trans. O'Malley).

Syruporum universa ratio. Paris, 1537.

[English translation] In Servetus Writings (trans. O'Malley).

Bibliography

Works Edited by Servetus

Biblia Sacra cum glossis. Lyons, 1545.

    Servetus worked on this edition in some capacity, but his exact role is not known.

Biblia Sacra ex Santis Pagnini tralatione. Second edition, Lyons, 1542.

    Servetus's introduction, and a selection of his marginal notes and chapter headings, are translated in Appendix B.

Claudii Ptolomaei Geographicae enarrationis libri octo. Lyons, 1535. Second edition, Vienne, 1541.

    [English translation] Portions of the first edition and the introduction to the second are translated in Servetus Writings (trans. O'Malley).

Scriptures

The Bible: Latin

Biblia sacra vulgata [The Vulgate].

    Many editions in the late fifteenth and early sixteenth century.

Biblia sacra. Translated by Santes Pagnini.

    First edition: Lyons, 1527-28.

    Unauthorized second edition: *Biblia sacra iuxta germanam Hebraici*. Edited by Melchior von Neuss. Cologne, 1541.

    Second edition: *Biblia sacra ex Santis Pagnini tralatione*. Edited by Servetus. Lyons, 1542.

Bibliae Sacrae cum glossa ordinaria et interlineari.

    Many editions in the late fifteenth and early sixteenth century.

Hebraica Biblia. Translated by Sebastian Münster. Basel, 1534.

Novum Testamentum. Translated by Erasmus.

    First edition: *Novum Instrumentum*. Basel, 1516.

    Second through fifth editions: *Novum Testamentu*m. Basel, 1519, 1522, 1527, 1535.

Sacra Biblia ad LXX interpretum fidem diligentissime tralata. Basel, 1526.

    Latin translation of the Septuagint.

Bibliography

The Bible: Greek

Sacrae scripturae veteris novaeque omnia. Edited by Aldus Manutius. Venice, 1518; reprinted with minor alterations as *Biblia Graeca*, Strasbourg, 1526.

Contains the Septuagint plus Erasmus's Greek New Testament.

The Bible: Hebrew

The First Rabbinic Bible. Venice, 1517.

The Second Rabbinic Bible. Venice, 1525.

The Psalter: Polyglot

Psalterium. Edited by Agostino Giustiniani. Genoa, 1516.

Contains 8 columns: Hebrew; Latin translation of Hebrew by Giustiniani; Vulgate; Septuagint; Arabic; Targum of Psalms; Latin translation of Targum; scholia.

Psalterium sextuplex. Edited by Santes Pagnini. Lyons, 1530.

Contains 6 columns: Hebrew; three Latin translations of Hebrew (Jerome, Pagnini, and Felice da Prato); Septuagint; Vulgate.

The Quran: Latin

Lex Saracenorum quam Alcoran vocant. Translated by Robert of Ketton. In Bibliander, *Machumetis Saracenorum*.

Servetus's Sources

The following list represents our best estimate of the non-Biblical sources that Servetus used in writing books 1 and 2 of *The Restoration of Christianity* and the corresponding portions of *On the Errors of the Trinity*. The list includes works that are explicitly mentioned in the text of *Errors* or *Restoration*, as well as others that have been identified, with varying degrees of certainty, as sources of quotations or information used by Servetus. All of these works were available in Servetus's day, some of them in multiple editions. The editions listed are ones that Servetus could have used, but not necessarily those that he did use.

Aristotle. *Auctoritates Aristotelis.* Paris, 1522.

A collection of excerpts from Aristotle, dating from c. 1300.

Athanasius. *De sancto spiritu, ad Serapion.* In Athanasius Works (1548).

[English translation] "Athanasius's Letters to Serapion on the Holy Spirit" in *Athanasius the Great and Didymus the Blind: Works on the Spirit*. Translated by Mark DelCogliano, Andrew Radde-Gallwitz, and Lewis Ayres. Yonkers, NY: St. Vladimir's Seminary Press, 2011.

———. *Epistola ad Epictetum*. In Athanasius Works (1548).

[English translation]
(1) In *Nicene and Post-Nicene Fathers*, series 2, vol. 4.
(2) Appendix I in John McGuckin, *Saint Cyril of Alexandria and the Christological Controversy*. Crestwood, NY: St. Vladimir's Seminary Press, 2004.

[Athanasius]. *De ariana et catholica confessione, ad Theophilum*. In Athanasius Works (1548).

———. *De assumptione hominis, contra Marcellionem haereticum, ad Theophilum*. In Athanasius Works (1548).

———. *De fide sua, ad Theophilum*. In Athanasius Works (1548).

———. *De nominibus sanctissimae Trinitatis, ad Theophilum*. In Athanasius Works (1548).

———. *De professione regulae catholicae, ad Theophilum*. In Athanasius Works (1548).

———. *De unitate fidei, ad Theophilum*. In Athanasius Works (1548).

———. *De unitate sanctissimae trinitatis, ad Theophilum*. In Athanasius Works (1548).

Augustine. *Collatio cum Maximino*. Included as book 1 of *Contra Maximinum*, in Augustine Works (1528-29), vol. 6.

[English translation] "Debate with Maximinus." In *Arianism and Other Heresies*. Translated by Roland Teske, S.J. Hyde Park, NY: New City Press, 1995.

———. *Confessiones*. In Augustine Works (1528-29), vol. 1.

[English translation]
(1) In *Nicene and Post-Nicene Fathers*, series 1, vol. 1.
(2) *Confessions*. Translated by Henry Chadwick. Oxford University Press, 1992.

———. *Contra Maximinum*. Books 2 and 3 of *Contra Maximinum*, in Augustine Works (1528-29), vol. 6. (*Collatio cum Maximino* is book 1.)

Bibliography

[English translation] "Answer to Maximinus the Arian." In *Arianism and Other Heresies*. Translated by Roland Teske, S.J. Hyde Park, NY: New City Press, 1995.

———. *De civitate Dei*. In Augustine Works (1528-29), vol. 5.

[English translation]

(1) In *Nicene and Post-Nicene Fathers*, series 1, vol. 2.

(2) *City of God*. Translated by Henry Bettenson. Penguin, 2003.

———. *De doctrina Christiana*. In Augustine Works (1528-29), vol. 3.

[English translation]

(1) In *Nicene and Post-Nicene Fathers*, series 1, vol. 2.

(2) *Teaching Christianity*. Translated by Edmund Hill, O.P. Hyde Park, NY: New City Press, 1996.

———. *De fide et symbolo*. In Augustine Works (1528-29), vol. 3.

[English translation] In *Nicene and Post-Nicene Fathers*, series 1, vol. 3.

———. *De praedestinatione sanctorum*. In Augustine Works (1528-29), vol. 7.

[English translation] In *Nicene and Post-Nicene Fathers*, series 1, vol. 5.

———. *De Trinitate*. In Augustine Works (1528-29), vol. 3.

[English translation]

(1) In *Nicene and Post-Nicene Fathers*, series 1, vol. 3.

(2) *The Trinity*. Translated by Edmund Hill, O.P. Hyde Park, NY: New City Press, 1991.

———. *Enarrationes in psalmos*. In Augustine Works (1528-29), vol. 8.

[English translation]

(1) In *Nicene and Post-Nicene Fathers*, series 1, vol. 8.

(2) *Expositions on the Psalms*. Translated by Maria Boulding. Hyde Park, NY: New City Press, 2000. 6 volumes.

———. *Enchiridion*. In Augustine Works (1528-29), vol. 3.

[English translation]

(1) In *Nicene and Post-Nicene Fathers*, series 1, vol. 3.

(2) *The Augustine Catechism: The Enchiridion on Faith, Hope, and Love*. Translated by Bruce Harbert. Hyde Park, NY: New City Press, 1999.

———. *Epistulae.* In Augustine Works (1528-29), vol. 2.

[English translation]

(1) In *Nicene and Post-Nicene Fathers*, series 1, vol. 1.

(2) *Saint Augustine: Letters.* Translated by Roland Teske, S.J. Hyde Park, NY: New City Press, 2001-2005. 4 volumes.

———. *In evangelium Iohannis tractatus.* In Augustine Works (1528-29), vol. 9.

[English translation]

(1) In *Nicene and Post-Nicene Fathers*, series 1, vol. 7.

(2) *Homilies on the Gospel of John.* Translated by Edmund Hill, O.P. Hyde Park, NY: New City Press, 2020. 2 volumes.

———. *Sermones.* In Augustine Works (1528-29), vol. 10.

[English translation]

(1) In *Nicene and Post-Nicene Fathers*, series 1, vol. 6.

(2) *Saint Augustine: Sermons.* Translated by Edmund Hill, O.P. Hyde Park, NY: New City Press, 1990-97. 11 volumes.

[Augustine]. *Contra Felicianum arianum de unitate Trinitatis.* In Augustine Works (1528-29), vol. 6.

———. *De fide ad Petrum.* In Augustine Works (1528-29), vol. 3.

———. *Dialogus quaestionum LXV, sub titulo Orosii percontantis et Augustini respondentis.* In Augustine Works (1528-29), vol. 4.

Basil of Caesarea. *Contra Eunomium* (books 1-3). In *Basilii Magni … Opera.* Paris, 1520.

[English translation] *Against Eunomius.* Translated by Mark Del Cogliano and Andrew Radde-Gallwitz. Washington, DC: Catholic University of America Press, 2011.

[Basil of Caesarea]. *Contra Eunomium* (books 4-5). In *Basilii Magni … Opera.* Paris, 1520.

Boethius. *De consolatione philosophiae.* Basel, 1522.

———. *De Trinitate.* In *Boethii opera et castigatiora et plura.* Venice, 1523.

[English translation] Translations of both *De consolatione philosophiae* and *De Trinitate* are included in *Boethius: Tractates and The Consolation of Philosophy.* Translated by H. F. Steward, E. K. Rand, S. J. Tester. Harvard University Press, 1973.

Bibliography

Clement of Alexandria. *Stromata*. Florence, 1551.

[English translation] In *Ante-Nicene Fathers*, vol. 2.

[Clement of Rome]. *Divi Clementis Recognitionum libri X*. Basel, 1526.

[English translation]
(1) *The Syriac Clementine Recognitions and Homilies*. Translated by Joseph Glen Gebhardt. Nashville, TN: Grave Distractions Publications, 2014.
(2) The Recognitions of Clement. Translated by Douglas F. Hatten. Printed by the translator, 2007.

Clichtove, Josse van. *Elucidatorium ecclesiasticum*. Paris, 1540.

Corpus juris civilis. Paris, 1511; many other editions with variant titles.

[English translation] *The Digest of Justinian*. Translated by Alan Watson. University of Pennsylvania Press, 1985; revised 1998. 4 volumes.

Cyprian. *Epistola ad Magnum*. In *Opera divi Caecilii Cypriani*. Basel, 1520.

[English translation] In *Ante-Nicene Fathers*, vol. 5.

Cyril of Alexandria. *In divi Joannis evangelium*. In *Opera divi Cyrilli Alexandrini*. Basel, 1546.

———. *Thesaurus de sancta et consubstantiali trinitate*. In *Opera divi Cyrilli Alexandrini*. Basel, 1546.

D'Ailly, Pierre. *Quaestiones super primum, tertium et quartum librum Sententiarum*. Paris, 1513.

De Oria, Juan. *De conceptu*. In *Johannis de Oria opera logica*, vol. 1. Salamanca, 1518.

———. *De enunciatione*. In *Johannis de Oria opera logica*, vol. 2. Salamanca, 1518.

Decretales d. Papae Gregorii noni. Lyons, 1528; many other editions.

Duns Scotus, John. *Ordinatio* [*Quaestiones in quattuor libros senteniarum*]. Venice, 1490.

[English translation] *The Ordinatio of Blessed John Duns Scotus*. Vol. 2, part 2, *On the Existence and Unity of God*. Translated by Peter L. P. Simpson. Militant Thomist Press, 2022.

———. *Quaestiones quodlibetales*. Venice, 1521.

[English translation] *God and Creatures*. Translated by Felix Alluntis and Allan B. Wolter. Princeton University Press, 1975.

———. *Reportata super primum sententiarum*. Paris, 1518.

Epiphanius of Salamis. *Panarion* [*Contra octoaginta haereses opus, Panarium*]. Paris, 1543.

[English translation] *The Panarion of Epiphanius of Salamis*. Translated by Frank Williams. Leiden: Brill, 1987-1996. 2 volumes.

Erasmus, Desiderius. *Adagiorum chiliades*. Venice, 1508; Basel, 1515; many other editions, some with variant titles.

First published in 1500; expanded in 1508 and subsequent editions. The sayings that Servetus appears to have found in *Adages* were in all of the editions starting in 1508.

[English translation] In Collected Works of Erasmus, vol. 30-36.

———. *Annotationes in novum testamentum*. Basel, 1516, 1519, 1522, 1527, 1535.

There is no complete English translation. A few sections (e.g. Romans, Galatians, Ephesians) are available in Collected Works of Erasmus, vol. 56 and 58.

The development of the work is shown in *Erasmus' Annotations on the New Testament: Facsimile of the final Latin text with all earlier variants*. Edited by Anne Reeve. London: Duckworth, 3 vols., 1986-1993.

———. *De libero arbitrio.* Antwerp, 1524.

[English translation] *A Discussion of Free Will*. Translated by Peter Macardle. In Collected Works of Erasmus, vol. 76.

———. *Moriae encomium*. Basel, 1522; many other editions, some with variant titles.

[English translation] *Praise of Folly.* Translated by Betty Radice. In Collected Works of Erasmus, vol. 27.

Eusebius of Caesarea. *Historia ecclesiastica*. Basel, 1523.

[English translation] *The History of the Church*. Translated by G. A. Williamson. Penguin, 1989.

Ficino, Marsilio. *De Christiana religione*. Venice, 1518.

[English translation] *On the Christian Religion*. Translated by Dan Attrell, Brett Bartlett and David Porreca. University of Toronto Press, 2022.

———. *Theologia Platonica*. Venice, 1525.

[English translation] *Platonic Theology*. Translated by Michael J. B. Allen. Harvard University Press, 2001-2006. 6 volumes.

Gregory of Nazianzus. *Orationes lectissimae*. Venice, 1516.

[English translation]

(1) In *Nicene and Post-Nicene Fathers*, series II, vol. 7.

(2) *On God and Christ: St Gregory of Nazianzus, The Five Theological Orations and Two Letters to Cledonius*. Translated by Frederick Williams and Lionel Wickham. Crestwood, NY: St. Vladimir's Seminary Press, 2002.

Gregory of Rimini. *Super primum et secundum sententiarum*. Venice, 1518.

Henry of Ghent. *Quodlibeta theologica*. Paris, 1518.

Herman of Carinthia (trans.). *Doctrina Machumetis summatim comprehensa*. In Bibliander, *Machumetis Saracenorum*, vol. 1.

Translation of an Arabic work, c. 7-8 century, in the form of a dialogue between Muhammad and Abdallah ibn Salam, a Jew who later converted to Islam.

Hilary. *De synodis*. In *Divi Hilarii pictavorum episcopi lucubrationes*. Basel, 1535.

English translation: In *Nicene and Post-Nicene Fathers*, series 2, vol. 9.

———. *De Trinitate*. In *Divi Hilarii pictavorum episcopi lucubrationes*. Basel, 1535.

[English translation]

(1) In *Nicene and Post-Nicene Fathers*, series 2, vol. 9.

(2) *The Trinity*. Translated by Stephen McKenna. New York: Fathers of the Church, 1954.

Holkot, Robert. *In quatuor libros sententiarum quaestiones*. Lyons, 1518.

[Ignatius]. *Epistolae*. In *Epistolae sanctissimorum*. Paris, 1515.

Includes epistles to the Ephesians, Magnesians, Philadelphians, Smyrneans, Tarsians, Trallians. The passages cited by Servetus are from versions of the letters (the so-called "long recension") that are now considered to have been edited and expanded after the time of Ignatius.

[English translation] In *Ante-Nicene Fathers*, vol. 1.

Irenaeus. *Adversus haereses*. Basel, 1526.

[English translation] In *Ante-Nicene Fathers*, vol. 1. The same translation is printed in book form as *Against Heresies*. Ex Fontibus Company, 2010.

Isidore of Seville. *Etymologiae*. Paris, 1520.

[English translation] *Isidore of Seville's Etymologies*. Translated by Priscilla Throop. Charlotte, VT: MedievalMS, 2005. 2 volumes.

Jerome. *Commentariorum in Matthaeum evangelistam*. In *Operum d. Hieronymi*, vol. 9. Basel, 1516.

John Chrysostom. *Evangelium secundum Ioannem commentarii*. Antwerp, 1542.

[English translation] In *Nicene and Post-Nicene Fathers*, series 1, vol. 14.

John of Damascus. *De fide orthodoxa*. Paris, 1519.

[English translation]

(1) In *Nicene and Post-Nicene Fathers*, series 2, vol. 9.

(2) *On the Orthodox Faith*. Translated by Norman Russell. Yonkers, NY: St. Vladimir's Seminary Press, 2022.

Josephus. *Antiquitatum Iudaicarum*. Basel, 1534.

[English translation] *The Works of Josephus*. Translated by William Whiston. (1736; Peabody, MA: Hendrickson, 1987).

[Bilingual edition] *Jewish Antiquities*. Translated by Henry St. John Thackeray, Ralph Marcus, Allen Wikgren, Louis H. Feldman. Harvard University Press, 1926-1965. 9 volumes.

[Justin Martyr]. *Iustini philosophi et martyris admonitorius Gentium*. Translated into Latin by Gianfrancesco Pico della Mirandola. Paris, 1538.

Also known as *Cohortatio ad Gentiles* or *Cohortatio ad Graecos*.

Kimhi, David. *Commentarium in decem primos psalmos Davidicos*. Translated into Latin by Paul Buechelin (Paulus Fagius). Constance, 1544.

Lactantius Firmianus. *Divinae institutiones*. Basel, 1521.

[English translation]

(1) In *Ante-Nicene Fathers*, vol. 7.

(2) *Divine Institutes*. Translated by Anthony Bowen and Peter Garnsey. Liverpool University Press, 2003.

Lax, Gaspar. *Arithmetica speculativa*. Paris, 1515.

———. *Termini*. Paris, 1511.

———. *Tractatus de oppositionibus propositionum categoricarum*. Paris, 1512.

———. *Tractatus syllogismorum*. Paris, 1509.

Liberatus. *Breviarium causae Nestorianorum et Eutychianorum*. Cologne, 1538.

Lucian of Samosata. *Luciani Samosatensis opera*. Frankfurt, 1538.

[Bilingual edition] *Lucian*. Translated by A. M. Harmon. London: William Heinemann, 1919. 7 volumes. The relevant dialogue (here called "Zeus Catechized") is in vol. 2.

Luther, Martin. *De servo arbitrio*. Wittenberg, 1525.

[English translation] In *Erasmus and Luther: Discourse of Free Will*. Translated and edited by Ernst F. Winter. 1961; reprint, New York: Comntinuum, 2005.

Mair, John. *In quartum sententiarum*. Paris, 1510-1512. 4 volumes.

Maxentius. *Dialogi contra Nestorianos*. In *Opuscula Maxentii Joannis*. Hagenau, 1520.

Melanchthon, Philip. *Loci Communes*, 2nd edition. Wittenberg, 1535.

Melanchthon's comments on Servetus were added in the second edition, and retained with minor changes in the later editions.

[English translation] *The Chief Theological Topics: Loci Praecipui 1559*, 2nd edition. Translated by J. A. O. Preus. St. Louis, MO: Concordia Publishing House, 2011.

Nicholas of Cusa. *Cribratio Alcorani*. In Bibliander, *Machumetis Saracenorum*, vol. 2.

Ockham, William. *Quodlibeta*. Paris, 1487.

[English translation] *Quodlibetal Questions*. Translated by Alfred J. Freddoso and Francis E. Kelley. Yale University Press, 1991.

———. *Summa logicae*. Venice, 1522.

[English translation] *Ockham's Theory of Terms: Part 1 of the Summa Logicae*. Translated by Michael J. Loux. University of Notre Dame Press, 1974.

———. *Super quatuor libros sententiarum annotationes*. Lyons, 1495.

Origen. *Contra Celsum*. In *Operum Origenis*. Paris, 1512.

[English translation] In *Ante-Nicene Fathers*, vol. 4.

———. *De principiis*. In *Operum Origenis*. Paris, 1512.

[English translation]

(1) In *Ante-Nicene Fathers*, vol. 4.

(2) *On First Principles*. Translated by G. W. Butterworth. 1936; reprint, Notre Dame, IN: Christian Classics, 2013.

Pagnini, Santes. *Hebraicas institutiones*. Lyons, 1526.

———. *Thesaurus linguae sanctae sive lexicon Hebraicum*. Lyons, 1529.

Peter Lombard. *Sententiarum libri quatuor*. Paris, 1514; many other editions.

[English translation] *The Sentences*. Translated by Giulio Silano. Toronto: Pontifical Institute of Mediaeval Studies, 2007-2010. 4 volumes.

Pico della Mirandola, Gianfrancesco. *Examen vanitatis doctrinae gentium et veritatis christianae disciplinae*. Mirandola, 1520.

Pico della Mirandola, Giovanni. *Apologia*. In *Ioannis Pici Mirandvlae Omnia Opera*. Reggio Emilia, 1506.

Polycarp. *Epistola ad Philippenses*. In *Epistolae Sanctissimorum*. Paris, 1515.

[English translation] In *Ante-Nicene Fathers*, vol. 1.

Quran. *See under* **Scriptures**.

Riccoldo of Monte Croce. *Confutatio Alcorani*. In Bibliander, *Machumetis Saracenorum*, vol. 2.

Richard of St. Victor. *De Trinitate*. Nuremberg, 1518.

[English translation] *On the Trinity*. Translated by Ruben Angelici. Eugene, OR: Cascade Books, 2011.

Rufinus. *Historia ecclesiastica*. In Eusebius, *Historia ecclesiastica*. Basel, 1523.

Sozomenus. *Historia ecclesiastica*. In Eusebius, *Historia ecclesiastica*. Basel, 1523.

Tertullian. *Adversus Marcionem*. In Tertullian Works (1521).

[English translation] In *Ante-Nicene Fathers*, vol. 3.

———. *Adversus Praxean*. In Tertullian Works (1521).

[English translation] In *Ante-Nicene Fathers*, vol. 3.

———. *Adversus Valentinianos*. In Tertullian Works (1521).

[English translation] In *Ante-Nicene Fathers*, vol. 3.

———. *De carne Christi*. In Tertullian Works (1521).

[English translation] In *Ante-Nicene Fathers*, vol. 3.

———. *De idolatria*. In *Opera Q. Septimii Florentis Tertulliani carthaginensis*. Paris, 1545.

[English translation] In *Ante-Nicene Fathers*, vol. 3.

———. *De praescriptionibus adversus haereses omneis*. In Tertullian Works (1521).

[English translation] In *Ante-Nicene Fathers*, vol. 3.

[Tertullian]. *Adversus omneis haereses*. In Tertullian Works (1521).

In PL, this is included in Tertullian, *De Praescriptionibus adversus haereticos*, starting in chapter 45.

[English translation] In *Ante-Nicene Fathers*, vol. 3.

Theophylact. *Commentarius in epistolam ad Philippenses*. In *In omnes divi Pauli epistolas enarrationes*. Cologne, 1527.

———. *In quatuor evangelia enarratione*. Basel, 1524.

Valla, Lorenzo. *De libero arbitrio*. Basel, 1526.

———. *Elegantiae linguae latinae*. In print from 1471, many editions.

———. *In novum testamentum annotationes*. Basel, 1526.

Vives, Juan Luis. *Adversus pseudodialecticos*. Strasbourg, 1520.

Bilingual edition: *In Pseudodialecticos: A Critical Edition*. Translated and edited by Charles Fantazzi. Leiden: Brill, 1979.

Other Sixteenth-Century Works

Calvin, John. *De scandalis, quibus hodie plerique absterrentur, nonnulli etiam alienantur pura Evangelii doctrina*. Geneva, 1550.

———. *Des scandales qui empeschent aujourdhuy beaucoup de gens de venir à la pure doctrine de l'Évangile et en desbauchent d'autres*. Geneva, 1550.

Calvin's French version of *De scandalis*.

———. *Defensio orthodoxae fidei de sacra Trinitate contra prodiciosos errores Michaelis Serveti Hispani.* Geneva, 1554.

———. *Déclaration pour maintenir la vraie foi que tiennent tous Chrestiens de la Trinité des personnes en un seul Dieu.* Geneva, 1554.

Calvin's French version of *Defensio*.

———. *Institutio Christianae religionis.*

First edition: Basel, 1536.

[English translation] *Institutes of the Christian Religion.* Translated by Ford Lewis Battles. Grand Rapids, MI: Eerdmans, 1975.

Second edition: Strasbourg, 1539.

Third edition: Strasbourg, 1543.

Fourth edition: Geneva, 1550.

Fifth edition. Geneva, 1559.

This edition of Calvin's *Institutes* contains a number of references to Servetus and refutations of his theology.

[English translation] *Calvin: Institutes of the Christian Religion.* Translated by Ford Lewis Battles. Philadelphia: Westminster, 1960. 2 volumes.

La Conferencia de Valladolid en 1527 en torno a la doctrina de Erasmo. Edited by Vicente Beltrán de Heredia. In *Cartulario de la Universidad de Salamanca (1218-1600)*, vol. 6 (1972), pp. 9-120.

Transcript of the conference with an introduction in Spanish.

Dávid, Francis. *De regno Christi.* Alba Iulia, 1569.

Gribaldi, Matteo. *Declarationis Jesu Christi filii Dei.* Unpublished manuscript, c. 1557.

This work, at one time believed to be by Servetus, is now known to be the work of Matteo Gribaldi.

The original Latin text was never published, but a bilingual Latin/English edition has been published as Matteo Gribaldi, *Declaratio: Michael Servetus's Revelation of Jesus Christ the Son of God; and other antitrinitarian works.* Translated by Peter Zerner et al. Providence, RI: Blackstone Editions, 2010.

Luther, Martin. *Tischreden.* Eisleben, 1566.

[English translation] *Table Talk*. Translated by Theodore G. Tappert. In Luther's Works, vol. 54. Philadelphia: Fortress, 1967. This volume contains a selection from *Tischreden*, using the same numbering system as the standard *Weimar Ausgabe* edition.

Selected Secondary Works

Adams, Marilyn McCord. *William Ockham*. University of Notre Dame Press, 1987. 2 volumes.

Alcalá, Ángel. Introduction to *Miguel Servet: Obras Completas*. Zaragoza: Larumbe, 2003.

Ancín, Miguel González and Otis Towns. *Miguel Servet en España (1506-1527)*. Tudela, 2017.

Bainton, Roland H. *Hunted Heretic: The Life and Death of Michael Servetus, 1511-1553*. 1953; revised edition, Providence, RI: Blackstone Editions, 2005.

Barth, Karl. *The Theology of John Calvin*. Translated by Geoffrey W. Bromiley. Grand Rapids: Eerdmans, 1995.

Cavard, Pierre. *Le procès de Michel Servet à Vienne*. Vienne: Syndicat d'Initiative, 1953.

Cross, Richard. *Duns Scotus*. Oxford University Press, 1999.

D'Artigny, Antoine Gachet. "Mémoires pour servir à l'histoire de Michel Servet." In *Nouveaux mémoires d'histoire, de critique et de littérature*, 2:55-154. Paris, 1749.

Friedman, Jerome. *Michael Servetus: A Case Study in Total Heresy*. Geneva: Droz, 1978.

Froehlich, Karlfried. *Biblical Interpretation from the Church Fathers to the Reformation*. Farnham (Surrey): Ashgate Publishing, 2010.

Gilmont, Jean-Francois. *John Calvin and the Printed Book*. Translated by Karin Maag. Kirksville, MO: Truman State University Press, 2005.

Gordon, Alexander. "Miguel Serveto-y-Revés." *Theological Review* 15 (July 1878), 281-307, 408-443.

Hillar, Marian. *Michael Servetus*. Lanham, MD: University Press of America, 2002.

Hughes, Peter. "The Christology of Michael Servetus." *Journal of Unitarian Universalist History* 40 (2016-2017), 16-53.

Bibliography

———. "In Search of Servetus's True Birthdate." In Sergio Baches Opi and Ana Gómez Rabal, eds., *Miguel Servet, Eterna Libertad* (Villanueva de Sijena: Michael Servetus Institute, 2012).

———. "Michael Servetus's Britain: Anatomy of a Renaissance Geographer's Writing." *Renaissance and Reformation* 39:2 (Spring 2016), 85-109.

———. "Servetus and the Quran." *Journal of Unitarian Universalist History* 30 (2005), 55-70.

Impartial History of Michael Servetus. London, 1724

La Roche, Michel de. *Historical Account of the Life and Trial of Michael Servetus*. London, 1712.

Lane, Anthony N. S. *John Calvin, Student of the Church Fathers*. Edinburgh: T & T Clark, 1999.

Lawson, John. *The Biblical Theology of St. Irenaeus*. 1948; reprint, Eugene, OR: Wipf and Stock, 2006.

Newman, Louis. *Jewish Influence in Christian Reform Movements*. 1925; reprint, Skokie, IL: Varda Books, 2002.

Noreña, Carlos G. *Studies in Spanish Renaissance Thought*. The Hague: Martinus Nijhoff, 1975.

Rezi, Elek. "The Influence of Michael Servetus on Dávid Ferencz (Francis Dávid) and the Beginnings of Transylvanian Unitarianism." In Clifford M. Reed (ed.), *A Martyr Soul Remembered*. Prague: Inernational Council of Unitarians and Universalists, 2004.

Rosemann, Philipp W. *Peter Lombard*. Oxford University Press, 2004.

Rudolph, Kurt. *Gnosis*. Translation edited by Robert McLachlan Wilson. Harper & Row, 1987.

Wilbur, Earl Morse. *A History of Unitarianism*. Vol.1, *Socinianism and its Antecedents*. Boston: Beacon Press, 1945.

Williams, George Huntston. *The Radical Reformation*, 3rd edition. Kirksville, MO: Truman State University Press, 2000.

Willis, Robert. *Servetus and Calvin*. London, 1877.

Wright, David. "The Edinburgh Manuscript Pages of Servetus' *Christianismi Restitutio*." In Elsie Anne McKee and Brian G. Armstrong (eds.), *Probing the Reformed Tradition*. Louisville: Westminster/John Knox, 1989.

Index

Abbreviations

The following abbreviations are used in the indexes.

A	Annotation	Reference is to book and annotation number, e.g. **A.R1.20** indicates annotation 20 for *Restoration* book 1.
Err	*On the Errors of the Trinity*	Reference is to folio number in the original 1531 printing, e.g. *Err*: **25r**
Rest	*The Restoration of Christianity*	Reference is to page number in the original 1553 printing, e.g. ***Rest*: 30**
SN	Servetus's notes to 1542 Pagnini Bible	Reference is to note number in Appendix B, e.g. **SN: No.35** indicates note no. 35 (Isaiah 42:7).

Index of Biblical References

Genesis

1:3, 6, 9, etc.	*Rest*: 51
1:14	*Rest*: 53
1:26	*Rest*: 48
1:27	*Rest*: 89
2:3	*Rest*: 64
2:7	*Rest*: 78, 83
2:24	*Err*: 24r
4:12-14	*Err*: 15v
5:1	*Rest*: 89
5:24	*Rest*: 80-81
6:2	*Rest*: 81
6:3	*Rest*: 83
6:4	*Rest*: 79, 81, 85
6:5	*Rest*: 83
9:16	*Rest*: 89
14:5	A.R2.50
14:18	*Rest*: 60, 66
15:7	*Rest*: 26; *Err*: 29v
15:20	A.R2.50
16:7-13	*Rest*: 27; A.R1.53
18:1-3	*Rest*: 27; A.R1.55
18:33	*Rest*: 27; A.R1.56
19:1-2	*Rest*: 27
19:18	A.R1.56
19:24	*Rest*: 88-89
22:7	*Rest*: 12
22:11-18	*Rest*: 27
24:27	*Rest*: 65
26:24	*Rest*: 26; *Err*: 29r
28:13	*Rest*: 26; *Err*: 29r
31:13	*Rest*: 27
32:9	*Rest*: 26; *Err*: 29r
35:1	*Rest*: 89
41:40-44	*Err*: 19r
48:5	*Rest*: 62
49:8-12	*Rest*: 61-62; A.R2.18, A.R2.20

Exodus

3:2	*Rest*: 48; *Err*: 30r
3:6	*Rest*: 25-27; *Err*: 29v; A.E1.30
3:14	A.R1.56
4:21	*Rest*: 83
6:2-3	*Rest*: 26; *Err*: 29v
6:12	*Err*: 12r
6:30	*Err*: 12r
7:1	*Rest*: 16; *Err*: 11v, 14r; A.R1.25
12:23	*Rest*: 81
12:29	*Rest*: 81, 84
12:42	*Rest*: 84
13:2	*Rest*: 10; *Err*: 6v
13:12	*Rest*: 10; *Err*: 6v
13:13	A.E1.8
16:7	*Rest*: 89
16:28-29	*Rest*: 89
17:6-7	SN: No.14
19:4	*Rest*: 91
20:2	*Rest*: 26, 34; *Err*: 29v, 35v
20:3	*Rest*: 34; *Err*: 35v
25:1-9	*Rest*: 67
31:3	*Rest*: 89
32:34	*Rest*: 27
34:19	*Rest*: 10; *Err*: 6v
35:21-22	*Rest*: 67
35:31	*Rest*: 89
36:2-3	*Rest*: 67

Leviticus

7:16	*Rest*: 68
9:24	*Rest*: 89
19:15	*Err*: 36v
21:8	*Err*: 30r
22:18	*Rest*: 68
23:38	*Rest*: 68

Index of Biblical References

Numbers

7:3	*Rest*: 67
8:16-17	*Rest*: 10; *Err*: 6v
10:29	*Rest*: 89
11:16-17	*Err*: 30v
11:31	*Rest*: 89
14:20-23	SN: No.14
15:3	*Rest*: 68
16:35	*Rest*: 89
24:17	*Rest*: 89
29:39	*Rest*: 68

Deuteronomy

1:17	*Err*: 36v
4:29	*Err*: 44r
4:35	*Err*: 37r
4:39	*Rest*: 34; *Err*: 35v
6:4	*Rest*: 34; *Err*: 35v, 37r; A.R1.79, A.E1.40
8:3	*Rest*: 78; *Err*: 16v
12:6	*Rest*: 68
18:18	*Rest*: 49
30:4	*Rest*: 91
32:17	*Err*: 43r
32:39	*Rest*: 34

Joshua

11:20	*Rest*: 83
18:1	*Rest*: 61

Judges

16:7	*Rest*: 22; *Err*: 20v
16:17	*Rest*: 22; *Err*: 20v

1 Samuel

2:10	A.R1.6
4:3-4	*Rest*: 61
9:6	*Err*: 38r
10:1	A.R1.6
12:1-5	*Rest*: 6; *Err*: 3v
15:17	A.R1.6
16:7	*Err*: 36v

1 Samuel, continued

Chapter 23	SN: No.4
24:3-7	*Rest*: 55
24:6	*Rest*: 6; *Err*: 3v
25:9-12	SN: No.10
25:28-31	*Rest*: 65
26:9	A.R1.6
26:12	*Rest*: 89

2 Samuel

5:1-16	SN: No.9
7:14	*Rest*: 60, 90
7:16	*Rest*: 62
17:1-4	SN: No.1
19:22	*Rest*: 59
22:12-14	*Rest*: 50
22:17	*Rest*: 91

1 Kings

1:40	*Rest*: 63
3:12	*Err*: 31r
4:21	*Rest*: 69
5:3	*Rest*: 66; SN: No.15
8:1	*Rest*: 88
8:55	*Rest*: 66
8:62	*Rest*: 66
10:10-22	*Rest*: 69
11:37	*Rest*: 91
12:21	*Rest*: 89
18:30-39	*Rest*: 10

2 Kings

2:9	*Rest*: 10; *Err*: 30v
15:29-16:9	*Rest*: 72; A.R2.30
Chapter 16	SN: No.21
16:2	A.R2.33
Chapter 18	SN: No.21
18:2	SN: No.22; A.R2.33, A.R2.37
19:19	*Rest*: 34
19:32-36	A.R2.36
20:1-5	*Rest*: 71

440

Index of Biblical References

1 Chronicles

5:1-2	*Rest*: 57, 62
11:1-9	SN: No.9
16:29	*Rest*: 69
17:13	*Rest*: 60, 90; SN: Introduction
22:5	SN: No.53
22:10	*Rest*: 60
28:6	*Rest*: 60, 61; SN: No.53
29:6-9	*Rest*: 67
29:23	*Rest*: 65-66, 68

2 Chronicles

9:8	*Rest*: 60
9:9-21	*Rest*: 69
11:1	*Rest*: 89
Chapter 28	*Rest*: 69
Chapter 29-32	SN: No.56
29:1	SN: No.22; A.R2.31
36:22-23	SN: No.34

Ezra

1:3	SN: No.34
1:4	A.R2.28

Job

1:6	*Err*: 14v
10:11	*Rest*: 90
26:5	*Rest*: 81-82; A.R2.50, A.R2.51
33:4	*Err*: 31v
38:7	*Err*: 14v
40:20	A.E1.44
41:25	*Err*: 14v

Psalms

1:1	SN: No.1
Psalm 2	A.R2.16
2:2	*Rest*: 60
2:7	*Rest*: 57-60; SN: No.2; A.R2:15
2:8-9	*Rest*: 58, 60

Psalms, continued

Psalm 3	A.R2.16
8:2	*Rest*: 28; *Err*: 27v
8:5	*Err*: 14v, 38r; SN: No.3; A.E1.1
8:6	*Err*: 5v
11:1	SN: No.4
12:6	*Err*: 5r, 12r
18:13	*Rest*: 50; *Err*: 16v
21:5	*Err*: 38r
22:16	SN: No.5
29:2	*Rest*: 69
29:7	*Rest*: 50
32:9	*Rest*: 43
33:6	*Rest*: 51
33:9	*Rest*: 51
36:9	*Rest*: 48
40:6	SN: No.6
45:6	*Rest*: 60; *Err*: 14r; SN: No.7; A.E1.10
45:7	*Rest*: 14, 16; *Err*: 5r, 12v, 38r; A.R1.26
45:11	*Rest*: 65 ; SN: No.8
47:2	*Err*: 15v
47:9	A.R2.28
54:6	A.R2.28
68:18	SN: No.9
68:29	*Rest*: 69
69:21	SN: No.10
72:5	SN: No. 11
72:6	*Rest*: 9
72:10	*Rest*: 68-69
72:17	*Rest*: 52, 53; A.R2.8
74:12	*Rest*: 83
78:25	*Err*: 15r
78:56-72	*Rest*: 62
81:10	*Rest*: 26; *Err*: 29v
82:1	A.R1.54
82:6	*Rest*: 14, 17; *Err*: 12v, 38r
82:6-7	*Rest*: 22; *Err*: 20v
82:8	SN: No.12

Psalms, continued

86:10	*Rest*: 34
89:3-4	*Rest*: 62
89:6	*Err*: 14v
89:27	*Rest*: 57; SN: No.13
89:29	*Rest*: 62
89:30-32	*Err*: 44r
89:36	*Rest*: 62
90:4	*Rest*: 53, 80, 84
90:5	*Rest*: 80
94:11	*Rest*: 85
95:7-11	*Rest*: 62-65; SN: No.14; A.R2.23
96:6	*Err*: 38r
96:9	*Rest*: 69
97:5	*Rest*: 65
97:7	*Err*: 14v
98:1	*Rest*: 63
104:4	A.R1.44
105:6	*Rest*: 90
110:1	*Rest*: 60, 65-67; *Err*: 20v; SN: No.15
110:3	*Rest*: 66, 67-69; SN: No.16; A.R2.25, A.R2.26, A.R2.27
110:4	*Rest*: 60, 66; SN: No.17
110:7	*Rest*: 67
118:26	*Err*: 17r
145:10	*Err*: 43r

Proverbs

1:24	*Rest*: 56
9:18	*Rest*: 81; A.R2.50
31:1	*Rest*: 70
31:4	*Rest*: 70

Song of Solomon

1:15	*Err*: 38r
6:9	SN: No.18
7:5	*Err*: 44r

Isaiah

Chapter 2	SN: Chapter heading
2:2	SN: No. 9
Chapter 3	*Rest*: 69; SN: Chapter heading
Chapter 4	*Rest*: 69
4:2	*Err*: 38r; SN: No.20
7:14	*Rest*: 89; *Err*: 6v, 11v; SN: No.21; A.R2.29, AR2.31
7:14-16	*Rest*: 69-72
7:18	*Rest*: 71
7:21	*Rest*: 71
8:3	*Rest*: 71; SN: No. 22; A.R2.31
8:10	SN: No. 23
Chapter 9	SN: Chapter heading
9:2	*Err*: 5r; SN: No. 24
9:5	*Rest*: 70; SN: No.25; A.R2.35
9:6	*Rest*: 15, 72; *Err*: 10r, 11v, 12r, 13v, 15v; A.R1.27
Chapter 11	SN: Chapter heading
11:1	*Rest*: 49, 89
11:2	*Err*: 31r
11:4	SN: No. 26
11:11-16	*Rest*: 70
12:2	*Err*: 38r
14:9	A.R2.50
16:1	SN: No. 27
19:20	SN: No. 28
21:5-9	*Rest*: 84
24:10-12	*Rest*: 85
26:14	*Rest*: 84
33:22	*Err*: 13v
35:5	SN: No.29
37:2	SN: No.61
37:16	*Rest*: 34
37:30-32	*Rest*: 71

Isaiah, continued

Chapter 40	SN: Chapter heading
40:3	SN: No. 30
40:5	*Err*: 38r
40:9	SN: No. 31
40:18	SN: No. 32
Chapter 41	SN: Chapter heading
41:2	SN: No. 33
41:4	*Rest*: 52; A.R2.6
41:8-9	*Rest*: 90
41:25	*Rest*: 52; SN: No.34; A.R2.6
42:1	*Rest*: 16; *Err*: 11r
42:7	SN: No.35
Chapter 43	SN: Chapter heading
43:4	*Err*: 38r
43:10	SN: No.36
43:11	*Rest*: 34; *Err*: 37r
44:6	*Rest*: 34
Chapter 45	SN: Chapter heading
45:1	*Rest*: 6, 71; *Err*: 3v
45:3	*Rest*: 15, 16; *Err*: 13v; A.R1.18
45:5-6	*Rest*: 34; *Err*: 37r
45:8	*Rest*: 9, 48, 50, 89
45:21	*Rest*: 34
46:8-9	*Rest*: 35
46:11	*Rest*: 52; SN: No. 37; A.R2.6
Chapter 47	*Rest*: 85
48:4	A.E1.7
48:12	*Rest*: 26; *Err*: 29v
48:16	*Rest*: 11, 44; *Err*: 41v; A.R1.12
Chapter 49	SN: Chapter heading
49:1	*Rest*: 52; A.R2.6
49:6	SN: No. 39
Chapter 50	SN: Chapter heading
Chapter 51	SN: Chapter heading
51:4	SN: No. 40
53:1	SN: No. 41
53:3	*Rest*: 7, 52; *Err*: 4v

Isaiah, continued

53:5	SN: No. 42
53:7	*Rest*: 52
53:8	*Rest*: 52; SN: No. 43
54:5	A.R1.27
55:5	*Err*: 38r
55:10	*Rest*: 9, 48, 49, 50
56:11	*Rest*: 85
60:6	SN: No. 44
61:1	*Rest*: 11, 44; *Err*: 42r
61:11	*Rest*: 49
62:2	*Err*: 38r
63:9-10	A.R1.44
66:9	*Rest*: 14; *Err*: 9v

Jeremiah

2:28	*Rest*: 26; *Err*: 29v
8:8-10	*Rest*: 85
11:13	*Rest*: 26; *Err*: 29v
17:14	*Err*: 38r
23:1-2	*Rest*: 85
23:5	SN: No.45
23:6	SN: No.46
29:13	*Err*: 44r
30:21	*Rest*: 20, 89; *Err*: 19r; SN: No.47
Chapter 31	SN: No.30
32:39	*Err*: 23v
33:14-17	*Rest*: 62
Chapter 50-51	*Rest*: 85
50:20	SN: No. 48
51:16	*Rest*: 50
51:39	*Rest*: 84
51:57	*Rest*: 84

Ezekiel

3:8-9	A.E1.7
9:3	SN: No. 49
11:19	*Err*: 31r
18:31	*Err*: 31r
22:26-28	*Rest*: 85

Index of Biblical References

Ezekiel, continued

34:2-6	*Rest*: 85
36:26	*Err*: 31r
37:5	*Err*: 31v
40:3	SN: No. 50
46:12	A.R2.28

Daniel

2:34	*Err*: 6r
5:2	*Rest*: 84
5:30	*Rest*: 84
6:3	*Err*: 30v
7:13-14	*Rest*: 20; *Err*: 18v
7:19	*Err*: 43v
9:24	*Rest*: 6; *Err*: 2v
9:25	SN: No. 51; A.R1.6
9:26-27	SN: No. 42
10:13	A.R1.55
10:21	A.R1.55
Chapter 12	SN: Chapter heading
12:1	A.R1.55

Hosea

Chapter 3	SN: Chapter heading
6:2	*Rest*: 71; SN: No.52
11:1	*Rest*: 11; *Err*: 7r; SN: Introduction, No. 53

Joel

Chapter 1	SN: Chapter heading
Chapter 2	SN: Chapter heading
2:28	SN: No.54
2:31	SN: No.55

Jonah

1:3	*Rest* (Edinburgh manuscript): E3

Micah

Chapter 2	SN: Chapter heading
4:1	SN: No.56
4:5	SN: No.57
4:7	SN: No.58

Micah, continued

4:13	SN: No. 59
Chapter 5	SN: Chapter heading
5:2	*Rest*: 78, 89; SN: No.60
5:5	SN: No.61
5:8	*Rest*: 85
Chapter 6	SN: Chapter heading

Zechariah

3:8	SN: No. 62
4:6	SN: No. 47
6:12	*Rest*: 7, 49; *Err*: 4v; SN: No. 45, No. 63
9:9	SN: No. 64
9:11	SN: No. 65
Chapter 11	SN: No. 66; Chapter heading
11:8	SN: No. 67
11:10	SN: No. 68
11:13	SN: No. 69
11:14	SN: No. 70
13:7	*Rest*: 20
Chapter 14	SN: Chapter heading

Malachi

3:1	*Rest*: 65; *Err*: 20v
4:2	*Rest*: 89

Matthew

1:16	*Rest*: 6; *Err*: 3v
1:18	*Err*: 6r
1:20	*Rest*: 9, 11; *Err*: 6r, 42r
1:21	*Err*: 6v
1:23	*Err*: 6v, 11v
2:13-15	*Rest*: 11; *Err*: 7r
2:15	SN: Introduction
3:9	*Rest*: 55
3:11	*Rest*: 10
3:16	*Rest*: 10, 12, 23; *Err*:30r
3:17	*Rest*: 12, 23, 42; *Err*: 8r, 25r, 30r
4:4	*Rest*: 48, 49, 78; *Err*: 16v

444

Index of Biblical References

Matthew, continued

5:13	*Rest*: 85
5:14	*Rest*: 88
5:15	*Rest*: 4
7:24-27	*Rest*: 23; *Err*: 10v, 42r, 43v
11:5	*Rest*: 19; *Err*: 18r
11:27	*Rest*: 16, 28, 37; *Err*: 11r, 28r
12:18	*Rest*: 16; *Err*: 11r
12:38-42	*Rest*: 69
13:3-8	*Rest*: 49
13:18-23	*Rest*: 49
13:33	A.E1.25
14:32-33	*Rest*: 6, 8; *Err*: 5v
15:6	*Err*: 36v
16:3	*Rest*: 4; *Rest* (Edinburgh manuscript): E3
16:6	*Err*: 36v
16:13-15	*Rest*: 7; *Err*: 3v; A.R1.7
16:16	*Rest*: 7, 23; *Err*: 4r, 26r
16:18	*Err*: 26r, 43v
16:20	*Rest*: 7; *Err*: 4r
17:2	*Rest*: 75
17:5	*Rest*: 48, 51; *Err*: 25r
18:10	*Rest*: 31; *Err*: 33r
18:20	*Err*: 44r
19:6	*Err*: 24r
19:17	*Rest*: 33; *Err*: 13r, 34r
19:24	*Rest*: 55
20:30	*Rest* (Edinburgh manuscript): E5
21:1-5	SN: No. 64
21:16	*Rest*: 28; *Err*: 27v
21:25	*Rest*: 18; *Err*: 16r
22:32	*Rest*: 27; *Err*: 29r
22:39-40	*Err*: 37r
22:41-46	*Rest*: 60, 66;
23:9-10	*Rest*: 28; *Err*: 27v
23:10	*Err*: 10v
23:37	*Rest*: 56
24:1-2	SN: No.66

Matthew, continued

24:23-24	*Err*: 3v
24:43	*Rest*: 84; AR2.53
25:41	*Rest*: 89
26:48	*Rest*: 8; *Err*: 4v
26:53	*Rest*: 20, 55; *Err*: 18v
26:64	*Rest*: 58
27:7-10	SN: No. 69
27:17	*Rest*: 5; *Err*: 2v
27:22	*Rest*: 5; *Err*: 2v
27:24-25	A.R2.9
27:34	SN: No. 10
27:46	*Err*: 13r
27:50	*Rest*: 23
27:54	*Rest*: 13; *Err*: 8v
27:64	*Err*: 39r
28:18	*Rest*: 15, 58; *Err*: 10r; A.E1.17
28:19	*Rest*: 22, 24; *Err*: 28v
28:20	*Err*: 16v, 43v, 44r

Mark

1:10	*Rest*: 10, 12, 23; *Err*: 30r
1:11	*Rest*: 12, 23, 42; *Err*: 8r, 25r, 30r
3:29	*Rest*: 56
4:27	*Rest*: 49
5:30	*Err*: 30v
7:21	*Err*: 44r
8:38	*Rest*: 29; *Err*: 28r
9:1	*Rest*: 58
9:7	*Rest*: 48; *Err*: 25r
10:8	*Err*: 24r
10:18	*Rest*: 33; *Err*: 13r, 34r
10:25	*Rest*: 55
11:30	*Rest*: 18; *Err*: 16v
12:26-27	*Rest*: 27; *Err*: 29v
12:29-32	*Err*: 37r
12:35-36	*Rest*: 66
13:1-2	SN: No.66
13:21-22	*Err*: 3v
14:7	*Rest*: 55

Index of Biblical References

Mark, continued

14:36	*Rest*: 55
14:44	*Rest*: 8; *Err*: 4v
14:61-62	*Rest*: 13, 58; *Err*: 8v
15:34	*Err*: 13r
15:36	SN: No. 10
15:39	*Rest*: 13; *Err*: 8v
16:15	*Err*: 44r
16:19	*Rest*: 65; *Err*: 20v

Luke

1:15	*Err*: 31r
1:17	*Rest*: 10; *Err*: 31r
1:31	*Rest*: 5, 9; *Err*: 2v, 3v, 6v
1:32	*Rest*: 9, 90; *Err*: 6v
1:35	*Rest*: 9, 10, 11, 14; *Err*: 6r, 6v, 38r; A.R1.11
1:41	*Err*: 31r
1:42	*Rest*: 11
2:8	*Rest*: 84; A.R2.53
2:21	*Rest*: 5, 10; *Err*: 2v
2:22	*Rest*: 10
2:23	*Rest*: 10, 11, 14; *Err*: 6v
3:16	*Rest*: 10
3:21	*Rest*: 10
3:22	*Rest*: 10, 12, 23, 42; *Err*: 8r, 25r, 30r
3:23	*Rest*: 7, 11; *Err*: 3v
4:4	*Err*: 16v
4:18	*Rest*: 44; *Err*: 42r
6:47-49	*Rest*: 23; *Err*: 110v, 42r
7:22	*Rest*: 19; *Err*: 118r
7:26	*Rest*: 10
8:5-15	*Rest*: 49; *Err*: 17r
8:16	*Rest*: 4
8:23-25	*Rest*: 8; *Err*: 15v
8:30-31	*Rest*: 80
8:46	*Err*: 30v
9:20	*Err*: 13r
9:26	*Rest*: 29; *Err*: 28r
9:35	*Rest*: 48, 65, 91; *Err*: 25r

Luke, continued

10:22	*Rest*: 16; *Err*: 11r
11:13	*Rest*: 4
12:8	*Rest*: 29; *Err*: 28r
12:10	*Rest*: 56
12:38	*Rest*: 84; A.R2.53
14:34	*Rest*: 85
15:12-13	*Rest*: 25; A. R1.50, A.E1.17
17:26-31	*Rest*: 84
18:19	*Err*: 13r
18:25	*Rest*: 55
19:2-7	*Err*: 17r
19:38	*Err*: 17r
19:40	*Rest*: 28; *Err*: 27v
20:4	*Rest*: 18; *Err*: 16v
20:37-38	*Rest*: 27; *Err*: 29v
20:38	*Rest*: 53
21:5-7	SN: No. 66
21:8	*Err*: 3v
22:69	*Rest*: 20, 58; *Err*: 18v
22:70	*Rest*: 13; *Err*: 8v, 37v
23:36	SN: No. 10
23:46	*Rest*: 23
23:47	*Rest* (Edinburgh manuscript): E13
24:19	*Rest*: 7; *Err*: 4v
24:39	*Rest*: 8; *Err*: 4v
24:49	*Rest*: 10; *Err*: 25v, 30v

John

1:1	*Rest*: 12, 18, 47-52, 90
1:1-18	*Err*: 20v
1:2	*Rest*: 48
1:3	*Rest*: 20, 51, 75; *Err*: 18v
1:4	*Rest*: 47
1:6	*Rest*: 18; *Err*: 16v
1:9	*Rest*: 18, 47, 88; *Err*: 17r; A.R1.30
1:12	*Rest*: 13, 55; *Err*: 9r
1:14	*Rest*: 49, 50, 86; *Err*: 7r, 10v

Index of Biblical References

John, continued
1:15	*Rest*: 78-79
1:16	*Rest*: 63, 79
1:18	*Rest*: 72; *Err*: 24r
1:20	*Rest*: 7; *Err*: 3v
1:27	*Rest*: 79
1:29	*Rest*: 12
1:30	*Rest*: 7, 79; *Err*: 4v
1:31	*Rest*: 12, 79
1:32	*Rest*: 23; *Err*: 26r; A.R1.44
1:33	*Rest*: 12; *Err*: 8r
1:34	*Rest*: 12; *Err*: 8r, 9r; A.E1.4
1:36	*Rest*: 12
1:47-50	*Rest*: 8; *Err*: 5v
1:51	A.R1.44
2:19-22	*Rest*: 69
3:2	*Err*: 5v
3:3	*Rest*: 59, 73
3:6	*Rest*: 41; *Err*: 10r
3:7	*Rest*: 73
3:13	*Rest*: 72-73; A.R2.38
3:26-27	*Rest*: 24
3:34	*Err*: 30v
4:24	*Err*: 10r, 30r
4:25-26	*Rest*: 8; *Err*: 5r, 37v
4:29	*Rest*: 6, 8; *Err*: 4v
5:18	*Rest*: 19; *Err*: 17v, 37v
5:19	*Rest*: 19, 75; *Err*: 18r, 33r
5:19-30	*Err*: 20r
5:19-47	*Err*: 18r; A.E1.13
5:20	*Rest*: 20
5:21	*Rest*: 19; *Err*: 18r
5:22-23	*Rest*: 19; *Err*: 18r
5:26-27	*Rest*: 20
5:31	*Err*: 41r
5:33	*Err*: 26r
5:35	*Rest*: 88
5:36-37	*Rest*: 17, 23; *Err*: 5v, 26r
5:39	*Rest*: 23

John, continued
6:15	*Rest*: 20; *Err*: 18r
6:31	*Rest*: 18
6:32	*Rest*: 18; A.R1.14
6:32-58	*Err*: 16v, 18r
6:33	*Rest*: 17; A.R1.14
6:35	*Rest*: 49; A.R1.14
6:38	*Rest*: 17; *Err*: 16r
6:41	*Rest*: 18
6:42	*Rest*: 17; *Err*: 16r
6:46	*Rest*: 31
6:48	*Rest*: 49; A.R1.14
6:50	*Err*: 16v
6:51	*Rest*: 72; A.R1.14
6:56	*Err*: 25r
6:58	*Rest*: 17
6:62	*Err*: 16r
6:63	*Rest*: 17; *Err*: 16r
6:69	*Err*: 6r
7:27	*Rest*: 53
7:41	*Rest*: 8
8:12	*Rest*: 88
8:15	*Err*: 16r
8:16	*Rest*: 28; *Err*: 27v
8:18	*Err*: 25r
8:23	*Rest*: 18; *Err*: 16v
8:28	*Rest*: 49
8:40	*Rest*: 7; *Err*: 4r
8:42	*Rest*: 41
8:44	*Rest*: 75
8:54	*Err*: 37v
8:58	*Rest*: 77-78, 90
9:5	*Rest*: 88
9:11	*Rest*: 8
9:22	*Rest*: 5; *Err*: 2v
9:37	*Rest*: 13; *Err*: 8v
10:17-18	*Rest*: 87
10:25	*Rest*: 17
10:27-29	*Err*: 24v
10:30	*Rest*: 25; *Err*: 22v, 24v, 25r; A.R1.51, A.E1.15, A.E1.19

Index of Biblical References

John, continued

10:33	*Err*: 15v
10:34	*Rest*: 16; *Err*: 12v
10:35-36	*Rest*: 14, 17; *Err*: 12v, 15v, 37v-38r
10:38	*Rest*: 87; *Err*: 16r, 25r
11:27	*Rest*: 6, 13, 18; *Err*: 8v
12:35	*Err*: 39v
12:42	*Rest*: 5; *Err*: 2v
12:45	*Rest*: 31
14:3	*Rest*: 91
14:10-11	*Rest*: 75-77, 87; *Err*: 22v, 24v-25r, 40v
14:13-14	*Err*: 28r
14:15	*Err*: 24v
14:16	*Err*: 30r, 36v
14:20	*Rest*: 75; *Err*: 24v
14:21	*Err*: 24v
14:23	*Err*: 24v
14:25	*Err*: 25v
14:28	*Err*: 13r, 19r; A.R1.34
15:1	*Rest*: 12
15:10	*Err*: 24v-25r, 44r
15:11	*Err*: 25v
15:16	*Err*: 28r
15:27	*Err*: 25v
16:2	*Rest*: 5; *Err*: 2v
16:3	*Rest*: 28; *Err*: 27v
16:15	*Rest*: 20, 86, 87; *Err*: 8v
16:23-26	*Err*: 28r
16:32	*Rest*: 28; *Err*: 27v
17:2	*Rest*: 49; A.E1.17
17:3	*Rest*: 28, 34; *Err*: 13r, 27v
17:5	*Rest*: 49
17:14	*Err*: 17r
17:16	*Err*: 17r
17:18	*Rest*: 18; *Err*: 17r
17:21	*Err*: 23v, 24r, 25r
17:22	*Rest*: 25; *Err*: 23v, 24r
17:26	*Err*: 25r
18:4-5	*Rest*: 8; *Err*: 4v
18:36	*Rest*: 20; *Err*: 18r

John, continued

19:7	*Err*: 37v
19:29	SN: No.10
20:17	*Rest*: 26
20:21	*Rest*: 18; *Err*: 17r
20:22	*Rest*: 22
20:28	*Rest*: 15, 16, 67; *Err*: 10r, 11v, 13v
20:30-31	*Rest*: 8; *Err*: 5v

Acts

1:8	*Rest*: 10, 11; *Err*: 25v, 30v
1:16	*Err*: 30r
2:3-4	*Rest*: 22, 48; A.R1.44
2:4	*Err*: 30v
2:17-19	SN: No.54
2:22	*Rest*: 7; *Err*: 4v
2:24	*Rest*: 87
2:32	*Rest*: 8; *Err*: 4v
2:36	*Rest*: 6, 8; *Err*: 3r, 4v
2:38	*Rest*: 24; *Err*: 28v
3:13	*Rest*: 26; *Err*: 29r
3:15	*Rest*: 87
3:18	*Err*: 30r
4:8	*Err*: 30v
4:10	*Rest*: 87
4:12	*Rest*: 24; *Err*: 28v
4:27	*Rest*: 6, 14; *Err*: 2v, 6v, 38r
4:30	*Err*: 6v, 38r
4:31	*Err*: 30v
4:32	*Err*: 23v
4:33	*Rest*: 10
4:34-37	*Rest*: 68
5:1-11	*Rest*: 55
6:3	*Rest*: 10
7:32	*Rest*: 26, 27; *Err*: 29v, 30r
7:55-56	*Rest*: 28; *Err*: 18v, 27v
8:9-24	*Rest*: 18, 77
8:10	*Rest*: 88
8:15	*Err*: 30v

Index of Biblical References

Acts, continued

8:17	*Err*: 30v
8:19	*Err*: 30v
8:26	A.R1.44
8:29	A.R1.44
8:33	*Rest*: 52
8:35	*Rest*: 53
9:20	*Rest*: 13; *Err*: 8v, 9r, 37v; A.E1.4
9:22	*Rest*: 6
10:34	*Err*: 36v
10:36-37	*Rest*: 6; *Err*: 2v
10:38	*Rest*: 6, 11, 16, 75; *Err*: 3r, 11r
10:42	*Rest*: 6; *Err*: 3r
13:23-25	*Rest*: 7; *Err*: 3v
13:28	*Rest*: 7
13:33	*Rest*: 57
17:3	*Rest*: 6
17:31	*Rest*: 7; *Err*: 4v
18:5	*Rest*: 6; *Err*: 2v
18:24-28	*Rest*: 6; *Err*: 2v
19:36	*Rest*: 50
20:28	*Err*: 43v
28:25	*Err*: 30r

Romans

1:3	*Rest*: 38
1:4	*Rest*: 57, 58
1:7	*Err*: 28r
1:17	*Rest*: 63
1:20	*Rest*: 75
1:28	*Rest*: 83, 84
2:4-5	*Rest*: 56
2:11	*Err*: 36v
3:4	*Err*: 41r
4:17	*Rest*: 53
4:24	*Rest*: 87
5:11	*Rest*: 24; *Err*: 28v
5:15	*Rest*: 8; *Err*: 5r
7:22	*Err*: 10r, 17r
8:2	*Rest*: 63

Romans, continued

8:6-8	*Err*: 16r
8:9-11	*Err*: 30v, 31v; A.E1.32
8:11	*Rest*: 87
8:15	*Rest*: 13, 63; *Err*: 9r
8:23	*Rest*: 13; *Err*: 9r
8:29	*Rest*: 14, 38
8:32	*Rest*: 13; *Err*: 9v
9:1	*Err*: 25v
9:5	*Rest*: 15; *Err*: 10r, 12r, 15v; A.R1.19, A.R1.27
9:14-16	*Rest*: 56
9:21	*Rest*: 57
10:17	*Err*: 26v
11:36	*Rest*: 86; *Err*: 26v
14:4	*Rest*: 55
15:6	*Err*: 34v
15:7	*Rest*: 91
16:27	*Err*: 7r

1 Corinthians

1:3	*Err*: 28r
1:17	*Err*: 5r
1:24	*Rest*: 46, 87; A.R1.11
1:30	*Rest*: 79
2:1-2	*Err*: 5r
2:9-10	*Err*: 30v
3:16	*Err*: 30v
3:20	*Rest*: 85
6:3	*Err*: 15r
6:14	*Rest*: 87
6:17	*Err*: 24r
7:37	*Rest*: 55
8:6	*Rest*: 28, 33, 85-87; *Err*: 16r, 27r, 27v, 34v
9:16	*Rest*: 4
9:17-18	*Rest*: 55
10:11	SN: Introduction
11:3	*Err*: 13r
12:3	*Err*: 22v
13:1	*Err*: 15r

Index of Biblical References

1 Corinthians, continued

14:32	*Err*: 31r
15:20	*Rest*: 57
15:21	*Rest*: 8; *Err*: 5r
15:45	*Rest*: 79; *Err*: 5r
15:47	*Rest*: 18; *Err*: 10r, 16v

2 Corinthians

1:2	*Err*: 28r
1:3	*Err*: 12v, 34v
1:11	*Err*: 36v
1:21	*Err*: 30v
2:10	*Err*: 36v
3:6	SN: Introduction
3:7	*Err*: 36v
3:13	*Err*: 36v
3:18	*Rest*: 3, 63; *Err*: 36v
4:6	*Rest*: 75, 88; *Err*: 36v
4:14	*Rest*: 87
5:1-4	*Err*: 17r
5:19	*Rest*: 74, 75
6:5	*Rest*: 84
6:16	*Err*: 29r
8:24	*Err*: 36v
9:7	*Rest*: 55
10:1	*Err*: 36v
10:7	*Err*: 36v
11:20	*Err*: 36v
11:23	*Rest*: 84
11:31	*Err*: 34v

Galatians

1:1	*Err*: 12v
1:3	*Err*: 12v, 28r
3:16	*Rest*: 39
3:19	A.E1.6
3:26	*Rest*: 13; *Err*: 9r
3:28	*Err*: 23v, 36v
4:4	*Rest*: 79
4:5	*Rest*: 13; *Err*: 9r
4:6	*Err*: 31v
5:18-21	*Err*: 44r

Ephesians

1:2	*Err*: 28r
1:3	*Err*: 34v
1:5	*Rest*: 13; *Err*: 9r
1:17	*Rest*: 41; *Err*: 13r
1:21-23	*Rest*: 20; *Err*: 18v
2:2	*Rest*: 83
2:15	*Rest*: 16, 59
2:16	*Rest*: 16
2:18	*Err*: 34v
2:20-21	*Err*: 26v
3:8	*Err*: 11v
3:9	*Rest*: 85
3:10	*Rest*: 80
3:15	*Rest*: 14; *Err*: 9v; A.R1.16
3:16	*Err*: 17r
3:17	*Err*: 25r, 26v
3:20	*Rest*: 55
4:3	*Err*: 23v
4:6	*Rest*: 33; *Err*: 27r, 34v
4:12	*Err*: 26v
4:15	*Rest*: 57
4:29	*Err*: 12r
4:30	*Err*: 31r
5:6	*Rest*: 48
6:12	*Rest*: 83
6:23	*Err*: 28r

Philippians

1:2	*Err*: 28r
2:5-11	A.R1.34
2:5	*Rest*: 21
2:6	*Rest*: 19-22; *Err*: 9v, 17r-20r; A.R1.35, A.R1.36, A.R1.37, A.R1.40, A.R1.41, A.R1.42, A.E1.12
2:7	*Rest*: 20, 21; *Err*: 17v, 20r
2:8	*Rest*: 22; *Err*: 12v, 20r
2:9	*Rest*: 15; *Err*: 10r, 11v, 12v, 19v

Index of Biblical References

Philippians, continued
2:11	*Err*: 10v
3:9	*Rest*: 63
4:13	*Rest*: 87, 88

Colossians
1:2	*Err*: 28r
1:3	*Err*: 34v
1:15	*Rest*: 52-53, 56-57; *Err*: 13r
1:16	*Rest*: 20, 78, 85, 86, 88; *Err*: 18v, 27r
1:17	*Rest*: 78
1:18	*Rest*: 14
1:24	*Err*: 26v
2:3	*Rest*: 88
2:8	*Rest*: 85
2:9	*Rest*: 14, 16, 49, 73-75; *Err*: 11v
2:12	*Rest*: 59
2:17	*Rest*: 74
3:3	*Rest*: 78
3:11	*Err*: 36v

1 Thessalonians
1:1	*Err*: 28r
5:2	*Rest*: 84
2:7	*Err*: 5r

2 Thessalonians
1:1	*Err*: 28r
1:2	*Err*: 28r
2:8	SN: No.26
2:16	*Err*: 28r

1 Timothy
1:2	*Err*: 28r
1:7	*Rest*: 32; *Err*: 33v
1:17	*Err*: 13r
2:5	*Rest*: 7, 28, 33; *Err*: 4r, 27v, 34v
3:15	*Err*: 43v

1 Timothy, continued
3:16	*Rest*: 3
5:21	*Rest*: 28; *Err*: 28r
6:3	*Err*: 12r
6:4	*Rest*: 46; *Err*: 32r, 35v, 36r, 42v
6:16	*Rest*: 72
6:20	*Err*: 32r
6:20-21	*Err*: 35v

2 Timothy
1:2	*Err*: 28r
1:13	*Err*: 12r
2:7	*Err*: 31r
2:14	*Err*: 36r
2:16	*Err*: 32r, 35v, 40v
2:26	*Rest*: 83
3:5	*Rest*: 85

Titus
1:4	*Err*: 28r
2:13	A.R1.27

Philemon
1:3	*Err*: 28r
1:14	*Rest*: 55

Hebrews
1:1	*Err*: 30r
1:2	*Rest*: 85-86
1:3	*Rest*: 86, 87; A.R2.3
1:4	*Rest*: 58; *Err*: 5v
1:5	*Rest*: 58
1:6	*Rest*: 65; *Err*: 14v
1:7	A.R1.44
1:8	*Err*: 14r
1:9	*Rest*: 14; *Err*: 38r
2:7	*Err*: 5v, 14v; A.E1.1
2:9	*Err*: 7r, 15r
2:10	*Rest*: 85
2:14	A.R2.57
2:16	*Rest*: 90-91; A.R2.57

Index of Biblical References

Hebrews, continued

2:17	A.R2.57
3:3-6	*Err*: 5v, 14r
3:7-11	*Rest*: 63-65; A.R2.23
3:13-15	*Rest*: 63-65; A.R2.22
4:4	*Rest*: 64
4:7	*Rest*: 63-65; SN: No.14; A.R2.24
4:12	*Rest*: 4, 66, 71; *Err*: 19r; SN: Introduction, No.46
4:13	*Rest*: 53
5:5-6	*Rest*: 58
5:7	*Rest*: 55
5:9	*Rest*: 79
7:3	*Rest*: 53, 79
8:6	*Err*: 34v
9:3	*Rest*: 58
9:12	*Rest*: 58
9:14	*Rest*: 78
9:15	*Err*: 34v; A.E1.6
10:1	A,RIn.1
10:5	SN: No. 6
10:12	*Err*: 20v
11:5	*Rest*: 81
11:36	*Rest*: 84
12:9	*Rest*: 41
12:14	*Rest*: 3-4
12:24	*Err*: 34v
13:2	*Rest*: 27
13:9	*Err*: 35v-36r

James

1:17	*Rest*: 24, 41; *Err*: 28v
1:18	*Err*: 7r
2:1	*Err*: 36v

1 Peter

1:3	*Err*: 12v
1:10-11	*Rest*: 82
1:11	*Err*: 31v
1:17	*Err*: 36v

1 Peter, continued

1:23	*Err*: 7r
3:18	*Rest*: 17, 82
3:19-20	*Rest*: 79-85
4:6	*Rest*: 82
4:11	*Err*: 10v, 12r

2 Peter

1:13	*Err*: 17r
1:16	*Err*: 5r
1:17	*Err*: 7r, 12v
2:1-3	*Rest*: 83
2:4	*Rest*: 80-81, 84; *Err*: 14v, 15r
2:5	*Rest*: 82, 84; A.R2.52
2:12	*Rest*: 32; *Err*: 33v
3:8	*Rest*: 53, 80
3:10	*Rest*: 84

1 John

1:1	*Rest*: 12, 49; *Err*: 26r
1:3	*Rest*: 28; *Err*: 28r
2:1	*Err*: 30r
2:3-6	*Err*: 44r
2:5	*Err*: 25r
2:7	*Rest*: 78
2:13-14	*Rest*: 78
2:15-16	*Err*: 17r
2:22	*Rest*: 6; *Err*: 3r
2:24	*Rest*: 78
2:27	*Err*: 30v
3:1	*Err*: 11v
3:24	*Err*: 25r
4:2	*Rest*: 18, 19
5:1	*Rest*: 6, 23; *Err*: 3r
5:5	*Rest*: 23
5:7-8	*Rest*: 22, 23; *Err*: 22v, 25v, 26r; A.R1.43, A.R1.109, A.E1.19, A.E1.21
5:20	*Err*: 13r, 31r; A.E1.9
5:21	*Err*: 13r

Jude

1:6	*Rest*: 80-81; *Err*: 15r
1:14-15	*Rest*: 81

Revelation

1:4	*Rest*: 29; *Err*: 28r
1:5	*Rest*: 14, 29; *Err*: 28r
2:21	*Rest*: 56
2:26-27	*Rest*: 58
3:5	*Rest*: 29; *Err*: 28r
3:19	*Rest*: 56
5:12	*Rest*: 16; *Err*: 7r, 11v. A.R1.24
5:13	*Err*: 7r
8:2	*Rest*: 85
9:1-11	*Rest*: 80
11:15	*Err*: 27v
12:7-9	A.R1.55
14:10	*Err*: 15r
16:13	*Rest*: 32, 35
17:4-5	*Rest*: 85
18:2	*Rest*: 82
19:10	*Rest*: 60, 66; *Err*: 25v; SN: Introduction, No.10
19:11	*Rest*: 49
19:13	*Rest*: 49
19:15	*Rest*: 58
20:1-3	*Rest*: 80
20:10	*Rest*: 81
21:22	*Rest*: 28; *Err*: 27v
22:3	*Rest*: 28; *Err*: 27v
22:4-5	*Rest*: 75

Judith

15:9	*Rest*: 88

Wisdom of Solomon

2:18	*Rest*: 13; *Err*: 9r
4:10-11	*Rest*: 80
7:26	A.R2.2

Wisdom of Solomon, continued

12:10	*Rest*: 56
17:16-17	*Rest*: 84
18:15	*Err*: 16r

Ecclesiasticus

16:8-9	*Err*: 15v
31:10	*Rest*: 55
37:23	*Err*: 36r
42:21	*Err*: 38r
44:16	*Rest*: 80-81
45:9	*Err*: 38r
49:14	*Rest*: 80-81

2 Maccabees

5:11-14	SN: No. 65

4 Maccabees

5:13	*Rest*: 55
8:22	*Rest*: 55

Index of Authorities Cited

Abelard, Peter, A.R1.73, A.R1.106, A.E1.29
  Theologia Christiana, AR1.119
Albert of Saxony
  Quaestiones circa logicam, A.R1.123
Albertus Magnus, A.R1.75, A.R1.106
Ambrose
  De fide, A.R1.53
  De spiritu sancto, Rest: 44
[Ambrose] a.k.a. Ambrosiaster
  Commentary on Phil 2:7-8, *Rest*: 19, 21; A.R1.34
Anselm, A.R1.73
Aquinas, Thomas, A.R1.17, A.R1.72, A.R1.75, A.R1.87, A.R1.106, A.E1.29
  Expositio de Ave Maria, A.R1.57
  Summa theologica, A.R1.117
Aristotle, *Err*: 32v; A.R1.17, A.E1.34
  Metaphysics, Rest: 44; *Err*: 41v; A.E1.34
  On Sense and the Sensible, A.R1.75
  On the Soul, Err: 33r; A.R1.72, AR1.75
  Nicomachean Ethics, A.E1.34
  Physics, Rest: 44; *Err*: 41v; A.R1.15, A.R1.87
  Posterior Analytics, A.R1.75
  Topics, A.R1.71
  See also: *Auctoritates Aristotelis*
Asterius of Tyana, *Rest*: 79; A.R2.44, A.R2.45
Athanasian Creed, *Rest*: 30; A.R1.70
Athanasius, *Rest*: 79; A.R2.17, A.R2.44
  De sancto spiritu, ad Serapion, Rest: 41, 75; A.R1.102
  Epistola ad Epictetum, Rest: 38, 39

[Athanasius], A.R1.96, A.R1.109
  De ariana et catholica confessione, Rest: 38, 43
  De assumptione hominis, Rest: 38; A.R1.96
  De fide sua, Rest: 42; A.R1.96, A.R1.109
  De nominibus sanctissimae Trinitatis, Rest: 38, 41; A.R1.96
  De professione regulae catholicae, Rest: 41
  De unitate fidei, Rest: 42; A.R1.109
  De unitate sanctissimae Trinitatis Rest: 25, 42; A.R1.109, A.E1.30
Auctoritates Aristotelis
  A.R1.72, A.R1.87
Augustine, A.R1.92
  Ad Donatistas, A.E1.7
  Confessiones, A.R1.10
  Contra Maximinum and *Collatio cum Maximino, Rest*: 21, 37, 40, 41, 42; *Err*: 24v, 38v, 39v, 40v, 41v; A.R1.38, A.R1.53, A.R1.91, A.R2.38, A.E1.15
  De civitate Dei, A.R2.10, A.R2.46
  De doctrina Christiana, Rest: 29, 32, 39; *Err*: 39r; A.R2.43
  De fide et symbolo, Rest: 43; *Err*: 40r
  De praedestinatione sanctorum, Rest: 43
  De Trinitate, Rest: 24, 25, 26, 27, 28, 29, 30, 32, 39, 40, 41, 42, 43, 44, 45, 46, 65, 75, 76; *Err*: 26v, 30r, 39v, 41v; A.R1.34, A.R1.39, A.R1.48, A.R1.52, A.R1.53, A.R1.56, A.R1.61, A.R1.63, A.R1.74, A.R1.101, A.R1.113, A.R1.116, A.R1.117, A.R2.40, A.R2.41, A.E1.24

Augustine, continued
  Enarrationes in psalmos, Rest:
    57, 76; A.R1.101, A.R2.26,
    A.R2.42
  Enchiridion, Rest: 39, 43; A.R1.98
  Epistulae, Rest: 32, 37, 39;
    A.R1.90
  In evangelium Iohannis, Rest: 11,
    25, 37, 39, 40, 41, 76; *Err*: 22v;
    A.R1.49, A.R2.41
  Sermones, Rest: 37; A.R1.106
[Augustine]
  Contra Felicianum, Rest: 39
  De fide ad Petrum, Rest: 75, 77;
    A.R1.39, A.E1.20
  Dialogus quaestionum LXV, Rest:
    30, 41, 43; *Err*: 41v; A.R1.39
  Liber seu diffinitio ecclesiasticorum
    dogmatum, Err: 40v
Averroes (Ibn Rushd), A.R1.75
Avicenna (Ibn Sina), A.R1.17,
  A.R1.75
Bacon, Roger, A.R1.75
Basil of Caesarea, A.R1.89
  Contra Eunomium (book 1-3),
    Rest: 30, 43; *Err*: 41v;
    A.E1.18
[Basil of Caesarea]
  Contra Eunomium (book 4-5),
    Err: 23r; A.E1.18
[Bede], A.R1.75, A.R1.115
Bibliander, Theodore
  Machumetis Saracenorum,
    A.R1.80, A.R1.81, A.R1.85
Biel, Gabriel, A.R1.71
Boccaccio, Giovanni
  Genealogia deorum gentilium,
    Rest: 42
Boethius, A.R1.17, A.R1.104
  De consolatione philosophiae,
    A.R2.10
  De Trinitate, A.R1.100, A.R2.10
Bonaventure, A.R1.17, A.R1.75

Bonaventure, continued
  Quaestiones disputatae de misterio
    trinitatis, A.R1.100
Buridan, John, A.R1.75
Burley, Walter, A.R1.123
Calvin, John, A.R1.4, A.R1.26,
  A.R1.62, A.R1.87, A.R1.106,
  A.R1.124
  Institutes (1539), A.R2.14
  Expositio psalmorum, Err: 41v
Chrysostom, John. See John Chrysostom
Cicero
  De amicitia, A.R1.23
Clement of Alexandria
  Stromata, Rest: 50-51, 79
[Clement of Rome]
  Recognitiones, Rest: 6, 24, 33, 77;
    Err: 3r-v, 15r, 28v, 34v-35r;
    A.R1.5
Clichtove, Josse van
  Elucidatorium ecclesiasticum,
    A.R1.58
Conferencia de Valladolid, A.R1.19,
  A.R1.43, A.E1.14
Corpus juris civilis, Err: 32r
Cyprian of Carthage, A.R1.40
  Epistola ad Magnum, Rest: 25;
    Err: 23v; A.R1.51
Cyril of Alexandria, *Rest*: 38, 43;
  A.R1.17, A.R1.95
  In divi Joannis evangelium, Rest: 25
  Thesaurus, Rest: 21, 30
D'Ailly, Pierre, A.E1.14
  Quaestiones, Rest: 29; *Err*: 32v;
    A.R1.60, A.R1.61
De Oria, Juan, A.R1.17, A.R1.117
  De conceptu, A.R1.72
  De enunciatione, Rest: 44; *Err*: 41v;
    A.R1.71, A.R1.118
Dionysius of Alexandria, *Rest*: 79
  Epistolae ad Sixtum Papam,
    A.R2.45

Index of Authorities Cited

Duns Scotus, John, *Rest:* 42, 45; *Err:* 41r; A.R1.28, A.R1.72, A.R1.73, A.R1.75, A.R1.87, A.R1.106, A.R1.107, A.R1.117, A.R1.122, A.R2.55, A.E1.29
  Ordinatio [Quaestiones in quattuor libros senteniarum], Rest: 44; A.R1.76, A.R1.105
  Quaestiones quodlibetales, A.R1.104
  Quaestiones super priorem et posteriorem analyticorum, A.R1.119, A.R1.123
  Reportata super primum sententiarum, Rest: 41
Epiphanius of Salamis
  Panarion, Rest: 37; A.R1.31, A.R1.32, A.R1.89
Erasmus, Desiderius
  Adagia, Rest: 23; *Err:* 12r; A.R1.23, A.R2.12, A.E1.3
  Annotationes, Rest: 19, 21, 22; *Err:* 23v; A.R1.16, A.R1.19, A.R1.27, A.R1.34, A.R1.41, A.R1.43, A.R2.3, A.E1.1, A.E1.12, A.E1.19, A.E1.21, A.E1.25
  Apologia ad Stapulensem, A.E1.1
  De libero arbitrio, Rest: 55; A.R2.13
  Ecclesiastes, A.RIn.1
  Moriae encomium, A.R1.1, A.R1.23, A.R1.111, A.R1.118, A.R1.121, A.R1.122, A.R2.12
  Responsio ad ... Eduardi Lei, A.R1.16
  Translation of New Testament, *Rest:* 59, 84; *Err:* 36v; A.R1.16, A.R1.19, A.R1.24, A.R1.27, A.R1.40, A.R1.43, A.R2.3, A.R2.46, A.R2.57, A.E1.1
  See also: *Conferencia de Valladolid*
Estienne, Robert
  Libri Moyse quinque, A.R2.56

Euclid
  Elements, A.R1.100
Eusebius of Caeseara, A.R1.4
  Historia ecclesiastica, Rest: 34, 37
  Praeparatio evangelica, A.R2.11
Faber, Johannes
  Doctoris Joannis Fabri ... orthodoxae fidei Catholica defensio, A.E1.6
Ficino, Marsilio
  De Christiana religione, Rest: 35; A.R1.81, A.E1.45
  Theologia Platonica, A.R2.11
Glossa Ordinaria, Err: 25v; A.R1.11
Gregory of Nazianzus, A.R2.17
  Orationes, Rest: 30, 43; *Err:* 41v
Gregory of Nyssa, A.R1.17, A.R1.89
Gregory of Rimini, A.E1.14
  Super primum et secundum sententiarum, Rest: 41; *Err:* 39v
Gregory the Great (Pope Gregory I), A.R1.73, A.R1.101
  Homiliae, A.R1.53
Haimo of Auxerre
  Expositio in diui Pauli epistolas, A.E1.6
Henry of Ghent, A.R1.17, A.R1.75
  Quodlibeta theologica, Err: 31v-32r; A.E1.33
Herman of Carinthia
  Doctrina Machumetis, Rest: 36
Hieracas, *Rest:* 37; A.R1.93
Hilary, A.R1.40, A.E1.20
  De synodis, Rest: 30; A.R1.68
  De Trinitate, Rest: 24, 25, 26, 30, 37, 44, 46, 75, 76-77; *Err:* 24v-25r, 31v, 41r; A.R1.48, A.R1.52, A.R1.101, A.E1.15, A.E1.32
  Tractatus super psalmos, Rest: 76; A.R2.42
Holkot, Robert, A.E1.14
  Quaestiones, Rest: 29; *Err:* 32r-v; A.R1.59

Index of Authorities Cited

Horace
  Satires, A.E1.3
Ibn Ezra, Abraham
  Commentary on Isaiah, A.R2.31
Ibn Rushd. See Averroes
Ibn Sina. See Avicenna
Ignatius, A.R1.29
[Ignatius], *Rest*: 19, 33-34, 79; *Err*: 34v; A.R1.33
  Ad Ephesios, Rest: 19
  Ad Phildelphios, Rest: 33; *Err*: 34v-35r
  Ad Smyrnaeos, Rest: 19
  Ad Tarsenses, Rest: 34; *Err*: 35r
  Ad Trallios, Rest: 19; *Err*: 7v-8r
Innocent III, *Rest*: 39; A.R1.73, A.R1.106
Irenaeus
  Adversus haereses, Rest: 6, 11, 18, 19, 24, 25, 29, 33, 34, 37, 46, 48, 49, 50, 51-52, 77-78, 79, 80, 86; *Err*: 26v, 34v, 35r, 38v, 39v, 42v; A.R1.29, A.R1.32, A.R1.46, A.R1.47, A.R1.88, A.R1.110, A.R1.124, A.R2.5, A.R2.7, A.R2.54, A.E1.2, A.E1.26, A.E1.28, A.E1.41, A.E1.42
Isidore of Seville
  Etymologiae, Rest: 37, 40; *Err*: 38r-v, 39r; A.R1.53, A.R1.67, A.R1.94, A.E1.2, A.E1.5
Jerome, *Rest*: 38; A.R1.73, A.R1.97
  Epistola ad Damasum, A.R1.65
  In epistolam ad Ephesios, A.R1.16
  In evangelium Matthaei, Rest: 50, 76; *Err*: 27r; A.R2.42, A.E1.25
  In Isaiam prophetam, A.RIn.1
  Translation of Bible, A.R2.25, A.R2.27, A.R2.51
[Jerome]
  In evangelium Marcum, A.E1.30
Joachim of Fiore, *Rest*: 39-40; *Err*: 39r; A.R1.99

John Chrysostom
  Evangelium secundum Ioannem, Rest: 63
  In epistolam ad Philippenses, A.R1.42
John of Damascus, A.R1.17
  De fide orthodoxa, Rest: 38-39, 41, 42-43; *Err*: 39v, 41r; A.R1.11
Josephus
  Antiquitatum Iudaicarum, Rest: 80; A.R2.52
Justin Martyr, *Rest*: 6, 34, 52; *Err*: 35r; A.R1.4, A.R1.78, A.R2.5, A.R2.17
[Justin Martyr]
  Admonitorius gentium, A.R1.4
Kimhi, David
  Commentary on Psalms, *Rest*: 59-60
  First Rabbinic Bible, A.R2.31
Lactantius Firmianus
  Divinae institutiones, Err: 34r; A.E1.37
Lax, Gaspar, A.R1.118
  Arithmetica speculativa, A.R1.100
Lefèvre d'Étaples, Jacques, A.E1.1, A.E1.6
Liberatus of Carthage
  Breviarium causae, Rest: 38; A.R1.95
Lombard. See Peter Lombard
Lucian of Samosata, *Rest*: 55; A.R2.12
Luther, Martin, AR1.96, A.R1.106, A.E1.9
  De servo arbitrio, Rest: 54; A.R2.12, A.R2.14
Maimonides, Moses
  Guide for the Perplexed, Rest: 61
Mair, John, A.R1.17, A.R1.62, A.R1.117, A.E1.14
  In primum sententiarum, Rest: 29-30; *Err*: 21r-v, 22r; A.R1.66, A.R1.118
  In tertium sententiarum, A.R1.111
  Introductorium in Aristotelicam dialecticen, A.R1.123

Index of Authorities Cited

Malvenda, Tomaso
  Commentariorum in s. scripturam,
    A.R2.35
Marsilius of Inghen
  Quaestiones in metaphysicam,
    A.R1.71
Maxentius, Joannes
  Dialogi contra Nestorianos, Rest:
    38; *Err:* 38v; A.R1.95
Melanchthon, Philip, A.R1.75,
  A.R1.106
Münster, Sebastian
  Hebraica Biblia, A.R2.18,
    A.R2.19, A.R2.34, A.R2.51
Nanni, Giovanni
  Berosi sacerdotis, A.R2.48
Nicholas of Amsterdam
  Exercitium in Porphyrium, A.R1.71
Nicholas of Cusa, A.R1.75
  Cribratio Alcorani, Rest: 36;
    A.R1.81, A.E1.45
Nicholas of Lyra, A.R1.11
Numenius of Apamea, *Rest:* 54;
  A.R2.11
Ockham, William, *Rest:* 45; A.R1.17,
  A.R1.66, A.R1.71, A.R1.75,
  A.R1.117, A.E1.14, A.E1.29,
  A.E1.33
  Dialogus, A.R1.73
  Quodlibeta, A.R1.104
  Summa logicae, A.R1.21,
    A.R1.118, A.E1.36
  Super sententiarum, Rest: 42; *Err:*
    41r, 42r; A.R1.108, A.R1.111
Origen, A.R1.65, A.R1.101
  Contra Celsum, Rest: 25; *Err:* 23v;
    A.R1.51
  De principiis, Rest: 33; *Err:* 34v
Pagnini, Santes
  Bible (1542), *Rest:* 52, 53, 69, 80;
    A.R1.25, A.R1.27, A.R2.8,
    A.R2.23, A.R2.27, A.R2.29,
    A.R2.51
  Hebraicas institutiones, Rest: 53

Pagnini, continued
  See also: Servetus, Introduction
    and notes to the Pagnini Bible
    (1542)
Pardo, Jerónimo
  Medulla dyalectices, A.R1.118
Paul of Venice, A.R1.75
  Logica magna, A.R1.123
Pelagius
  Libellus fidei ad Innocentum
    papam, Rest: 38; A.R1.97
Peter Lombard
  Sentences, Rest: 24, 26, 28, 29,
    30, 37, 38, 39, 40, 41, 42,
    43, 44, 45, 46, 52, 75, 77;
    Err: 22v, 24v, 26v, 27v, 28v,
    30r, 31v, 32v, 38v, 39r, 39v,
    40r, 40v, 41r, 41v, 42r, 42v;
    A.R1.11, A.R1.48, A.R1.52,
    A.R1.69, A.R1.73, A.R1.97,
    A.R1.99, A.R1.101, A.R1.106,
    A.R1.113, A.R1.117,
    A.R1.120, A.R2.38, A.E1.20,
    A.E1.24, A.E1.30, A.E1.32
Pico della Mirandola, Gianfrancesco
  Examen vanitatis, A.R1.75,
    A.E1.34
Pico della Mirandola, Giovanni
  Apologia, A.R1.5, A.R1.111
Polycarp
  Ad Philippenses, Rest: 19
Quran, *Rest:* 35-36, 46; *Err:* 43r;
  A.R1.80, A.R1.81, A.R1.82,
  A.R1.84, A.R1.85, A.R1.86,
  A.R2.52, A.E1.45
Richard of St. Victor
  De Trintate, Err: 31v
Ricoldo of Monte Croce
  Confutatio Alcorani, A.R1.81
Robert of Ketton
  Alcoran (Latin version of Quran),
    Rest: 35-36; A.R1.80, A.R1.81,
    A.R1.82, A.R1.84, A.R1.85,
    A.E1.45

Index of Authorities Cited

Rufinus
  Historia ecclesiastica, Rest: 37
Scotus. See Duns Scotus
Sefer Nizzahon, Rest: 61; A.R2.18, A.R2.19
Septuagint, *Rest*: 61, 80, 84; *Err*: 15r; SN: No.5; A.R1.56, A.R2.25, A.R2.26, A.R2.46, A.E1.1, A.E1.11
Servetus, Michael
  Introduction and notes to the Pagnini Bible (1542), *Rest*: 66, 68; Appendix B; A.R2.9, A.R2.16, A.R2.23, A.R2.35
Sozomenus
  Historia ecclesiastica, Err: 38v
Stunica. See Zúñiga, Diego Lopez de
Talmud, *Rest*: 46
Targum, *Rest*: 58-59, 60; *Err*: 15r; A.R2.15
Tertullian, *Rest*: 48, 79; A.R1.29, A.R1.40, A.R1.47, A.R1.77, A.R2.17
  Ad nationes, A.E1.8
  Adversus Marcionem, Rest: 25, 33, 50; *Err*: 3r, 34v, 38v
  Adversus Praxean, Rest: 6, 15, 24, 86; *Err*: 2v, 3r, 7v, 9v, 22v-23r, 29r, 36v; A.R1.2, A.R1.3, A.R1.13, A.R1.94, A.R2.54, A.E1.15
  Adversus Valentinianos, Rest: 11; A.R1.124
  De idolatria, A.R2.46
  De praescriptionibus, A.R1.31
[Tertullian]
  Adversus omnes haereses, Err: 38v-39r; A.R1.94
Theophylact
  Commentarius in epistolam ad Philippenses, Err: 19v; A.E1.12
  In quatuor evangelia, Err: 25v
Thomas Aquinas. See Aquinas

Valla, Lorenzo
  De libero arbitrio, Rest: 55; A.R2.13, A.R2.14
  Disputationes dialecticae, A.R2.17
  Elegantiae linguae latinae, A.R1.63
  In novum testamentum annotationes, A.R2.53
Valladolid. See *Conferencia de Valladolid*
Vives, Juan Luis
  Adversus pseudodialecticos, A.R1.118, A.R1.123
  De conscribendis epistolis, A.R1.23
Westheimer, Bartholomeus
  Troporum theologicorum, A.R2.56
William of Ockham. See Ockham
William of Sherwood
  Syncategoremata, A.R1.123
Zúñiga, Diego Lopez de
  Annotationes contra Erasmum Roterodamum, A.R1.19

www.ingramcontent.com/pod-product-compliance
Lightning Source LLC
Chambersburg PA
CBHW071114080526
44587CB00013B/1337